Urban Triage

Critical American Studies Series

George Lipsitz, University of California–San Diego, series editor

Urban Triage

Race and the Fictions of Multiculturalism

James Kyung-Jin Lee

Critical American Studies

University of Minnesota Press

Minneapolis | London

The University of Minnesota Press gratefully acknowledges assistance provided for this book by a University Cooperative Society Subvention Grant awarded by the University of Texas at Austin.

"Nigger Song: An Odyssey" from Rita Dove, *Selected Poems* (New York: Pantheon Books, 1993). Copyright 1993 by Rita Dove. Reprinted by permission of the author.

"Beware of the M Word," by Russell C. Leong, first appeared in *High Performance Magazine* in a special issue on the Los Angeles Rebellion, summer 1992, titled *The Verdict and the Violence,* edited by Wanda Coleman. Reprinted with permission by Russell C. Leong.

"Oakland Blues" from Ishmael Reed, *New and Collected Poems* (New York: Atheneum, 1988). Copyright 1989. Reprinted with permission by the author.

An earlier version of chapter 2 appeared as "Fictionalizing Workers, or The Abuse of Fiction: Violence, Reading, and the Staging of Barrio-Space in Alejandro Morales's *The Brick People,*" in *Re-placing America: Intercultural Conversations and Contestations,* edited by Ruth Hsu et al., *Literary Studies: East and West* 16 (Honolulu: University of Hawai'i Press, 2000); originally published by the College of Languages, Linguistics, and Literature, University of Hawaii at Manoa. Portions of chapter 4 appeared as "Where the Talented Tenth Meets the Model Minority: The Price of Privilege in John Edgar Wideman's *Philadelphia Fire* and Chang-Rae Lee's *Native Speaker,*" *NOVEL: A Forum on Fiction* 35, nos. 2/3 (2002); copyright 2003 NOVEL Corp.; reprinted with permission.

Published by the University of Minnesota Press
111 Third Avenue South, Suite 290
Minneapolis, MN 55401-2520
http://www.upress.umn.edu

Library of Congress Cataloging-in-Publication Data

Lee, James Kyung-Jin.
    Urban triage : race and the fictions of multiculturalism / James Kyung-Jin Lee.
        p.   cm. — (Critical American Studies series)
    Includes bibliographical references (p.) and index.
    ISBN 0-8166-4180-3 (HC : alk. paper) — ISBN 0-8166-4181-1 (PB : alk. paper)
    1. Multiculturalism—United States.   2. United States—Race relations.   3. Minorities—United States—Social conditions—20th century.   4. Inner cities—United States—History—20th century.   5. United States—Social conditions—1980–   6. United States—Intellectual life—20th century.   7. Minorities—United States—Intellectual life—20th century.   8. American literature—Minority authors.   9. Inner cities in literature.   10. Race relations in literature.   I. Title.   II. Series.
    E184.A1L415 2004
    305.8'00973—dc22

                                                                                2003023682

Printed in the United States of America on acid-free paper

The University of Minnesota is an equal-opportunity educator and employer.

12   11   10   09   08   07   06   05   04   10   9   8   7   6   5   4   3   2   1

Contents

Acknowledgments

"Words are witnesses," E. J. Hobsbawm once mused, "which often speak louder than documents." And if certain words settle in us history's sediments that layer who we are onto who we were, then the clarity of words' meanings, and the importance we ascribe to them, take on added significance long after the speaker or writer has uttered them. Such is the task of academic wordsmiths.

Many pillars and hands held me as I brought this book to completion. So to the witness of words, I add the testimony of names who remind me that intellectual labor is wrought collectively, that whatever value this book holds rests in the communities that speak through it. Begun as a dissertation, *Urban Triage* was made possible initially by funding from the UCLA Department of English and Graduate Division, whose Project 88 fellowship (a vestigial legacy of the school's formerly proud commitment to affirmative action), alongside a special grant from the Institute of American Cultures, gave material sign to support. The University of California President's Postdoctoral Fellowship provided much-needed space, time, and resources to complete most of the book's re-creations and revisions, and I am especially thankful to the staff in Oakland who tirelessly worked to make sure that we Fellows would not falter for reasons structural: Sheila O'Rourke, Kim Adkinson, Jane Gonzalez, Jahleezah Eskew. In my brief time here at the University of Texas at Austin, I have been honored to receive, almost immediately, signs of faith. I thank UT's College of Liberal Arts for the David Bruton Jr. Regents Chair Fellowship and the Summer Research Assignment to help me bring this book to its final version, and especially acknowledge the college's dean, Richard Lariviere, for his trust, guidance, and the unexpected invitations to lunch.

The staff at the Van Pelt Library at the University of Pennsylvania and the Charles E. Young Research Library at UCLA provided invaluable assistance. I am indebted to Marjorie Lee of the UCLA Asian American Studies Reading Room for her wise guidance. Special thanks are due Laura Tosi of the Bronx County Historical Society and Susan Zimmer of the New York City Landmarks Preservation Commission for helping me uncover the history of the Bronx County Courthouse. Lindsey Schell and Gera Draiijer of the Perry-Castañeda Library at UT opened their doors to me even in the busiest moments of semesters as I sought out end-of-the-hour citations.

As part of the three-legged stool that makes up university departments and programs (students and faculty being the other two), support staff are the most permanent and vital. A person would be hopelessly lost in places as big as UCLA, UCSD, and UT without their presence. I am grateful to those in the Department of English and the Asian American Studies Center: Michelle Harding, Jeanette Gilkinson, Nora Elias, Rick Fagin, Doris Wang, Lynda Tolly, Mary Uyematsu Kao, Brandy Worrall, Christine Wang, Cathy Castor, and Irene Soriano. To the staff at UCSD's Department of Literature, I offer my appreciation for their warm welcome to someone who was but a brief interloper: Debbie Morrow, Lucinda Rubio-Barrick, and Nancy Ho-Wu. At the UT Department of English, I have received nothing but the best in graciousness from its staff: Anda Wynn, Emil Kresl, Justin Leach, Ramona Van Loan, Geneva Walton, Allen Graham, Marshall Ryan Maresca, Cristina Zambrano, Tim Campos, Susana Castillo, Debbie Rothschild, and Clay Maer. And UT's Center for Asian American Studies survives on a shoestring budget because of its incredible staff, who have made that space sanctuary for its faculty and students: Barbara Jann, Vicente Lozano, and Monica Rivera.

The original readers of this project exemplify the best in academic life: intellectual brilliance, humility, and integrity. Valerie Smith admonished me to move past my initial insecurities, and Don Nakanishi taught me never to forget a student's idiosyncratic needs—Val and Don never forgot mine. Two others never speak of themselves in superlatives, but I will: Richard Yarborough and King-Kok Cheung embody intellectual and political commitment, and are examples of what faculty mentors should be: models who open and show the way. Even more have nurtured this project in immeasurable ways: Helen Deutsch, Felicity Nussbaum, Rachel Lee, Sonia Saldívar-Hull, Jenny Sharpe, Shu-mei Shih, Ali Behdad, Jinqi Ling, Rafael Pérez-Torres, Harryette Mullen, Kimberlé Crenshaw, Henry Yu, Valerie Matsumoto, Sid Lemmelle, Herman Beavers, Lisa New, Lindon Barrett, Traise Yamamoto, Connie Razza, David Witzling, Debbie Banner, Russell Leong, Glenn Omatsu, Steve Louie, Theresa Delgadillo, Tracy Curtis, Helen Jun, Barry Masuda, Lisa Cacho, Randy Williams, Boone Nguyen, Grace Hong, Victor Bascara, Viet Nguyen, Asale Angel-Ajani, and Dylan Rodriguez. David Lloyd was a true intellectual comrade, offering advice, assistance, and wine for no reason but the sheer joy of collegiality. Lisa Lowe read and commented on early drafts of my project, for which I am truly thankful, but I am equally grateful for her unfettered encouragement well before she'd read a word. Rosaura Sánchez was the perfect mentor for a postdoctoral fellow, helping me ask new questions and then graciously inviting me to deliver a version of chapter 2 at UCSD. Her ongoing critique of my work sharpened the project's blunt edges. During the summer of 2002, Min Hyoung Song and I exchanged drafts of each other's respective work, and besides his incredible generosity, Min's contribution in improving my book is everywhere. George Lipsitz read each word of multiple drafts. His belief in my project was the book's "tipping point" and pushed me forward and showed me when to stop. That he invited me to include this book in the Critical American Studies series only scratches the surface of the quality and immensity of his support. I also thank David Eng and Michael Awkward for being such astute readers, for the stringent criticism they offered accompanied by their belief that this book was important enough to continue, transform, and complete. The editorial and production staff at the University of Minnesota Press never wavered in their nurturing of this project from start to finish: Mike Stoffel, Andrea Kleinhuber, Brian Wiedenmeier, Alison Aten, Laura Westlund, Linda Lincoln, Catherine Clements, and Mary Poggione. I'm especially grateful to my editor, Richard Morrison, for his unwavering belief in this project even when I, at times, faltered.

UT's Department of English and Center for Asian American Studies let me stay in Southern California for a couple of years after they hired me, and I especially thank my chair Jim Garrison for his patient good cheer. When I did arrive in Austin, I was greeted by an amazing array of colleagues, and I am particularly grateful to the following for their friendship and counsel: Gerry Heng, Art Sakamoto, Ann Cvetkovich, Lisa Moore, Evan Carton, Sam Baker, Phil Barrish, Elizabeth Butler Cullingford, Brian Doherty, José Limón, Neville Hoad, Khaled Mattawa, Helena Woodard, Shelley Fisher-Fishkin, Julia Mickenberg, and Shirley Thompson. My Asian American Studies comrades, Kim Alidio and Sharmila Rudrappa, show me what is possible and exciting in the field, and my trips to that small office are always a joy. The cohort of new junior faculty who drove into Austin with me—Jennifer Wilks, Doug Taylor, John González, Domino Perez, and James Cox—made the transition to Texas not only bearable but actually, at times, pleasant. Barbara Harlow is not only an example but an exemplar of teaching me how and why what we do in the academy matters politically. And three people deserve special attention: Mia Carter, my fellow traveler in English and interim director of Asian American Studies, always made her office open as I stumbled through my first year; and Joanna Brooks and David Kamper, whose footsteps I followed from Los Angeles to Austin, keep my memories of California and my hopes for Texas alive. Students at UT have been wonderful to teach and, more important, to learn from. Too numerous to mention all, these few will stand in and stand for themselves:

Mari Kobayashi, Murtaza Surtawalla, Andrew Tolentino, Esther Wang, Asra Syed, Jentso Hwang, Neesha Davé, and Dixon Deutsch.

I name wonderful friends, both old and new but always everlasting, who continue to show me why I should not give up, whether in a book or the world: Eric Wat, La'Tonya Rease Miles, Rob Miles, Jabari and Zoe Miles, Joni Jones, Laura Kim, Lois Leveen, Michael Jasny, Michelle Levy, Andrea Brewer, Arthur Ago, Amy Seif, Cyrus Yang, Kathy Fu Yang, Lee Hayakawa, Brenda Kwon, Angela Deaver Campbell, Nancy Yoo, Kelly Jeong, Minh Nguyen, Anna Alves, Jennifer Tseng, Darlene Rodrigues, Earl Patterson, Elisa White, Gayle Isa, Jane Park, and kt shorb. I give special thanks to the people of All Saints Episcopal Church in Pasadena and St. James Episcopal Church in Austin, who remind me that the arc of the moral universe is long but bends toward justice: Ed Bacon, Tim Safford, Gary Hall, Scott Richardson, Greg Rickel, James Baer, Anne Peterson, Terry Gock and David Caley, and Abel López. I met Liz Muñoz, Renee Hill, Mary Foulke, and Helena and Matthias Foulke-Hill in Pasadena, and while we are now all scattered in places distant, their fierce and incisive commitment keep me in check in a constellation of conscience.

Four people are in my thoughts constantly. These fantastic four are un-compromising in their commitment to authentic liberatory politics, true intellectual rigor, and genuine friendship, and they have taught me that these are the real master narratives. Ruth Wilson Gilmore and Craig Gilmore invited me into their home time and again, and when I finally accepted, I realized that I should have done so much earlier. Their work to abolish the death-making prison-industrial complex in California and beyond compels me to imagine our world anew, their vision matched by their generosity of heart and brilliance of mind. My plumblines of justice, against which I measure what I do daily, are the dynamic duo of Laura Pulido and Mike Murashige, who teach me that joy is always a part of struggle.

Thanks to Drs. Kun Ho Cho and Jiyoun Elizabeth Lee Cho, as well as James, Joseph, and Jane, for showing without reserve their pride in their newly adopted family member. My brother, Ted Lee, once told me to either "have a nice life" or "get a life." I don't remember, but in his taciturn way he meant both. My parents, the Rev. Dr. John Lee and Young Ja Lee, taught me that life's purpose is to serve people, and they never failed to remind me to do so but also never failed to demonstrate that with such admonishment comes the deepest in faith and love.

Julie Cho shows me daily how to live a courageous life. I am grateful that she shares hers with me. Beyond these, words would fail to bear adequate witness to what she means to me.

All these names uttered point to a history and community of new possibility in social recognition, but some more words require immediate attention. As I complete this project with these prefatory sentences to illuminate, however inadequately, the community with whom I've labored to bring this book to this form, these final words are marked also as a response to wordless chambers of power, whose silence testifies to a tragic passivity toward the possibility of mass human death. This book ends with my putting my books down in order that, as AIDS activists of the 1980s made for deep correspondence, silence might not equal death. To put it very simply: we in the United States are at the brink of war, and yet, as Robert Byrd chastised his colleagues on the U.S. Senate floor on February 12, 2003, for their "haunting silence," "we are truly 'sleepwalking through history.'" If anything, finishing this book at this time makes clear that the best way I can honor the community that lifted me throughout these years is to stop writing for the moment and fill power's silent somnolence with the voice of protest. For all I have to offer are the fallible witness of my word and the fragility of my body, whether in these pages or on the streets of Congress Avenue, the hue and cry of things written and spoken.

Austin, Texas
February 15, 2003

Introduction
Lines and Walls

> Beware of the M word
> Motherfucker
> Multiculturalism
> Everyone's wearing it
> on their lips
> and on their cheeks
> it's the latest cosmetic
>
> —Russell Leong, "Beware of the M Word"

The United States neither invented the word "multicultural" to describe its polity, nor has it ever adopted multiculturalism as a matter of social policy. But ever since the word captured the imagination of a few U.S. scholars in the last decades of the twentieth century, multiculturalism has held the honor (dubious or deserved, depending on where you stood during the "culture wars" of the 1980s) of becoming the nation's operative fantasy as it worried itself into the twenty-first century. Those in the business of reading, writing, and thinking about literature in American colleges and universities have, over the past three decades, taken on multiculturalism as both descriptive of what they do when they teach literature to the next generation of young readers and prescriptive of what they would like to see as the wineskins of older, canonical syllabi give way to newer, many-hued vintages. Embracing multiculturalism is now considered one answer to the troubling racial question that Du Bois posed to himself with simultaneous eloquence and wit: "How does it feel to be a problem?" Du Bois would not throw the same question back to his white interlocutors in *The Souls of Black Folk,* at least not directly. Still, the rise of multiculturalism as a guiding principle barely masks a deeper social concern that in some way, throughout U.S. history and in its cultural reproduction, we are all part of the problem.

Indeed, Du Bois's response to that initial question was to lay the problem at the feet of social relations and those who manage those relations, particularly those "of the darker to the lighter races of men." And these relations, he tells his readers, are built by the nation's operative fantasy, whose metaphor is a line. From this two-dimensional metaphor three-dimensional walls have been erected—legal, political, economic, cultural—to control the destinies of those living on either side of the walls constructed on the fantasy of the line, to facilitate on one side privileged life and on the other organized death. Du Bois has shouted throughout this long and terrible century to take notice of this line and to do something about its symbolic power and the real, material barriers that it can create. In the latter days of the twentieth century, people heard him and held aloft multiculturalism (among other things) as a possible solution. And multiculturalism's axiomatic principle to do something about the color line was simple: cross it.

But, as this book premises, it is much easier to cross a metaphorical line than to break down real walls. It is easier to imagine a new fantasy than to dismantle the actual racial legacies that a previous fantasy permitted the United States to nurture. If multiculturalism has become our new national and even, I might boldly venture, global story to stop the organized killing inherent in racism and to try to live differently, it remains unclear whether the practice of this agenda can live up to the promise of its parable. Both lines and walls demarcate space, one the space of lived imagination, the other the space of territorial life. Multiculturalism imagines anew how to reorganize the heretofore unequal representation of American life; its more difficult task lies in its capacity or even its willingness to redistribute uneven resources in American communities. The fantasy of multiculturalism's practitioners depends on this parallel movement of more equitable representation and resources: to win hearts and minds in the space of our imagined communities, to gain the bread and land for those living in the landscapes of our real neighborhoods. This book contends, however, that this recent history of multiculturalism and those who have written literature in its era have noticed an altogether different movement, one in which the work of representing race differently, the work of crossing lines, has not resulted in the work of redistributing resources. In many ways, it has not helped break down walls, but has instead helped to build them higher.

Nowhere does the shattering of multiculturalism's dream become more apparent than in U.S. cities during the "belle epoque" of the Reagan era. In the eight years that marked his official tenure and the four-year extension of the senior Bush's regime, cities and their residents suffered economic, political, and cultural hemorrhage so great that it constituted nothing less than a great urban crisis of terminal proportions. Certainly, U.S. cities have always struggled through crisis and change. Carl Sandburg captured boisterously the great transformation at the turn of the twentieth century of a sleepy Midwest town called Chicago into an industrial giant that became the "Hog Butcher, Tool Maker, Stacker of Wheat, Player with Railroads and Freight Handler to the Nation." The ascendancy of the United States into a world capitalist power in the aftermath of World War I and its eventual supremacy after World War II created great interlocking urban belts, stretching from the factories of the Northeast to the automobile manufacturers of Detroit to the defense contractors of Southern California's megalopolis. U.S. economic expansion in the post–World War II era accelerated some of the greatest internal mass migration ever seen in the world and, with the delinking of national origins as a de jure criterion from immigration policy in 1965, it brought on fundamental changes in the spatial configurations of American cities. By the time students absorbed as holy writ Robert Park and his Chicago School's classic paradigms of urban sociology and its concentric circles of racial and class-based residential patterns, the city was already morphing into something different. And no sooner had landmark judicial cases such as *Brown v. Board of Education* in 1954 and crucial laws like the Civil Rights Act of 1964 and the Voting Rights Act of 1965 been enacted to challenge the racial dictatorship that squeezed and shortened life for millions of people of color in the United States did many within these communities experience a wholly new kind of racial and urban misery. As lunch counters and public schools were desegregated to the joy of liberal and religious civil rights workers, and as restrictive covenants in Los Angeles and other cities were struck down to allow materially privileged families of color to buy homes in formerly all-white neighborhoods, a new kind of "American Apartheid" took shape that made even the most optimistic analyst pause, lapsing into silent apoplexy over how much had been lost in the midst of what had seemed like significant gain (Massey and Denton). Lyndon B. Johnson's oft-quoted "affirmative action" speech at Howard University in 1965 and the implementation of such policy under the Nixon administration in the early 1970s enabled a record number of Black and Brown students to enter the most elite universities, producing a cadre of intellectuals of color that would have thrilled Du Bois. But at century's end, the promise of productivity in a multicultural workforce had given way to the social death of more than two million men and women locked in the cages of federal, state, and municipal detention centers: prisons and their affiliated economies have made some urban communities the frontline for what can only be called genocide, where industries of punishment rather than institutions of learning have become the primary definers for racialized and poor people, the tragic bridge to this, the twenty-first century.

It is within this contradiction, between the dream of multiculturalism and its racial awakening, that intellectuals—artists, academics, activists, and other cultural workers—committed to the belief that the crossing of lines can point to ways to break down walls, find their struggle both crucial and desperate. It is also this contradiction that this book, *Urban Triage*, takes seriously as a crucial and desperate intellectual and political dilemma that demands critical investigation. I am not, of course, alone in this thought; practitioners of multiculturalism in the U.S. academy face this dilemma almost daily, even if they do not want to, sometimes as soon as they walk out of their classrooms. Two examples. The first took place the day after the fiftieth anniversary of the Japanese attack on Pearl Harbor— December 8, 1991—when the late poet and professor June Jordan delivered a speech to students at Mount Holyoke College in Massachusetts entitled "Toward a Manifest New Destiny" (195–211). Ostensibly a consideration of anti-Japanese stirring in the weeks before the Pearl Harbor commemorations, as well as a reflection on the protracted legacy of ethnocentric bias against people of color by lily-white institutions and white leaders, Jordan's address culminated in a celebration of demographic projections that forecast the superseding of people of color over whites in California by the year 2010. The numbers—"[O]verall, 61 percent people of color; 39 percent non-Hispanic white; 38 percent Hispanic; 16 percent Asian; 7 percent black"—provided Jordan with the evidence to assert that the sheer masses of people would fulfill the march of history as multicultural promise. And after quipping that such shifts toward increasing racial diversity compelled educators like herself to be ready to justify their homework assignments, Jordan called for the abolition of the canon: "[T]here can be no canon, there can be no single text for the education of our multicultural, multilingual, multiracial population!" (210). In its stead, she provided the following alternative: "And so I propose that we undertake to make of the teachings of public education in America a politically correct, a verifiably sane basis for our multicultural, multiracial, and two-gendered lives on this infinitely multifaceted, multilingual planet. I propose that we undertake this awesome work with pride and yes, fanatical zeal" (211). Such abolition of the literary canon would serve the eschatological hope that, in Jordan's assessment, would be fulfilled in the messianic promise of the majoritarian moment for people of color. But less than six months later, Jordan and those in her audience would awaken from their American multicultural dream—as would the rest of the United States—as the first flashpoints of violence erupted in pockets of South Central Los Angeles, whose fires would burn for days and whose racial rage and frustration continue to smolder.

The second example occurred about ten years earlier. The year 1981 saw the publication of a seminal collection of works by women of color; the title of the anthology, *This Bridge Called My Back: Writings by Radical Women of Color*, underscored the connection between literary production and self-conscious political mobilization. Here, the term "radical" was deployed to move beyond (but still encompass) its 1970s usage in feminist circles, the notion that "women" could be viewed as a "collective whole, a singular noun, its diverse elements part of its commonality" (MacKinnon, 40). The cumulative effects of patriarchy were said to act upon women of color differently than they do on white women, the ideology and violence used to enforce male power over women also enforcing racial domination to exact its toll of "multiple oppression" against women of color. Writer and coeditor Cherríe Moraga framed the construction and publication of *Bridge* as a necessary gesture of survival: "The materialism in this book lives in the flesh of these women's lives: the exhaustion we feel at the end of the day, the fire we feel in our hearts when we are insulted, the knife we feel in our backs when we are betrayed, the nausea we feel in our bellies when we are afraid, even the hunger we feel between our hips when we long to be touched" (Moraga and Anzaldúa, xviii). The anaphora that Moraga uses here—"we feel"—bears witness to the idea that the bringing together of diverse, and in many ways, divergent women writers of various racial and ethnic backgrounds is not merely a self-fabrication of "radical ideology," but the cultural production emerging out of lived experience. But it is Moraga's claim of the "materialism" of the book that gives her statement an added charge: this textual coalition not only reflects a socially based reality of the commonality of women of color in their shared systemic oppression, but is itself the productive working out, the formation of, this radical community. Cultural production, here exemplified by the textual coalition forged through the mantle of racial and sexual domination, is not just the flora to the root "reality" of material life; the work of the writers put together is itself "material," its expression and constitution more than a description of the felt experiences of "lives in the flesh," more like the creation of common experience in the textual act.

By 1983, with the publication of the second edition of *Bridge*, Moraga would cast her political commitment to this radical coalition of women writers of color in a more foreboding tone, simultaneously more urgent and more somber. The intervening two years were a period of intense political turmoil, an onslaught of repressive action instigated around the world, including the right-wing insurgencies in Nicaragua, the installment of U.S.-backed terror regimes in El Salvador and Chile, the marine invasion of Grenada, the hardening of apartheid in South Africa, the assassination of dissident Benigno "Ninoy" Aquino in the Philippines, and the new right social policies of the Reagan administration in the United States. The incipient "Third World" feminism imagined by the editors and writers of *Bridge* found a formidable enemy in this general front of conservative coalescence, which forecast the remaining years of the 1980s to be ones in which the celebration of new literary achievements by women of color would be severely tempered by their limited political efficacy in the face of this reinvigorated Right. Moreover, Moraga writes of a new "reality" emerging in this coalition, the emergence of visible cracks in the sutured alignment of political solidarity and literary community. Again, she positions this realization within the context of survival, reaffirming the political necessity of a book such as *Bridge*. But in 1983, the task of building and maintaining this cultural/political nexus proved more difficult: "The *idea* of Third World feminism has proved to be much easier between the covers of a book than between real live women" (Anzaldúa and Moraga, foreword). The shift not only in tone, but in theoretical claim is significant. Whereas in 1981 Moraga asserted the material immediacy of the writings lodged in *Bridge*, the notion that culture is not false ideology but is materially constituted and performed, in 1983 she inserts a distinction between the idea of solidarity and the difficulty of that community actually emerging "between real live women." Somehow, Moraga worries, *Bridge*'s stated purpose was missing its mark; thus, the new foreword warns its readers that the "political necessity" of the anthology underscores more the exercise of frustrated political will than the culmination of the book's transformation of actual—"real live"—social relations. Moraga's new foreword reads with more restraint, a fettering of vision that nevertheless, or perhaps even more so, stresses a coterminous exigency: "I must confess I hate the thought of this. . . . But . . . this world on fire provides us with no other choice."

The reservation reflected in the second inauguration of *Bridge* is not so different from the worries produced by the disjointed events of the early 1990s. If the initial celebration of Moraga's preface in the first edition provided readers with the chance to see the vision of "Third World" feminist solidarity in literary practice, her second edition remarks suggest less a vision and more a certain awakening on the part of the two coeditors. This movement from vision to awakening, from promise to a hampered reality, would mark a pervasive anxiety throughout the decade, a concern that writers in the 1980s would struggle with in understanding why the idea did not coincide with felt experience. Revisiting this question again ʾain, writers in this brief period produced works that strove to make f this awakening. Some sought to heal this apparent rift between ideal and anxious realization; others wrote to provoke, even exac- ʾs tension to perhaps expose the undercurrents of cultural worry in this decade. The 1980s would still prove a productive decade for artists of diverse hues, but the age would restrain their imaginations from unmitigated celebration of multicultural achievements.

What has thus far been implicit in these stories, and must be brought to light, are the racial dynamics of the discrepancy between, for example, Moraga's audacious celebration of 1981 and her palpable retreat in 1983, or the relation between Jordan's imperative of 1991 and Los Angeles's statement in 1992. An understanding of the historical movement of race will offer critical insights into the shift from the dream of multicultural promise to the awakening of racial contestation, if not antagonisms. *Urban Triage* thus contends that within the decade of the 1980s, a particular high point of a particular kind of multiculturalism into which cultural workers located their work, the production and representation of urban space took on a central status in diagnosing this social contradiction, whose dialectical impasse—between idea and experience, promise and nightmare—registered both the limits and value of such cultural production during this period. More specifically, this book tells the story of how the 1980s produced both possibility and constraint for writers attempting to examine their participation in the realignment of racial identity, in the reproduction of racial power and social inequality, and in the reassessment of literature's value in their broader social context. I argue that the very anxieties that writers display in their work, like the concerns made explicit or implicit in the examples of Jordan, Moraga, and the Los Angeles uprisings, signal literature's vital, because contested, insights into an understanding of this decade. The writers investigated in this study engage an era whose questions about race, representation, and resources we continue to ask today, and in whose shadow we also work, as multiculturalism ascends to become a legitimate, increasingly official discourse in American institutions and an accepted social warrant. This legitimated warrant of multiculturalism's promise takes shape in the 1980s even as, or as this study asserts, precisely because attention to the urban spaces that multiculturalism was designed to address, are increasingly abandoned as places where such social transformation might take place. These writers testify to the process of social triage in the diagnosis of the American city and to those who live in these spaces: as the contemporary U.S. political economy has engaged in what David Harvey insightfully calls the "organized abandonment" of racialized urban communities, the writers discussed in *Urban Triage* reflect on, take issue with, and at times participate in the tragic consequences for those who are, literally and figuratively, written off the map of power.

The chapters that follow study four literary narratives written by U.S. writers and the writers' engagement with the historical period in which they work. I situate these narratives in the 1980s, assuming that this decade constitutes a distinct historical formation as a definitive, if vexed, era of both multicultural promise and racial nightmare. Politically, this era is often referred to as the decade of Reagan-Bush and the rise of neoconservatism; coterminous with the ascendancy of the political right, the 1980s saw the dismantling of what little was left of Keynesian "welfare-warfare" economic policy and installed a new economic regime that dramatically shifted state and corporate resources away from vast sectors of the U.S. population. Thus the *political economy* of the 1980s determined the cultural production of multiculturalism and the cultural work that this formation would perform during this period. The era of multiculturalism was simultaneously an era of racial realignment, and the ensuing chapters reconstitute this period as a crucial moment in U.S. racial history. Central to this premise and my argument is the claim that these literary works display racial anxieties that threaten the very foundations of multiculturalism upon which the narratives rest. Readers of these urban fictions confront a contradiction that the writers themselves worry about: placing these works within a multiculturalist rubric brings multiculturalism itself into crisis. To the extent that the formation of racial anxiety is, in this book, a response to the interracial constitution of American identity and culture in general, the chapters place literary study in the circuitry of urban and ethnic studies, uncovering the layered and contingent construction of racial meaning and its material consequences as they took place in U.S. cities during the 1980s. For it is through the relation to, the respect of, and the transgressions toward these different approaches that readers of the city, of race, and of literature can better understand this period and perhaps imagine social relations in ways even beyond those the writers themselves or I can offer.

Thus I begin this tableau of literary work by first showing off its canvas. Chapter 1 provides the discursive frame around which and the material conditions under which the literary narratives considered in this study are placed. It begins with a brief theoretical discussion of racial formation as a dynamic and contingent process within specific historical and spatial circumstances. Given this idea of race as always a mirror and a filter through which to "read" one's world, the chapter then moves to cast a general outline on the political economy of U.S. cities during the 1980s. I locate three trends: first, economic restructuring within late U.S. capitalism incapacitated the life choices of those residing in these areas. Second, with this shift in the structure of the U.S. political economy arose a new configuration of state formation and capacity, one no longer arranged on the principles of Keynes (welfare), but rather on increased repression, what Toni Negri has called the "warfare state." Third, the state, in this new repressive capacity,

waged a low-intensity war against various collectivities of color. The decimation of these groups from the 1970s on produced an intellectual vacuum
for racialized people to mount a visible critique against their increasing
isolation. Alongside this reading of urban political economy, I examine the
extent to which sociological, ethnographic, and public policy accounts of
the "urban crisis" of the 1980s cast this crisis in racial terms, both descriptive and prescriptive. I take in particular the work of William Julius Wilson
and Charles Murray as examples of academic and popular accounts of
urban communities whose intent to reinvigorate studies of racial communities with economic analysis (Wilson) was overdetermined by a rhetoric of
racial pathology (Murray). To illuminate the contingency of racial meaning,
the contemporary U.S. political economy, and the discourse of urban crisis,
I provide a reading of Rita Dove's poem, "Nigger Song: An Odyssey," as a
dress rehearsal for the kind of analysis that subsequent chapters follow.

Chapter 2 considers the challenge that Chicana/o writers faced in re-
imagining their history of labor struggle and racial resistance while employing the rhetoric and ethos of the culture of triumphant individualism pervasive in the 1980s. I look closely at Alejandro Morales's 1988 narrative—his
most well known to an English-reading audience—*The Brick People*, ostensibly a historical novel that tells the story of the emergence of an East Los
Angeles barrio in the period preceding the Second World War. Morales
fictionalizes this cornerstone of Chicana/o historiography through the narrative strategy of *lo real maravilloso*, a tactic of literary resistance closely
associated with the magical realism of other Latin American writers. My
reading of *The Brick People* critiques the notion that narrative innovation
can be equated with political resistance. While contemporary critics of
Morales celebrate his use of "magical realist" techniques and episodes of
fantastic violence, I believe that such narrative strategies must be viewed
in the light of the redirection that Chicana/o studies and more generally
Chicana/o communities needed to take in the Reagan/Bush era. It is in
this light that I believe that Morales's innovations actually obfuscate the
forces that worked to maintain Chicana/os within the cordoned spaces of
the barrio, while displacing insurgency into the hands of an "exceptional"
figure—Morales as writer. This chapter opens up a paradigm that I maintain, even if I vary, throughout the project: collective resistance is sacrificed
at the altar of the writer's exceptionalism.

The third chapter examines the issue of solidarity between racialized communities, particularly between Asian Americans and African Americans.
Asian Americans have persistently looked to and borrowed from the processes and rhetoric inherent in the formation of Black identity, especially
those approaches aligned with 1960s and 1970s Black Power struggles, to

[margin annotations, handwritten:] magical realism? — eg lo real maravilloso? An aesthetic convention or theme tied to its subject matter? intent?

limn their own racially constituted identity. But in the 1980s these link-
ages underwent a fracture between the rhetoric of racial solidarity and the
practical possibilities of coalition based on shared racial experiences. As
I demonstrate in my reading of Hisaye Yamamoto's memoir, "A Fire in
Fontana" (1985), Asian American writers anxiously articulated the pro-
nounced difficulty of aligning their racial identity with the experience of
African Americans several years prior to more publicized tensions between
Blacks and Asians in 1992. My analysis of "Fire in Fontana" engages
Yamamoto's deeply layered metaphor of being "burnt black." For it is this
provocative image that enables her narrative to relay not only the social
history that generates the metaphor (the atrocities against Blacks in Los
Angeles), but also to atone for her reticence to act in the past (burning as
sacrifice, atonement) and to hope for future solidarity (blackness becomes
a unifying color for Asians and African Americans). Yet her intentions are
exceeded by the structural forces to which she as an Asian American is
subject: her final celebration of Black revolt is viewed at a distance. Her
story inevitably cannot fully resolve the guilt that fuels the story, for the
material contradictions between Asian Americans and African Americans
in Los Angeles during the 1980s belie a fully resolved ending to her story.
"Fire" highlights an undercurrent of anxiety and even racial guilt when the
story's implicit and understated thematizing of Asian American identity
cuts against the political and economic backdrop of Los Angeles in the
late 1970s and early 1980s. The story's complex rendering of racial constitution and identity points to a tacit acknowledgment of Asian American
complicity in the processes of economic restructuring commonly referred
to during this period as "urban redevelopment."

My reading of Wideman's *Philadelphia Fire,* the subject of chapter 4,
reveals a narrative that tries to be as honest as possible about one writer's
distance from the community that he wants to represent and attend to, and
the knowledge that he is unable to be part of that community. The novel
begins and ends with political paralysis. The series of narrative failures
in *Philadelphia Fire*—the failure of Cudjoe's novel, of the neighborhood
production of *The Tempest,* of the narrator's communication with his
incarcerated son, and of finding alliance with men and nonsexualized
relations with women—exposes how the trauma of the violence in 1985
underscored the state's capacity and willingness to eradicate alternative racial formations and normalize material "difference" through urban Black
fragmentation. Moreover, Wideman's novel highlights the instrumental
role that contemporary Black intellectuals have played in this creation of
normative "difference," a social position afforded the privileged sanction
in institutional, multicultural discussions of race, but also dependent on

the idea of permanent Black poverty located in deindustrialized, gentrified urban cores. I suggest in this chapter that maintaining this vision of black intellectual leadership (not unlike the energy undergirding the Million Man March) does not account for the alternative benchmarks to social struggle: the ethic of collectivity (beyond institutional realms) explored most often by Black women writers, the project of politicizing communities outside the boundaries of "legitimate institutions" like the academy or the government, the capacity for alliances to be generated between "intellectuals" and the Black working class without the Du Boisian "talented tenth" assumption of those in leadership. For Wideman, it is the destruction of MOVE that knells the larger trajectory of Black cultural formation in the 1980s: to borrow from the language of *The Tempest* used in the novel, the figure of Black agency is no longer insurgent Caliban, but ambivalent Ariel.

Chapter 5 contends, through an examination of Tom Wolfe's *Bonfire of the Vanities,* that whiteness, like other racial identities, undergoes significant changes in the political economy of the 1980s. I argue in this chapter that Wolfe's satire tracks and exposes the underpinnings of white privilege—a triangulation of power determined largely by the privatization of space, the continuation of white supremacy through property relations, and the attendant ethos of individualism—in 1980s New York, but that his mode of critique becomes the fundamental obstacle to an outright attack on the power of whiteness. Wolfe's narrative, centered primarily around Sherman McCoy, whose encounter with the "other" New York as a result of his hit-and-run accident/assault against a Black teenager propels him into the New York criminal justice system, tells the story of a man who has, in effect, lost his whiteness. Yet even as the novel attempts to dismantle one man's dependence on white privilege through satire, Wolfe's narrative must reassert whiteness in a more aggressive, masculine, and violent form. In so doing, Wolfe's novel displays the fundamental anxiety endemic to white identity in the 1980s, and his satire paradoxically remains invested in the whiteness that he struggles to expose. In doing so, Wolfe recuperates the vigilant brand of whiteness that resorts to violence and aggression to claim the power that was once structurally embedded as property. Thus, in satirizing one form of whiteness, Wolfe calls forth the palpable ghost of another—whiteness as violence—whose primitive mode (aggression) helps to further consolidate the normalized modes of accumulation and power (private property).

The book concludes with a brief discussion of the necessity of literary criticism as an institutional and intellectual endeavor and, paradoxically, the dire and urgent need to read and act beyond the protocols of institution and discipline. More meditation than manifesto, but with the rhetorical trappings of the latter, the conclusion proposes that in the contemporary intellectual search for cultural "resistance," literary critics are compelled to move beyond finding oppositional modes within literature itself and into the world of other ideas, other actions, even as those in other disciplines increasingly find their way into the sanctioned spaces of literary and cultural production to find hope from their desperate analyses. If, in fact, the labor of literary criticism and of literature in general is to make available "spaces of hope" (David Harvey's phrase) and terrains of possibility, if not calculable action, the future can only be hopeful and possible if the utterances of literary critics are taken seriously for what they are: utterances. Intellectual honesty about institutional limits can bring about disciplinary crisis. But it is the crisis of our own speech—what we are institutionally trained to do—that might just be enough for something new to happen. And if in thinking through the limits of what we say we discover just how valuable we are, we might more humbly and more effectively think through the work and value of literature, and the difference it might bring in the world in our newest age of multicultural privilege and racial misery.

The argument set forth in this book takes seriously the materiality of culture and on good days dreams the dream of Marx, that even theory—"the weapon of criticism"—might become a material force gripped by the masses. Culture, in this view, is not simply a reflection of the political and economic forces that propel a society forward, or backward as the case may be, but itself becomes a productive force, registering, pushing, gesticulating a way out of a social dialectic that appears impassable. Of course, culture is *also* a reflection of these objective forces; it is still, in part, the bladder of history, taking in and often spilling back out what society at large has consumed. Given canonical status by our intellectual institutions, this view of culture is called art and literature: it is, perhaps, what has given a text like Eliot's *The Wasteland* such sanctified status in the American academic industry. But before any cultural work is afforded, even lauded as, a moment of individual genius, it is first the assemblage of available material in the artist's world, or to put it in academic garb, it is a productive instance of historical determination. This dual definition of culture or cultural production as both reflection and transformation is held aloft together, for as Raymond Williams has shown us, determination itself is not simply a "setting of limits . . . it is also an exertion of pressures" (87). Against unqualified abstractions of determination, Williams proposes a notion of society that is at once more dynamic and generous of cultural production, and more rigorous and demanding of culture's critique: "Society is . . . a constitutive process with very powerful pressures which are both expressed in political, economic, and cultural formations and, to take the full weight of 'constitutive,' are internalized and become 'individual wills'" (87). To the extent that the four narratives under investigation manifest racial anxiety as their internalized expressions of a determination's "pressures," they perform a kind of cultural work that on the level of "individual will" provides some glimmers of possibility, but while spun in the constitutive realms of political and economic formations do an altogether different kind of work. What makes these particular narratives distinctive, and so appealing, is that their creators are all too aware of this contradiction, which is why their specific anxieties register even greater social ennui. To put it analogically: if multiculturalism as racial anxiety indexes or defines the approach of the writers' fictions, multiculturalism as urban triage determines the larger reception and function of these narratives.

The title of this study and its metaphorical lens—urban triage—demands further explanation. Derived from the French *trier,* which means to pick or to cull, triage first appears in agricultural contexts as a process of assorting products of different quality. For some inexplicable reason, perhaps because in English the word approximates the etymological prefix "tri," the Latinate "three," the attribution and division of quality has usually gone along segments of three. Fleece or coffee beans, for example, would be separated by determining best, middle, and worst specimens, and this last group, not worthy of being sold on the market, would invariably be tossed out or left for the scavenging poor to glean. Triage today is more commonly used in specific professional vocabulary, most notably medicine and especially in emergency medicine, field medicine, or other modes of trauma and immediate care (DeGowin and DeGowin, 1–2). Its principal definition as a way of assorting quality, however, has not changed much from its agricultural roots. Triage as a way of classifying patients' need for treatment was first used in the mid-nineteenth century, but became widely popular at the turn of the twentieth century, and was first used as a diagnostic method en masse during World War I (Winslow, 1–4). Indeed, triage is almost always associated with moments of crisis; thus it is no surprise that the crisis of war pushed triage to the forefront of intellectual technologies, as new forms of destruction demanded new ways of saving as many broken bodies as possible. Medical professionals use various forms of triage, almost always sorting patients into groups of three. In hospital emergency, triage nurses and doctors assign "levels" to determine the length of time a person can endure his or her ailment before receiving proper treatment: tagged Level One, the patient must be provided care immediately; labeled Level Three, she might have to wait all day. During wartime, triage can be even more stark. Patients are literally tagged or marked to correspond to those who need urgent attention, those who require medical care but can wait, and those whose injuries are so extreme that they are beyond help. In other words, triage can tag someone as "dead" even before the person stops breathing (Winslow, 9–10).

While triage usually corresponds to the assigning of urgent medical care, the term also is harnessed by social intellectuals who use the term to describe the problem of how best to distribute scarce resources in explosive demographic situations. In times of food shortages, for example, triage determines which groups in the population would be best served with meals and which, sadly, must be unfed or underfed for the greater good of that society (Rubenstein, 196). In the context of population studies, triage tends toward Malthusian assumptions, where the taxonomies of people and the qualitative judgment of their survivable value is often judged as cold-hearted, callous, cynical justifications for existing unequal relations to power. Bob Moses, legendary civil rights activist, organizer of the Mississippi Freedom Democratic Party in 1964 and now founder of the Algebra Project, has argued as much, labeling the current state of U.S. public education as a calculated triage, in which public policy makers, politicians, and educators decided that the United States could not afford to fund public education fully and thus created a hierarchical system of reward that would save a select few and leave the greater mass of other students behind.

Leaving aside for the moment (but only a moment) moral judgment, we can ascertain a common thread between mundane, medical, and demographic definitions of triage. Triage is diagnosis infused with power, a decision made with authority. It is not healing, but it is the way to healing and therefore can be, and often is, a choice literally of life and death. Triage is a tool for making order out of chaos, and most importantly for assigning value to that order. And lest we condemn at the outset the seeming heartlessness of triage practitioners, we must also acknowledge the extent to which triage pervades almost all professional academic disciplines and indeed helps to shape the very basis and structure of our disciplines. In political science, it is called "rational choice"; we in literary studies extol it as the "canon"; in psychoanalysis, it is the difference between neurosis and psychosis; in the liberal arts in general and during times of war it is referred to as "civilization." So whither multiculturalism in this discussion of triage? Multiculturalism has usually been regarded as the antidote to American cultural triage, the "canon wars" a sign at the very least of shifting the terms of what counts as legitimate literature. Multiculturalism can be taken to mean a form of a particular "exertion of pressures" on the boundaries of cultural products worth reproducing, and in this case, it matters who is granted or affords himself the authority to make such decisions. But this book contends that multiculturalism, when placed in the circuit of its particular formation during the 1980s alongside its attendant political and economic formations, played a crucial role in determining the racial terms of urban triage. And the stakes of urban triage are akin to the stakes of war and the calculating callousness of overpopulation demographers: multiculturalism and literary rubric in the 1980s laid the ground upon which one could rationally diagnose and then decide who would thrive, who would die, and who would remain the walking wounded in American cities.

It is in and because of the conceptual configuration of multicultural-ism as urban triage that these writers express racial anxiety in their work. Multiculturalism has granted space to these writers, many of whom would not have been read in earlier, more stringent versions of the literary canon, and some of these writers are still not read regularly in U.S. literature classrooms. With the exception of Tom Wolfe, the book's sole white writer, none of these writers' works can be said to have achieved popular acclaim. Thus, their literary expressions are qualified by relatively small audiences. Whatever political interventions these narratives make are even smaller in scope. Nonetheless, each of these narratives consciously performs a kind of intervention, if only because they are each harnessed within the auspices of multiculturalism as justifications for the expansion of creative and intellectual space for U.S. people of color, and they do the work that U.S. intellectuals of color have struggled so hard and so long to claim should be included as legitimate objects of study. Despite Henry Louis Gates Jr.'s admonition against anthropological fallacies and others who refuse to reduce these narratives to simple mimesis, and perhaps to the artists' own chagrin for the muting of their individual creativity, these works are seen—and the writers themselves know this—as somehow purporting to represent communities previously unstudied or understudied. They are, in the first instance if not the last, granted representational status. Of course, they do not end there, and the narratives themselves resist this status, but the fictions' entry into larger social consciousness begins with their representational claim to the multicultural impulse.

Racial anxiety therefore emerges in these works just as concern over the racial representation in cultural formations during the 1980s went, for the moment, underground. This is, after all, the decade that enabled David Palumbo-Liu to make the following claim in the early 1990s: "The battles for the inclusion of ethnic literature in the curriculum of American literary studies have been fought, and in many cases, won" (*Ethnic Canon,* 1). And yet racial anxiety over multiculturalism's triumph asks: What has been won, and for what end? Feeding their worries, an answer returns in the form of a whisper that the writers cannot bear but also cannot avoid: triage. These writers evince individually through racial anxiety what is collectively understood as multiculturalism's implicit, if not intentional project, that recognizing and nurturing a racial renaissance in the realm of cultural production could address, even trump, the paucity of attention given to the political economic poverty of racialized urban communities. And as the politics of representation took center stage over the politics of resource, these narratives writhed on the uncomfortable island of multi-cultural "victory" in a sea of urban woe and loss. Called upon to represent this generalized racial sadness, these writers do try to take on that call, but in the process write more about the distance that separates them from the experience of the urban many, a signal crisis in writing that mirrors the terminal crisis of urban triage.

But crisis leads to creativity, and racial anxiety in these fictions brings with it a certain amount of critical admiration, at least from a literary standpoint. Chapters 2 and 3 dramatize fictional works that most explic-itly struggle with the weight of history, and show how particular stories of racialized communities—Chicana/o and Japanese American in these cases—embed themselves in the terms of limit and liberation that are part of each writer's cache. In the case of *The Brick People,* Chicana/o labor historiography is punctuated by scenes of fantastic racial violence, and such magical moments produce crises in the lives of the barrio's residents. Yet it is this same commitment to formal innovation that ultimately leads to a resolution that consolidates, rather than dissipates, racial power to reconsti-tute Chicana/o identity and community in a logic of capitalist legitimation. In Yamamoto's memoir, "A Fire in Fontana," ironic distance and skepticism toward her narrator enable ever so briefly a glimmer of glee that readers are invited to share in the potential destruction of civil society. Left suspended in this momentary exuberance is a definitive crossing over into racial trea-son, and the story leaves open the unresolved disappointment of broken soli-darities between Blacks and Asian Americans in Los Angeles, and portends a future dangerous crossroads at which, as Viet Nguyen has implied, Asian Americans may someday become racially white, take on the privileges ac-corded to whiteness, and enjoy the demands of white supremacy—even though they may have different ethnic features. The narratives teach us how to abandon people even as they cling to hopes that this might not come to pass. But failed political projects are not, I believe, the last word. Rather, they offer up brief episodes of irrationality, moments of crisis that are at once signposts to a present absence and a future anterior, and a reminder of lost but not forgotten social warrants for greater change.

cf essay by Kara Keeling in GLQ 2009
"Looking for M___"

Chapters 4 and 5 even more explicitly confront this question of what difference aesthetic innovation can make beyond the spaces of the book. *aesthetic* Whether it is Wideman's agonized devotion to modernist meditation or Wolfe's wild but deliberate satire, formal strategies such as these distend time and space in the city and allow the critic to look deeply into what went so terribly wrong in Philadelphia and New York. More than Morales or Yamamoto, Wideman and Wolfe confront the urgency of urban triage in their respective cities—operatively coined "redevelopment" by planners, politicians, and pundits—and offer up narratives that, again, provide provisional glimpses into the uneven relationship between multicultural power that feeds off and fuels urban triage, and the death of so many who are left in its wake. They show, quite accurately, the cognitive map of urban triage and the institutions of culture that undergird and justify that map. Where these two narratives part, aside from their distinctive approach to language, is in the nexus of language and politics, and the conclusions drawn from that meeting place. Regarding urban space leads one to political paralysis, barely above despair, and in the other a kind of Nietzschean glee that reaffirms with laughter the death drive and maintenance of white supremacy and its total destruction of the city. These writers teach and reaffirm Raymond Williams's paradigmatic statement about determination and agency, structure and culture: ideology and political economy do not tell us everything about individual agency and social choice; on the other hand, neither can narrative displacements fully transcend the history into which they write.

The journey that this book takes, then, is a modest proposal to discover and recover an urban palimpsest from celebrations of easy multicultural promises and even easier visions of racial pathologies. It offers the story of how artists and their creations have been used to concoct the parable of multiculturalism through the redaction and excision of the racial nightmare from which the dream emerges. To return to the agricultural roots of triage, I metaphorically reconstruct the story in this way: chapter 1 explores how the ground was tilled; chapters 2 and 3 dig up the roots; and chapters 4 and 5 look closely at what has grown, what fruit has been borne of this historical soil. Urban space, my conceptual plot, has often been the preeminent arena through which intellectuals offer social judgment on their society and existential value on their very position as observers (and sometimes prophets) of society. Because of their seemingly intrinsic ability to display communities in contestation, to work out various diversities, and to mitigate unequal relations of power, cities tell us what, how, and why we value what we do. The urban, unlike other spaces, does not allow us to escape from our built realities, refusing the call to light out into territories, which are, after all, social constructions themselves. Where literature can register the possibilities and disappointments of urban space, as they emerge in the 1980s, it makes the task of the critic as a figural Foucauldian archaeologist or Benjaminian translator all the more crucial. But we still see through the looking glass darkly, and although we see much through this lens, we can, like the artists we study, register crisis but can rarely incite it. Thus this study is a production of racial anxiety as much as it is a critique of it; it is indebted to the promise of multiculturalism that it can never fully expiate. As much as we want to do more, we are wedded structurally more to crossing lines than to breaking down walls, to diagnostic cutting rather than recuperative healing. This is the condition of academic racial anxiety, felt individually but determined collectively. It is my belief, as a young literary critic who willingly and modestly takes on the task and hopes to recover, discover, and point elsewhere, that the best of answers will be in the provisional spaces that institutions tolerate but do not fully sanction, and in the conversations that compel us to read all kinds of different books and nudge us, at times, to put our books down.

1

Mapping Urban Triage and Racial Crisis

> In the 1980s, things changed, for many reasons. One, of course, was the Reagan era.
>
> —Renee Tajima

> Well it's six o'clock in Oakland
> and the sun is full of wine
> I say, it's six o'clock in Oakland
> and the sun is red with wine
> We buried you this morning, baby
> in the shadow of a vine
>
> —Ishmael Reed, "Oakland Blues"

Looking out from his home on Fifty-third Street in Oakland, California, Ishmael Reed wrote the opening lines of "Oakland Blues" in 1988. Defying the satirical invective for which he is most well known as a novelist and essayist, Reed turns his creative energies into a poem full of urban pathos in that most apt and oft-used of Black verse: the blues. Images of the evening sun "full" and "red" with wine echo the beginning of W. C. Handy's twelve-bar "St. Louis Blues" (1914): "I hate to see de evenin' sun go down." But while Handy's song tells the story of a woman pining for a lover who has abandoned her for a white woman, Reed's poem voices even more explicitly the pain of collective loss, the deeper pang of absence for a dead lover who belongs to no one in particular and thus is shared by all. Elsewhere in *Points of View,* the collection where we find "Oakland Blues," Reed writes

1

of love again as "full of wine," and notes very quickly that love kills "if you're gay." Such intertextual repetition provides clues to the source of the sorrow in "Oakland Blues," evinced by the lines later in the poem: "they told you of the sickness/almost eighteen months ago." The disease is not named, but it is not hard to read these lines, and the poem itself, as a reminder about the genocidal impact of AIDS on the Black community and as an elegy for the suffering of those who otherwise would remain out of sight, out of mind. In the midst of the general AIDS crisis, as activists called on a complacent Reagan administration to boost funding for disease prevention and to fast-track experimental drugs like AZT, urban communities of color felt the impact of an even more sinister urban triage.[1] It was as if in drawing the map of the AIDS epidemic, Gertrude Stein's horrible claim about Oakland—"there is no there there"—was public health's dictum.[2] Reed's blues tap into the form's historical incarnation of Black injury and its contemporary manifestation of communal crisis, the result of an authorized politics of forgetting against which Reed, like the dead lover, fights "Death," with characteristic pugilism, "toe to toe."

Death is a singular experience, but inflected as social crisis. The era in which Reed wrote this poem has been described by Ruth Wilson Gilmore in a different, but not so dissimilar, context as an age of human sacrifice. Draw maps, as David Harvey does, and they tell stories about what he calls "organized abandonment," forgotten places and forgotten people buried by the creative destruction of capital's movement in and out of lands, and the discursive and territorial spaces cleared by political bulldozers: "The accumulation of capital and misery go hand in hand, concentrated in space" (Harvey, *Limits*, 418). Death is what we are left with, and where the writers studied in this book begin, the operative term of the cost and consequence of revolutionary defeat. Theoretically, death is the metaphorical placeholder for a terrain of political absence, the cards that white supremacy's regime deals that entail physical death for many, and social death for an even greater number. Death is the result and logic of urban triage, "durable inequality" writ large and embraced by the primary definers of U.S. society: the state, the media, and other cultural and economic institutions (Tilly). The 1980s brought into sharp relief once again the opportunity to define racism in these terms, the capacity for individuals and collective bodies in power to shorten life for whole segments of a population, and nothing less than that. For is this not what Daniel Patrick Moynihan's infamous "benign neglect" thesis was all about, to hasten death for urban communities of color deemed pathological and therefore expendable, and to justify that principle as a matter of social policy? When commentators wonder about the causes, rational or not, of contemporary urban uprising, why Black and

Brown people burn down their own neighborhoods, their eyes and ears fail to see and hear that amidst chaos and violence is our own reflection: you are killing us. Paul Beatty's satirical novel, *The White Boy Shuffle* (1996), makes clear that racism and our apathy, in the last instance, follow the path to genocide, as his characters of color flock to Los Angeles to engage in mass suicide, to participate in "the ultimate sit-in." It is in this context that this chapter sets out to trace the decade during which the structural and discursive realignment of U.S. racial formation mitigated, harnessed, and ultimately legitimized the cultural logic of racism through urban triage, of urban triage as death's calculus.

If the story of U.S. ascendancy as the world's superpower has followed from a historiography that chronicles domestic expansion from its eastern seaboard to the Pacific coast and beyond, then the story of urban triage, conversely, moves from west to east, as an imaginative trajectory of a new imperialist sweep. The 1980s might rightfully begin in California, the gestation of urban triage coinciding with the rise of Ronald Reagan from his mediocre movie résumé to his assumption of the California governorship in 1967, from which he would then meteorically rise to the U.S. presidency in 1980. The "ping" of Sputnik that terrified Americans in 1958 precipitated an unprecedented national project to produce a new strata of technicians, engineers, and other professionals to offset the seeming superiority of Soviet intellectual capital. In California, such anxiety over U.S. educational complacency resulted in the Master Plan for Higher Education of 1960 during the administration of Edmund G. "Pat" Brown, which guaranteed affordable postsecondary education to every high school graduate in the state. With its now well-known three-tier system of community college (two-year), state college (four-year with nonresearch graduate), and university (four-year and graduate research), higher education in California became a benchmark for ways the state could invest in its future specialized labor force, its putative cold war soldiers.[3]

Under the successive administrations of Brown and Reagan, California led the way in showing how vigorous Keynesianism could actively manage social relations. But the state also would show the rest of the country that political change could outstrip the parameters of state mitigation. The passage of the Voting Rights Act of 1965, the crown jewel of the nominally Christian-led civil rights movement, was overshadowed later that summer when Black and Brown people in Watts vented their rage over police brutality and general systemic betrayal. In the fall of 1966, Oakland's Merritt College housed two obscure Black students who drafted a Ten-Point Platform to circulate within the city's Black community, armed themselves with shotguns, and started monitoring police as Oakland's finest routinely stopped Black youth. Within two years, the Black Panther Party for Self-Defense set up chapters in almost every major city in the United States, started breakfast programs and free clinics, and threatened to send "brigades" to support the North Vietnamese, while other young people of color copied almost verbatim the model of the Ten-Point Platform and tweaked it for their respective communities' needs. By 1968, the Black Panther Party became, in the eyes of FBI director J. Edgar Hoover, "America's greatest internal security threat," prompting a terrified Governor Reagan in 1967 to pass, ironically, a gun-control law designed to criminalize what was then the Black Panther Party's constitutionally sanctioned right to bear unconcealed arms. The new militancy of these antiracist formations soon captured the imagination of college students, first at San Francisco State College, where students revolted against an education designed to create in them a pliant technical workforce and demanded a Third World College attentive to their working-class, raced communities. Later, in less than a year, strikes emerged in places like the University of California at Berkeley and UCLA, and in fact, in almost every state college and university so that by 1970, ethnic studies became a permanent, albeit still tenuous, fixture in California higher education. On the streets and on campuses, liberation struggles emerged on various fronts—antiwar, anticolonial, free speech—and connected globally faster than the forces of authority could put them out: "[N]o sooner had the smoke cleared in one place than fires of revolt flared up in another" (Gilmore, "Globalisation," 176).

Urban rebellion and campus unrest thus brought to a critical limit the Keynesian social wage, even as this same revolt was largely conditioned by this self-same state demand. If the state sought to expand its guarantees onto populations as a bulwark against further mutiny, thereby managing those who had formerly been excluded from the social wage, it could not fully contain the energies—at least for the moment—of a multiracial population stirred to redefine the terms of *how* they were to be included. The students at San Francisco State did not simply call for a department of Ethnic Studies to affirm previously unacknowledged identities living in the midst of Eurocentric curricula, to see themselves nudged into a glorious American story of assimilationist inclusion. Their target was twofold. First, consciously regarding the ways in which the Master Plan of 1960 dispensed fully funded higher education while at the same time maintaining hierarchy in its three-tiered structure, students rejected this educational functionalism that would place them, those in the second tier, into specific roles as future laborers in California's great economic engine.[4] They noticed the disproportionate funding granted to research universities to the detriment of schools serving more working-class communities and communities of color, and also criticized the new elitism that the Master Plan implemented—the cutoff for students eligible for a seat at the University of California narrowed from the top 15 percent in California's high schools to the top 12.5 percent; eligibility for entrance into a state college was narrowed from the top 50 percent to the top 33⅓ percent. Second, related to this critique of the Master Plan's ultimate goal of creating a new army to fill California's labor needs, students struck to dispense completely with the imposition of admissions standards and to refocus higher education's mission to address the immediate needs of their communities, which were just beginning to feel the effects of a prolonged urban abandonment. The campus would become a space in which community concerns could be addressed and argued; theory would derive from their material conditions, and not the other way around. The demand for full admissions and a "Third World College" that would be "relevant" to its surrounding neighborhoods of color therefore took the logic of the Keynesian guarantee and flipped it on its head. What so infuriated the school's president, S. I. Hayakawa, and Governor Reagan was not only that Black, Chicana/o, Asian, Native, and white students brought San Francisco State to a virtual standstill for months, but that this brand of multiculturalism, ironically created by the conditions laid by the Master Plan eight years earlier, sought expansion rather than containment, anarchy rather than pliable social order, democratic crisis rather than republican diversity management. Students endured tear gas and police batons to bring their communities into light, for fear that their entry into the world of college would further accelerate their communities' growing obsolescence.

The spirit of national treason as a badge of honor—signaled by widespread draft dodging, pitched battles with police forces and National Guard units, constant mass protests, and urban uprisings in cities as big as Chicago and as small as Newark—spread across the United States and indicated that inclusion needed to be radical. Thus, it was the dispossessed, the U.S. wretched of the earth, those such as students, wage earners, welfare recipients, feeling the immediacy of the state's mitigation, which could easily turn into brute violence, who revolted, struck, and claimed historical and moral supremacy over the forces that struggled to hold back social disorder. Asian Americans saw right through the duplicitous praise that reporters heaped on them in the mid-1960s and railed for the next three decades against their racialized portrayal as loyal model minorities who could shame Black and Brown people out of their insurgency.[5] White students engaged in racial betrayal and aligned themselves with people of color to resist the confluence of white supremacy, U.S. imperialism, and police and penal brutality. Sidney Lumet tapped into this rage as late as 1975, his film *Dog Day Afternoon* featuring a young Al Pacino as an incompetent bank robber who temporarily staves off police bullets by screaming "Attica! Attica!" to the delight of a multiracial cast of bystanders and the movie's audience. In 1969, Black and Puerto Rican transsexuals in New York finally lashed back against constant police raids, and soon Stonewall became the historical benchmark for the gay and lesbian liberation movement; a couple of years later, Black Panther Party leader Huey P. Newton pronounced that gays constituted the most radical and vanguard of liberation movements in the United States, thus forging in public speech, if not necessarily in practice, political movements based not simply on identities, but in their intersections. Even in Frank Rizzo's town, Philadelphia, groups like the Black Panther Party, whose members included a young North Philadelphia resident-turned-reporter named Mumia Abu Jamal, established offices for a brief period before they were brutally repressed by Rizzo's police henchmen. Remnants of these earlier groups would transmogrify into the MOVE organization, which itself was dispatched by a satchel bomb and thousands of bullets in 1985. Nonetheless, the cultural politics of radical inclusion stretched state legitimacy to its limit and, however unevenly, created wholly new capacities for social imagination, in the words of Toni Cade Bambara, "to see what the factory worker sees, what the prisoner sees, what the welfare children see, what the scholar sees . . . what the ruling-class myth-makers see as well" (quoted in Lipsitz, *American Studies,* 289). More than anything else, what was let loose was a fundamental skepticism in ruling-class mythmaking, as disenfranchised people set to work to build new stories for themselves and hope that new myths might actually form the basis for a new world.

But these tectonic shifts in U.S. social relations that emerged first in California and then spread across the country must be seen along an even greater and longer fault line, one whose effects traveled with surprising speed. And indeed, even as poor people and students sought to bring to crisis historiographies of U.S. triumphalism, repression and punishment were just around the corner, the result of a crisis in political economy that coincided with the revolts of the late 1960s. During the 1950s and 1960s, the United States led the greatest economic expansion the world had ever seen, immediately after World War II had effectively demolished most of the world's markets. It did so through three arenas. First, the U.S. government, through the Federal Reserve, operated as the world's central bank and let loose a spectacular amount of liquidity in order to sustain this unprecedented expansion in production and trade—the Marshall Plan was, among other things, an attempt to do something with this surplus money. But expenditures can never be legitimated through mechanistic means; the United States needed a political rationale. Thus, second, the creation of the "communist menace" provided ideological backbone for the incredible peacetime military buildup, of the United States domestically and Europe and Japan internationally.[6] In no other moment of world history has a country held (and continues to hold) so many military outposts around the world during peacetime. James O'Connor, who dubbed the United States a "welfare-warfare state," sums it up this way: "[T]he military-industrial complex and U.S. militarism are inconceivable outside of the context of world capitalist development" (*Fiscal Crisis*, 153). Finally, the United States encouraged and compelled newly decolonized nations to help feed its economic expansion by providing the West with a seemingly unlimited reservoir of natural resources to exploit and control. And for about twenty years, this strategy seemed to work and work exceptionally well. The Cuban missile crisis all but signaled to the world U.S military supremacy over the Soviet Union, the revitalization of Western Europe and Japan gave credence to U.S.-financed economic expansion, and the rising rates of per capita income seemed to suggest that world capitalism would indeed "lift all boats."

But just as this *pax Americana* seemed absolutely triumphant, cracks and eventually crises began to form. Vietnam became the flashpoint of this crisis. As Giovanni Arrighi argues, First World dreams of a Third World bloc flexible and amenable to corporate exploitation of its resources faced up to the contradictory impulse of national sovereignty over these same resources. In other words, the United States encouraged decolonization in hopes of securing the Third World as its reservoir of cheap natural resources, but the very process of decolonization encouraged the spirit of self-determination that proved an obstacle to U.S. interests. As Arrighi puts it,

> The exercise of full sovereignty rights by Third World states was bound to reduce this flexibility, and eventually eliminate it completely. Should these states feel free to use their natural and human resources as they saw fit—including hoarding or mobilizing them in the pursuit of domestic, regional or world power, as sovereign states had always felt free to do—the pressure on supplies generated by the expansion of the U.S. regime of accumulation would inevitably implode in the form of "excessive" competition within and among First World states. (321)

This is what we saw in Vietnam. At the very moment that the United States had reached its highest level of global reach militarily, ideologically, politically, and economically, it also sowed the seeds for its undoing. What resulted after the mid-1960s was a deep military and legitimacy crisis for the United States—a military crisis, because it could not defeat one of the poorest countries in the world, and a legitimacy crisis, because it could no longer scare the American people into pouring money and shedding American blood for a communist menace that it seemed to have defeated after the 1962 crisis. Finally, by the end of the 1960s the great economic boom across the world began to contract: corporate competition, along with worldwide rising wage rates, began to cut into profits, which precipitated, among other things, the abandoning of the fixed exchange rate of the dollar toward a flexible rate based on a pure dollar standard, the decreasing ability of the U.S. government to regulate monetary supply, and the consequent rise of oil rents to the First World, which culminated in the first oil shock of 1973. Alongside legitimacy and military crises and coterminous with the Vietnam War, the United States and the world suffered the first great economic crisis in two decades.

Thus, the age of urban triage in the 1980s can also be called the long decade, to borrow from the historical analyses of capitalism's "long centuries" put forth by Ferdinand Braudel, Immanuel Wallerstein, Eric Hobsbawn, and Giovanni Arrighi. The "signal crises" that emerged between 1968 and 1973—the very years of ethnic studies' flowering, the days of rage, long hot summers, and North Vietnamese victory—resulted in major structural adjustments to mitigate the decline in the profitability of U.S.-produced goods. The same year that Arab nations began to embargo oil reserves, the United States abandoned the gold standard, devalued the dollar, and sent the world into recession for two years. As inventories gathered dust and corporate profits from production and trade began to contract, the state was under enormous pressure to fill its coffers elsewhere. At the end of the 1960s, U.S. capital began its inexorable flight out of its domestic territory into two primary domains: the first was an outsourcing of production that helped stem the rise in wages that U.S. workers had enjoyed for two decades. The second was a shift of mobile capital out of production and into the speculative financial realm. This corporate offensive, as Glenn Omatsu calls it, coincided with a new reluctance among corporations to bear most of the burden of the tax base, something that they had agreed to decades earlier as part of Roosevelt's New Deal. Capital's ability to convince federal and state governments to reduce its tax contributions laid the groundwork for the middle-class tax revolts of homeowners in the mid- to late 1970s, which further accelerated the dismantling of the Keynesian bargain. The crisis in state legitimacy, exemplified by corporate retreat from the state as the site of social capital, threatened to erode state capacity. For working people, the "fiscal crisis" of the state meant the loss of high-wage jobs in the industrial sector, the erosion in real wages for those who managed to stay working, and an increasing tax burden disproportionately placed on wage-earning renters.

Activists and urban revolters soon found themselves the target of U.S. militarism come home and still smarting from the global shame of Vietnam. Nixon's invocation of a "silent majority" answered questions of state legitimacy by pointing the finger at the "source" of the problem: Black and Brown people scripted by primary definers as drug dealers and users, violent criminals, gang members, welfare abusers, and promiscuous reproducers. This finger shook with a fear and loathing that spread into a general "moral panic" (Stuart Hall's phrase). And yet the sources of this moral panic, generalized into a fear of racialized urban space as the United States entered the 1980s, must be effectively read against the political and economic panic that produced a range of public anxieties, which the state harnessed to retool itself into a new toothy force. In previous years, starting from the rise of American political and economic hegemony in the capitalist world after World War II, the United States fashioned its economy along Fordist lines of control, while Keynesian principles guaranteed effective demand for capital and protection from calamity for labor in a tense but mutually beneficial dance: mass consumption would follow and complement mass production of goods for the majority of people, while the state would assume the responsibility of absorbing those on the margins of this economic bargain through a combination of corporate incentives and welfarism.[7]

As Mike Davis has noted, Fordism enabled American workers to reap the fruits of their labor. High consumption of durable goods led to the increasing suburbanization and privatized mobility (the automobile purchase boom) of the American landscape: "By 1950 and 1960, suburbs grew *forty* times faster than central city areas, while automobile registration increased by 22 million" (*Prisoners*, 191). Unlike their European counterparts, whose gains in wage levels coincided with the enlargement of a political bloc for organized labor, American workers opted for a more sedate "collectivity of privatized consumers" (191). Thus although George Lipsitz is at pains to argue that the 1940s produced some of the most revolutionary and radical activity among rank-and-file workers—whose unauthorized "wildcat strikes" of 1945 antagonized even their national unions—he concurs with Davis in noting that "individual economic mobility and ethnic loyalty have been class strategies for survival as well as individual means of escape" (*Rainbow*, 12). While this confluence of personal mobility and racial chauvinism was most clearly manifested in the exclusion of workers of color from gains posted by white workers during the post–World War II era, nonwhite workers were also compelled by this ideology of individualist gain. In Alejandro Morales's *The Brick People*, as we will see in chapter 2, Octavio leads a bitter and eventually failed attempt to unionize the brickyard workers, deciding in the aftermath that "in the future no one would help him" (246). By the end of the novel, Octavio's dismissal of a class-based collective struggle gives way to its logical end, even more strident as Morales narrates this postwar scene through the lens of the 1980s: Octavio and his son Arturo displace potential resistance to racial violence and opt instead to rebuild their home, which represents a future built on the ethos of patriarchal control of private property. Their identities remain connected to the racialized barrio only insofar as such racial solidarity enables them to achieve personal success. Buying a car, accumulating appliances, but especially owning a house to clear space for oneself and one's family: these are the markers of the postwar American Dream that resulted from the deliberate principles of Fordism, whose consumerist rewards to workers enabled U.S. capitalism, even in the midst of the civil rights challenge, to expand with little dispute from organized labor.[8]

The "Fordist climacteric" (Davis's term) precipitated shifts in the demography, patterns of employment, and culture of accumulation during the 1970s, forces that began to unravel this high productivity/high consumption pact. An increasing number of people graduating from colleges (thanks to federally subsidized affirmative action programs like the G.I. Bill) aided an explosion of nonproductive, managerial positions in an increasingly service-oriented economy. By 1977, professionals, managers, and technicians composed almost 24 percent of the entire U.S. labor population (Davis, *Prisoners,* 213). And the rise of these members of a "new" professional-managerial class, who benefited from the social capital invested in educational "Master Plans" at the start of the 1960s, brought along a correlative culture of *overconsumption,* a system of accumulation built not on the notion that the social surplus of productivity would be transferred back into the broad expansion of real wages, but on the premise that productivity served the consuming needs of this growing cadre of professionals, managers, and other nonproducers. But the underbelly of the broken promise of Fordism and Keynesian state regulation was profound. As Davis notes in his critique of this emerging occupational stratum, "Between 1966 and 1981, twenty-eight million new jobs were created: for each job added in goods-production . . . *ten* jobs were added in the tertiary sector" (*Prisoners,* 214). This "tertiary" demographic, mostly women and poor men of color, encompasses those at the bottom of the wage scale, including a burgeoning population of low-skilled health care labor (nurses' aides, medical technicians, clerical workers), business services (secretaries, janitorial work, cashiers), and fast-food employment; many of these jobs are also part-time or temporary. "Overconsumptionism" and professional salaries have emerged, resulting in the "ongoing degradation of job creation and the erosion of mass Fordist consumer norms" (*Prisoners*, 219). Displaced and disassembled, the "break" and "brake" in wide-scale economic expansion in the United States as a result of this crisis in Fordism has led to a downward spiral of wages and mobility for the vast majority of Americans.[9]

While Fordism has not been completely eclipsed, its economic hegemony has been challenged by new forms of social and labor control, most prominently by the rise of new regimes of regulation and accumulation, especially that of "flexible accumulation." David Harvey defines the term in the following manner:

> *Flexible accumulation* . . . is marked by a direct confrontation with the rigidities of Fordism. It rests on flexibility with respect to labour processes, labour markets, products, and patterns of consumption. It is characterized by the emergence of entirely new sectors of production, new ways of providing financial services, new markets, and, above all, greatly intensified rates of commercial, technological, and organizational innovation. It has entrained rapid shifts in the patterning of uneven development, both between sectors and between geographical regions, giving rise, for example, to a vast surge in so-called "service-sector" employment as well as to entirely new industrial ensembles in hitherto underdeveloped regions. (*Condition*, 147)

Harvey's portrayal of this new economic and cultural logic not only assists in understanding the loosening of the American economy from its prior Fordist bolts, but also provides an analytical language for understanding the emergence in the early 1980s of what Robert Reich has called "paper entrepreneurialism," the rearrangement of corporate assets through inflation of stock and bond value, hostile takeovers and "friendly" mergers, and short-term investments (95). Such vast tinkering with the financial side of American business has brought about a logic of short-lived profit at the expense of long-term productivity.[10] The beneficiaries of "paper entrepreneurialism" are those we will meet in chapter 5, whom Tom Wolfe satirically dubs the "Masters of the Universe": Wall Street bond traders like Sherman McCoy, who maintain insulated, segregated lives by spending exorbitant amounts of money, but who never actually produce anything. The divorcing of the financial sector from the productive economy—spatially marked in *Bonfire of the Vanities* as the difference between riding a ten-dollar taxi cab and taking the subway—has led to the well-documented widening gap between rich and poor, white and nonwhite, those dwelling in gentrified downtown cores and those living in deindustrialized fringes. Moreover, flexible accumulation aptly describes the reintroduction of older forms of labor-intensive, unregulated but highly controlled sectors of the tertiary economy, most visible in the huge sweatshop-driven industries of Los Angeles, San Francisco, and New York.[11] The replacement of manufacturing-based, industrial work once available to working-class communities with a postindustrial, flexible model of accumulation has pushed urban dwellers of color into poverty-level jobs with bottomed-out wages or into semi-permanent states of worklessness.[12]

The notion that the crisis in Fordism has propelled new trends in capitalist control of flexible accumulation is not surprising, nor particularly original. Flexible accumulation is, after all, a return to an older form of control, a neocraft specialization of sorts. What is surprising is the extent to which flexible accumulation does not view crisis as a necessarily bad condition that warrants a complete mitigation of forces always threatening to spill beyond the boundaries of recognizable structures. Instead, flexible accumulation views such crises as constitutive within its practices, a kind of economic "uncertainty principle" that allows capitalism to expand its boundaries when and where selective spurts of growth occur.[13] Again, Harvey is helpful here, as he characterizes capital's "spatial fix" as an addictive behavior, but also as a feature not of capitalism's failure, but of the very contradictions of its success: "Under capitalism there is a perpetual struggle in which capital builds a physical landscape appropriate to its own condition at a particular moment in time, only to have to destroy it, usually in the course of crisis, at a subsequent point in time" (*Urban Experience*, 83).

Thus the culture of "overconsumptionism" (or the "culture of triumph," as Nicolaus Mills puts it) at the beginning of the 1980s as a response to the economic crisis of the 1970s emerges not merely as an instrumentalist component to the demands of the labor sector, but also as an index to the sea change in the structure of the U.S. political economy (Mills, "The Culture of Triumph," 12–13). Coterminous with the ascendant logic of flexible accumulation was a reconfigured role for the state and the enlargement of the state's capacity in ensuring the smooth operations of capital in this period of economic transition. Contrary to the popular "government-off-our-backs" discourse pervasive throughout the 1980s and 1990s (which in many ways began during the tax revolts of the mid-1970s), state capacity—its ability to regulate and command the functionings of social relations over its given territory—has expanded in its instruments and practices of social control. In the name of fiscal austerity and economic scarcity—what President Carter dubbed the "malaise" of the nation—the scope of state intervention in economic and social policy increased dramatically as a conscious, concerted effort to buttress the incipient forms of the emerging economies driven by the Fordist "crisis."[14] Indeed, the vision of the state during this period has been termed by Italian Marxist intellectual Toni Negri as the emergence of the "crisis of the crisis-state." Mirroring the warrant seized by flexible accumulation of harnessing "crisis" itself as a way to refashion operative demands, Negri's notion of the "crisis-state" takes as its assumption that the state not only is in crisis, but uses its very crisis as the contingent basis to employ new practices of control, many of which have become increasingly repressive. The development of the "crisis of the crisis-state" emerges most profoundly in the 1980s as a shift from the "welfare state" of Keynesian planning and regulation to a "warfare state" attending to "flexible" economies:

> By transition from "welfare" to "warfare" state I am referring to the internal effects of the restructuration of the state machine—its effect on class relations. . . . Development is now planned in terms of ideologies of scarcity and austerity. The transition involves not just state policies, but most particularly the *structure* of the state, both political and administrative. The needs of the proletariat and of the poor are now rigidly subordinated to the necessities of the capitalist reproduction. . . . The state has an array of military and repressive means available (army, police, legal, etc.) to exclude from [the arena of bargaining or negotiating] all forces that do not offer unconditional obedience to its austerity-based material constitution and to the static reproduction of class relations that goes with it. (Negri, *Revolution Retrieved*, 181–82)

The tenor and vehicle by which Negri formulates the "crisis-state" as one based in "warfare" are important to consider. Capitalism in this vision cannot sustain itself unless through the management and sustenance of the state, a state that for Negri is inherently violent and coercive in order to maintain the "static reproduction of class relations." Here, Negri echoes what Marx refers to in *Capital* as "primitive accumulation," the historical process of "divorcing the producer from the means of production" (874–75). Yet unlike the implied or hidden "violence" of social control in a welfare state, contemporary "primitive accumulation" has returned to an invigorated militarism to bolster capitalist accumulation. The state, in this regard, returns to a capacity not of mitigating social contradictions through uneven and partial redistributive means, but to a project that engages actively in the dispossession of people from their tenuous connections to labor, land, and citizenship. In chapter 5, we will see this principle of "primitive accumulation" not only affecting the planned contraction of public space in New York, but also helping to shape the ways in which Sherman McCoy, after his fall from white privilege, reconstitutes his whiteness along a similar "primitive," masculinist aggression.

Nowhere are the effects of the contemporary economic "crisis" and correlative state repression more pronounced than in U.S. cities, and especially
within urban communities of color. Consider, for example, the case of Los
Angeles. As Melvin Oliver, James Johnson, and Walter Farrell have noted
in their article on the "Anatomy" of the 1992 Los Angeles rebellion, the political economic "seeds" for such a conflagration were laid by deindustrialization of the city's manufacturing infrastructure, which portended at best
wage cuts for those lucky enough to maintain employment and job "security" that gave little solace to those who suffered most from the labor hemorrhaging of the 1980s (117–41). Between 1978 and 1982, South Central Los
Angeles lost 70,000 high-wage, unionized manufacturing jobs; by 1989,
124,000 more people had found themselves without work (122, 125).
Most of these industries, in their attempt to absorb labor costs and increase
profit margins, closed their plants and fled either overseas (Mexico, Asian
regions) or to new "technopoles" in other parts of Los Angeles County and
Orange County (122). Replacing high-wage work were service-sector jobs,
many of which paid (if legal) minimum wage or (if under the table) worse;
such poorly paid work relied heavily on Latino immigrant (often times undocumented) labor moving into what was since the midcentury considered
a "Black" community. Alongside the decimation produced by the economic
"bottom line" was an invigorated effort on the part of local, state, and federal agencies to criminalize whole portions of the burgeoning unemployed.
Davis writes of the virtual war against primarily Black and Latino youths
(in the name of the "War on Drugs"), which by 1989 gave the police license to sweep and detain indiscriminately 50,000 of the 100,000 Black
youths in Los Angeles, to "seal off" or barricade whole communities (renamed "narcotics enforcement zones") from the rest of Los Angeles, and to
infuse tactics of fear into the popular media with images of gang "armies"
whose numbers supposedly reached the flagrantly inflated total of 100,000
(City of Quartz, 267–322). Actual gang violence, its most infamous instance fueled by the Bloods-Crips rivalry, exploded into ultraviolent form
as community-based organizations designed to serve, advocate for, and
organize youths of color collapsed either because of federal defunding or,
in the case of local organizations forged under the dynamic and diverse
ideology of Black or Chicano nationalism, through violent means (City of
Quartz, 297–99; Oliver, Johnson, and Farrell, 126).[15] In place of radical
spaces of politicization or even sanctioned spaces of labor are new zones
of incarceration, as Los Angeles's relative surplus population has become a
primary source for the growing prisoner populations and the expansion of
the cages that house them in California.[16] The dissipation of public arenas
in which people in impoverished communities are afforded provisional in-

tellectual space has increased the urgency to work through the question of racial meaning in the context of a racial realignment that anathematizes urban space and creates, as Ruth Gilmore puts it, "public enemies" of those living in communities of color ("Public Enemies," 76).[17]

The military-carceral ring that surrounds and determines Los Angeles's spatial configuration is mirrored by a ring of poverty in east coast cities such as New York and Philadelphia. Even as Southern California's megalopolis competes to claim status as the nation's global city, New York has enjoyed the advantages of its relative seniority, including a longer and greater reach to centralize, in the last three decades of the twentieth century, the internationalization of the financial and commercial sectors. Manhattan's position as a world broker has provided the island's managerial and professional class top-heavy earnings, which has enabled it to stay in check with even more exorbitant housing cost increases. A classic reconstitution of core-periphery spatial relations, formerly working-class neighborhoods that once housed waves of poor immigrants—Southern European, Yiddish, Asian, Latino—have been transformed into gentrified zones of a new nouveau riche sector. To signify their class mobility and distinction from an area's historical origins in poverty, places such as the Lower East Side were renamed "East Village," transformed into a coextension of its fashionably and conspicuously consumptive neighbor, Greenwich Village. Manhattan, on the other hand, has become all but unlivable for the city's poor, who have been pushed completely out of the southern tip of the island and squeezed into little more than Harlem and East Harlem to the north. Professionals who have bought or rented units with inflated prices in places like Chinatown and Soho have their lives made easier by this population of service workers, mostly women, Black and Brown, who can barely afford a Manhattan-priced lunch, let alone the rent for a studio in the borough in which they labor. "There is a ring of poverty," observes Saskia Sassen in her description of New York as a global city, "that runs through northern Manhattan, the South Bronx, and much of northern Brooklyn" (261). Sassen adds that the trend in New York tends toward greater racial and class polarization: "In 1980 New York City contained a larger number of census tracts with higher levels of poor households than in 1970" (261). And while the city's real estate industry gleefully built luxury housing in the 1980s, to the virtual exclusion of other kinds of housing projects and to the benefit of its moneyed "paper entrepreneurs," the burgeoning poor were increasingly Black, Brown, female, and young; Sassen remarks that most of New York's poor are children, "reminiscent of Third World cities" (264). If Los Angeles excavates a future of increased containment and repression as its mode to exact urban triage, New York pronounces a

Victorian policy of abandonment for its children of color, orphaned in a sea of wealth.

Philadelphia lost its status as a world city in the nineteenth century, but its impact as a regional center for industry and commerce and the effects of post-Fordist, post-Keynesian policy have been equally stark. White flight to outlying suburban tracts in Montgomery, Bucks, and Chester counties, as well as to tax havens in southern New Jersey, began as early as the end of World War II, but white people fled in earnest during the 1960s and this movement out of the city limits continues apace, at least for those who can afford the move. Inverting New York's core-periphery model, Philadelphia takes on an urban form more akin to Robert Park's concentric zones, in which suburban commuters fill downtown offices in the daytime and empty the streets of Center City by sunset. Its predominantly Black communities of North, West, and portions of South Philadelphia collapsed under the brutal weight of chronic under- and unemployment, defunded public schools, and shrinking social services, mirroring the crises of larger cities like New York and Los Angeles but in intensified fashion because of the city's smaller urban scale. And although its local economy was more mixed than those of cities dependent on a single industry, like Detroit and Pittsburgh, Philadelphia suffered its own share of economic hemorrhage during the 1970s and 1980s. By the time Wideman traversed the city's landscape in *Philadelphia Fire* in 1990, Philadelphia's largest employers had been whittled down to two: the city government and the University of Pennsylvania, two institutions that required of its higher-paid symbolic analysts a high degree of postsecondary education, and of its janitorial, clerical, and other service workers bottomed-out wages. Blacks who had only recently enjoyed unionized work in the city's manufacturing companies lost it just as quickly, and excitement over the benchmark election of the city's first Black mayor, Wilson Goode in 1984, was soon tempered and then soiled by the city's crushing fiscal crisis—precipitated by the capital flight of its productive industries and the residential flight of white middle managers over two decades—which eventually resulted in Philadelphia's near bankruptcy in 1991. Urban planning that would attend to this crisis, spearheaded by the city and the university, began as early as 1980, and by the 1990s Center City enjoyed a kind of cultural renaissance as suburban workers began staying out during the evenings, dining, shopping, and theater-hopping. Meanwhile, the University of Pennsylvania began to attract faculty and staff to relocate to West Philadelphia, offering financial incentives to buy homes in the blocks just north and west of campus, creating magnet schools for the intellectuals' offspring, and all the while slowly but inexorably pushing West Philadelphia's Black residents further west, north, and south: Philadelphia's newest Black Belt can be mapped along City Line Avenue, which marks the border between Philadelphia and its "mainline" satellites (the old-moneyed and college towns of Ardmore, Bryn Mawr, Haverford, Villanova, and Swarthmore). Black Philadelphians, if not isolated in hypersegregated areas like North Philadelphia, are conveniently pushed out of the sight of the city's newly revitalized cultural edifices and correspondingly pushed out of mind in Philadelphia's ongoing urban "redevelopment."

The decimation of public space (and the criminalization, if not eradication, of radical social movements), the destruction of low-income housing, and the flight of industrialized zones have exacted a huge toll on the city's residents of color, but the narrative of urban decline has also produced its beneficiaries. There is a reason why the 1980s are considered years of "prosperity." Pundits, politicians, and public policy planners have been quick to talk about the "city in crisis" if only to use this language of crisis to mitigate the acceleration of a wide-scale transfer of resources and power. Most economists concede, as previously noted, that in the midst of governmental "fiscal crises," the United States actually experienced a glut of cash. Where did this money come from, and where did it go? Part of the answer to the overabundance of money lies in the shift toward a service economy; with the decline of an economy of goods, and a concomitant drying up of investment for actual production, more cash was freed up for financial speculation. More importantly, city governments, struggling to compensate for fleeing businesses or to attract new ones, offered not only huge tax breaks for these companies, but also submitted "private-public partnership" proposals to real estate speculators and developers to, in effect, help finance expensive construction projects. "Urban redevelopment," as it is called, was not new for city governments in the 1980s, but such projects were seen, by this decade, more and more to be the panacea for municipal fiscal and social woes. Thus, rapid development of downtown skyscraper offices, the creation of tourist- and consumer-friendly commercial strips, the selective gentrification of neighborhood blocks, and increased investment in specific public transit lines (linking the city core with outlying, affluent suburbs) emerged as the practical responses to the urban crisis. For communities of color trapped in the path of the redevelopment, urban renewal coded its more insidious practice of urban removal: whole communities were displaced, low-income apartments were torn down to make way for high-rent luxury condominiums and co-ops, mom-and-pop shops were squeezed out by larger national and multinational corporations, and public funds were reallocated to make the city's suburban and urban "yuppie" commuters comfortable, while their poorer neighbors were more or less neglected. If money was taken out of production lines and out of Keynesian coffers providing the last vestiges of a "safety net," the abundant circuits of cash found their way into the pockets of developers, managers, and speculators, all with the blessing of the city council: this coalition of what Roger Sanjek calls the "permanent government" in, for example, New York City, keeps as its mantra, "Public policy for private gain" (34). Although the actual cases of urban redevelopment differ from city to city, this narrative of renewal and removal, investment and displacement, or what Joseph Schumpeter famously and oxymoronically coined "creative destruction," looms large in each of the four works considered here. The effects of urban redevelopment not only provide the spatial and historical backdrop of the narratives, but also produce deeply felt responses both for the city's marginalized dwellers of color and the narrators who traverse the places where the other half lives while still enjoying the comforts of the glittery side of the tracks.

These political economic stories provide only a glimpse of the far-reaching effects of racial realignment in the long decade of urban triage, shifts in the material constitution of U.S. racial formation of which works considered "multicultural" have agonizingly struggled to make sense. John Edgar Wideman's character J. B. in *Philadelphia Fire*, the novel discussed in chapter 4, laments this almost intractable difficulty in making sense of the urban landscape, borne out of the conjunction of public policy, fiscal austerity, and capital flight. J. B., a homeless Vietnam vet, one who bears on his own racialized body the brunt of these political economic forces, wishes to make objective sense of a city leaving behind whole communities in its push toward urban renewal, but finds that such clarity of vision remains elusive: "What we need is realism, the naturalistic panorama of a cityscape unfolding. Demographics, statistics, objectivity" (157). J. B.'s internal monologue seems to echo Wideman's sentiments throughout the novel, as the story of Philadelphia's slide into urban decline, its increasing population of destitution, its polarized racial history, and its uneven march toward redevelopment provokes both unfulfilled hopes for understanding and resigned realizations of cynicism.

On the other side of the new racial "enclosures" are writers whose articulation of racial identity becomes troubled at the moment they confront these borders, material lines that pronounce all too clearly the distance that the racial order of the 1980s has created between those called to "speak for" these communities and those spoken of. The issue of finding "resistance" in literary works, an analytical goal so pervasive in critical works of multicultural literature, becomes a profoundly mediated task, to say the least. Alejandro Morales's *lo real maravilloso* comes to mind here:

his narrative instances of violence are designed to expose and disrupt the larger institutional violence circumscribing the racialized barrio of the Simons workers, but his characters remain trapped in ideologies that, I would argue, Morales fails to dismantle by narrative prowess. Margaret, in *Philadelphia Fire*, dons the ideological garb of MOVE's resistance to capitalist "progress" by employing the radical group's practice of "willful destitution": mirroring the Greek Cynics' renunciation of Roman imperial civilization, members of MOVE intentionally looked like the city's expendables and bodily foregrounded the enervating effects of exploitative, racist social institutions and structures. But Cudjoe meets Margaret only after she has been "normalized," her Cynical protest devolved into a more general cynicism in which social resentment can no longer be expressed through collective anger. More prevalent than attempts at narratives of resistance are the anxieties of writers who, in recognizing that their entry into the racial world of the 1980s looks so very different from the lives of most other people of color, work to create imaginative worlds that attend to these material and therefore social differences.

The key, then, to understanding the multicultural politics of identity of the 1980s revolves around the manner in which writers produce narratives that do *not* underscore or make central a project of "resistance," but instead craft works to highlight the concerns implicit in realizing that such resistance may not easily arrive by the end of their story. Wideman's alternative to resistance is survival, when he invokes a painfully autobiographical account of his all-too-brief conversations with his son in prison. His last words to his son in the novel do not conceal the anguish palpable in this ironic rendering of a father giving advice for which he has no reference: "Make do. Hold on. Each day will be slightly different. . . . Hold on" (151). Yamamoto's answer is the story she has written: her retelling of the racial atrocity in Fontana—the murder of Short and his family—four decades later tries to work as a kind of narrative penance even as she retains her sense of guilt. But, as chapter 3 will demonstrate, her attempts at what Grace Hong regards as a moment of "cross-racial solidarity" exemplify more the disjunction between a rhetorical stance against and material complicity with the spatial arrangements in Los Angeles already driving Asian Americans and African Americans apart. Even in the best-intentioned pursuits of antiracism, narratives written in this decade cannot fully overcome the oppression they seek to expose. As George Lipsitz has noted, identities must emerge out of political struggle, and not vice versa (*American Studies*, 285).

What emerges from these political economic changes—the move away from the Fordist-Keynesian hegemony toward the "post-Keynesian militarism" of the 1980s, the divestment and deindustrialization of urban cores throughout the United States and their replacement economies of selective service-attending and craft-based modes of production and accumulation, the resegregation of American cities, the emergence of "fiscal crises" at the municipal, state, and national levels of government, the expansion of state capacity in the form of increasing police/military presence, prison economies, and social regulation, and the changing status of the state's role toward managing social relations—is a preponderance of rhetoric and discourse on race that points not only to the changing and complex status of racial meaning during this decade, but also to the terms by which race as a material activity of cultural agency becomes politically mobilized. Indeed, what occurs throughout the 1980s amounts to nothing less than the persistent use of race to advocate for and struggle against social policies designed to reshape, even smooth over, economic and political relations between different racial groups. The economic landscape of the 1980s does not precipitate a quantitative change in discussions around race, but rather effects a qualitative shift in the race talk of this decade.

Race is better imagined as a verb than as a noun; it is not so much a description of a particular human condition as it is the production of one. The activity of race provides all Americans with a profound sense of agency, a way to place themselves in a terrain of social struggle and to derive meaning from that landscape. The interaction of social beings with one another or with a larger social system such as the federal government creates the vocabulary through which race is communicated. But these terms are not created equally: the recognition and conferral of racial meaning into social intercourse are the result of negotiations whose rules of engagement set the zones of legitimate conversation. To engage in the activity of race, then, is to talk about the boundaries within which the discussion takes place. The moral panic over racialized people in the 1980s sharply delineated conversations over how best to manage those who struggled to refuse the call of state and capital to become pliant urban subjects, flexible even unto death. Thus, increasingly, these terms of management were defined with principles of punishment, containment, and abandonment in mind, as the legitimacy of racial grievance was heard more and more as complaint borne of irrationality and pathology. The great retreat from race of the 1980s, as Dana Takagi has called this era, has sharpened the tools of death and blunted the ethical demand for life as the decade ushered in a confluence of economic and moral panics.

To elucidate this conjunction between political economy and the rhetorical realignment of race in the 1980s, we might consider William Julius Wilson's 1978 book, *The Declining Significance of Race,* as a paradigmatic example and instigator of these changes in racial meaning. Wilson's study is important here because it serves not only as a response to and a reflection on the severe changes in the political, economic, and social lives of African Americans in the wake of the changing material conditions beginning in the 1970s and taking firm hold in the 1980s; even more important for the purposes of this introductory chapter is the way in which *Declining Significance*, as both sociology and social policy, tries to make those very connections between political economy and the changing status of Blacks in the United States. Writing against the then prevalent discourse of Black nationalism, whose calls for radical action among Blacks and sharp critique of white institutions were falling on fewer and fewer ears willing to listen, Wilson claims that "the life chances of individual blacks have more to do with their economic class position than with their day-to-day encounters with whites" (1). Wilson's larger point in arguing what then seemed a radical or reactionary assertion is that structural arrangements in the changing political economy of the United States in the 1970s compel one to rethink the terms through which race and in particular charges of "racism" are voiced. In many ways, in investigating the social lives of African Americans in the light of declining material circumstances and opportunities afforded to Blacks, Wilson wants not simply to assert that race no longer matters, but that discussing "ideologies" of race no longer holds much validity unless one accounts for and attends to the altered state of the U.S. political economy.

Yet in bringing a "materialism" back into debates about race that were predominantly presented in "cultural" terms, *The Declining Significance of Race* set into motion discussions in academic circles and in more popular arenas that appropriated Wilson's rhetoric over race—race's decreasing importance in explaining the consistency of Black "underclass" poverty—while virtually ignoring the substance and vision of his book, of greater attention to the structural barriers allowing for the persistence of Black ghetto communities.[18] Much of the language that Wilson deploys in *Declining Significance*—the obsolescence of racial discrimination, the "culture of poverty," the Black "underclass," the importance of class over race—would become key terms in numerous studies on race written by neoconservatives of the 1980s.[19] A case in point is Charles Murray, whose 1984 book, *Losing Ground*, both crystallized and bolstered the policy of indifference and antagonism toward racial issues by the Reagan administration.[20] Murray writes within the discursive space opened by writers like Wilson and appropriates the rhetoric of "declining significance," but recasts the "structural" explanation so central to Wilson's thesis: the problem is not that the political economic structures have become "impersonal" barriers to Black progress, but that these structures help Black folks too much. Programs like AFDC and affirmative action, Murray argues, designed to combat "structural obstacles" have produced a culture of dependency among African Americans, and thus the emergence of the "Black" underclass of unemployed, unskilled men and women within urban communities is the result of years not of "benign neglect," but of overattention. This rhetorical sleight-of-hand became the hallmark of prevailing discussions over race in the 1980s; if Wilson wanted to displace a racial language to focus more directly on poverty, Murray uses Wilson's space to explain poverty in racial terms.[21] While Wilson and Murray would be at political cross-purposes with one another, the proximity of their rhetorical usage can help us understand how racial realignment operates in this decade. The crisis over racial meaning in the 1980s is predicated on a simultaneous retreat from a rhetoric of race given credence in the crucible of the civil rights and liberation movements of the 1960s and 1970s, and the rearticulation of racial meaning no longer considered analytically useful for understanding concrete social relations.

Murray and other neoconservatives, whose "scholarship" received increasing media attention and foundation support while avoiding the time-honored system of peer review to which other intellectuals were beholden, sedimented so well the "underclass" thesis in the popular imagination that it set the general discursive terrain within which liberal scholars responded. Discussions of what to do about pervasive urban poverty turned into "underclass" debates, and no matter how much liberal and progressive scholars bristled and tried to qualify the term, "underclass" became shorthand for Black and Brown urban pathology, and cities became the crucible for cultures of poverty. The state's crisis and eventual transformation from a Keynesian broker into a militarized creative destroyer of communities could be smoothly displaced and recast as a problem of those it had once unevenly been called to protect. Meanwhile, those who opposed Murray and those among his cultural cohort such as Allan Bloom, Dinesh D'Souza, William Bennett, Shelby Steele, and Lynne Cheney busily retooled their syllabi in university courses with writers who had somehow managed to escape the repressive armature of containment and punishment and, in the process, managed to garner significant accolades from American literary patriarchs. These writers' purported task was to, in the words of Cisneros's Esperanza in her critically acclaimed and newly canonized novel *The House on Mango Street* (1986), "write for those who cannot out," and certainly these authors' groundbreaking, breathtaking prose and poetry made it that much easier for teachers to reconstruct the American literature syllabus: it is hard to argue against the inclusion of a Nobel Prize winner like Toni Morrison. The work that writers and academics engaged in during this period changed the ways in which we ascribed quality to works written by people of color forever, and answered claims by monoculturalists of the supposed aesthetic inferiority of multicultural writers with a confident and resounding rebuke.

Yet a pervasive anxiety, like a whisper, seeps into the ears of U.S. multiculturalists celebrating their newly won gains. Writers especially hear this still small voice, a reminder that other voices are shouting the discourse of a recalcitrant, amoral, unsalvageable urban underclass that multiculturalism can sometimes cite, but cannot fully explain. After all, how can writers, who so elegantly tell stories heretofore unheard, qualify for cultural inclusion in the most elite educational institutions and American readerships' affection, and the simultaneous political and economic disaggregation of the very communities whose cultures helped produce these literary artifacts? For writers in the 1980s, even a self-conscious invocation of race provides only partial epiphanies of contemporary situations, a literary language of race anachronized by the changing dimensions of an ever complicating territorial scope. Such difficult strivings in writing about race in increasingly opaque circumstances are apparent in a poem by Rita Dove, who would eventually become the nation's poet laureate. This short lyric is about a journey one night of six, presumably Black, adolescents cruising around their town. The explicit reference to the racialized nature of this excursion appears immediately, the poem's title a profoundly certain declaration of its Black inflection—"Nigger Song: An Odyssey":

We six pile in, the engine churning ink:
We ride into the night.
Past factories, past graveyards
And the broken eyes of windows, we ride
Into the gray-green nigger night.

We sweep past excavation sites; the pits
Of gravel gleam like mounds of ice.
Weeds clutch at the wheels;
We laugh and swerve away, veering
Into the black entrails of the earth,
The green smoke sizzling on our tongues . . .

In the nigger night, thick with the smell of cabbages,
Nothing can catch us.
Laughter spills like gin from glasses,
And "yeah" we whisper, "yeah"
We croon, "yeah."[22]

A quick reading almost instantaneously reminds us of another poem about a Black teenage "odyssey," Gwendolyn Brooks's "We Real Cool." The collective and repetitive "we" of both pieces foregrounds the adolescent nurturing of group social behavior; the comparison of the raucous laughter spilling from Dove's kids to "gin" evokes the rebellious tone of Brooks's speakers, who "Thin gin" to prove they're acting "real cool." Helen Vendler has argued that Dove's poem withholds what Vendler regards as "the prudishness of Brooks's judgmental monologue," her authorial castigation of these pool players, whose constant yearning to find new ways to "Sing sin," ultimately ends with the somber declaration that they will "Die soon" (384). Brooks's tone in her poem is, in fact, more despondent than judgmental; her speakers' move toward an inevitable death provokes for Brooks an attempt to suspend pedantry and to find meaningful rhythms in the face of her speakers' existential tragedy.[23] Thus, what appears at first as pounding, almost parental downbeats in "We Real Cool" is displaced in its utterance by Brooks's syncopated spacing, demanded by a hesitant enjambment of each line's last word, "we." The tension, then, between tragic theme and the poem's almost playful execution (which also includes numerous chiasmic rhymes) produces an irony, but not embittered satire against her speakers. In place of fatal tragedy, Dove grants her teenage speakers the ability to live on, their emphatic rebellion that "Nothing can catch us" not tempered by any semblance of impending doom. Indeed, contrasted with the syncopated tension of Brooks's poem, the lines of "Nigger Song," although tightly controlled by its confederation of iambic feet and trochaic and anapestic substitutions, move with regulated fluidity. And the alliterative and sonorous playfulness of the "gray-green nigger night" and of "gravel gleam[ing] like mounds of ice" suggests an improvisational sensibility on the part of the teenagers, even as such lines bespeak more Dove's careful poetic endeavor. Dove's poem seems to "laugh and swerve" in its shifting sensory references as much as her speakers do as they refuse to drive along prescribed routes, unlike the linear trajectory of impending doom in the lives of Brooks's speakers, whose odyssey ultimately marches toward young, abrupt death. Instead, "Nigger Song" suggests a celebration that Brooks cannot afford her speakers, the excessive racialized laughter spilling as easily as "nigger" seems to fall out of the mouths of the adolescent speakers of Dove's poem.

Yet the repetitive affirmation of rebellion in Dove's speakers belies an undercurrent of worry, the preemptory "yeah" whispered, only later to be voiced more confidently in their "croon." With more spastic reactions like hiccups, provoked more by fear than a defiant celebration of their laughing excess, the adolescents' journey registers a vision that makes their laughter and crooning more deliberate than rebellion warrants, an awareness that such laughter in the "nigger night" sounds much like the nervous titter of a scared child left alone in alienating darkness. If the "nigger night" avails the six to revel in their hidden insouciance, protected by the "Black entrails of the earth," its capacity to screen overwhelms in its darkening blindness. "Nothing can catch us," they sense, because like Ralph Ellison's protagonist, nobody can see them and they are seen by nobody: by the end of the last stanza, the group attains their assertive voice only at the expense of any access to visual markers. The loss of sight is partially compensated for by vestigial senses ("the smell of cabbages"), verbal excess ("yeah . . . yeah . . . yeah"), and strained, isolated simile ("laughter . . . like gin from glasses"), but these remnants left for Dove's adolescent speakers offer only at best a "tree-in-the-forest" kind of celebration. We are then left wondering whether, like that other mythic figure whose own "odyssey" ended in blindness, the six move from vision to voice, from observant sight to blind tongue, with intention, with reckless will, or with uncontrollable abandon. We also are compelled to wonder whether this journey has taught the poem's speakers anything. Was their attainment of voice worth the cost of vision? Central to these considerations, and to an understanding of what is at stake in the teenagers' nervous defiance, is the line that signals the speakers' turn away from the town and their descent into the "Black entrails" of the "nigger night," the line that ends with the participle "veering." The ambiguity of intention rests in this word. It suggests a bounded action, in the sense that a detour is a route taken when circumstances prevent direct movement. "Veering" is both an "escape from" and a "travel toward." Just as the poem here takes a decisive turn away from a description of the town anchored by sight, so the speakers at this moment make a critical decision to drive from the familiar roads into the uncharted terrains of the "Black entrails of the earth." The "yeah" of racial celebration cast in the palpable "nigger night" then strains with anxiety to affirm what still remains liminal in the poem. The speakers continue to "veer" as the poem ends, and if their overstated ebullience in the "yeah" registers slightly the potential for new poetic sight-cum-Black voice, what remains unacknowledged are the reasons why they were "veering."

The deliberate yet anxious movement in the poem compels us to consider what the speakers "swerve away" from, what prompts this shift from a visual description of the town to the paradoxically controlled but rebellious voice of Blackness. Glimpses of the landscape from the perspective of the speakers' car indicate a decidedly urban setting, a quick sweep of major landmarks of industrial space. But the teenagers seem to give these places little thought, their reference to the "factories" and "graveyards" only mentioned after they have gone "past" these sites. Despite the apparently rugged terrain of the streets, best exemplified by the poetic texture of the "gravel gleam[ing] like mounds of ice," there is a peculiarly mundane quality to this town. The poem stages the six in the car against the backdrop of a palpably lifeless landscape, the only hint of the speakers' presence in the town coming from the deadening gaze of the "broken eyes of windows": no one else besides the six seems to exist here. It is therefore not surprising that the teenagers drive through—"sweep past"—and never linger on an isolating place so bereft of life and imagination. Indeed, insofar as the road trip is also a journey of poetic imagination, "the engine churning ink," the poem makes tacit gestures to the familiar geography of urban setting, but never finds in the town anything poetic worth looking at with attention. In fact, not only is the town so uninspiring that its structures can only be acknowledged without passion, but it also emerges as a place that holds back the movement of the car, an implicit fettering of the imaginative capacities of the speakers and, presumably, the poem itself: "Weeds clutch at the wheels." Left with this vision of apparent urban blight, the "veering" or escape of the teenagers "away" from the town and toward the yet unrealized, unseen, even blinding "nigger night" does not surprise at all: there is nothing in this town worth looking at.

Yet one should not easily dismiss this peculiarly mundane town, nor should the speakers' escape from such a boring place seem the obvious answer to the enervating existence led in a city such as this. That Dove poses a nascent yet possibly exuberant voice of Blackness against the tedium of urban Black life in "Nigger Song" might lead us to believe that the difference between the familiar visions of urban Black experience and an emergent Black poetics of "nigger night" articulation is only productive for poetry when one is on the other side of the tracks, in the space of "Black entrails" and not in "excavation sites." Embedded in this poem are competing notions of Blackness cast in the phrase "nigger night," with all of the racially charged connotations that the term "nigger" implies. On the one hand, the "nigger night" serves as the pent-up landscape in which the speakers heave or "croon" a generative racial imagination, a "nigger" imagination, if you will, that poses the racial term with defiance. On the other hand, the "nigger night" also invokes its racist ghost, the destructive capacity of the term following the speakers even as they traverse the boundaries of its familiar meanings, its familiar landmarks. To this extent, "nigger night" suggests not just the fervor of the speakers' "yeah" of affirming Blackness, but it also testifies that the attempt to turn the loaded term "nigger" from its conventional usage to apaphatic uncertainty predicates a concomitant abjection of the racial space of the town that the teenagers (and Dove, in this context) leave behind. Both the speakers' journey and the movement of the poem itself leave a place construed as a racialized "ghetto" in which the impoverished imagination in the town embodies the scarcity of poetic material for celebratory Black identity.

Indeed, there was little to celebrate in Pittsburgh, and in particular for the city's Black residents, in the late 1970s and 1980s, the period in which Dove wrote this poem. Driving past this region during this time, a traveler might peer with astonishment at the extent to which deindustrialization had so rapidly decimated the city's once vibrant industrial past. If she tried to relate to others what she observed, our driver might very well have referenced the same urban landscape of devastation that the six riders in "Nigger Night" swerve and veer by. Steel factories literally turned into labor's graveyards, as Pittsburgh's population melted from a high of 676,000 in 1950 to less than 370,000 by 1990 (Lubove, 258). The green smoke of the teenagers' tongues is metaphorical for what were once belching smelt furnaces and mills that spewed the smoke of U.S. Steel, Donora Works, Wheeling-Pittsburgh, and Jones and Laughlin (now LTV Steel). Precipitated by the planned recession of the early 1980s, by the end of the decade these industrial workhorses all but closed shop, their plants rotting metal skeletons symbolic of the deep hole in the lives of their former workers and their families. The grumbling signs of Pittsburgh's decline began in the late 1960s, around the same time as the nation's signal crisis, which moved liquid money out of fixed industrial capital and into speculative finance and the service sector. Dove's poem was written during the years when the region lost 100,000 manufacturing jobs—two out of every five—and 75,000 of these workers applied for unemployment after 1980 (Lubove, 29; Ferman, 29). "Attrition [in the Pittsburgh area]," writes the late Roy Lubove, "turned into swift decapitation of an entire industry built over the course of a century" (7). And as Big Steel died in Pittsburgh, the city hemorrhaged, tagged "dead" even as those left struggled to breathe air even more toxic than its older miasma of coke and iron.

Even during better times, the city's Black community did not receive equally the protection and wealth afforded to white workers in the post–World War II expansion. This said, the decline of Pittsburgh's economy appears to have trounced the futures of all of its residents, and begs the issue of why Dove inflects her portrait of a landscape in decline with such powerful racial terms. Wilson's analysis may well have applied to the urban tableau that Dove draws, his thesis that structural adjustments and not race would determine the sad future of the six men in the car. But in the 1980s, it was not Wilson but Murray whose warnings of Black pathology defined the ways in which the teenagers' lives would be read. It is in this light that we might consider Dove's poem as both absorbing the primary definition of Black youth as dangerous elements of the so-called underclass, and imbuing them with the capacity to realign, perhaps even interrupt, this racialized moniker by "spilling ink" themselves. Their drive through and out of town is an odyssey, and their vision of "nigger night" turns into song. This poetic stance is certainly nervous, and the affirmative "yeah" finally spoken at the end of the poem is ambiguous, tenuous at best. Dove's anxious stance betrays the distance felt in the struggle to understand six men whose social options are so far removed from hers, the racial anxiety of representing urban Blackness from afar. The poem cannot answer whether the six voices' crooning "yeah" is a rebellious cry to survive, or their fantasy of absolute freedom before their social death becomes a physical one, before someone with a badge catches up with them. But Dove invites her reader to assume this very ambiguity and receive different sensory messages: listen to their song, watch my anxiety, feel the gasps of an abandoned city.

Pittsburgh displays vividly the post-Keynesian, post-Fordist urban world that our six teenagers inhabit, and from which Dove derives the material to fashion her verse. It is the world with which the writers of the subsequent chapters must contend. The ground upon which they write is a stark picture of cities in decline, of oppositional politics in absentia, and of buried social warrants for future change. The 1980s bring into sharp relief once again that in representing race and its effects, one must take that representation to its limit, its logic: racism is not simply dehumanizing, it is human sacrifice; it is the legitimation of the wholesale abandonment of communities and punishment for those who dare to say "yeah" despite urban triage's tagging, "no, you're dead." Both Reed and Dove, both Wilson and Murray, are writers and scholars whose work flourished in this world, in which the political will to save lives and livelihoods was tempered by the economic fear that in doing so, we might all go the way of Oakland and Pittsburgh. For Murray, his answer is glaringly simple: if we can't lift all boats, we should save some and let others sink. For the others, especially Reed and Dove, who in different ways have been beneficiaries of multiculturalism's call to represent, such surgical removal is not so easy. The answers they offer are unsatisfying, the racial tragedy suffered by communities during the 1980s almost too unbearable to sublimate. But even in the midst of spaces urban triage deems unsalvageable, these writers show us something else is happening. And they invite us to join in their anxious discoveries: to listen to their pain, to watch our anguish, and to hope that this might in some way offer solatium. It is this search through racial pain that propels writers like Alejandro Morales and Hisaye Yamamoto to plumb the past to help give them answers to their present, to hear through history what might alleviate, even transform, the scenes of misery of those around them now. It is their reimagined narrations of history that abet in giving multiculturalism its truncated shape and cities their boundless sorrow, to which we now turn.

2

Fictionalizing Workers in the Barrio

Drive east from the glassy skyscrapers of downtown Los Angeles, past the hilly barrios of East Los Angeles, the landscape flattens and the cloud cover of Southern California's marine layer burns away in the hot San Gabriel Valley sun. Ensconced between the new Chinatown suburbs of Alhambra and Monterey Park to the west, the white and nouveau riche Asian households of San Marino to the north, and the extended Latino satellites of Temple City to the east is smallish San Gabriel, whose demographics include both aging post–World War II neighborhoods of Chicana/o, Japanese American, and white residents and Chinese newcomers. In the middle of town, on aptly named Mission Street, stands the San Gabriel Mission, an anachronistic Spanish-tile fortress that seems eons apart from the newly built shopping complexes less than three miles away. For seven dollars, devout visitors can walk through the mission's gardens, poke heads into its wood-burning kitchens, amble through former living quarters, and place four-dollar candles in front of a statue of the Virgin in the long and narrow old chapel, a stone's throw from the larger "modern" building, where Mass is still held and sacraments are still performed. On the far end, where painstakingly crafted miniature models of California's twenty other missions stand just outside, is housed a tiny museum that documents, through artifacts, photographs, and books, the history of San Gabriel Mission, the richest of them all.

Inside the museum, glass cases contain pictures and personal effects of one Eulalia Pérez, a nineteenth-century housekeeper and supervisor of the mission, whose devotion to the Church and to this western outpost was marked by her commitment to the *indios,* who were kept at bay by the high walls and cautiously filtered in through sanctifying gates. Rosaura

Sánchez, in her study of *testimonios* narrated by the Californios, the original Spanish-speaking settlers of Alta California, takes up the story from here. Sánchez describes Pérez's everyday routine of supervising daily chores and the in-house production of food and clothing, labor that was performed by Indian neophytes in order to free the missionaries to proselytize to the willing and condemn the resistant, all the while eating and sleeping in segregated quarters (75–77). Pérez buffered the friars from immediate contact with the mission's Indian workers by acting as taskmaster and disciplinarian, and assisted in building San Gabriel's wealth by trading and selling the goods produced inside the mission's walls. For this, Sánchez writes, "The missionaries gave Pérez land for a *rancho* and an orchard" (89). Such generous economic compensation put Pérez somewhat at odds with the general violence and expropriation perpetrated against Californios, Mexicans, Indians, and other people of color by white immigrants from the U.S. northeast in the latter half of the nineteenth century, and demonstrates the uneven and often contradictory transformation of Alta California into the "racial fault lines," to use Tomás Almaguer's phrase, of the Union's thirty-first state.

This Eulalia Pérez is reconceived in Alejandro Morales's novel *The Brick People* (1988), rechristened honorifically as "Doña Eulalia" at the beginning of the narrative. History bleeds into folktale and myth when Joseph Simons, a white brickyard owner, notices a painting of a man and woman in a restaurant and asks his foreman, Rosendo Guerrero, who the woman is. A waiter overhearing the conversation breaks in, explaining that her tale is shrouded in mystery, so much so that when Doña Eulalia died in 1878, documents put her age at one hundred and seventy years (11). The waiter continues with Doña Eulalia's story, which in the novel begins after she and her husband had petitioned for and received land from the San Gabriel missionaries. She plants an oak tree in Pasadena, and soon gives birth to three sons in her *rancho*, dubbed "El Rincón de San Pascual." But soon tragedy befalls Doña Eulalia: her husband, Juan Marine, dies, and immediately her right to the land is threatened. On a fateful Sunday, the waiter proceeds, she returned from Mass to find her home ransacked, and her beloved oak tree chopped into four pieces, placed on the ground to form the outline of a man, next to a pit that once rooted the tree. Eulalia screams, has a vision of her husband and sons, and falls into the pit and dies. After reluctantly deciding to exhume Eulalia, neighbors are horrified to discover hundreds of "indescribably large brown insects" that cause paralysis, and gossip spreads that Doña Eulalia has turned into the insects, overtaking El Rincón de San Pascual in a kind of territorial revenge for her untimely and violent death.

"Absolutely astonishing," Joseph replies after the tale is told, and so begins the first in a series of violent episodes that mark the origins and maintenance of Simons, the fictionalized brick company and adjacent barrio of Morales's characters in his novelistic account of Chicana/o labor in Southern California. That the novel opens with this fantastic story of Doña Eulalia puts into immediate focus the tenacious intellectual knot that one encounters when literary representation collides with historical re-creation. Namely, how does one say something new about a larger historical experience? Such anxious adumbrations of cultural fancy are not new with Morales, or with any of the writers considered in this study: they are as old as U.S. literature, made most manifest and given most primacy in Emerson's "Divinity School Address" in the first half of the nineteenth century. Yet within this drive toward originality are what Emerson called the constant "offices of relation"[1] that constrain a work's horizons, make knowable its innovation, and give its craft social meaning. This seeming paradox—that originality is born of its historical relationality, between what has been written and what can (and what can't) be—takes on particular salience in this chapter.

Straddling, or more accurately, highlighting the constitutive, narrative character of both fiction and historiography, George Lipsitz reminds us that History is never fully immanent. Rather, "the complexities and pluralities of the past always resist definitive evaluation and summary" (*Time Passages*, 21). But Lipsitz's caveat prevents neither fiction nor history from being written, nor does it negate the intellectual and social value that such narrative might offer; the past's "resistance" to reductionism need not slip into a general grand suspicion of narrative or knowledge as such. The plurality of history and its necessary distillation into historiography may indeed tell us much more, the resistance of the past more diagnostic than taxonomic.[2] Thus to tell an original story about racial history: this is the perforce challenge that Alejandro Morales faces and makes explicit in *The Brick People* (1988), a novel that tells in historical terms and dimensions a story of an avowedly Chicana/o experience. But literary storytelling is not simply one of artistic freedom and innovation, though it is of course partly that as well. It is also distillation and refraction—and in some cases, displacement—of received historiographical narratives under which we construe the boundaries of identity and community, and a reconstitution of history into one that might be productive for identities and communities reimagined. The struggle to write something new is, in a word, ideological; and insofar as ideology marks the capacity for people to understand and believe smoothly their relationship to a given historical moment—Althusser's hailed subject—writing is as much a struggle of *reading* history into legibility as it is assessing where and why it remains unreadable.

The Brick People negotiates delicately its coverage of a formative era in Chicana/o historiography, namely the history of Chicana/o labor from the turn of the twentieth century until the period immediately following World War II. And yet it is a novel written in an entirely different historical moment—1988—when Chicana/os both within academic circles and at large in communities felt a palpable shift in how a Chicana/o collective consciousness would be configured. From the beginning of the 1980s, scholars looked with not a little apprehension at the fact that many of the institutional and ideological gains of which Chicana/o activists, artists, intellectuals (both organic and traditional) could be proud were withering under the conservative regime of Reagan-Bush. Far from its heyday of activism and agitation for self-determination and drastic social and political change—in essence, the struggle to alter radically social relations in the United States—to which Chicana/o studies is a lasting testament, Chicana/os in the 1980s faced a different kind of urgency, one that threatened to diffuse Chicana/o insurgent opposition of the 1960s and 1970s into a milquetoast 1980s, known now as the "Decade of the Hispanic." The 1980s, in other words, inflect Morales's revisitation of Chicana/o labor history of an earlier period, just as others looked to this decade as a period in which the *movimiento* of Chicana/o struggle and liberation was at a definitive "crossroads."[3]

Indeed, Morales himself reflects a similar ambivalence regarding the salience of positioning his oeuvre within specifically Chicana/o contexts. In an interview with José Antonio Gurpegui, Morales responds to the question about the context in which he places Chicana/o literature: "I consider it to be a part of American literature. At the beginning of the Chicano movement there was a tendency to consider it as separate from American literature and I felt it was really a part of the American experience" (Gurpegui, "Interview," 5). Morales continues this line of reasoning by aligning Chicana/o literature with an ethnic canon: Irish American, German American, Italian American, African American, all of which form the "American literary mosaic." Citing but not critically indulging in the revelatory implications of his foregrounding of ethnic white literatures (Irish, German, and Italian), we can simply note for the moment the extent to which this exchange brackets, however provisionally, Morales's work within a Chicana/o literary history, itself a member of a U.S. multicultural confederation. Left out, again provisionally, are other possible frames, those in which his work has been more often read, in courses housed in Latin American studies and even "Spanish" literature. Certainly, Morales's recent works, written more often now in English than in Spanish, might account for his own shift in literary critical paradigm. But we can begin to meditate on *The Brick People* not simply as a deliberate, conscious choice retooled for a multicultural machinery, but at the determining forces that made such a choice productive. We might also wonder at the extent to which the disavowal of a "separatist" Chicana/o literary stance, against his more favored American ethnic configuration, has something to do with his conception of literary history, of literature as history, and of the contested political histories that inhere in the two different formations.

It is into this historical and, by extension, political dilemma that we enter Morales's novel, one fraught with the concerns of a collective history on the one hand and the forces of contemporary exigencies on the other. All the while *The Brick People* strives to claim creative space for itself, to open up what Wahneema Lubiano calls the "terrain of possibility" imagined and available in literary work ("Toni Morrison," 327). And it is the three arenas of literary palimpsest—those revealing buried moments of the era described (Chicana/o labor history), those evinced as markers of the period in which the work is written (the 1980s), and those claimed, as a result of this tension, as wholly the artist's own—that Morales struggles to reconcile in *The Brick People.* As if to remind his readers of this last bit of disclosure, that of his own original contribution to this narrative of Chicana/o history, Morales writes the following as his closing epigraph: "*The Brick People* is a work of fiction. Any similarity between the characters and people, living and dead, is coincidental."

We tend to forget that this conventional kind of epigraph, a declarative disclaimer, masks an insistent imperative to read—even in our most skeptical, postmodern moments—within the spaces of disciplinary authority. To begin, there is the logic of the epigraph's universal applicability: what makes such a claim generic is that its continual repetition in the marginal spaces of novels reinforces the normal (and normalized) boundaries of genre with the most subtle exercises of power. These final sentences to Morales's novel seem so much an afterthought that a blank page following the last punctuation mark and closing the story proper would almost suffice to do the work of nudging the reader to turn her/his back to the boundary that simultaneously enables and limits the task of reading. The assertive impulse of the epigraph is one to which we must all assent, yet it hardly feels painful given the critical tools we are granted to enjoy what takes place in this fictional world. So long as the two primary terms holding up fiction remain oppositional categories to one another—similarity/coincidence—we are ensured of the privilege that any enclosed or planned community, in this case a readerly community, eventually assumes is a right. But the moment we shift our eyes to the epigraph's border, it becomes clear that the opposition is installed with a rhetorical violence whose force is hidden by the simple slash between words, or by the signpost that polices the good neighbors from those other bad ones out there.

For a writer of color such as Morales, the exceptional status granted fiction by the recitation of its coincidental relation to the more contested terrain of "history" cannot be underestimated. The late Barbara Christian wrote with eloquence when she signaled the importance, even necessity, of the space literature has afforded people of color against the monochromatic, expurgated version of U.S. social history: "I can only speak for myself. But what I write and how I write is done in order to save my own life. And I mean that literally. For me literature is a way of knowing that I am not hallucinating, that whatever I feel/know is" ("Race," 335). Morales himself has echoed the salience of fiction writing as a way to recuperate and validate an experience all too often lost in the general American narrative: "*The Brick People* is more of a personal work. It is based on the lives of my parents. . . . *The Brick People* . . . traces the experiences of my family. However, they represent a large sector of the *mexicano* population, namely, the working class. In the past we used to have novels of the working class but authors don't seem to write them anymore" (Grandjeat and Rodríguez, 109, 110).[4] The ethos established in both Christian's and Morales's statements about literature is profound; the stakes are high, particularly if we accept (which I do) the political warrant embedded in their assertions: both employ literature, and in the specific case of Morales, use fiction to undertake a project of historical recovery.[5] Reading "properly" in this light gathers an urgency that the epigraph, with all the ease of its conventional wisdom, almost betrays and with which I identify.

It is the acknowledgment of this urgency that has driven the small but contentious debate to critical distraction around *The Brick People*. Those who have written on this novel have done so in curiously pedagogical terms, curious because the premise on which the arguments are based have to do with the most basic of questions, concerns that are implied in both the closing epigraph to the novel and the more general relationship between "original" fiction and history: how are we supposed to read Morales's work? Ostensibly, *The Brick People* is a historical novel that fictionalizes the emergence of a Southern California barrio in the period preceding the Second World War. But critical engagement with the novel begins with the disciplinary and generic tension that "historical fiction" suggests, and whose definition is the barometer by which critics judge the work. Recent scholars point to the first extended consideration of the novel, Mario García's review, which faults the novel for failing to imbue its characters with the capacity to change the conditions of those collectively laboring and living in the Simons barrio. García carefully regards the attention that Morales gives to uncovering the dialectical tension of the Chicana/o struggle in the early part of the century, and credits the novel for bringing to a fictional world "the major contributions of Mexicans to the building of California" (199). What troubles García in the final analysis is the narrative's inability to "channel" the racial and material dialectic of white capitalist exploitation against the robbed labor of Chicana/o workers into a novel celebrating the tenacity, even in the face of constant defeat, of collective struggle. Demarcating a "working-class literature" whose point of view is decidedly "middle class" from a "proletarian" one whose working-class perspective would reflect the political value of class struggle, García makes quite clear to which category he thinks *The Brick People* belongs: "But what Morales' novel is not, and here it differs in a very fundamental way with recent Chicano *[sic]* historiography, it is not a history of people's struggles. Of struggles which have not only manifested the grievances of Chicanos, but which have given rich meaning to their lives" (199).

What makes this reading "improper," even "retrogressive," according to recent critics, is García's inability to grasp the literary techniques that Morales employs to offer what is elsewhere regarded as *The Brick People*'s "delegitimation of the hegemonic discourse" of the "totalization of history" (Waldron, 105). García's amounts to a "bad" reading for failing to move beyond, as Antonio Márquez has chided, an anachronistic, Lukácsian straitjacket in which social realism acts as the critical plumbline for literature. For Márquez, Morales's blending of Chicana/o history with "surrealism, dream-narrative, magic realism, ample touches of the grotesque, and elements of the fantastical ('metafiction')" mandates that the critic attune herself to the protocols of the "postmodernist tack and distance from the traditional historical novel" (76–79). By extension, the relationship of the novel to its historical subject is not one of constant and servile indebtedness. Rather, reading Morales's novel begins an opportunity to offer a postmodernist critique of the "grand narrative" of History—and in this case, the collectivist historiography of the Chicano movement of the 1970s that García regards as foundational—through the multiplicity of the contemporary fictional form in Chicana/o literature.[6] Complementing Márquez's celebration of Morales's literary sophistication, Carl Gutiérrez-Jones specifies the terms through which *The Brick People* suggests strategies for political resistance against the "hegemonic discourse" of white domination. Gutiérrez-Jones concentrates his reading on the consistent cycles of violence in Morales's novel, citing these specific passages as emblematic instances of *lo real maravilloso,* a tactic of literary resistance closely associated with the magical realist strategy of other Latin American writers. These moments of violence underscore the ways in which communities such as the Simons barrio and its white counterpart, Montebello, are racially constituted through the expression and infliction of power, both coercive and ideological. Central to this exposure of power through Morales's use of *lo real maravilloso* are for Gutiérrez-Jones the "homeopathic rhetorical manipulations whose value lies, in part, in [their] emphasis on the constructed character of panoptic, disciplinary tools" (101).[7] The unmistakably Foucauldian usage in his analysis enables Gutiérrez-Jones's reading to script in political terms what Márquez asserts in literary ones: *The Brick People* complicates and exposes the despotic control of powerful, received discourses, and thereby resists the imprisonment of discursive boundaries and all the assumptions wedged into those borders.

At the risk of overly emphasizing the instrumental nature of this debate, let me pose the arguments presented by García, Márquez, and Gutiérrez-Jones as indices of an academic, disciplinary contest. Simply put, what amounts to a "bad" reading is premised on the differing hermeneutics of "fiction" and "history." García, the historian in this case, considers Morales's fictional interventions into the realm of Chicana/o historiography lacking for the novel's inability to underscore the political ethos of the Chicano movement that he is at pains to maintain. On the other hand, Márquez and Gutiérrez-Jones regard "History," even a Chicana/o version of it, as the problem that Morales's fiction seeks to circumvent and even undermine for both aesthetic and political purposes. What each regards as "bad" reading amounts to the "infection" or "violence" of alien interpretive protocols of one discipline into another; each "horizon of expectation" finds fault with the warrants of the other. The terms of critical judgment in this debate therefore bring us again to Morales's epigraph and compel us to take seriously the relation, in spite of or even because of its "coincidental" connection, between the fictional staging of a community's history and the historical implications of such fictional intervention. In order to attest to this relation, we can assume that both sides of the debate are correct: Morales does perform in the novel a historical revision that evacuates political agency from its characters (García's claim) *and,* through "magical," narrative manipulations, exposes the violence inherent in the construction and maintenance of the Simons barrio as a racialized community of labor (Gutiérrez-Jones's reading). Emerging from an acknowledgment of both claims are ramifications not only for the question posed earlier—how do we read *The Brick People?*—but also to the violence that inheres in such a reading, whether it is the rhetorical violence of interpretive value or the political violence that fashions and frames a community.

If violence as it is underscored through "magical" strategies draws our attention to the relations of power that are installed and reinforced to maintain the racial construction of Chicana/o communities; if magical realism, as it is generically called, attempts to transform our ways of thinking and reading so that "new and deeper dimensions of existence are revealed" (Walter, 21); if spectacular, and altogether "fictional," acts of violence foreground in *The Brick People* the "novel's embattled ontologies" (Gutiérrez-Jones, 85), we are still left to consider if and how such moments reshape the worldviews of the characters in the novels, those who also experience this violence in more visceral ways. While both Márquez's and Gutiérrez-Jones's critiques correctly point out that Morales's magical realism prompts the novel's readers to think again about the political forces shaping Chicana/o history in Los Angeles, their readings are notably silent on another, equally important facet of how magical realism, or even the more conventional use of violence, recalibrates the capacities for the characters themselves to read their particular social situation any differently from before.[8]

Numerous examples emerge, of novels merging myth and history, the fantastic and the mundane, in which central characters, after having gone through a "magical" or spiritual experience, wake up the next morning to see the world with critical lenses more sharply focused on the structures undergirding social relations. Sterling, for example, one of the primary characters in the ensemble cast of Leslie Silko's *Almanac of the Dead*, learns of and experiences the myth of Quetzalcoatl, the spirit god who, in Chicana/o and Native American mythography, is poised with her armies of the South to retake the American Southwest. Sterling begins as a rather staid figure who measures his success by lily-white American standards— "Education, English, a job on the railroad, then a pension . . . self improvement"—and ends thoroughly transformed ("haunted," as the narrative tells us), with an eye toward an eventual social apocalypse ready to revolutionize the United States (760–61). For Silko, it is as important for the characters to open their eyes as it is for her readers to do so; resistance against oppression takes place imaginatively within the story by the characters as well as along the story's borders, in the readers' engagement with the novel.[9]

But this double agency that magical realism, which also encompasses for the purposes of this chapter novelistic examples of violence, can achieve is staged in Morales's narrative as mutually exclusive, even antagonistic, possibilities of critical engagement. Insofar as *The Brick People* enacts examples that attempt to pose competing social logics that countervail one another, and even tilt momentarily relations of power toward those with whom we are meant to sympathize, the novel also blindfolds these characters, the Chicana/o workers of the Simons barrio, with a social vision that prevents them from overcoming the boundaries of racial space and their identities as laboring consumers. In this fictional revisitation of

Chicana/o labor history through the story of one Los Angeles barrio, novelistic innovations telescope the structures of racial power that underwrite the spatial—both material and ideological—construction of the Chicana/o community, but from which a critical social vision is posed as a limiting horizon rather than an enabling one. In this sense, *The Brick People* is a narrative that denies its characters exactly what they need to do and what the novel's readers ironically are granted, the capacity to read "badly": to read power in social arrangements beyond the disciplinary protocols of sanctioned interpretive tools. Such a novelistic enterprise that uses the spectacular and violent to foreground the limits of agency rather than the possibilities of transformation gestures at the conditions under which Morales produces this narrative vision—the 1980s, a moment in which Chicana/os, both from within their own intellectual communities and from external forces redefining their condition and "place" in U.S. social formation, were undergoing a sea change in their position within a new racial order. *The Brick People* provides an opportunity to read its narrative ruptures and closures as instances of larger racial anxieties that pervade discussions of Chicana/o identity and its political projects in the 1980s. This is a social, contextual consideration of the novel that I will offer toward the end of the chapter.

It is not unimportant that many of the novel's readers deem the representations of violence in the narrative central to Morales's vision of the formation of the Simons barrio, and that indeed this fictional attention toward spectacular acts of violence marks the primary means by which Morales integrates elements of *lo real maravilloso*, or magical realism, into the story. In this light, violence is integral to understanding the diagetic construction of this Los Angeles community and the undercurrent of disruptive energy circumscribing the narrative itself. Consider, for example, our introduction to the inauguration of the Simons brickyard, the original one set up by Joseph Simons. This site, as the narrative recounts, was founded on two acts of violence: the first, as we have seen, is the death of Doña Eulalia and the murder of her family. The second is told almost immediately afterward, and chronicles the historical massacre of the Chinese laborers in Los Angeles. Both are accounts of violence and death that imbue the work site in historical moments; they parabolically distill into interwoven stories the birth of Mexican labor as emerging from the remains of a disenfranchised and debilitated *Californios* population and of a former indentured labor force suffering from the whims of white nativists. Between these two historical accounts, the narrative tells us that Joseph orders the excavation of the primary site of clay extraction, a process of labor exacted by newly hired Mexican laborers: "An immense red hole began to form, a wound located in an unnoticeable place on the earth's precious skin. Rosendo hired more Mexicans who fell into the pit as laborers who dug, molded, and created the material that built small to large pyramids" (Morales, 16). Later on, these workers discover the remains of the murdered Chinese, but let us first take notice of the language used to describe this initial breaking of the ground as Simons's property. As the earth's skin is "broken," from which an "unnoticeable wound" oozes, the anthropomorphized ground signals the shattering of a supposedly precarious balance between people and the land. From here, small incidents of revenge take place against the perpetrators of this infliction of violence on the land: the brown insects eventually return to take Joseph's life as other members of the Simons family are also overwhelmed by these mysterious creatures. Just as the death of Doña Eulalia brought about the initial reporting of brown insects, an immediate act of revenge against the men who destroyed her family and her tree, so does the breaking of this ground reenact the same organic retribution that time and again emerges to claim the lives of various people involved in this brickmaking process (Orin, Joseph, Walter). As Gutiérrez-Jones observes, this revenge of the "brown insects" exemplifies Morales's use of *lo real maravilloso,* the strategy that "reveals institutional languages as perpetuators of particular worldviews, ontologies that appear inescapable only so long as their legitimacy remains a sheltered part of a political unconscious" (85). The brown insects, as one emblem of this "magical" aspect of the landscape, challenge the status of reality and rationalized time, as the insects enact revenge in seemingly spontaneous and unpredictable moments in the narrative that in turn disrupt the space, interrupt the time, and claim the lives of the white characters and their institutions.

In this way, Morales opens up a discursive opposition between rationalized, white patriarchal temporality and spontaneous emergences of a feminized, magical, and violent earth. The brickyard becomes a space of a crisis, in which ideologies clash to control the status of reality. As the earth is wounded by a metaphorical "rape," the red earth broken open for capital accumulation of the Simonses—mirroring the castration of the virile tree that Doña Eulalia grieves over—we see the staging of an embattled terrain over which barrio/work-space is established.[10] As Gutiérrez-Jones notes, "Doña Eulalia . . . [creates] an omnipresent force that asserts its own brand of justice" (87). Violence inflicted onto the Simons brothers exposes the violent origin of the Simons barrio, constituted as a community of laborers. Extending this metaphor of "rape" of the land by inserting a fictional metaphor of "justice," Morales reproduces the template of the Chicana/o narrative of "Reconquista": like the myth of Quetzalcoatl, the plumed serpent whom El Eco dreams will retake the "homeland" of

California (60). The mythic history of Doña Eulalia provides the narrative energy to remind us that the origins of the Simons barrio and its laboring inhabitants are premised on the violence of constructing the people as mere sources of labor for expropriating profit. The elements of *lo real maravilloso* that inhere in the violence that the brown insects inflict onto the Simons brothers make explicit that social relations—and by implication, social identities—in the barrio emerge, at its origin, from conditions of a political economy based in racial violence.

This portrait of Doña Eulalia is a far cry from the actual Eulalia Pérez of the San Gabriel Mission, whose supervisory brilliance in exploiting *indio* labor won her high praise from Spanish missionaries and a place in the reconstruction of the mission's history, absorbed into a larger conversion narrative that elides the contradictions and conflicts of Southern California's white conquest. That the novel imbues Doña Eulalia with power through death *after* she tumbles into the pit suggests that Morales makes mythic connection between her and another Doña: Marina, better known in Chicana/o studies circles as La Malinche. Often viewed as the betrayer of *la raza*, Malinche actually occupies a double symbolic position for Chicana/os, divergent views cut across gender lines. For Chicanos, she can never be forgiven; Malinche's seduction by Hernán Cortés and her aid in Cortés's genocide of the Aztecs made her not only a *chingada,* the passive, violated mother of Chicanos, but also, in more active ways, a co-conspirator in the relentless devastation of *la Conquista*. Chicanas, on the other hand, have bristled at this deeply misogynistic reading of Doña Marina, and have retooled the constitutive terms of Chicana/o history to reclaim Malinche and the year 1519 as a moment of syncretic origins: *mestizaje* overtakes passivity, and flexibility and hybridity determine Chicana/o community, not disavowal. As Ramón Gutiérrez argues, "The only public models open to Mexican women were those of the virgin and whore. If women were going to go beyond them, then they had to begin by rehabilitating Malinche" (52).

Doña Eulalia, then, derives much of her mythic power in this recasting of la Malinche as an adaptive figure who worked within the boundaries set by a dominant regime but whose legacy also invokes a more pervasive and insidious potential for disruption, rebellion, and revenge. But Doña Eulalia is not a strict descendant of Doña Marina. Rather, by framing her death, not her life, in the historical origins of the Simons brickyard, Morales not only puts into motion 1519, but also layers 1848—the fateful year of Mexico's defeat by the United States, the collective loss that inhered in the ultimately broken Treaty of Guadalupe Hidalgo, and the more conventional, modern "origin" of Chicana/o history—as yet another mediated historical trope embodied in Doña Eulalia's death. In both cases, whether 1519 or 1848, Chicano history arises out of instances of violation, shame, defeat, and death, all of which demand vengeance if not justice for lost culture, land, and historical continuity. The inclusion of a feminist reconsideration of 1519 and Malinche nudges 1848 out of its construction as decisive defeat: Doña Eulalia screams "¡Mi familia! ¡Mi vida!" and willingly jumps into the pit—"falls forward," in fact. Her death signifies not defeat but defiance, and she becomes, in effect, the mother of Chicana/os, the Malinche who traverses 1519 and 1848 to bring terror anew, in the form of flesh-eating insects to those who would dare torture her children in Simons, land stolen, descendants exploited, but never forgotten.

On the other side of this violent origin, however, is the excavation of Chinese bodies, which provokes a retelling of the Chinese massacre that took place two decades prior to the brickyard groundbreaking. Another scene in which we see that the historical origins of this community are contingent on the infliction of racial violence, here the narrative takes on a decidedly unmagical aura. Rather, Morales writes of the massacre of the Chinese with no countermemory of mythic revenge; it is a story of brutal victimization. Strangely, the remnants of this story are quickly forgotten by not only the residents of the area, but also the narrator. The bodies are burned, and the "only physical evidence left of the dead were five mounds of ash, blown away that evening by a strong warm wind that came from the east and flew to the sea" (24). This sentence is the last we hear of the Chinese in Simons. Profoundly reminiscent of the "historical amnesia" that the narrator chastises the city of Los Angeles for suffering from after the massacre, the story of this violence is quickly subsumed by the narrative as well. The excavation of the story of the Chinese massacre yields little more than a brief pause, and the narrative eerily mirrors Joseph's reasons for erasing the visible signs of this unearthed memory: "Joseph was prepared to eliminate anything from the past that might halt the successful progress of the plant" (24). The Chinese have no witness here; their remains are scattered, and the narrative moves along to record the building of the brickyard once again.

What is peculiar in this rendition of the doubled inaugural violence of the brickyard's origins is that although Morales recuperates and negotiates competing temporalities between white institutional domination and brown insect revenge that suggest a narrative struggle between the organic (and rightful) owners of the land—those who will take part in La Reconquista—and the white invaders who steal and exploit the land, the violent end of another laboring community is suddenly cited and just as suddenly dismissed. As historians have flagged, violence, repression, and exclusion of the Chinese helped facilitate and were predicated on the arrival of cheaper and more available labor from the south, as impoverished Mexicans from poor states such as Guanajuato immigrated north to fulfill the labor needs of the burgeoning white capitalists.[11] Whereas the eyes of the earth and the infusion of the insects can "magically" see the workings of Anglo exploitation and the incipient racial division of labor, the eyes of the Chinese dead register blank stares and impotent anger and fear in the hearts of the new Mexican laborers: although the workers consider this mass burial site "sacred ground" (17), they offer little resistance when Joseph orders them to burn the remains of the Chinese (23–24). The unearthing of the Chinese bodies points, in effect, to a dead end regarding the ability of an excavation of historical memory to pose a challenge to the Simons brothers' emerging empire of brick.

The "brick people" then, the Mexican laborers who arrive in the aftermath of these initial moments of violence, encompass a double metaphorical position. Hypostatizing them as clay, the narrative figures these men and women as "natural" people of the land, while also reifying the Simons residents as workers whose activity of labor forces them to "contemplate [their] own activity in the alienated form of commodities interacting in accord with their own laws of motion . . . toward the objectified constructs of [their] own mind[s]" (Porter, 25). Yet Morales presents these cognitive moments as skewed and split, since it is only the former metaphorical translation that is considered seriously in the narrative. The memory of enchanted space, which signals the return of the brown insects, is excavated and kept as a repetitive drive whose undercurrent can formidably and consistently disrupt the machinery of the Simons capitalists. On the other hand, by foreclosing and forgetting the violence inflicted on Chinese laborers, Morales narrows the scope of the laborers' vision and renders them unable to assert an agency that would align their history birthed in traumatic violence with the eradication of another. If Morales's narrative strategy of *lo real maravilloso* integrates the fantastic violence of Doña Eulalia's revenge to expose to his readers the inherent violence in the relations of power between the white owners of the brickyard and those who labor in that space, this same strategy necessitates that the structures that determine these social relations are *not* seen by the actors in this struggle differently, perhaps seeing in the dead Chinese workers their own possible future. The Simons workers dig up the Chinese bodies, the women mourn for "the unknown dead, for the loss that had never been recognized" (24), but there the connections end. Unable to forge what Vijay Prashad calls "horizontal assimilation" with the legacy of racial death that these Chinese bodies represent, the Simons workers' descent into the pit to excavate bodies and their later descent to collect clay for the production of brick are not posed as mirroring activities. Crossracial historical memory fades away with the ashes of the Chinese, blown significantly out into the Pacific—back to China?—and the newer immigrants labor on, waiting for the next eruption of violence to reconstitute again the space of the Simons barrio.

Certainly, the workers' fall into the pit and into a political economy of a racial division of labor stems from the Mexicans' urgent necessity to move into this relation. As Tomás Almaguer shows in a "world-systems" analysis of nineteenth-century capitalist development in California, the uneven development between California as an annexed part of an industrialized U.S. economy and the remnants of feudal despotism and peasantry in Mexico generated the influx of immigrants into an incipient labor force for rapid capital accumulation ("Interpreting Chicano History," 8).[12] Morales evinces this connection between the processes of capital and the movement of people as labor when his narrative depicts the appalling conditions that Walter confronts in his trip to Hearst's "Rancho Mexicana" in Chihuahua. But the narrative's response to the dominating logic of economic dependency and white supremacy that determines the migration patterns and labor of the Simons workers ironically constructs the racialized barrio as the primary space in which opposition can emerge. In this sense, the logic of resistance depends on the logic of domination. The story of Doña Eulalia and her resurrection through the insects renders legible the workers' connection to a larger Chicana/o historiography, which turns historical defeat into organic possibilities of countermemory. Memory, however, is selective, often to justify and make readable present conditions. The narrative makes clear that the workers themselves do not act specifically upon either myth to change their circumstances. Revenge against the Simons family simply happens; Doña Eulalia's mythic rage is simply part of the landscape. The workers' entry into this Chicana/o historiography is organic, their *intention* not part of the calculus of resistance, but this same organicity is precisely what prevents their imagined racial community from seeing that the forces that killed the Chinese workers are the same that reify them as pliant labor. At the same time that the workers are placed into the vein of a cultural politics at whose heart is the reconstitution of a fabled betrayer of the race into its first dissident, they must erase, render illegible, another possible "origin," in which the very terms of Chicana/o insurgency might be recast not simply in terms of racial origin but also through a crossracial historical trauma of death.

The consequences of placing the workers in one cultural relation of power at the elision of another are profound, as we shall see later in this chapter. For the moment, let us pause and look briefly at how another novel about California labor works to bring to light that which Morales's narrative shields. In very different historical, literary, and cultural contexts, Carlos Bulosan's autobiographical novel *America Is in the Heart* (1946) foregrounds as the main terms of struggle the capacity for Filipino workers, usually but not exclusively migrant laborers, to join in the larger, impossible claim of "America," in which the state's workers of color recast the American dream of ethnic assimilation into a socialist dream left in interregnum at the book's end. Both *America* and *The Brick People* share similar historical structures of migration: like Morales's characters' journey from Guanajuato to Los Angeles, Bulosan's narrator Allos/Carlos depicts the Philippines as a country devastated by and dependent on U.S. colonialism, global patterns that compel him and thousands of other pinoys to risk the long voyage to the U.S. West Coast. Despite four decades of separation, both novels are concerned most explicitly with their *raza*, and document the pain that racialized labor suffered at the hands of white bosses and equally white violence.

Patricia Chu and Rachel Lee have both considered rightly what they view as *America*'s dependence on gendered codes of "fraternity"—most clear in the narrator's obsessive construction of sexually desirable but chastely unavailable white women and in his imagination of a feminized American landscape—which in their minds constitute, but ultimately undermine, Bulosan's political and even authorial claims. But as Viet Nguyen shows, in exposing the masculinist matrix of power that Bulosan employs in the novel, what emerges also is the centrality of labor as a material determination of how race, gender, and sexuality constitute the bodies of Brown men: "The Asian American body politic is deeply embedded in the movement of labor and capital, and its bodily, material shape is inevitably partially determined by work" (68). However troubled his relation to a greater politics that might include women, especially women of color, Bulosan's claim to America rests squarely in imagined multiracial workerist collectivities, fed by his affiliations to national liberation movements in the Philippines and his rhetorical embrace of the Communist Party in the United States (San Juan). Bulosan's gendered ethics of erasure turn on a not unproblematic transformation of labor *in itself* into labor *for itself*.[13] Morales makes up for the amnesia of coalitional labor by construing a vengeful feminized landscape, a productive inversion that results in quite different conclusions. Bulosan sees, if partially, the promises of labor reading itself into a national, even international script; Morales's workers read neither labor nor the land that fights for them: for them, violent crises that interrupt their regulated workdays seem to occur as naturally as Los Angeles's weather patterns. In a word, they cannot read themselves—they must be read.

Not only, then, are violence and death the ways in which the community emerges, but they also suggest to us *how* a community is constructed, *what* narrative it follows, and *why* such a narrative of the community is asserted. The space of the barrio in Morales's novel works in doubled fashion. The first is one in which the characters struggle in their daily lives to make the best of things: to raise and support a family, to maintain one's job at Simons, to build a house of one's own, all of the things that exhibit a certain ideological space that the workers inhabit and understand well, despite the daily grind and pain. But this is challenged by the second one, the energy of the brown insects, the moment of *lo real maravilloso,* which prevents us from reading this novel as one where white institutions and individuals and their power can be absolutely exerted, unchallenged by a Chicana/o subject of resistance. Instead, the barrio, the community, remains a vibrant one, a place where white domination is checked and contested, so that the people of the barrio can continue to struggle in realizing a subjectivity afforded by their work and their buying power, and their reproduction of the family into something called tradition. But the resistant energy of the barrio community comes from outside of it, outside the space and time of their existence. The narrative, a confluence of magical and naturalist tendencies, retains ownership of that energy, and legible correspondence occurs solely between writer and reader, production and reception, creation and consumption. To this extent, *The Brick People* ironically disrupts the fiction of white supremacy by consolidating the very boundaries of the barrio, constructed as laboring subjects, determined by violent white rule. Resistance depends on the very space afforded by racial power; the terms of Chicana/o freedom, set by the walls that separate Simons from the white suburbs of Los Angeles, ensure historical continuity of the barrio, but also limit the workers' capacity to reimagine the barrio itself. As George Sánchez has observed, Los Angeles's political economy during the 1920s largely determined the choices available for the barrio's residents: "Certainly living within the barrio allowed Mexican immigrants a measure of control over their future. Yet economic and political developments outside the barrio continued to impinge on these decisions" (205).

This limited narrative strategy of limiting white domination while strengthening the boundaries of the barrio is posed in the puzzling scene in which William Hickman, a strange white man who has even stranger visions, abducts a little girl and later kills her, dismembers her body, tries to collect ransom money offered by the father, and is later arrested and executed. Appearing in the middle of the novel, the Hickman episode offers few signs that would suggest its relevance to the rest of the story, besides its coincidental relation to an actual, historical William Hickman who abducted and killed little Marion Parker. At first glance, Morales seems to juxtapose the relative safety of those within the barrio against the background "in Los Angeles [where] an eternal and terrible fear began" (172). The fear of violence is now situated in "white" Los Angeles, as a "monster" is loosed upon them. Hickman's "obscene acts" seem to continue what occurs sporadically in the novel: retribution and revenge against whites take on uncalculated, spontaneous forms. White violence doubles back on itself, and the fear and violence that racial exclusion had exerted against those living in the barrio return to the white community in the form of a deranged white man. The same energy that, from the body of Doña Eulalia, comes forth as the brown insects to wreak havoc on white characters such as Joseph and later Walter also produces a Hickman to terrify a white public.

What emerges from this energy, as it is personified and embodied in Hickman, however, are discourses of criminality and madness. Even the Mexicans in Simons vilify Hickman as an "animal" who shatters their sense of safety: "Hickman came from the mass society outside of Simons, a society that rejected them, and now a beast created among the gringos was infiltrating and interacting psychologically with them" (173). A peculiar union of mind between Anglo and Mexican emerges as both communities mourn over the dismembered body of Marion Parker and are enraged by this atrocity committed by "the Fox." The paranoia that spreads across all of Los Angeles is ironically another instance in which people reassert ties with one another to fortify a certain idea of community, a moral one that eschews a mad figure. The madman, the criminal, is then justifiably hunted down, confined, and eliminated. "In the shadows of the bourgeois city," Foucault reminds us, "is born this strange republic of the good that is imposed by force on all those suspected of belonging to evil. This is the underside of the bourgeoisie's great dream and great preoccupation . . . the laws of the state and the laws of the heart at last identical" (61). The madman is the nightmare of the "good" society, but he is also its dream: evil, Nietzsche would say, scares people into imagining what is good, what is utopian. Like madness, crime functions precisely as a way for irrational fear and moral outrage to be rectified by the arm of the state. And in the aftermath of Hickman's crime, this is just what occurs:

> Now, in front of Octavio Revuelta's home, Don Vicente stopped to say hello to Octavio and Federico who chatted with Ignacio. Federico read from the *Los Angeles Times,* whose headline roared "This Fiend Must Not Escape!" The entire force of two thousand Los Angeles police were mobilized to search for Hickman. The department requested the cooperation of Los Angeles's leading citizens and the surrounding police agencies.

An unpredictable, volatile hysteria settled over the city. People gathered and circulated aimlessly through the streets, waiting for more news about the progress of the search. Fearful citizens donated funds for a reward for information leading to the arrest of the killer. By Sunday morning authorities had amassed twenty-five thousand dollars to capture the Devil. (173)

From the reversal of violence inflicted onto a white girl's body to the outrage that issues forth to capture Hickman, this passage coalesces three ideas of staging the Simons barrio in relation to itself and to its neighboring white constituencies. First, the residents in the barrio become interpellated into a shared ideology with that of the rest of white Los Angeles. Federico reads from the *Los Angeles Times,* whose demonized portrayal of Hickman produces a shared readership that is developed by the coverage of the crime by the Spanish-language *La Opinión.*[14] The murdered body of Marion Parker brings about a community's outrage, whether Mexican or white, and thus ensures an ideological coherence of justice permeated and reinforced by the newspaper. The barrio fortifies its symbolic meaning as a "real" community in establishing this connection to a larger ideology of outrage against a white, "American" body. Whether it is Don Vicente reading *La Opinión,* Federico reading "This Fiend Must Not Escape" from the *Los Angeles Times,* or white folks circulating "aimlessly" through the streets waiting for "news," the criminalization of Hickman through the mutilation of the girl's body produces an imagined community, one predicated on a circulation of shared moral codes, sedimented ideas stemming from the aversiveness of criminalized violence and the violated, female body.[15] This adoption of "universal," national, and transracial ideologies in the barrio community has its consequences, displayed later during World War II, when Mexican boys give up their own bodies to "die for" their "country" and to give meaning to their respective barrios.[16]

But second, this production of "shared" codes also proceeds to fashion community with a racial difference. If the death of Marion Parker allows violence against one body to stand in for violation of a body politic, then it is her *white* body that signifies the perpetuation of racial ideologies. The Mexicans in the barrio are aware of this difference. After Federico reads the *Los Angeles Times,* he points out that the connection of Simons to the white communities surrounding the barrio demonstrates an antagonistic contingency, alongside one of commiseration: "'Like I've said, Don Vicente, it will become dangerous for Mexicans. The newspapers are saying that the Fox has black curly hair. They will stop all of us who have hair like that. You'll see how the police will harass the Mexicans,' Federico said assuredly" (174). The qualifier "assuredly" presumes that Federico's analysis of how the investigation will affect the residents of the barrio is a well-established and lingering effect of the racialization of Mexicans as potential "deviants" from the moral codes of the white communities. Indeed, the narrative seems to assume a barrio voice when it remarks, "In the back of their minds lurked the possibility that the gringo beast could enter their world, or that Walter Simons would allow the police to go into Simons Town and invade their homes in search of the beast" (173). As a counterstance, Octavio points out that whites' racial fear against Mexicans would bar them from an imminent invasion by the police: "The gringos don't enter here, nor will criminals like the Fox" (174). Whether the fear is one of invasion or not, the criminal act of a white man generates a racial crisis, as the residents contemplate how they will again be scripted as racial bodies. The consequences of this investigation, in other words, will verify and reaffirm the prevailing racial ideologies of Los Angeles. Marion Parker's violated body will be sanctified, in this crisis of racial representation as read by the Simons residents, by reasserting race.

Dialectical oscillation between a shared intercommunity interpellation of outrage in Los Angeles and its racialized difference within the barrio, however—and this is my third point—elides the important narrative of the *enclosure* of barrio-space between this collusion of ideological codes and a repressive state regime. Unacknowledged in the discourse of justice and moral rage within the "universal" set of assumptions about criminality and unread in the critique of racial ideologies by the Simons residents is the border erected to separate white from Mexican, labor group from labor group, which simultaneously threatens and protects each community from one another. And on the eve of the Great Depression, consolidation of police power serves to regulate and manage communities that are replete with worker unrest. The two-thousand-member police force, which combs the streets of Los Angeles to search for Hickman, is sanctioned by a white public concerned about "justice" and is feared by a Mexican community concerned about encroachments on their civil rights by an overzealous, racist police force. But both imagined communities of differential fear erase the police's crucial role as primary definers in cordoning off the neighborhoods and facilitating the creation of criminality, madness, and goodness in a seamless professional discourse.[17] The cause, as it were, becomes the effect: crisis generates its own mitigation; the Los Angeles police force turns singular madness into collective crime and thus comes into its own as the thin blue line of combating the evil it has helped to create. "The state, and the state only," Stuart Hall asserts, "has the monopoly of *legitimate* violence, and this 'violence' is used to safeguard society against 'illegitimate' uses" (68). Regarded as legitimate in the chaos of Hickman's monstrosity, the police force now enjoys its elevated role in defining and protecting against illegitimate social action, whether individual or communal. Long after the Hickman affair is forgotten by both white and Mexican communities, the police remain, only to reemerge later to displace and contain the Simons residents in ever smaller residential spaces as adjoining white, homeowner communities push to control more sections of the region. The police force pursues and enacts a self-fulfilling ideology of paranoia and surveillance, in which a small body of police can efficiently enforce the patrol of communities with little knowledge of them.[18] But it is precisely this silent enclosure that determines for its residents the contours of Simons's activity—read as Mexican, it becomes a Chicana/o barrio, its borders swallowed by the residents as constitutive of their communal identity.

One should not underestimate the transformation of the state, in the guise of police containment, in the consolidation and determination of the Simons barrio. From its fictional origins in the violence inflicted on and by Doña Eulalia, Simons is embedded in the struggle of Aztlán, to reclaim land pilfered, labor reified, lives managed. The barrio remains a place where its residents can forge identities heretical to the paternalism of Walter Simons's fantasies of recreating dependent *ranchos* in Southern California. But the terms of contestation against white violence, already contracted by the erasure of the Chinese and the originary loss of the laborers' multiracial recognition, increasingly cluster around ever smaller spaces in which the workers can maneuver. Forged in the dialectical crucible of white domination and Chicana/o dissent, violent injections move Morales's novel forward to specify under what conditions and in what language change is to take place. And as these terms of resistance are honed for Simons's workers, the logic of urban triage becomes clear. As the police state reconfigures, redefines, and regulates the anarchic forces that spill out of the barrio, it sanctions barrio-space to determine the patterns and modes of future Chicana/o opposition. As the residents claim Simons as their home, their identification as Chicana/os—those who rightfully belong—aligns the language of dissatisfaction with the language of complacent containment.

The spectacular account of the Hickman case and its attendant but largely silent police containment of the barrio serve to displace concern over working conditions at the Simons's brickyard and temporarily stall union sentiment. Not much is made at this point in Morales's narrative that would account for the unrest that begins to filter into the minds of Octavio and the other Simons workers, in the beginning of this chapter, or the fear they feel in the layoffs of Mexican workers resulting from a slowdown in brick production: "'There's no job security at any brickyard,' Ignacio responded. . . . 'That's why we need a workers' union to protect the workers and their jobs,' Octavio said in a strong tone" (164–65). News about the criminality of an individual overshadows the potential "news" of an insurgent labor struggle, one that shields even the Mexicans from looking beyond the sensationalized event. Morales occludes the visions of the workers from drawing the connection between a spectacular discourse of criminality and racial ideology, and its material foundations in the division of labor and its ensuing contraction of barrio-space. Moreover, like the foreclosure of the Chinese massacre story, this passage of the Hickman affair offers the limits of a narrative that attempts to display the irony of a barrio community that derives its meaning through a contradictory ideological struggle between "universal justice" (outrage at the murder of Marion Parker) and incipient racism and exclusion (fear of police reprisal). Like the episode with the Chinese dead, the Hickman murder case ends not with a bang, but with a whimper: the initial hysteria over the murder wanes to barely passing interest, and the crisis of social formation and community reconfiguration is sealed once again in the wake of another moment of historical amnesia.[19] And just as the earlier episodes of violence do not afford the workers new forms or models of action to challenge the structures of white domination that contain them in the barrio, so this violent crime does not facilitate for Octavio or the others different capacities besides that of merely going to work the next day.

The occlusion of social relations blanketed through the Hickman affair leads us to consider Morales's novel not as a narrative that seeks to retrieve the memory of Chicana/o labor from the auspices of history and its textual closures, but one that highlights a process of denial and displacement that rather regards violent upheavals as events taking place in a space that must be narrated differently, even perhaps muted. Community stability necessitates a dispersal of labor insurgency, to render order out of chaos. Crises brought about by violence and the proliferation of dead bodies are rationalized through a presentation of the consequences of violence as naturalized occurrences (the brown insects), or as fleeting moments of spontaneity (Hickman). The movement of capital, first in the construction of Simons modeled after Hearst's *rancho,* then in Walter's rationalization and expansion of the brickyard, and finally in Simons's eventual industrial obsolescence, produces a Chicana/o laborer whose identity mirrors and bristles against capital's expropriations of land and appropriations of people. And in the novel, nature helps the worker, at least temporarily. But in each case, the potential disruption of social formation and a politicization of barrio-space are jettisoned for the sake of a narrative that fashions itself as the agent through which the ideological force of white capitalism and its ability to delineate barrio-space is undermined by an even greater vision of the narrative and its maker. The story of *The Brick People* leads us closer and closer to the idea of the primacy of reading as resistance. And, like the mythic, atemporal energy of Doña Eulalia's revenge through nature, the novel invites those outside the time and space of the workers—we, the readers—to look for that resistance with capacities unavailable to the workers themselves.

It is not surprising, then, that Morales inserts a photograph of the Simons brickyard in the middle of the novel, as it displays a Chicana/o work-space that, on the one hand, could be read as the white capitalists' point of view to regulate the brickyard's activity; on the other hand, the narrative seeks to wrest this viewing privilege from white institutional, visual power to a position even higher, to produce a perspicacity available to a narrative that evacuates the power of white, capitalist control. Fantastic and spectacular violence leads to such capacity of vision—the ability to read and expose racialized relations of power—through which the forces containing the barrio become ever more evident to the reader. The presentation of violence enables us and affords us the tools to read this photograph against its grain; the issue invoked here is whether the workers in the photograph can do so as well. And greater still is why.

The narrative has led us to a space in which Chicano work-space is now "readable" as a *Chicana/o* means of limiting white institutional power, where the violence that inheres within the barrio and also occurs on its borders ultimately gives meaning to its space as a community. But in this scenario, the Chicana/o worker, who not only views the violence but is threatened by it and lives through the events, becomes virtually illiterate.[20] Insofar as violence produces bodies that rupture the continuity of social formations in a given space, these relations of racialized power produce both a worker's regulated behavior and the possibilities of escape from such reification. The effect of rendering legible the Chicana/o in this narrative makes the worker a productive producer and consumer, but proves disastrous when a crisis revolves around the potential disruption of these relations. One such case is in the pathetic attempt to unionize the Simons workers. Feeling frustrated by the failure to make gains during the strike, the workers, especially the one set up as the "leader," Octavio, lay blame on the union organizers, Armando, Caroline Decker (we will return to Caroline at the end of this essay), and Lanzetti: "'You are a bunch of sons-of-bitches. You're the same as the old man Simons. Your only interest is in what you're going to gain. You're thieves and exploiters!' Octavio allowed his hatred to speak" (240).

To Octavio and the other workers, the strike fails because of the union's misappropriation of the strike-fund money, and less because of Walter's manipulation of his company's use of scab labor. There is, for the workers, no alternative but to return to work under the same or even worse conditions than when they started; any other way of living and reading their lives is ridiculous, even hopeless. Their inability to read beyond their own specific working and living conditions results in a complete disintegration of a potential labor energy that emerges out of their initial readings of their exploited condition in relation to their boss, Walter Simons. Their "illiteracy" thus propels them to fortify their hope, and to consolidate a barrio subjectivity in a profound adoption of a spurious rendition of American domestic bliss and consumerist individualism, as exemplified in Octavio's thoughts of both the failed strike at Simons and the collapse of the workers' collective store: "Octavio walked out into the evening and for the first time in his life in the United States he felt alone. He felt that he had been cut off from the groups and organizations that he should support or that should support him. He headed home, realizing that in the future no one would help him—only Nana, Micaela, Arturo, Javier, Flor and himself" (246). Although the climax of the novel is yet to come, the rest of the narrative follows through as a denouement on Octavio's moment of isolation. As the last of the Simons brothers dies, and the brickyard, once buzzing with work, falls into capitalist anachronism, Octavio, the other Simons workers, and their families set out to realize their dreams in barrio-space encoded through an embrace of a particular brand of "success." Morales's narrative, which opens up potential sites of reading resistance through various moments of violence, begets a contraction of barrio vision that pushes the community farther away from its white neighbors through violent exclusion (the maintenance of white Los Angeles against the barrio, Montebello versus Simons) and the barrio's ironic embrace of a Fordist ethic by the end of the novel. Yet Octavio's embrace of patriarchy and consumerism as coterminous avenues of mobility is staged in *The Brick People* as a logical, even preferred response to the barrio's permanence in the Los Angeles area.

If this whole appraisal of "reading resistance" encounters a fundamental contradiction between alternative narrative spaces produced through violence and the foreclosure of that same space to the workers; if ideology is shown to be limited by Chicana/o mythos but also to be that which sediments the workers and pushes them along already trodden paths of identity, making them illiterate of their predicament; then this contradiction is poised and demonstrated in its most ruptural figure in Arturo, Octavio's son. Not illiterate, Arturo is, literally, dyslexic. Dyslexia serves as a counterpoint to the reading abilities of the other residents in Simons. Indeed, Morales seems to suggest through Arturo that the contradictory forces delineating barrio-space coalesce and become embodied in Arturo, whom everyone in the community considers more or less an idiot. Yet because his seeming stupidity revolves around his inability to read properly and his entrance into social formation comes about somewhat skewed, this slightly aberrant vision enables Arturo to see far beyond the other residents of his family and the barrio. Morales highlights Arturo's troubled vision and crafts him as the "reader" of the social semiotic par excellence.

Consider the first encounter with Arturo, as the narrative recounts the manner in which his teachers castigate him. After knocking down another boy, Mikey Rodelo, who had bullied him with a stick, Arturo hears this from the priest, a salutation with which he has become familiar:

> "Bad boy!" Father Charles repeated while Mikey faked crying.
> Now the priest whom everybody respected and even Arturo liked had identified him as a bad boy. He was bad for defending himself and worse because he did not learn from his teachers. He tried, but when he repeated or wrote or solved math problems the teachers always said he was wrong. Arturo never said or wrote the answers correctly. Although to Arturo his letters and numbers seemed written well, to the teachers, parents, sisters, brother and friends, they appeared distorted. (247)

No doubt poor Arturo lives in a time when such a learning disability could not be handled with care. He himself internalizes a feeling of inadequacy, so that "[a]t times he considered himself the most stupid person in the world" (281).

Since, however, his relationship to the processes of "properly" reading is not transparent, he provokes a series of responses to those in positions of authority, retributions that expose the fact that reading and understanding must be ascertained through pregiven codes that are employed by dominant ideological structures. He is, therefore, a "bad boy," not just in the mind of Father Charles, but also in the conceptual structures that attempt to enclose him as a subject in and of ideology. Arturo's dyslexia provokes uncertainty for himself surely, but more important it disrupts the ideological apparatus of education, the institution that is supposed to make an action like reading a simple one. Not a good student but a "bad boy," Arturo fails to be interpellated "properly," to borrow from Althusser's comment on those who do not recognize the hailing of ideology. Not only a bad boy, Arturo is Althusser's bad subject, the one who exposes ideological codes in his very failure to read them and thereby fails to be absorbed by ideology's narrative. The priest, in this sense, is absolutely right: Arturo is a bad boy because the child transgresses the imperative of ideological "goodness." If the residents of the Simons barrio give meaning to their community by positing a certain relation to ideological codes of "reading," an "imaginary representation of individuals to their real conditions of existence" (Althusser, 162), Arturo's dyslexia interrupts this transmission of representation.[21] Instead of extracting meaning from words in the linear way that one is supposed to read, Arturo mixes the letters around, breaks syntactical coherence, and highlights the intrusive, arbitrary nature of words and their meanings. His "disability" decodes the ideology of reading as he ponders the violating condition of word making and word meaning: "Words to him manifested themselves into pictures and images, and these entities that he saw should be expanded and not locked in words, in sentences, on pages, in books. Ink violates a space; words imprison themselves in themselves" (282).

Two moments are significant in this passage. By pronouncing the sheer physicality of words, "ink on paper," Arturo disrupts the seeming transparency of the reading act by referring to it as an act of violence, something utterly unnatural, intrusive, and imprisoning. "Proper" reading means being complicit in an act of violence, and therefore it engages in a movement that imbues meaning only by closing itself off to other possibilities. The second salient observation that Arturo makes as he contemplates the materiality of the reading process is his opening up of reading, which allows words to "manifest themselves into pictures and images." That is, reading does not merely encompass the replication of what one has been taught in the school; the process of reading opens up to entail a much larger semiotic economy, in which cultural signs assign and are assigned meaning. Arturo reads books poorly, but his capacity to learn goes far beyond the transmission of meaning through already scripted acts. Indeed, by presenting words as material instances of ideological persuasion, he also implies that "pictures and images" can also serve to highlight the relationship between ideology and the material. Clothing, for instance, like reading, encodes certain ideas of propriety that immediately inform a logic of social control; the hyperdisplay of bizarre clothing draws attention to a symbolic order in crisis, which then exposes the differential power relations by provoking a response to the "improper" display of one's body.[22] As in improper reading, improper clothing rips at the semiotic seams of social control by displaying itself so much that the "style" becomes jarring.

In this way, Arturo's belief in a system of signs beyond books, "into pictures and images," is realized and exercised when he takes part in this semiotic manipulation of clothing: he buys a zoot suit in the aftermath of what is now known as the "Zoot Suit" riots of 1943. What is striking in Morales's narrative is how Arturo's dyslexic condition correlates with the concerted effort of the *pachucos* to perform an impropriety through a semiotics of protest.[23] By doing so, the zoot suiters offer a dyslexic vision that paradoxically exposes and destabilizes a cultural economy that continually portrays the Chicano as a "bad boy." The narrative conflates Arturo's own dyslexia with the dyslexic performance of the zoot suiters, in which strange talk and strange clothing are exemplified instead of denigrated: "'Mama, sharp this is!' Arturo showed off the newly learned language of zoot suit-ism. He was proud to wear the zoot suit that Saturday night" (257). His dyslexic language actually helps facilitate this particular mode of protest, in which language, clothing, and attitude bespeak a larger negotiation and struggle with prevailing ideologies. Nana responds by pleading with her son to take off the zoot suit and buy "real" clothes: "Return the suit. . . . [Your father] gave you money to buy clothes for work" (257). But it is Arturo who recognizes the limit of this ideology of work that Octavio, Nana, and the rest of the Simons barrio cling to, an ideology that also rei-fies them as necessitous labor: "Arturo saw the thousands of men and their families with crowns of bricks on their heads, burdens of unrecognized labor carried forever by the Mexicans who worked, lived and called Simons home" (258). Importantly, Arturo's dyslexia gives him a capacity to make alternative meaning through which the fictionality of a community forged through work is exposed by the hypervisible display and fictionality of the zoot suit. Holding up two bricks as a demonstration of their reified relation to the Simons brickyard, Arturo uses this gesture to signal his rebellion against the totalizing force to which his parents are blind, and therefore, illiterate.

Showcasing Arturo as a privileged character of reading crystallizes Morales's attempt to punctuate the ideology of the "real," which in this case is constructed as a belief in a community of work, with possibilities of the outlandish to put forth the notion that these other moments of vision are valuable moments in which resistance might lie. Arturo is Morales's model reader and agent of Chicana/o resistance, since he alone translates seemingly unreadable spaces into acts of defiance in order to refuse a transparent entry into a social order that would eventually sediment him into a piece of brick as well. Likewise, Morales wants to envision his nar-rative built on these violent aberrations and fantastic spaces to undermine a scripted ideological relation that retains Chicana/o space, barrio-space, in the service of capitalist progress.[24] Consequently, Morales directs us to look at those energies outside, that have been cordoned off by the bound-aries of the barrio, the peripheral areas whose violence displaces the com-munity as it has been set up, but also displaces the structures of domination that attempt to maintain such borders in the service of exploited labor.

But even as this novel proffers a figure who relies on a different narra-tive than one that relies on an ethos of work, a character who manages to engage in alternative reading strategies, Morales's narrative does not construct a community built on these differences, but envisions the progress of the barrio within a logical extension of capitalist development. As the abject energy of difference—embodied in Arturo—is assimilated back into the barrio, in the wake of the Simonses' fires that destroy many of the homes in the barrio, the narrative shifts into a subjective account of a personal history, told by Octavio. With a now comprehensible Arturo at his side, Octavio recounts his family's history of immigration and struggle as he thinks of a future home for himself and his family. Illiteracy and dyslexia give way to a reconstruction of the community whose morphology is based on an idyllic family, in which father and son no longer fight, but whose cooperation can forge a new home and community: "Arturo untied the bundle of wood and separated it by lengths. He stood proudly before his father, silently telling him that the wood was ready for cutting and that they should begin building their new home" (318). There seems to be very little, if any, irony here. The pride of father and son working together—the utopian fantasy of a patriarchal community—leaves out the larger analysis that Arturo's dyslexia would have caught, that such seeming self-sufficiency is a limited response to the massive displacement of the Simons workers from their previous homes. Mirroring the driving out of the Chinese earlier in the novel, the destruction of Octavio's home exemplifies the contraction of social space afforded to this emerging and struggling Chicana/o community, a collapse of barrio-space in the name of (white) redevelopment and renewal.[25] Strangely, Arturo does not read his pride as a retreat into an economic logic that bears no guarantees of this new home's permanence or resistance from further white encroachment; nor does either father or son recognize that such logic reinforces social relations through property relationships, a contractual system to which they have been manacled as racialized workers in the barrio.[26]

This final gesture is not just, as Mario García writes, "a more individualistic and conservative model of social change founded on each worker's dream of achieving private home ownership" (197). It is, moreover, the final consequence of staging community, barrio-space, as a place in which people cannot recognize their own conditions of material deprivation and their relation to the violence that opens up and momentarily ruptures the smooth layering of ideological meaning production. Bulosan's blindness toward women and feminized landscape in *America Is in the Heart* leads to an imagination of an America that has yet to come; he is offered no home for his labor, and so looks for it, and works for it, in a socialist fraternity. *The Brick People* offers characters who build actual homes, but in the process lose sight of the boundaries—those enacted by white violence and those absorbed by adopted dreams of consumerism—that they cannot but live within. For if Arturo's dyslexic capacities, Simons's last best hope, become assimilated and diffused through his return to conventional social practices of labor and family, property and patriarchy, the barrio and its inhabitants remain subject to—not dialectically opposed to—the spatial nature of white supremacy and its attendant, exploitative political economy in which men like Arturo and Octavio exercise their limited power within the sanctioned spaces of the fantasy of home.[27]

Why, after encountering narrative strategies that illuminate the racial and economic underpinnings of the barrio, *The Brick People* prevents the larger narrative's trajectory from imagining a social ethos different from that undertaken by Morales's characters remains a crucial question, not unrelated to the reasons for why it is so important for us to read this novel as a "work of fiction." The novel's connection to history, and more specifically to a particular brand of Chicano historiography, is more than coincidental; the nexus of these two disciplines exposes an explosive reconsideration of what constitutes political agency in contemporary Chicana/o social struggle. In the shadows of the waning light of what is considered the "Chicano movement" of the 1970s, whose ideological allegiance to popular mass protest and collective struggle corresponds to movement historiographies of this era, *The Brick People* rewrites this subject with a "post-movement" lens, as Gutiérrez-Jones observes (101–2). Embedded in this contest between fictional and historiographic representation of Chicana/o labor history is the implied vision of Chicana/o political struggle in this recent period of cultural reaction to mass social movements.

To illustrate this discursive battle cloaked in disciplinary garb, let us turn to the figure of Caroline Decker, a union organizer in the novel and an actual historical communist activist working in Chicana/o communities in California before World War II. Not only does Caroline's presence in the novel once again seriously qualify Morales's claim of "coincidental" relationships to actual people, her depiction microscopes the divergent perspectives that *The Brick People* assumes Caroline is meant to represent. Morales borrows almost verbatim the characterization of Caroline Decker from Rudolfo Acuña's second edition of *Occupied America,* a veritable "classic" of Chicano historiography. Acuña quotes Decker as she speaks about her role as a communist organizer in a predominantly Mexican union:

> Actually, most of the young people in the CAWIU [Cannery and Agri-cultural Workers Industrial Union] were starry-eyed, dedicated idealists with a mission to save the agricultural workers. They were poorly paid and overworked. If someone had asked them if they were Communist,

they would have replied "Yes." They were ideological communists. Communism was the thing to believe in if one were a radical with a social conscience. (219)

And here is *The Brick People*'s rewriting of Decker as Caroline:

"We are a group of people dedicated to our mission to save the exploited workers of this country. We are poorly paid and overworked. If someone were to ask me if we had Communist affiliations, I would have to say yes, we do. We are ideological communists, progressive Americans with a social conscience who believe that with the organization of workers we can achieve equality." . . . Caroline considered her beautiful, powerful words. She scratched her nose. (207)

The historical Caroline Decker would be arrested and jailed in 1934 on charges of "criminal syndicalism," and the union would be demolished by the Sacramento police; fictionally transported to Los Angeles, Morales's Caroline, along with her fellow organizers, simply and self-righteously walks away from the Simons workers after the union botches the strike effort. Despite their ideological rigidities, the leaders of the CAWIU are praised by Acuña, for the "communists must be commended for doing something about conditions" (228); in contrast, Caroline in *The Brick People* speaks of her communist affiliations with arrogance, her nose-picking signaling the novel's sarcastic disdain for the union leader.

The transformation of Decker into Caroline, and the rewriting of historical representation of Chicana/o labor into the subject of fictional imagination, tells us something about social horizons.[28] The movement from Acuña's Decker to Morales's Caroline reflects a shift in contemporary Chicana/o thought of the capacity of political agency to contest racialized social structures: Gutiérrez-Jones rightly concludes that Morales's novel asks implicitly, "What typifies a utopian process?" (102). For movement historians, the answer was clear: the struggle of Chicana/os in "occupied America" constituted a larger unfolding of a dialectic of social liberation: the promise of Aztlán. For Morales, the historical process is not so eschatological, as the 1980s unfurled a series of political setbacks that canceled the gains posted by Chicana/os and other groups of color in the 1970s.[29]

Gutiérrez-Jones points out that *The Brick People* should be read in the context of "conservative political pressures," not the least of which are the recent anti-immigrant measures designed to contain the potential political power of Latino immigrants (87). The passage of sundry ballot initiatives in California only touches the tip of this racial backlash: Proposition 187 (the denial of public services to undocumented immigrants), Proposition

209 (the anti-affirmative action initiative gaining steam across the nation), and Proposition 227 (the dismantling of bilingual education). These three ballot initiatives, an unholy trinity of sorts that were barely transparent for their anti-Chicana/o and Latina/o coding and explicit anti-immigrant energy, all passed overwhelmingly, even in the wake of mass protests against them.[30]

But the passage of the ballot measures tail-ended a much larger contestation emerging between Chicana/o and Latina/o communities and between those communities and the larger U.S. social formation. By the early 1980s, scholars working within decade-old Chicano studies programs in various colleges and universities began to voice concern over disturbing trends that threatened the foundations, both ideological and institutional, of what student activists and scholars had fought for at the height of the protest period of the movement. Chicano studies, like other ethnic studies programs, bore the brunt of the universities' fiscal austerity projects; added to these political and economic problems was a growing conservatism, which looked upon Chicano studies as a marginal field that deserved intellectual ghettoization or even disestablishment. As Luis Ramón Burrola and José A. Rivera observe in their 1983 study of Chicano studies programs, Chicano studies and its scholars faced "an increased emphasis on academic quality and program expansion into research and other missions," at the expense of community outreach and organizing (13). Even more significantly, unlike the activism that birthed these programs, Chicano studies would not enjoy broadened support as a result of "renewed militancy on college campuses" (13). Burrola and Rivera's assessment of the state of Chicano studies in the 1980s makes evident the idea that Chicano studies, in any form, could only survive and flourish from efforts toward greater professionalization and administration from "above," rather than support and advocacy from those on the ground, namely from students and those in Chicana/o communities.

By 1996, when a book-length study on the "crossroads" situation of Chicana/os emerged, the condition of not only Chicano studies but also the larger communities these programs were purported to represent appeared even more dire. As David Maciel and Isidoro Ortiz maintain, the advances of Chicana/o communities during the 1980s remained, at best, uneven: "The advent of a Republican presidential administration in 1980 signified a retreat and the initiation of a dismantling by the federal government of many of the triumphs of the Chicano Movement and other progressive movements. . . . [These] came under constant attack during the 1980s." As a result, Ortiz asserts, the leading Chicana/o advocacy groups, many of which had lost up to 20 percent of their staff as a result of state defunding, realigned themselves to garner corporate sponsorship and to focus their energies on self-starting business enterprises and the creation of viable and distinctive "Hispanic" markets (Maciel and Ortiz, 110–23). At the same time, rates of poverty within Chicana/o communities soared during the 1980s, with one in four Chicana/o families deemed poor and one in three Latino children living in poverty, according to the 1990 U.S. Census (cited in Maciel and Ortiz, 15). Faced with the necessity of greater professional and corporate demands and the possibility of institutional obsolescence, Chicana/os attuned to these deep, social contradictions in the 1980s struggled to make relevant these realities. But these self-inventories of Chicana/o studies and its scholars demonstrate the extent to which the ability to expose systemic problems within communities could not generate a concomitant capacity to imagine alternative political and economic models.

The 1980s are also the decade in which the term "Hispanic" was coined, an administrative racial classification celebrated and officiated by the Reagan administration, which superseded and diluted the politically constituted term "Chicano." The shift in terminology is partially a result of the increasing number of non-Mexican Latina/os immigrating to the United States, many of whom (at least in Southern California) hail from Central America and find new homes in the congested areas of Koreatown, "South Central," and downtown Los Angeles. Brought together under the rubric of "Hispanic," Latina/os compose the largest group in Los Angeles's plurality, and are at least one-third of the population in the states in the U.S. Southwest, and in Texas, Florida, and New York. More important, however, as Carlos Muñoz suggests, the shift to "Hispanic" signals a generational change, in which younger activists, while perhaps appropriating the rhetoric and symbolism of the *movimiento* period, invest their actual political energy in more "legitimate" forms of activity, such as electoral politics or small business ventures, always driven by demography.[31]

Indeed, part of the political project that inheres in the shift to "Hispanic" mirrors the ways in which *The Brick People* treats the workers in its narrative. Rather than being seen as a group agitating and disrupting the fundamental social relations in the United States, Latina/os in the United States are regarded, both by the state and by private industry, as a "market" to which products and services are disbursed. The Adolph Coors Company, among others, labeled the 1980s as the "Decade of the Hispanic," a claim that encouraged business and governmental interests to coordinate their efforts to tap into a growing number of Latina/o potential consumers. As Nicolas Kanellos observes about the effects of the demographic explosion of Latina/os on U.S. culture, "It was really during the 1980s with the growing awareness in the media and business communities of burgeoning Hispanic populations, school enrollments, market potential, and voting power that finally a demand or 'market' was identified for a literary culture that had always existed" (3). Celebrating the "unique position" that "Hispanics" enjoy in the Western hemisphere, Kanellos considers Latina/os as the prime mediators of a new multicultural world, and Latina/o writers as the agents to facilitate this pluralism, brought about (of all things) by new economies emerging as a result of the 1993 North American Free Trade Agreement (NAFTA).[32]

But if "Hispanic culture" is indeed part of an ascendant hemispheric hegemony whose cultural base is no longer monolithic or monocultural in the United States, what remains are the material underpinnings that reproduce the same market conditions that relegate many of these celebrated "Hispanics" to labor-constituted, super-exploited barrios.[33] Multiculturalism in the 1980s has assisted in bringing "Hispanics" into symbolic, even cultural legibility. But the Chicana/o struggle to bring into light a different kind of relation, one attentive to those whose material poverty cannot be altered by symbolic legibility, warns that in reading for resistance or into ownership, other spaces and people must be written out, cast into urban triage's darkness. Arturo's bundle of wood at the end of Morales's novel may be a sign of "Hispanic" progress—the capacity to build for oneself. In light of this kind of progress, *The Brick People*'s reconstruction of a narrative of Chicana/o revenge—from Doña Eulalia's violent ruptures of magical and natural brown insects, to the barrio's self-identification during the Hickman affair, to the dyslexia of Chicana/o youth that jars parental injunctions to work—moves toward this kind of triumphant end: to build a Chicana/o house of one's own out of the wood carried by Arturo and used by Octavio. But nowhere in the novel or in current discussions of the shift to "Hispanic" does anyone ask from where the wood was bought, under what working conditions the wood was chopped, to whom the money for that wood might go, and which communities this wood might displace or leave behind. That story of horizontal relationships, of labor's refusal to read itself in synchronicity with the movement of capital and white supremacy, is foreclosed, and indeed must be so.

The novel's magical revisitation compels us to reconsider with suspicion the ideological (and idealist) underpinnings of movement historiography. But such spectacular fictional accounts of Chicana/o workers also present a literary and political horizon of interest in, and not liberation from, a calculable political economy whose logic, even if exposed by an alternative magical reality, compels us to remain within the ever-shrinking spaces of property, patriarchy, and power. It does not imagine home with a difference, or imagine what is possible politically beyond the home, perhaps with the historical dead of different origins. Fictionalizing workers, in this case, retains a primary bifurcation in which theorized resistance remains a privileged site of an *idea* of oppositional politics within a community, but in which the *practice* of those politics reaffirms a larger ideological imperative to build it on the same grounds momentarily broken open. Fictionalizing workers, even in celebrating them, also means limiting them within the vision of a narrative whose own boundaries are circumscribed by the political enclosures of the contemporary Chicana/o situation. Whether such scribal, magical "resistance" is sufficient to replace the historical popular resistance registered but not embraced in this narrative remains to be seen as Morales's novel tells us why we—workers and readers, all—should learn how to read and revolt, but can't.

3

Appropriations of Blackness

| Does literature have any impact on what goes on day
to day?
| —Hisaye Yamamoto

"We had finally made it to Simons," the penultimate paragraph to *The Brick People* reads, a passage doubled in meaning to reflect the Revueltas family's immigration to Southern California from Mexico and the moment in which they, particularly the father and son, could claim Simons as their home (318). It is a passage that reflects the novel's own horizon of reception, from *mexicano* to Chicana/o to American. Unspoken here is the fact that Arturo and Octavio and the rest of the family have "made it" into a barrio whose delineated boundaries continue to constitute them as exploited, racialized workers in the political economy of post–World War II Los Angeles. Morales's final image of the novel, of the patriarchal promise of safety in property, does not displace the irony of the conditions under which their new home is built—still in segregated space, still locked within social relations girded by racial terror (the arson that burnt their previous home), still necessarily proximal to the industries in which they must labor. Even in the building of their new home, Octavio's individual, masculinist will is determined by the social axes of race, space, and economics that mandate his family to build *there,* and not elsewhere.

Historically, as Chicana/os set definitive root in the barrios of Southern California in the aftermath of World War II, another group of people remigrated to Los Angeles, quietly rebuilding homes and livelihoods uprooted by the war. Among the thousands of Japanese Americans returning to the

West Coast after years of incarceration in makeshift prison camps in the "heartland" of the United States, a young Hisaye Yamamoto came with them and soon found herself walking along the familiar streets of First and San Pedro, the heart of Los Angeles's Japanese American community, Little Tokyo. A budding writer, Yamamoto quickly accepted a job as a reporter for the *Los Angeles Tribune,* a local weekly that catered to a Black community that had grown exponentially as a result of wartime employment in naval shipyards and other war industries. Within three years, however, she quit this post and moved to New York to write for *The Catholic Worker,* an experience that honed the pacifism for which she is well known today. All the while, Yamamoto slid stories into literary journals, building with slow deliberation a writing career of distinction. By the time she returned to Los Angeles with her husband in the late 1950s, many of the stories for which she is most celebrated—"Seventeen Syllables," "The Legend of Miss Sasagawara," "Yoneko's Earthquake," "Wilshire Bus," "Epithalamium"— were already in print in places like *Kenyon* and *Partisan Review.* While the volume of her writing decreased over the next few decades, Yamamoto has continued to produce, mostly in local newspapers and magazines in Los Angeles. With the rise of interest in Asian American literature during the 1980s, she has enjoyed canonical status and critical acclaim as a crucial figure in the multicultural reconstruction of U.S. literature.

Why did Yamamoto, after returning to Los Angeles from internment, leave so quickly thereafter, only to return a decade later? Admittedly, Los Angeles immediately following the end of World War II remained a difficult place to live for Japanese Americans, although in substantially different ways from their experiences of prewar racial hostility. But like Chicana/os and Blacks, Japanese Americans and other Asian Americans suffered from the exclusionary practices of residential segregation, patterned in law not only through the pernicious Alien Land Laws of 1913 and 1920, but also in the creation of restrictive housing covenants that prevented the resettlers and immigrants from moving into white enclaves, at least for the moment. Asian Americans, with African Americans, Chicana/os, and other groups of color, lived historically in material enclosures installed by the productive imagination of racial fault lines, which for much of the country's history have relegated each of these groups to conditions that always grant whites social privileges. But in Southern California, each group's experience with their particular racialization translated and affected other groups: in contrast to the histories of segregation in other U.S. cities, Los Angeles's is marked by a conscious set of exclusionary practices against Asian Americans that extended to bar other groups of color as well.[1] Japanese Americans found themselves in 1946 living and working alongside another group ostracized by the structures of racial exclusion; during World War II, as Japanese Americans were cordoned in desert prisons, African Americans filled up the vacuum of Los Angeles's Little Tokyo community and renamed the area Bronzeville. The simultaneity of two distinct spatial identities within the same district tells us something about the restrictions that people of color suffered during this era, a withering of public space that demanded such close quarters in a city beginning its massive urban (and suburban) sprawl. But, as longtime Los Angeles resident and writer Karen Tei Yamashita recounted of her life in the 1950s, the existence of Little Tokyo and Bronzeville in downtown Los Angeles provided apt examples of the visual, symbolic histories that compelled these two groups of color to live so close to one another.[2]

Chester Himes's *If He Hollers Let Him Go* (1945), a novel set in World War II–era Los Angeles, briefly touches on the symbolic proximity between Blacks and Asian Americans that the war facilitated. The protagonist Robert Jones works at a naval shipyard and endures the bitter, everyday confrontations with white racism. Each encounter with white people (both individual and collective) diminishes his sense of manhood, to the point that race invades his dreams, to the point that the simple act of walking down the street becomes a racial act. "But to me it was racial," Robert thinks, as he drives his car to the San Pedro naval shipyard encountering small moments of racial hatred from white drivers and pedestrians, which lead him to exclaim at the end of this infamous freeway chapter: "The white folks sure brought their white to work with them that morning." This section early in the novel highlights the deep irony and contradiction in the use of Black labor in wartime Los Angeles: building these ships of destruction in the service of American "democracy," Black workers endured the racial humiliation that denied them the capacity to claim full citizenship. In the course of the novel, Himes extends this critique: whiteness does not trump citizenship, whiteness *is* citizenship. In the midst of this tableau of white supremacy, Robert meditates very briefly, in fact only two times, on the internment of Japanese Americans. In the first chapter, he notes that a child in the neighborhood, little Ricky Oyama, sang "God Bless America" [!] as he and his parents were shipped to the Santa Anita Relocation Center in Arcadia and then off to camp. Robert muses, "It was taking a man up by the roots and locking him up without a chance. Without a trial. Without a charge. Without even giving him a chance to say one word" (3). Later, Robert signals his identification with little Ricky and other Japanese Americans: "I was the same color as the Japanese and I couldn't tell the difference. 'A yeller-bellied Jap' coulda meant me too" (4). Himes mirrors the wartime incarceration of Japanese Americans at the beginning of the novel with Robert's eventual induction into the Army at the end, a kind of imprisonment or punishment for his alleged rape of Madge, a white racist worker at the Atlas Shipyards. In both cases, neither Japanese Americans nor African Americans are given a trial: a decision is made for them, in their "best interests." That both internment and induction are expressed in *If He Hollers* as modes of imprisonment, framing the entire story, suggests what to Himes is the way in which people of color enter into their proper roles as citizens: to be cordoned off and left out. In other words, to be a proper racialized citizen, you must forgo all rights as a citizen and enter a kind of social death.

The second time that Asian Americans are referenced takes place after the lesbian encounter between Stella and Alice, Robert's on-and-off-again girlfriend. The next day, Robert takes a drive downtown: "I turned over to San Pedro and headed downtown toward Little Tokyo, where the spooks and spills had come in and taken over" (72). Of course, by this time there are no Japanese Americans living in Little Tokyo; it has become Bronzeville, as Blacks filled the residential and commercial vacuum left by the internment. The narrative's use of the term "Little Tokyo" rather than Bronzeville is deliberate. It is a reminder of the ghost of Asian American presence in the midst of real Japanese American absence. Asianless places, in Himes's formulation, become an index of both the impossible citizenship standards of white supremacy and the tenuousness of Black mobility within that space, even if, as Robert puts it, "spooks and spills" had "taken over" the area. Asianless places, such as Little Tokyo, remind Himes's audience that Blacks and Asians are connected only insofar as both groups are subject to the legal, political, economic, and cultural embargoes placed on them by a wartime political economy reconfiguring urban space to fit its needs. There is nothing more in Himes's novel that connects Robert Jones or the other Black characters with disembodied Asians, the absent presence in the novel. But in Himes's formulation, in 1945 that connection was enough.

Yet the deeply symbolic and ideological, and occasionally material, connections between Asian Americans and African Americans must be understood as moments of similarity in a larger process that racializes these two groups differently. Thus, even as Asians and Blacks share experiences that make them historically *not* white, the specific trajectories of these histories—even when they live alongside one another in the same neighborhoods—are, as Grace Hong puts it, "uneven and discrepant."[3] By the 1970s and especially in the 1980s, these differences would become much more apparent. The social histories of Asian Americans and African Americans in this later period, fraught with contestation as a result of shifting economic and political exigencies, would disturb the claim to solidarity between the two groups and threaten the symbolic coalition forged between the spatially contiguous communities of Bronzeville and Little Tokyo. By the 1980s, Bronzeville as a community identity was long gone, and Little Tokyo had changed dramatically from a place where formerly displaced Japanese Americans resettled (and lived) to a site in which people shopped and tourists converged, and from which (some) Asians and Asian Americans garnered much wealth. If Bronzeville evaporated quickly after World War II and returned to its older moniker, Little Tokyo, this space would mean something altogether different by the 1980s, which were marked by material transformations that portended even greater shifts in political and cultural identity for its dwindling inhabitants.

Symbolic connections have at their heart ideological underpinnings, as Himes deftly demonstrated in 1945. But it would take forty years for Yamamoto to make her statement on these relations, to answer why she left Los Angeles so soon after she arrived, to live through the fictional redaction of this period in her memoir, "A Fire in Fontana" (1985). As I concluded in chapter 2, *The Brick People* sought to align the history of Chicana/o labor in Los Angeles with the social realities of the 1980s and thereby provide its readers with a portrait of Chicana/o Los Angeles evacuated of its more radical possibilities. So, too, does "A Fire in Fontana" serve as an instance of intervention negotiating both the connections and contestations of a period of Asian American social existence in which race, space, and economics in Los Angeles portended new relations and therefore new identities between Asian Americans and their neighbors, particularly their neighbors of color. Unlike Morales, Yamamoto reaches back to a history of crossracial interaction—namely the period shortly following World War II up to the catalytic Watts rebellion of 1965—not to diffuse but to deploy as a way of understanding how Asian Americans and African Americans coalesce in struggle, and suffer in their failure to come together. But Yamamoto's story is more than merely reflective of this period; her story serves as a prophetic instrument to warn her predominantly Asian American readers of the consequences arising from a forgetfulness of this interracial history. In the wake of the oft-cited, but even more often misrepresented, events in Los Angeles in 1992, in which apparent tensions between Asians and Blacks were foregrounded, Yamamoto's thematic concern seems prescient.

So this chapter sets out on an exploration in the spirit of this desperately hoped for imagined community, once called Third World solidarity, which is all the more crucial as this new century lays out a new set of terms that enhance, rather than diminish, racial misery for many, and offer a jittery multicultural privilege to a few. It is this anxiety over such conflict and the hope of racial solidarity among groups of color that motivate this reading of "Fire," a story that narrates Yamamoto's own concerns about this issue. Set in post–World War II Los Angeles, "Fire" recounts her transformation in racial identity through her experience of racial exclusion and violence against African Americans when she worked as a reporter at the Black-based *Los Angeles Tribune* just before her brief respite from Los Angeles's racial crucible. The symbolic gesture made in this narrative, of an Asian American becoming "black," serves as the primary sign around which all the events she tells circulate. More specifically, "Fire" attempts to correlate the material deprivation exacted on the Black bodies of African Americans and Yamamoto's ensuing outrage at such racism, an anger that spurs her transformation. As such, the narrative presents Asian American identity formed through the suffering of Black bodies set against the spatial arrangements of Los Angeles's post–World War II urban political economy. Racial ideologies, in other words, are evinced through her visualizing of Black bodies, whose exposure of these ideologies serves as an emblem for an Asian American racial formation.

But in heightening the image of Black bodies into an abstraction to signify a transformation in identity, the narrative undercuts the efficacy of this political realignment in the very image that inaugurates her change—the Black body. That is, what is posed as a means for making connections also serves to distance Asian Americans from African Americans. The story stages scenes in which attention to the Black body, her or his condition of deprivation and racial violation, is deflected for an image of Blackness. Black bodies constitute the form that serves to imbue the Asian American with racial consciousness, but the content of these bodies—what they have to say about their racial experiences—is effectively evacuated. Thus, in writing this highly personal memoir to recuperate a history of racism, Yamamoto exposes an ambiguous, highly contestable relation between rhetoric and materiality, and threatens to disrupt the connections she continually tries to assert and affirm. Asian American political consciousness is both engendered and bound by its attempt to delineate the meaning of Blackness through Black bodies, a strategy that provokes the insurgent space offered to collapse under its analogical rhetoric.

In no way does this interrogation of Yamamoto's strategy of equating a certain idea of Blackness with an Asian American political identity attempt to diminish the problem or the urgency of a racial consciousness that promotes solidarity among people of color. Nor does this analysis argue for a narrowly defined nationalist politics in which different groups of color attempt to forge for themselves, and solely for their own "group," terms and images exclusive to their respective "groups." Rather, by asking how and why Blackness is displayed as a preeminent model for racial identity, we can further see to what extent such a strategy used on the part of Asian Americans has been productive politically, and brings into focus the ways in which this strategy is circumscribed by historically contingent structures of contemporary urban triage. Moreover, what is suggested here as a limit does not mean that an Asian American racial identity, infused with radical possibilities, is arrested at the moment when appropriations of Blackness are open to question. Indeed just as the nature of racial domination changes according to profound shifts in the U.S. political economy and social formation, so too do writers and activists struggle to confront changing space and time with radical and practical ways of fighting institutions of domination and violence. For Asian American as well as for African American cultural workers, this has meant that political action must be performed within spaces scripted by material conditions. In Yamamoto's case, her story works to model a kind of cultural transcription, from her experiences working with African Americans distilled into metaphor from which her Asian American readers might deploy themselves *for* themselves (and their racial identities) and for the service of coalition work. And as we shall see, it is the urgency of the latter—of struggling to create horizontal, communal relations between the two racial groups during the 1980s—that prompts Yamamoto to create the aesthetic of the former, of discovering Asian American identity through Blackness. But like Morales's revisitation of Chicana/o labor history, Yamamoto's imaginative telling is determined by, even if not merely and mimetically reflective of, the concrete dynamics taking place during the 1980s. As efficacious as a rhetoric of unity between Black and Asian subjects may be, activism—whether in the streets or in writing—cannot take place apart from the places and times in which real people's bodies and lives are affected by the collision of material and symbolic economies.

Published first in 1985 in the Los Angeles-based *Rafu Shimpo*, a Japanese American daily, "Fire," unlike Yamamoto's previous works, does not submerge racial issues but rather attempts to address them in a more explicit manner. Yet like her other works, this story is narrated through what King-Kok Cheung calls Yamamoto's "double structure," an external plot corresponding to the story's manifest actions, while latent movements bubble into an internal plot ("Dream in Flames," 128; *Seventeen Syllables and Other Stories,* xvii). Often, external and internal narratives work against each other, producing ironic disjunction and compelling the reader to derive meaning from Yamamoto's stories by the silent fissures opened by this double structure. This narrative strategy, Cheung argues further,

allows Yamamoto to tell stories that on the surface appear as if they document quiet, calm life in Japanese American communities, but all the while
they reveal seething emotions or indict the sear of racism. That she wrote
many of her stories in the 1950s, when voicing social critique might have
brought down on a writer the wrath of McCarthy's pogroms or at least
pushed the artist into societal margins reserved for madmen, renegades,
or subversives, makes Yamamoto's muted approach all the more politically
appropriate while still being aesthetically innovative. For a recently besieged, incarcerated, and vilified community, muted tales—essentialized
into "Nisei reserve"—made sense as Japanese Americans sought to prove
their soundness as loyal citizens, to steer clear of outlandish behavior that
might stoke racial animosity once again, and to act as the nation's model
minorities, never again to be thrown into desert prisons. "Not once,"
Cheung writes, "do the barbs of the author's covert social commentary
puncture the smooth narrative surface. It is by orchestrating telltale details, eroding narrative authority, and encoding volatile political allegory
that the author criticizes the ethnic community and the larger society for
their intolerance of difference and for their mechanisms of exclusion"
(*Articulate Silences,* 72).

For example, Rosie, the protagonist of "Seventeen Syllables" (1949),
struggles with an incipient and buoyant teenage sexuality, but this external
drama conceals and then explodes into its latent story, that of the mother's
silent but deep artistic, almost sexual drive in her haiku, which in turn is
smashed, both figuratively and literally, by Rosie's father. In moving into
adult sexuality, Yamamoto suggests, Rosie encounters the patriarchal
"no" of sexual and gender regulation within the community, shared by,
but never uttered between, daughter and mother. Likewise, in "Wilshire
Bus" (1950), the narrator, Esther Kuroiwa, travels along the busy Los
Angeles street in a bus and encounters a racist white man taunting an elderly Chinese American couple, who are consoled by other, sympathetic
white passengers. But barely submerged is the shame of racial recognition
through ethnic denial: Esther, a Japanese American, breathes a sigh of relief that the man attacks a Chinese couple, but realizes that she engages in
the same kind of abjection that Chinese and Korean Americans asserted
during the war as she and other Japanese Americans were interned. By the
story's end, her silence is complicitous with the white man's epithets, her
ethnic disavowal an emblem of Asian American internalized racism, all
while the bus lumbers down Wilshire Boulevard and lets on and off passengers that correlate to Los Angeles's segregated neighborhoods.

In "Fire," double emplotment assumes a similar chiasmic structure,
hinged around the emblem of Blackness, or more specifically the image of

being "burnt black." To summarize: Hisaye, just returned from the internment camp in Poston, Arizona, is hired as a staff writer for the *Los Angeles Tribune*, ostensibly to smooth relations between Bronzeville's Black residents and the Japanese Americans returning to Little Tokyo, and maybe even to generate some advertisements and a readership from the Japanese American community. Pulling together stories from other Black periodicals across the United States, Hisaye puts into brief news capsules stories of weekly lynchings, but her encounters with racism against African Americans is sharpened by daily conversations among her coworkers about racial violence and hostility. One day, a certain O'Day Short asks Hisaye to feature a story about threats he is receiving for moving into the lily-white city of Fontana, about sixty miles east of downtown Los Angeles. She does so without urgency, and shortly thereafter Short and his family are killed when a fire, presumably arson, consumes their home. It is after this incident that Hisaye leaves Los Angeles and travels around the country, up and down the eastern seaboard. The story ends with her return in the 1960s to Alhambra, a Los Angeles suburb adjacent to San Gabriel, newly married to a white man, as she takes on the role of a proper housewife, and watches coverage of the 1965 Watts rebellion on television. This external story line of spatial mobility out of Little Tokyo and into a white suburban tract is juxtaposed with her internal transformation, in which she slowly moves into alignment with the travails of African Americans. As she travels around the country, Hisaye recounts various episodes of individuals expressing deep hostility against Black neighbors; even her relatives express racial prejudice. But the crucial instance of transformation, that which sets her on this racial journey inward, is her guilt over her reticent response to O'Day Short: Hisaye feels the pang of guilt and responsibility over his and his family's deaths. For this and other injustices exacted but not rectified, Hisaye silently revels in the destruction she sees on television in 1965, a small retributive morsel to assuage the protracted horror of violence and discrimination inflicted against Blacks, crystallized in Short's racial hagiography.

The year 1985, when Yamamoto revisited this painful history in *Rafu Shimpo*, was the apex of Reagan's revolution, buoyed by his sound reelection the year earlier. Reagan's first four years in office appeared nicely attuned to the global rightward drift that utterly shattered earlier dreams of an expanded democratic process; the "excess of democracy" at home and abroad was fully reined in. Engineered recessionary policies in the early 1980s, tied to a tightening of U.S. monetary policy, sped up industrial dismantling of U.S. Rust Belt cities, while in Third World countries, particularly those in the south, high interest rates, deregulation, and restrictive monetary policy spelled disaster for their struggling economies. Fully abandoning the Rooseveltian vision of a global New Deal oiled by anticommunist rhetoric and enforced by U.S. military presence around the world, the United States allowed high finance to take control of international policy, triggering a crisis in the hemispheric south that enabled the nations of the north to consolidate a newfound, uneven hegemony. Britain's forays into the Falkland Islands in 1982, in the same year that Reagan sent U.S. marines into Grenada, exemplified all too well the extent to which states exercised their capacity of force to paralyze Third World attempts at stalling this global "Great U-turn." "As if by magic, the wheel had turned," says Giovanni Arrighi of this signal change in international relations. "From then on, it would no longer be First World bankers begging Third World states to borrow their overabundant capital; it would be Third World states begging First World governments and bankers to grant them the credit needed to stay afloat in an increasingly integrated, competitive, and shrinking world market" (323). The unidirectional realignment of economic and military force, unencumbered even by issues of legality—as the triangle of drugs, arms, and money of Iran-Contra would expose a few years later—jarred people out of rickety homes south of the U.S. border and on paths northward. The wave of poorer immigrants into the United States, mostly from the hemispheric south, which compelled lawmakers to pass the 1986 Immigration Reform and Control Act and sent California's electorate into fits of panic seven years later, can be partially explained by this larger global dynamic of financial mobility and military incursion creating mass movement: "they" moved here, because "we" were there first.

Meanwhile, arrogant displays of U.S. cultural superiority during the 1984 Summer Olympics in Los Angeles barely hid the political and economic orphaning of the U.S. people by their institutions, and in particular a calculated triage of chocolate cities. By 1983, the share of income taxes paid by corporations slid to an all-time low of 6.2 percent, having been already slashed to 12.5 just three years earlier (Pollack, 293). Tax regression and capital flight caused municipal and state officials to take belt-tightening measures that hit first those who had benefited from Keynesianism last. And people who continued to rage against this machine were given an extraordinary government gift of satchel bombs: in Philadelphia, the city we will examine in chapter 4, John Africa and ten other members of his MOVE organization were incinerated, along with an entire city block of West Philadelphia. Alongside state repression and corporate reconsolidation, the death of the Great Society facilitated a climate for a resurgence of racial violence to overtake the national scene. This violence cast ironic light on Reagan's "color-blind" vision of U.S. society, as its ideology was contradicted by events in which racial antagonism was all the more pronounced. This overt racism manifested itself in contemporary lynchings of African Americans in what Manning Marable has called the "Red Year of 1980"; the proliferation of racial epithets and "White Student Unions" on college campuses exposed the underlying tension of whites toward students of color, in an era where Black and Latino admissions were *declining*; for Asian Americans, the wave of anti-Asian sentiment as a result of the "Japan-bashing" by U.S. automobile companies in the early 1980s culminated in the 1982 Detroit murder of Chinese American engineer Vincent Chin, who became the model figure for what is commonly referred to as "anti-Asian violence."[4] In Los Angeles, this reactionary trend produced a police climate toward its African American and Latino residents through which, under the guise of the "drug epidemic" and its ensuing violence, areas spatially constructed as South Central and East Los Angeles were increasingly surveilled, criminalized, and imprisoned.[5] If Yamamoto wrote her story in the comforts of a period in which audiences readily consumed multicultural works, and indeed emphatically celebrated cultural pluralism, her story also bears witness to a crisis in which these kinds of celebrations were circumscribed by a general decline in the political agency of working poor people of color.[6]

Moreover, this political climate of crisis in which "Fire" was written also became visible in the dialogues between groups of color, particularly those between African American and Asian American communities, and especially in Los Angeles. By the mid-1980s, Japanese American demand for a formal apology and compensation from the U.S. government over the issue of the World War II incarceration of 120,000 Japanese Americans intensified, with groups such as the National Coalition for Redress and Reparations and the Japanese American Citizens' League soliciting aid from Black-based civil rights groups, and eventually resulting in the redress and reparations "victory" in 1988. Yet conversely, at this same time, relations between Black and Asian communities became strained: the most visible of these tensions resulted in the ensuing media representation of the "Black-Korean" conflict in the late 1980s and early 1990s, epitomized in the flow of literature on the issue after the 1992 Los Angeles rebellion.[8] But we can purview its beginning pains in the early 1980s, not in Korean merchant/Black customer conflict, but in the gentrification and eventual eviction of working-class residents of color in downtown Los Angeles through a complicit relation between Japanese American small-businessowners, downtown developers, and an influx of Japanese (and European) capital investment. This cooperative corporate effort reshaped the downtown skyline and geography with its transnational corporate offices, luxury hotels, and entertainment centers for the culture-hungry elite; its consequences were the contraction of space for low-income housing and the rise of homeless Black and Brown families. Little Tokyo, the symbolic if not material residential space for the Japanese American community in Southern California, quickly became a showcase of redevelopment planning to attract out-of-town tourism, especially the transnational elites from Japan.

Urban redevelopment, the plan to "revitalize" city centers, has been seen for decades by city mayors as the panacea to urban woes. But as chapter 4 will elaborate, such "renewal" also devastated Black communities around the nation, and Los Angeles was not an exception. Thus at the same time that *some* Asian Americans enjoyed economic, if not hegemonic, ascendancy during the 1980s as a result of this reconstitution of ethnically identified neighborhoods, other groups found their political and economic options pushed off the map of social attention in the wake of this period of restructuring. As Los Angeles embraced its status as a world city, the U.S. base of a Pacific Rim economic circuit, the surpluses of U.S. capital that moved to Saipan and the Asian capital that moved into Southern California resulted in a surplusing of people: as economic restructuring pushed predominantly, but not exclusively, Black and Brown people into spaces of permanent unemployment or underemployment, California embarked on a wide-scale expansion of prisons as its way to "fix" its surplus crises of capital, state capacity, and labor (Gilmore, "From Military Keynesianism"). As violent crime rates *fell* during the 1980s, *before* prison construction began and new crime legislation was enacted, Los Angeles's urban residents experienced removal that differed from Japanese American internment only by its scale, scope, and constitutionality. The age of urban development in Los Angeles, in which Asian American cultural and political power ascended to heights unimaginable since the late 1960s, depended on a simultaneous age of punishment for thousands of Black and Brown people living in unimaginable suffering. The contradiction and crisis in political affiliation and identity continue today, as Asian American activists struggle to find a vocabulary that would, on the one hand, avoid xenophobic, anti-Asian sentiment, and on the other, stave off the further splitting of political relations between Asian Americans and African Americans.[9]

These contemporary examples of the differential histories between groups of color are cast in "Fire" as a potential space of hope set against moments of significant pause. Highlighting the discrepancies between Asian Americans and African Americans, similar only in the systemic denial of property rights to both groups, Grace Kyungwon Hong convincingly examines

Yamamoto's story as one that cites the two groups' relational connection of grievance and loss by foregrounding their specific differences in their historical disenfranchisement through, respectively, internment and segregation. Hong explains: "Internment and segregation are disparate but related manifestations of the privileging of property rights that structures the liberal democratic state" ("Something," 293). Like Chester Himes's novel forty years earlier, "Fire" reconstructs for Yamamoto's *Rafu* readers an ideological net by which they might be reminded of the close and contiguous relationship that had been cultivated between Japanese Americans and African Americans in Los Angeles's social history. Yet in a more significant gesture, she hopes to convey not only a historical connection between the two communities of color, but to show how the experience of racism by each might give meaning to the struggles of both histories. To this end, she charts a personal journey that is intimately interwoven with both historical narratives. The story opens with this internal plot, a metaphorical kernel that the story unfolds into external difference, but holds together in the heart:

> Something weird happened to me not long after the end of the Second World War. I wouldn't go so far as to say that I, a Japanese American, became Black, because that's a pretty melodramatic statement. But some kind of transformation did take place, the effects of which are with me still.[10]

The dramatic "transformation" that Hisaye notes here is indelibly racial, and furthermore involved in her relation to historical events in modern U.S. history.[11] The "something weird" that produces the strange statement, of a Japanese American becoming Black, is elucidated soon, a few pages into the narrative, but it is important to recognize the extent to which the narrative already tries to guide its readers—Asian American ones—into a contiguous relationship between Blackness and Asian American formations of identity at the outset.

Hong correctly points out that the publication of "Fire" coincided with the "height of the movement for redress and reparations" on the part of Japanese American activists over World War II internment. In this light, the story captures a general spirit during the 1980s in which groups of color looked to the redress and reparations campaign as a way to flashpoint historical racial grievances and expose "the contradictions in demanding equal rights for people of color from a system created to protect white property rights" ("Something," 307). *Rafu*'s editors may well have had this ongoing campaign on their minds when "Fire" was published: the story was featured in a special two-part Christmas edition of the newspaper's occasional magazine. The opening story, written by staffer Takeshi Nakayama, chronicled the struggle of the Heart Mountain draft resisters, infamous "no-no boys" whose movement to expose the contradictions over Japanese American "loyalty" to the U.S. government during internment bitterly divided the community and was only recently acknowledged by the moderate Japanese American Citizens League as a legitimate campaign for Japanese American justice. Besides Nakayama's piece, the December 21 issue also included articles concerning Japanese American sanseis and their "dilemma" of straddling "the majority society" and their Japanese heritage, a fictional account of a Japanese American living on Los Angeles' skid row, and a special report entitled "Golf Boom," which documented Nikkei golfers from the previous forty years. A reader flipping through the magazine would have noticed not only accompanying artwork and photographs with these stories, but the advertisements that took up much of most pages' layout and defrayed the costs of the newspaper's production: Yamamoto's story is wedged against County Supervisor Kenneth Hahn, the Southern California Gardeners' Federation, and Union Federal Savings Bank, among other individuals and businesses, all wishing *Rafu*'s readers "Holiday Greetings!" along with seasonally appropriate drawings of mistletoe and wreaths. For Los Angeles's Japanese and other Asian American subscribers, redress may have been an important story to follow, but Christmas was just around the corner.

These semiotic ironies notwithstanding, the opening lines of "Fire" certainly jarred Yamamoto's readers out of holiday somnambulance, if only for a moment. And as if to cause further cognitive disjunction, Hisaye, Yamamoto's narrator, follows with a brief recounting of Bix Beiderbecke, a white musician who died for his association with "Negroes"; Hisaye then parenthetically inserts the following: "[I]n 1985, how odd the word has become!" (8). We read Hisaye's qualification perhaps to situate her readers in a different era by deploying this racial anachronism, perhaps to undercut the narrator's authority at the very beginning, perhaps even to suggest how far we have come by thinking this term so weird. Playing with all these possible expectations, Hisaye frames her "melodramatic statement" in a kind of temporal triangulation: readers are invited to revisit a bygone era that for Japanese Americans marked a low point in their history, in the relative comfort and progressivism of Christmas 1985, but are distanced from both historical moments in the reading experience. Suspended, if only for a moment, outside both temporalities, the story's readers hold both eras aloft to examine this woman's weird story and diagnose hers with theirs, or vice versa in the midst of holiday cheer.

Early on, Hisaye's weird metaphor of racial transformation coincides with correlative histories of racial injury, Yamamoto's internal and external plots folding together nicely in a scene that takes place during the war. While on a bus that would drop Hisaye off at the Poston internment camp in Arizona, the passengers stop in a town just south of Springfield and Hisaye's seatmate, a white girl, exults over a Black man being barred from drinking water in a restaurant. The girl's glee triggers in Hisaye a remembrance of her own social exclusion, as a Japanese American, during the internment in World War II: "Here I was on a bus going back to the camp in Arizona [the Poston Relocation Center] where my father still lived, and I knew there was a connection between my seatmate's joy and our having been put in that hot and windblown place of barracks" (367). Whether it is a Black man finding himself on the periphery, physically and symbolically barred from institutions deemed "for Whites only," or a Japanese American woman who must return to her home of incarceration in the desert in which she and her father are kept, Hisaye senses "a connection," a contiguous relationship between these spatial and material exclusions, engendering a narrative that suggests a shared relation, even if not an equivalent condition. The material effects of racial exclusion associate these two cases, history recorded in a spatial dynamic.

Readers of this passage would not be hard-pressed to elucidate further these connections of contiguous racial histories. Like Robert's metaphor of imprisonment that characterizes Japanese American internment and the induction of Blacks into the army in Himes's *If He Hollers,* Hisaye's ruminations about wartime racial exclusion suggest that the decision to push Japanese Americans into western deserts follows a similar logic to the one that keeps Blacks out of restaurants and other public facilities. Both examples highlight white investment in maintaining strict boundaries of citizenship by laying out specific, partial grounds of "inclusion" for people of color—containment—and the spaces of abjection afforded them that signal the barest signs of human tolerance, either stooped over in the back or behind barbed-wired fences. It is this legacy of white privilege, based on the protection of white property rights in U.S. law and social practice, that girds the denial of full citizenship rights to Asian Americans and Blacks, albeit manifested differently; this privileged status of "citizen," conversely, is assumed and protected for whites (Hong, "Something," 294–301).[12]

There are, however, important distinctions to be made, even as the narrative attempts to make analogous segregation against African Americans with the internment of Japanese Americans, differences that are implied in this scene by spatial comparisons between the African American and the Japanese American. U.S. social formation, as Lindon Barrett suggests, has been conditioned by post-Enlightenment Western thought, in which social relations are "so often redacted in the terms of the black/white racial dichotomy indispensable to the U.S. cultural imagination" ("African

American," 415). And insofar as this imaginary has been the predominant axis of identity and subjectivity, from the early religious justifications of race to the biologism of scientific racism up to the notion of race as social and political phenomena, "black" and "white" have been figured as the two primary antagonistic terms.[13] Thus, in material relations, African Americans and their oppressors share an intimate relationship, albeit one continually marked by violence, domination, and deprivation. In this sense, crises that emerge out of this relationship become highly visible, feeding into the racial "common sense" of the U.S. populace.[14] The fact that the white girl in the story expresses "glee" over the Black man's exclusion from the restaurant fuels the already sedimented ideological codes through which the girl ascribes and achieves meaning. That is, her history—"I was brought up this way"—is imbued with value and is "justified" through a set of meanings filtered through the black/white dichotomy, a relation that configures the idea of the American body politic.

On the other hand, and because of this intimate binarism of Black/white, Asian Americans have been cast in more complicated ways, no less racial in intention but ambiguous in effect. A brief schematic reading of Asian American social history will suffice in recording the systematic denial of citizenship rights to Asian Americans, beginning with the 1882 Chinese Exclusion Act up to the 1924 Immigration Act, in which race figured crucially in shaping immigration policy. Coterminous with immigration restriction were California's Alien Land Laws, which kept Asian, and in particular, Japanese American farmers from owning land; along with Los Angeles's restrictive housing covenants, which specifically sought to exclude Asian Americans from white enclaves, the impossibility of property ownership demonstrated materially what immigration law taught Asian Americans symbolically. Symbol and material, idea and land, reached a nadir with Roosevelt's 1942 Executive Order 9066, which sanctioned the detainment of "all persons of Japanese ancestry, both alien and non-alien." The conflation of "alien and non-alien" into a homogeneous category, through which the state could seize person and property, underscores the depth to which Asian Americans have been continually regarded as outside discussions of citizenship.[15] Moreover, this casting of Asian Americans as outside U.S. social discourse has inhibited Asians from articulating and delineating political and social identities in terms of legitimate struggle toward enfranchisement. As Sau-ling Cynthia Wong has so cogently put it, "Asian Americans are permanent houseguests in the house of America" (6). Because Asian Americans are regarded as perpetually foreign, scholars attempting to uncover Asian American social history have first had to establish a viable Asian *American* subject: it is no surprise that so many studies feature titles that include the phrase "Asian America," a linguistic rendering that, in a sense, tries to will Asians into the U.S. historical and cultural imagination precisely because they are so often left out. Asian Americans are conveniently displaced into either heightened "otherness," outside the domains of what constitutes an American identity, or pushed into sheer invisibility.

Scholars investigating the process and history of Asian American racial formation have had to access the more demonstrable Black/white paradigm to produce a political agency in order for Asian Americans to enter the racial discourse. Gary Okihiro once posed the question, "Is yellow black or white?" a query predicated on the shuttling of Asian American subjectivity between foreignness, invisibility, and appropriation: "Asians have been marginalized to the periphery of race relations in America because of its conceptualization as a black and white issue—with Asians, Latinos, and American Indians falling between the cracks of that divide. Thus, to many, Asians are either 'just like blacks' or 'almost whites'" (xi).[16] Okihiro and others have opted to look for the historical affiliations between Asian Americans and African Americans, highlighting the similar racial stereotyping and exploitation of labor in the two groups. Thus, they work against a prevailing contemporary dominant discourse of the "model minority" myth to ally Asians as honorable whites, all the while crafting a story of its own for Asian Americans, different from, but akin to, the miseries of Black history.[17]

Yet the conundrum of Asian Americans trying to fit themselves into one racial category or another highlights more than simply the spurious nature of the historical racial project, in light of Asian Americans who implicitly yet constantly remain in the shadow. Something behind the slide into inherent Asian foreignness takes place in "Fire." While the struggle to assert Asian Americans as *Americans,* who therefore have a legitimate stake on U.S. soil to voice racial grievance, works against the cultural logic of racial invisibility, the invisibility that is registered in Yamamoto's story has less to do with Hisaye's outsider status or even her substantive denial of citizenship. In fact, Hisaye's concern over disappearing, which propels her metaphorical claim to Blackness and her insistence on the contiguity of Asian American and Black historical loss, rests on her symbolic and structural alignment with whites. Her external observations of the restaurant scene and her inward transformation are mediated through an earlier snippet of wishful alignment with Johnny Otis, the famous white jazz musician who later settled down to become a minister in Watts. For Hisaye, Otis admirably lives out a jettisoning of his white identity, "from which there was no turning back" (8). This celebratory story is told just after a description of the life of Bix Beiderbecke, whose interactions with Black musicians led to an untimely death. "[Otis's] life, as I see it," Hisaye muses, "represents a triumph," and we can assume that despite Beiderbecke's "tragic end," she regards both musicians' lives with admiration. Both Beiderbecke and Otis have given up their normative status as white men, which in Hisaye's mind forever casts them into Black cultural space; they have given up, in a sense, the exclusionary social privileges assigned to them in order to experience a different kind of joy. Set against the examples of these two men, Hisaye gives herself diminutive Nisei features—"four feet ten, my hair straight, my vision myopic"—her physicality distinctive enough from white for her to reflect on her "connection" between her journey to Poston and the Black man's indignity at the restaurant. But at no point does Hisaye's seatmate make this connection: to the white girl, Hisaye's racial difference is invisible. The girl presumes that Hisaye shares in racial glee. And despite a silent "sign of protest," Hisaye never incurs the girl's racial ridicule, laughter, or wrath. In the very scene in which Black and Japanese American histories come together in the differential but critically connected histories, the crucial external nexus that might give material evidence to her internal movement toward Blackness, Hisaye is rendered so invisible that she might as well be white.

If Beiderbecke and Otis then become visible at the moment they "lose" their whiteness by inhabiting Black space, Hisaye's Asian American invisibility is made possible because of her structural alignment with whiteness. Even if she ascertains this certain connection between her identity as a Japanese American traveling back to an internment camp and the sad predicament of the Black man, Hisaye stays on the bus and observes the man with the white girl seated right next to her. Wartime incarceration forces her into silence—"I didn't dare shove her out the window"—but her quiet reticence born possibly of fear enables the white girl to enjoy company with an Asian American woman who inversely matches her hatred for the Black man standing outside the bus. The wartime era, in which exclusion against Asian Americans seemed to reach its feverish height, the most blatant example of systemic racial profiling, still offers a concurrent narrative of assimilation through racial invisibility. To the extent that her recognition of internment and segregation as reinforcing modes of white supremacy is not only mitigated by, but constitutive of, her structural alignment with whiteness, Hisaye's materiality of racial difference—her phenotypical presence—must be supplemented by a projection of this unacknowledged difference onto another body that does register the animus of difference: injured Black bodies.

Thus the spatial arrangement in the restaurant scene designed to analogize the historical exclusion of the Black man in the story to Hisaye's incarceration works to showcase both less and more of these connections.

Less, because the triangulation between the white girl, the Black man, and herself, a Japanese American woman, places Asian American identity in structural relation to enjoy, even if unpleasantly, the spectacle of Black denigration. But more, insofar as this very arrangement that compels both silence and invisibility in Hisaye prompts her to imagine a racial rhetoric that outstrips her semiotically inert body. Unlike Himes's story, contiguous racial history in "Fire" is not enough; Hisaye's desire to move toward visible racial solidarity, into Blackness, depends on eliding her body into invisible whiteness. We might then reread the passage in which she describes her transformation not as an alembic of solidarity between the disparate Japanese American and Black experiences of racial exploitation. Rather, her internal metamorphosis exacerbates and exposes the distance that she tries to bridge, the "connection" merely a moment of fictive origins:

> [W]hen I realized that something was happening to me, I scrambled to backtrack for awhile. By then it was too late. I continued to look like the Nisei I was, with my height remaining at slightly over four feet ten, my hair straight, my vision myopic. Yet I know that this event transpired inside me: sometimes I see it as *my inward self being burnt black in a certain fire.* (367; emphasis mine)

One should acknowledge the extent to which Hisaye's self-deprecating attitude toward her body can be seen as part of a "Nisei reserve," a mode of deference that is regarded as a virtuous cultural expression of Japanese Americans of her generation.[18] But while this may be the case, Hisaye makes her own body visible as a racialized woman in order to render it diminutive.[19] Foregrounding a nonthreatening, unassuming Asian body, contracting herself into a bodily space that sedates her seeming assertiveness, Hisaye's brief description of her own physical characteristics is overshadowed quickly by the "yet" of the next sentence, which juxtaposes her unthreatening body surface to a transformation within that is dynamic, unsettling, even violent. Although her outward characteristics remain the same—nothing has happened to change her phenotypical lineage—the transformation in her "inward self" produces a split and an antagonism between an Asian corporeality that bleeds invisibly and an invisible transformation that proclaims agency against this idea of Asian American quiescence.

Hisaye's staging of Asian American identity, then, hung between a structural proximity to whiteness and the desire of identification with Blackness, connotes two significant features of how and, more important, why Asian Americans are racialized in the U.S. political economy. First, Asian Americans derive racial identities through a constant mediation, not simply with the structures of white supremacy, even if those structures appear overwhelming and absolute, as in the case of state-sponsored internment. Rather, the mediation is triangular: Black experience emerges as a model through which Asian Americans might articulate another kind of consciousness beside one that poses Asian American identity simply as white negation. Second, that Asian Americans can occupy this racial "third space" makes the work of social choice all the more crucial in lifting Asian Americans out of invisibility within a Black/white binarism. This is not to say that Asian American racial identities are not determined by specific constraints placed upon them—the history of legal, political, and cultural exclusion certainly tells us otherwise—but that determining structures of whiteness and the alternative possibilities of Black response to white supremacy make social action on the part of Asian Americans defining moments in their racial constitution. Asian American response to racialization is itself constitutive of their racialization.

The fictive conjunction between internment and segregation in the restaurant scene elucidates the former feature of this racial process for Asian Americans, even if the certain connection that Hisaye imagines is undermined by the spatial arrangement of the scene. The episode that immediately follows corresponds to the latter issue of choice. If the Black body corresponds to a kind of racial violation that exacts disjunction between inward transformation and outward alignment, what difference does this make for Asian American action? In the very next paragraph, Hisaye steps off the bus at a rest stop to use the restroom and confronts a segregated toilet. Here we see a moment of flux for Hisaye, a place in which her racial identity is put into crisis in a racialized space that she cannot avoid, one that she cannot view from afar, behind glass:

> The toilets were a new experience, too, labeled Colored or White. I dared to try White first, and no one challenged me, so I continued this presumptuous practice at all the way stations of Texas. After I got back on the bus the first time, I was haunted by the long look given me by a cleaning woman in the restroom. I decided, for the sake of my conscience, that the Negro woman had never seen a Japanese before. (368)

Undoubtedly this passage is presented ironically, particularly when read alongside the previous scene. There, Hisaye feels but does not express a connection with the Black man; her understanding of Black segregation and Japanese American internment, however mediated, supplements her inactivity. Here, her act of choosing betrays that connection through a series of misrecognitions. First, in "choosing" the "White" toilet, she elects to elide the ways in which her "presumptuous practice" is itself encoded. Hisaye does not want to realize how she is herself "Colored," which she had just previously identified earlier with the Black man, even though the bus is taking her back to the Poston center. Nor does she admit that it is because of her racial invisibility, and not for any daring feat, that no one prevents her from choosing white over colored toilets. Thus Hisaye's decision, however daring or mundane, does not encompass an act of resistance by insinuating a colored body into white space (à la Rosa Parks) but instead manifests the ease with which an Asian American body, erased from this racial imperative, can opt to act out structural whiteness and thereby settle the crisis that the choice initiates.[20] Her body does not provoke a response from the institutions that keep in place the distinction between "White" and "Colored" toilets. Hisaye's "daring" choice loses its political meaning because her Asian body is rendered invisible, not even significant enough to be considered a racial subject that needs to be divided from whiteness. In this case, choice is calculated insignificance, if not structured impossibility.

In this symbolic exchange of language, bodies, and institutional protocol, Hisaye's body expresses nothing and angers no one, not daring at all but just an act of peeing—except in the encounter with the cleaning woman. Again, Hisaye "chooses" not to recognize the irony of her meeting this woman in the "White" restroom. The irony, of course, is that the cleaning lady's only access into this segregated space arises from her position as a laboring subject who cleans an area that she herself cannot use and whose perspective allows her to gaze upon an Asian woman who can use this restricted space because the Asian is invisible. The gaze of racial exclusion is returned to Hisaye by the Black woman, whose "long look" exposes how meaningless the act of entering this area is for the two women of color. And yet again, this only engenders a further misrecognition and rationalization on the part of Hisaye, who mistakes that gaze for the Black woman's ignorance.

The narrative affords Yamamoto's readers the opportunity to coordinate the correspondence between racially spatialized arrangements and their coterminous yet differential effects on Black and Asian bodies. This ironic passage does indicate a moment, as Hong suggests, in which the Asian American "does not really fit either category, 'White' or 'Colored,' and must, figuratively and literally, choose between them" ("Interethnic," 21–22). But this scene also offers an instance in which racialized space, the segregated restroom, performs its ideological function of exclusion by highlighting the Black (woman's) body disallowed from material access— the "White" toilet—and by erasing Hisaye's body, much in the same way that Hisaye herself displaces her body. Conversely, however, it is the cleaning woman's body that "speaks" with the "long look," a gaze that implies racial recognition and exposes Hisaye's inability or unwillingness to recognize hers. Blackness therefore highlights itself in bodily form against the backdrop of racial space, showcasing the material effects of Black bodies, whose condition is one of inaccessibility to that space. Through this comparison with racial exclusion implicit in the construction of Blackness, Hisaye's racial status comes into view, for she is produced paradoxically by the visual agency of Blackness and the erasure of the Asian body. What we see in this passage is the way in which racial fiction is substantiated. The Black body (of the cleaning woman) and her gaze (at Hisaye) serve to expose the racial structuring of the restroom, a racial overdetermination of Blackness that occurs because the Asian body does not evince enough meaning. The cleaning woman is in an area in which she is not supposed to be, but her inability to access that space is still as real as the Black man's inability to have a drink of water in the restaurant. The conflation between Blackness and the spatial-material effects of segregated institutions on Black bodies must occur for Hisaye, for in that clustering of material conditions and racial abstraction, Black bodies speak to her and make legible the racial dimensions of social space, a visuality that is foreclosed in her own Asian body.

The cleaning woman, significantly, does not say anything: she conveys her "haunting" message to Hisaye through a "long look." Hisaye in fact deplores the discussions that African Americans take on, as she describes what her colleagues at the *Los Angeles Tribune* talk about: "The inexhaustible topic was Race, always Race. . . . I got a snootful of it. Sometimes I got to wondering whether Negroes talked about anything else" (369). Casting her colleagues at work as incessant "whiners," Hisaye undermines the eloquent history of Black social protest: Black speech.[21] Even as spatial arrangements are exposed to their racially ideological underpinnings through the inscription of Black bodies, bodies that signify their racialized predicament, Hisaye continues to value injured Black bodies over their Black voice. "Race talk" is devoid of substantive matter; it is a "snootful" that can be and, in the case of the narrative, is disjuncted from the activities of the Black bodies through which such speech is uttered.

Implicit within this portrayal of African Americans split asunder, between voiced grievance and visual corporeality, is the forty-year historical passage traversed between Hisaye's experience and Yamamoto's retelling. It is well worth rehearsing the cultural production that shaped Asian American identity during these decades, as Asian Americans not only enjoyed less restrictive boundaries than had heretofore interrupted their mobility—immigration law, legal precedent, restrictive residential covenants, bounded labor markets—but in fact soon served as paramours for ethnic assimilation. What is commonly known as the model minority myth, and what David Palumbo-Liu specifies as "model minority discourse," emerged in 1965 and 1966, at the very moment that the civil rights movement took a decidedly different turn from its southern-based, Christian-inspired era of mass boycotts, lunch counter sit-ins, and principled nonviolence. The most well known of these model minority artifacts, a *U.S. News & World Report* article entitled "Success Story of One Minority Group in the U.S." (1966), found a readership that was reeling from a transformation and intensification of Black protest. Published in December, those living in 1966 saw on television screens beret-wearing Black men and women wielding shotguns, first in Oakland and, before anyone could blink, in cities across the United States. These urban Black activists, who dubbed themselves the Black Panther Party for Self-Defense, wrote up a Ten-Point Platform that sharply delineated Black demand and not request, and fearlessly organized urban communities that expressed inchoate rage a year earlier in Watts, the same year that civil rights supporters won the passage of the Voting Rights Act and two years after Johnson launched his War on Poverty while bombing Vietnamese in another war.

In the midst of Black insurgents' call for radical transformation, if not eradication, of civil society and state legitimacy, "Success Story" chronicled Chinese Americans in New York and San Francisco achieving economic success and cultural acceptance without similar demands for deep social change. "At a time," the article begins, "when Americans are awash in worry over the plight of racial minorities. . . . One such minority, the nation's 300,000 Chinese-Americans, is winning wealth and respect by dint of its own hard work" (6). Four paragraphs later, the author specifies a more pronounced agenda, a critique of governmental remedy to the problem of poverty within communities of color: "At a time when it is being proposed that hundreds of billions of dollars be spent to uplift Negroes and other minorities, the nation's 300,000 Chinese-Americans are moving ahead on their own—with no help from anyone else" (6). The prepositional repetition, "at a time," situates historically the racial triangulation between vociferous Black protest, white recalcitrance or ambivalence, and Asian American ascendance built on their reticence. Ever since, this racial template has haunted Asian American activists, as the model minority myth has solidified into a discourse that, according to Palumbo-Liu, "argues that an inward adjustment is necessary for the suture of the ethnic subject into an optimal position within the dominant culture," but ving intact and even strengthening "the sociopolitical apparatuses that ꜱetuate material differences" (*Asian/American*, 397). For Black and ʼn people, suffering even more under the auspices of urban triage beneath the banner of "benign neglect"—model minority discourse's policy mirror—the myth has been nothing short of a muzzle, a racial grievance turned into inexhaustible snootfuls, a Black voice silenced by apparent Asian American mobility.

The irony in Hisaye's denigration of Black speech about race comes later when she herself takes part in "race talk," when she castigates friends and family for exhibiting racist sentiment: "I was a curmudgeon, a real pill. . . . They got so they would do their occasional sho-nuffs behind my back, hushing up suddenly when I came into the room" (371). It is not only ironic that Hisaye is race talking, engaging in speech that she had earlier lambasted, but her own speech is also subverted by an imitation of black speech in its dialectal and corporeal attributes. Instead of engaging Hisaye on the issues that she brings up, her family and friends deploy a stereotypic strategy of mimicry, focusing rather on the physicality of Black vernacular speech, returning it to its "bodily" forms. Not interested in what African Americans are concerned about, they highlight how African Americans say it. Race talk is no longer a subject to be discussed seriously, but rather a dialect to be mimicked, made fun of, implicitly emptied of value for its proximity to denigrated Black bodies.

In this light, with the voice of African Americans diffused and relegated to mere bodily function; with the visual overdetermination of Black bodies presented as the *only* sign through which they can "speak"; and with concomitant dismissal and erasure of the Asian American body, we begin to see the limitations of an Asian American strategy for whom being burnt black can amply save them from racial invisibility. However necessary this abstraction of Blackness is for the development of an Asian American racial consciousness, being "burnt black" metaphorizes what remain real predicaments for African Americans, an evacuation of the content within this distilled form of Blackness in the service of constituting Asian American identity. Likewise, this process of abstracting the Black body and deflecting the Black voice does nothing to interrogate the structures that not only permit these symbolic moves to occur, but provoke material consequences of shunting aside the Black voice and highlighting Black bodies. This is the most serious effect of Asian American invisibility, racially swaddled in model minority discourse, which enables Hisaye and her family to "enjoy," albeit differently, Black violation on the one hand and white privilege on the other. The racial triangle remains intact and at best, Asian American identity remains in an intractable contradiction; at worst, and so often the case, such triangulation amounts to racial division between groups of color at crucial historical moments.

Hisaye's transformation of being burnt black refers directly to the climax of the story, the murder of O'Day Short and his family, whose house is destroyed in a fire in Fontana, where he had been receiving threats from his presumably white "neighbors." From what we have discussed so far, it is not insignificant that Hisaye does not take Short's prophetic warning seriously, dismissing the urgency of his situation as blithely as her reporting of "alleged [!] lynchings . . . combined . . . into one story" (150). For Hisaye, Short's "race talk" only seems to gain credibility after he has been killed. What is compelling to her actually is not what Short had said, but the fact that a dead body is produced. This production of a dead Black body serves as the catalyst, the emblem from which outrage pours. Ironically, the conferring of a dead Black body into a sign producing outrage provokes a bodily response from the Asian American: "It was something like an itch I couldn't locate . . . something was unsettling in my innards" (152). The viscerality of Hisaye's outrage brings around full circle the ideological circuit between Black bodies and its abstraction of Blackness grafted onto an Asian American identity and felt on an Asian body. Simply put, Hisaye physically reacts to racist violence because she is transformed inside; she is transformed inside because a dead body proves that the violence occurred. What remains ignored, even abjected, in this referential ideology is Short's voice, whose race talk is shunted aside. The Asian American body, which disappears again in its own physicality, becomes visible again through a cathartic abstraction of the dead Black one.

We therefore have our answer to the question posed earlier—why Hisaye leaves Los Angeles shortly after she arrives in the city from her internment camp. Her "unsettled innards" prompt "something" to change, the trauma of arson forcing her out of her complacency. It is this outrage that foments the process of her being burnt black and sends her on the road, yet the effects of this outrage continue to hinder Hisaye from moving toward a viable political insurgency. Instead, she is still trapped in a prison house of verbal inexpressibility, "as handicapped as the boy in the wheelchair, as helpless" (371). Again, as she recounts this conversion by fire, Hisaye compares herself not simply with a mentally and physically challenged Japanese American boy, but also with a white man—a priest—who is transferred out of Southern California for writing a play that critiqued the police version of the fire, whose half-hearted investigation exonerated Short's neighbors. As in the beginning of the story, in which she mediates her inaction to Black denigration at the restaurant through her stories of Beiderbecke and Otis, Hisaye offers two competing examples of mobility: while the white priest is forced to move for speaking up, she is free to roam because of her silence. It is this journey that will enable Hisaye to do what she was unable, or unwilling, to do in Los Angeles: to record further episodes of racial exclusion against African Americans and implicate all sorts of people, white and Asian alike, in racist ideologies and practices. Nevertheless, by posing the triumph of white action against the paralysis of Asian American reserve, Hisaye suggests that what unsettles her, what burns her black, is not so much her outrage at racism against Blacks as her utter silence in the face of these horrors.

Thus, in leaving Los Angeles, Hisaye enacts what Sandra Cisneros's narrator in *The House on Mango Street* desires at the end of that story: to write for those who cannot out, an ethos that is different only for those whom Hisaye and Esperanza consider are the ones who cannot escape racial misery and require someone else's record. But if by the end of the narrative Hisaye takes on a certain position of responsibility for exposing racial injustice, she recounts these scenes as a compensatory gesture of remembrance that tries to alleviate and rectify that which she did not do at the time. Certainly, the "race talk" that she attempts to voice is quickly squashed by those to whom she subjects her issues, her credibility undermined not by any fault of her own, but by the racist atmosphere in which she finds herself. In this sense, her narrative of compensation is not so much limited by the visceral transformation of Asian Americans from outward whiteness into a form of hidden Blackness as an analogical indication of solidarity as it is simply not heard. Yet even as she has taken on a new mission to expose racial violence—the murder of Short and his family, the numerous other acts perpetrated against African Americans—by narrating it, she also leaves absent a spatial interrogation of her position as an Asian American when she writes, an investigation that also places her outside the realm of action. The passage, from which we see Hisaye narrating the story with her racial transformation settling into a certain agency, takes place at the end, as she watches the Watts rebellion on television. I quote it at length:

> So it was that, in between putting another load of clothes into the automatic washer, ironing, maybe whipping up some tacos for supper, I watched the Watts riots on television. Back then I was still middle-aged, sitting safely in a house which was located on a street where panic would be the order of the day if a Black family should happen to move in—I had come there on sufferance myself, on the coattails of a pale husband.
>
> Appalled, inwardly cowering, I watched the burning and looting on the screen and heard the reports of the dead and wounded. But beneath all my distress, I felt something else, a tiny trickle of warmth which I finally recognized as an undercurrent of exultation. To me, the tumult in the city was the long-awaited, gratifying next chapter of an old movie that had

flickered about in the back of my mind for years. In the film, shot in the dark of about three o'clock in the morning, there was this modest house out in the country. Suddenly the house was in flames and there were the sound effects of the fire roaring and leaping skyward. Then there could be heard the voices of a man and woman screaming, and the voices of two small children as well. (373)

This is a narrative of revenge; Hisaye exults over the violence by relating the events on the television screen as a mode of justice to an imaginary movie, based on the previous scene of Short and his family. The two scenes, montaged together, enact a diegesis to posit for Hisaye a narrative revision and remembrance of Black bodies violated.

But the screen also screens. Her description suggests that those viewed, who enact the "burning and looting" in Watts, amount to nothing more than Black bodies going wild. African Americans become violent, but this violence, for Hisaye, seems without a clear sense of agency; intentionality is granted through the filmic splicing in Hisaye's imagination, but not in the Black bodies that perform for her. In watching the uprising on television, and in creating a narrative that completes her own predicament of being burnt black, Hisaye elides the political insurgency and urgent meanings of the rebellion.[22] Moreover, her imagined satisfaction in Watts's vengeance for the death of a Black family twenty years earlier is staged in spatial alignment that mirrors the restaurant scene at the beginning of the story. This time, the bus window that protects her from violation is the television that keeps her safe from violence; instead of sitting uncomfortably next to a white girl, Hisaye views urban unrest in the comforts of a white suburban tract, "on sufferance myself, on the coattails of a pale husband" (19). Where she had little choice but to stay on the bus to take her to internment in the 1940s, her social options are wider in the 1960s, but the story structures space and action in similar fashion. Asian Americans and whites still sit together and watch Blacks, humiliated or insouciant, through a glass screen of protection from violation of any sort.

Suturing then the Black bodies in the Watts rebellion with another set of Black bodies burnt in the fire in Fontana, Hisaye elides a critical spatial interrogation of herself. This final gesture toward Black bodies draws attention away from her displacement of the spatial-material positioning of her own Asian American body. The "trickle of warmth" that she feels serves to glide over the fact that she is enabled to feel such "exultation" long after she herself had moved away from the threatening places that she views on television. "Sitting safely in a house," situated firmly in suburban space with a white husband, Hisaye's moment of articulating her now scripted racial consciousness emerges precisely when and where her own material existence gives her access to a zone of comfort and privilege, a space that Black bodies themselves cannot enter. Her visual pleasure therefore indulges in extracting Black bodies as cathartic emblems with which to be affected vicariously but from which to be distanced as well. If beforehand Hisaye implicated herself in complicity with racial exclusion by placing her displaced body in proximity to spectacular Black bodies, her imagined film screens her from her complicit alignment with white flight and the increasing vanilla suburbanization of Los Angeles spatial politics.

Certainly, this passage is meant to be read as ironic, Yamamoto's oblique way of finally undercutting herself from a romanticized insurgent subjectivity. Pointing out that she arrived at this terrain of material distance— with its concomitant consumerist and consuming privileges—on the "coattails of a pale husband," she deploys a rhetorical distancing that seems to critique her final moment of racial transformation. But instead of debunking and destabilizing her claim to solidarity, the narrative's irony is, ironically, that which structures and girds the very currency of her fantasy of solidarity. Her newly arrived social reality, of writing her racial consciousness in white space, engenders her critique of racial ideology precisely because she tries to displace the arena to which she is firmly bound. Yamamoto's irony can therefore be considered as a specific function of ideology in the construction of social formation and in the partial masking of reality. Slavoj Žižek suggests that to ironize one's position within ideology does not expose it to be illusion, but conversely promotes the very force of ideology's control: "Cynical distance is just one way—one of many ways— to blind ourselves to the structuring power of ideological fantasy; even if we do not take things seriously, even if we keep an ironical distance, *we are still doing them*" (33). Žižek's cautionary statement of the limitations of irony in its contestation of ideological formation helps to expose how the narrative's resting place, however undercutting it may be of the narrator, recapitulates racial formation and in fact achieves the transformative racial consciousness only by leaving spatial alignments of "threatening" Black urban space in material deprivation and white suburban privilege intact.[23]

Within this circuit of narrative closure, then, is writing enough? Has Yamamoto, as Cheung argues, "vindicated and reclaimed her own voice," and thereby enacted writerly justice for Short and his family, and for violation against Blacks in general ("Dream," 128)? Yamamoto's penance for her narrator, Hisaye, stitched together in a narrative that weaves 1945, 1965, and 1985 in a story of "reciprocal solicitude and personal agency," is the writing itself, a reportage to awaken her Japanese and Asian American readers, enthralled in holiday cheer, to "foster a new sense of accountability across racial lines" ("Dream," 128). Not unlike the theme of writerly revenge that Maxine Hong Kingston asserts in *The Woman Warrior* (1976), in which "the reporting is the vengeance—not the beheading, not the gutting, but the words," the crafting of "A Fire in Fontana" can be read as a moment of deliberate literary intervention, to help a community come to terms with its responsibility and, indeed, debt to the struggles of another. But like Kingston's story, Yamamoto's story achieves neither justice nor future solidarity, but instead follows a trajectory that Palumbo-Liu regards as "*not* a political and collective act of vengeance, but an interpersonal reckoning" (*Asian/American*, 404). The trajectory of personal healing mitigates the politics of collective racial pain, particularly for others' pain.

Thus Hisaye's initial assertion of transformed racial subjectivity, of "being burnt black," can be seen, as mentioned earlier, as both compelling and troubling. Compelling, because the fictional alignment of Black bodies to structures that dominate them and enact violence onto them brings her to a different political alignment as an Asian American. This fictional arrangement of Black bodies with a critique of racial ideologies and institutions is the only one afforded to her, an Asian American consistently aligned with white bodies in zones of distanced safety. Still Hisaye's assertion is troubling, because the transformation of her subjectivity emerges at the expense of submerging engagement and exposure of the spatial-material changes that allow such a transaction. This is not an objection that would capitulate social choices to simplistic economism, or the kind of "bad" determination that Raymond Williams would rail against. Rather it is a warning that one must not dispense with an analysis that would account for the ways in which these constraints of material shifts in capital accumulation produce trenchant shifts in an urban/Black, suburban/white Los Angeles spatial landscape. And these structural changes inhere in the formation of political identities at the very instance when they are set into the motion of social relations as political choices.

Hisaye also does not simply implicate herself as a single perpetrator in this ascendancy into the privileged space of whiteness. Rather, she regards the formation of contemporary Asian American identity as deeply imbricated in its increasing reliance on a racial order that permits the entry of Asian Americans into the circuit of economic mobility previously denied to them and still denied to other groups of color. Describing a conversation with another Asian American, Hisaye pointedly does not respond to her colleague's actions enabled by uneven access to resources and space:

> An attractive Korean lady friend and real estate agent put her children
> in Catholic schools because, as her daughter explained it, the public

schools hereabouts were "integrated," while on the other hand she win-somely urged local real estate onto Black clients because, as she explained to me, "it's the coming thing," and her considerable profits ("It's been very good to me") made possible her upward mobility into less integrated areas. (373)

Hisaye's silence about her Korean acquaintance's business practices prob-ably has to do with her own participation in moving to "less integrated areas," which she acknowledges fully later on. But more important is what Yamamoto does articulate. Whereas prior to this scene Hisaye voiced her objection to the individual racist comments made by her Asian American friends and family, here she paints the larger social canvas that realigns but also reaffirms the racial order to block entry and access to people of color. Following the trajectory of whites in Los Angeles, the Korean American real estate agent does what is socially and economically expedient—profiting from the exclusionary system of racial housing and educational segregation—and places her bets on her newfound entry into the privileged and protected world of white property. What we as readers read with an intended incredulity as the Korean American woman's inability to see the contradictions of her actions, she takes as an almost natural course of ac-tion for social mobility, a "coming thing" that normalizes the racial power imbedded in such continued exclusion.

In the context of the story that Yamamoto has provided us, such prac-tice should be regarded as outrageous, a form of social hypocrisy at best and betrayal at worst: how can an Asian American participate in and bene-fit from a system of racial exclusion? But within the auspices of the con-temporary scene in which Hisaye engages in her own suburban shuffle and during which Yamamoto wrote the story, the contradictions of the Korean American's housing and schooling decisions come as little surprise. The fact that Hisaye's colleague seems not a bit troubled by the contradiction, and that Hisaye herself sees the contradiction and *still does the same thing* demonstrates not only how the differential effects of racial formation have enabled Asian Americans a certain entry into racial privilege, but also sug-gests that the formation of an Asian American racial consciousness through the catharsis of visualizing Black victimization and the symbolic appropria-tion of these experiences is not sufficient to keep Asian Americans from moving away as material circumstances change. Asian American choice, forged through the rhetoric of racial solidarity and expressed through out-rage at another's and even at one's own complicity, remains difficult and, as Yamamoto suggests in this story, perhaps impossible.

In this context of Los Angeles social history and political economy, the relationship between structure and subject undermines that which seems possible in the imaginary alignment between Black bodies and a nascent Asian American agency. If the abstraction of Black bodies is deployed to cope with real relations in which Asian Americans are an integral part, then this rhetorical gesture necessitates close attention to the proximity or distance of Asian Americans and African Americans to each other spatially, bodily, and politically, all in the limelight of history. In this sense, the salience and power of posing affinity between African Americans and Asian Americans, even through a fiction of differential analogy between Black and Asian bodies, cannot be understated. One might say that this connection is a fictional necessity, one that continues to be an effective one in bringing people of color together in political coalitions. An example of the coterminous efficacy of racial solidarity could be seen in the fiftieth anniversary commemoration of the Japanese American internment in 1992. In a special issue of *Amerasia Journal,* the editors chose African American civil rights activist Charles Lawrence to introduce the volume.[24] Expanding the meaning of the internment beyond its significance to Japanese Americans or even Asian Americans, Lawrence took this time and space to draw larger connections to a more protracted history of civil rights struggle in the United States. In this transcripted speech Lawrence states, "The internment was produced by the same culture that lynched over four thousand Black men; the same culture that invented Jim Crow, and wrote the Chinese Exclusion Acts" (3). Important historical connections are made between African Americans and Asian Americans by suturing them together as part of the racist configuration of U.S. social history. But I also think it is just as, if not more, important that Lawrence himself was exhibited for those participating in this commemoration, that is, for an audience of mostly Asian Americans to see and hear a Black man give this speech. The staging of a Black man to inaugurate this historical remembrance brings to bear the continued reliance on the politics of appropriating Blackness to reclaim a perpetually disappearing Asian American body and political voice. The visual connection is vital in establishing the groundwork for more invested multicultural coalitions.

But as we read "Fire" and open up similar rhetorical gestures in this narrative, we must also pay attention to how Yamamoto attempted to persuade her readers (the *Rafu Shimpo* audience) in 1985 to imagine these connections, just as she did for herself in her story. For this is a story in which the geographies that Asian Americans and African Americans share in Yamamoto's narrative compensate for, and mask Asian American complicity in racial restructurings of Los Angeles during this decade. Japanese American community "empowerment" in Little Tokyo took place at the doorstep of the internationalization of downtown Los Angeles; Little Tokyo was one of the "test cases" for redevelopers in this flight of transnational capital into Los Angeles. In the process, not only have the ensuing effects resulted in the decimation of "Black Los Angeles," as Mike Davis has described, but they have also sped the increasing "thirdworldization" of primarily immigrant labor in the Los Angeles economy, in which Black and Latina/o immigrant workers take the brunt ("*Chinatown*," 71–73). The gentrification of Little Tokyo that began in the late 1960s eventually spread into the entire downtown region and the Wilshire Corridor, resulting in sundry redevelopment projects that have crammed communities of color into areas surrounding downtown, with virtually no coherent housing policy, deteriorating infrastructures, structural worklessness, and a general crisis in relations between older residents of color and new immigrants of color. Elderly Japanese American residents in Little Tokyo and family-run businesses, reopened after World War II, were the first to experience displacement, and as one of Little Tokyo's last holdouts, Mas Umemoto, remarked in 1985, with a Nisei reserve and resignation that barely mask the sarcasm, "What the hell! You can't stop progress. You can't fight. Big business usually wins. People are fools to go against big companies." Preceding the publication of "Fire" in *Rafu*, articles also documented the closure of the Alan Hotel, a low-income residential hotel opened in 1946, whose older, multiracial tenant clientele were forced out, without any compensatory relocation payments, by a Japanese-owned Hong Kong–based company. The spirited protests against redevelopment during the 1970s by groups like the Little Tokyo People's Rights Organization (LT-PRO) gave way to the community's complete transformation, into a space in which corporate triangulation of Japanese conglomerates, city agencies, and commerce-oriented Asian Americans transformed the area into a zone of transnationalism whose success is evaluated by how many tourists it can bring in to purchase and consume Japanese and Japanese American culture. As much as Yamamoto's story can be indexed with the ascendant struggle and ultimate triumph of Japanese Americans over the issue of redress and reparations, "Fire" must also be read against an urban politics of contraction, in which the very spaces that made possible more radical formations and multiracial connections in the 1970s were effectively closed down by 1985. Members of LT-PRO, who fought valiantly to keep alive an imagined community of Little Tokyo from the bottom up, necessarily shifted their attention to issues of Japanese American redress, coalesced in the grassroots National Coalition for Redress and Reparations (NCRR), as they calculated that defeat in spatial politics could be reconfigured into political energies that may someday reemerge beyond its limited Japanese American scope.

But in 1985, in the midst of old Little Tokyo's swan song and in the waning light of political movements that imagined justice much more broadly, the readers of "Fire" were subjected to the new glare of Reagan's reality, in which Asian American cultural workers and activists were busy fending off incipient claims of Asian American neoconservatism, corporate complicity in redevelopment's swathe, and a state ready to lock up and criminalize in newer, tighter cages those who dared to revolt. And in the wake of the 1978 Bakke decision, which severely curtailed the constitutional justification for affirmative action programs, the model minority myth reemerged in the 1980s to dismantle further these uneven attempts at redistribution of cultural and political capital, and Asian Americans were once again structurally aligned with whites as unfair targets of reverse discrimination. Likewise, the "victory" of the redress and reparations campaign turned on two principal issues for debate: first, activists needed to put to rest the slippery yet consistent correlation between enemy "Japs" and those incarcerated in the camps. Japanese Americans, in essence, had to reaffirm their loyalty and commitment to the United States during World War II and into the present. Second, the campaign required that internment exemplified a breach in U.S. values of liberty, freedom, and due process; thus, redress and reparations signified an acknowledgment that American democracy had gone horribly wrong in the 1940s, and thus necessitated an action to make it "right." President Reagan's formal apology in 1988, followed by Bush's appropriation of reparations payments in 1990, effectively capped the campaign within these framing questions, that Japanese Americans, loyal to the United States, were treated unfairly and therefore justly deserved recognition of wrong in order to exonerate the state. As Reagan himself put it in his speech on August 10, 1988, amidst the tears of redress's supporters, "[W]hat is most important in this bill has less to do with property than with honor. For here we admit a wrong; here we reaffirm our commitment as a nation to equal justice under the law . . . that is still the American way" (quoted in Maki, 195). In this context, amidst the recuperation of Japanese Americans in the U.S. body politic and their exoneration from charges of disloyalty; within an era of a state relegitimizing itself by passing a bill of "honor" and again putting aside the question of stolen property and material loss not only for Japanese Americans but also for other people of color; in the historical reenactment of Asian Americans' structural alignment with whiteness to provide multicultural cover for a larger effort to mute the voice of Black social protest and grievance; and with the debilitating effects of capitalist reorganization taking place in urban spaces such as Los Angeles and especially in the lives of people of color bearing the burden of these spatial-material "adjustments," could Yamamoto's revisitation have been written any differently? What happens to the rhetoric of cross-racial affiliation in the face of the Asian Americans' disappearing act as the crisis in Los Angeles deepens? Or, as Yamamoto herself puts it, "Does literature have any impact on what goes on day to day?" The answers to these not-so-rhetorical questions can only be engaged if these spatial configurations are exposed, if what happens to Black bodies is vigorously put up against the backdrop of changing identities in changing chronotopes, and if we keep in mind what remains in shadow as Asian Americans are increasingly brought into the light.

Moreover, the rhetoric of racial transformation in "Fire" threatens to elide once again one of the central problematics that Asian Americans face: the categorization of Asian Americans as well-adjusted, perfectly interpellated subjects, as people without problems. Hisaye takes up Blackness as an inward manifestation at the very moment that she slides into spaces of whiteness. This racial choice is not contradictory at all; in fact, Hisaye's chiasmic movement highlights what Viet Nguyen argues is the critical dependence of Asian Americans on claiming both an identity of the Althusserian "bad subject"—of which Blackness is the primary emblem—and the reliance of such ideological resistance on the increasing inclusion of some Asian Americans into an assimilationist, multiculturalist imagination of U.S. social formation.[25] Armed with the moral saber of Blackness but shielded by the mantle of whiteness, Asian Americans thus become multiculturalism's perfection. Both bad subject and model minority, they teach us that such racial triangulation can substitute a politics of material transformation for a politics of individual therapy. Not only then are conditions of African Americans displaced in the celebration of commodified Blackness, but what cannot be accounted for are the Asian immigrants who themselves are displaced and exploited in these new spatial economies.[26] Capitalist restructuring, for example, has made the garment industry the second largest employer in Los Angeles County, with its oppressive subcontractorship organization siphoning off the work of Asian and Latino labor, shielded by lax and even hostile state regulatory bodies.[27] Therefore, to be burnt black continues the process of marginalizing Asian American material dilemmas, even as other Asian Americans enjoy appropriated Blackness and flexible whiteness and disappear into the suburbs of Los Angeles. The crucial dilemma, then, rests not simply in Gary Okihiro's query of "when and where" Asian Americans enter literary and cultural history, but also how and why they emerge when they do, and what consequences their strategic appearance entails.

Between complicity in the withering of Black Los Angeles and complicity in the displacement of Asian American concerns lies the insurgent activity of Asian Americans struggling to make visible both Black and Asian American bodies, not to consume them through commodified abstractions in the service of therapeutic multiculturalism, but to listen to what these bodies, injured yet still speaking, say. Instances of these actions on the part of Asian Americans reside in political work that underscores racism as integrally tied to a racialized political economy, a structure that compels them to call out racist practices by folks who may look like them, but are more affiliated with a white economy of corporate capitalism.[28] The fiction posited in this story of an Asian American woman recognizing racism through Black bodies reverberates in the cultural imagination of Asian Americans who are attempting to find alternative subjectivities to the "model minority," the most available model granted to them through their own U.S. racial interpellation. At the personal level, being burnt black is an exercise and resignification of the idea of Blackness as the preeminent racial signifier woven into one's individual identity, and which can clear a space for Asian American political identity. But the task of responsibility lies in preventing the Asian American disappearing act from occurring, rendering vigilantly the emergence of the Asian American in her social space in relation to the African Americans whom she views. Otherwise, the visible entry of Asian American identity into literature serves to justify urban triage through multicultural expansion, with Black bodies rendered silent in the desired racial imagination of a deliberate "Asian America" as a critical but nonetheless embraced constituent of the "racial frontier" of twenty-first-century U.S. manifest destiny (Palumbo-Liu, Asian/American, 2, 392). As the persuasive fiction of Black bodies burning Asian Americans black enters a collective Asian American imaginary, the contradictions inherent in the real relations between African Americans and Asian Americans must serve to expose the insidiousness of racialized restructurings of spatial alignments, and can direct the fiction, as fiction, to acknowledge when the fiction debilitates, and when it is actually useful.

These political questions lead us away from Yamamoto's narrative, only to bring us back to admit that this process is, in many ways, unavoidable in contemporary U.S. racial formation. Indeed, Blackness can serve as an efficacious mobilizing force to consolidate the real dynamic, both historical and contemporary, between Asian Americans and African Americans and create new political identities that struggle against a racialized economy that consumes racial bodies as it accumulates capital for a select few.[29] As one attempts to talk about racial politics in profoundly compromised spaces from which one can see people struggling against a spiraling logic of ideological intrusion and bodily infliction—and Yamamoto's story certainly struggles here—such narrative gestures toward political solidarity park us at provisional rest stops, temporary "answers" that nervously seem to settle the queasiness of political identity. But these should only lead us to answers that are in fact more questions, those that are passionately posed by longtime Asian American activist Glenn Omatsu: "Will we [Asian Americans] overcome our own oppression and help to create a new society, or will we become a new exploiter group in the present American hierarchy of inequality? Will we define our goal of empowerment solely in terms of individual advancement for a few, or as the collective liberation of all peoples?" (66). "These are," as one Los Angeles scholar has put it, "not academic but political questions."[30] Black bodies and Asian American bodies still remain in tension long after Hisaye's film has ended in "Fire," subjects who tell us that, in their struggle against abstraction in the service of multiculturalism, future spaces of possibility must be sought out elsewhere. And it is to another space, three thousand miles away, in a city older but no more teetering and triaged than Los Angeles, in communities equally left behind, that we turn next.

4

Intellectual Cynics, Cynical Intellectualism, and Brokered Masculinities

The palimpsest that we have unearthed in the battles of Los Angeles in the preceding chapters unravels multiculturalism's abstractions, narrative strategies that expose, yet leave intact, the ethos of urban triage. The primacy of dyslexia and disruption in Morales's novel gives way to a patriarchal recontainment and mythic reclamation of land that surreptitiously affirm community building through relations of property girded by the logic of capitalist domination. The barrio's resistance—and its constitutive Chicana/o identity—is constrained and enabled by that which determines its borders. Likewise, Yamamoto's story triangulates Asian American identity between structured proximity to whiteness and political desires toward Blackness. But "A Fire in Fontana" appeals to a utopian vision of horizontal assimilation that is stridently undermined not only by the material distance between Blacks and Asian Americans produced and enhanced during the 1980s, but also through the racial complicity that inheres in appropriations of historical violation against Blacks, which further cast aside racial injury from the multicultural conversation that Asian Americans have tried so hard to join. If racial anxiety in the age of multiculturalism compels writers like Morales and Yamamoto to reach back into their respective community's histories to say something, however partial and bounded, about present conditions, then attention to contemporary circumstances leads writers to an almost unbearable silence.

To underscore what fuels this pent-up silence, we might broaden the racial triangulation evident in Yamamoto's story and implicit in Morales's to encompass the anxiety of writing in the midst of urban triage in general.

100

For literary narratives are nothing more than sieves through which power, and those who wield power, might understand those for whom reaching the structures of reward remains difficult, perhaps even impossible. They are nothing less, conversely, than the work of bringing to light what Min Song refers to as "negative spaces" into the imagination of those who make the maps and decide which communities are made legible, and which are left indecipherable. In short, writers of multiculturalism might be rightly deemed cultural brokers. Brokers are not simply middlemen, mediating and controlling access to societal power; brokers benefit from and, through their social being, affirm the asymmetrical relationships between the owners of capital and capital's owned, and manage that which is seen by the powerful and that which is left behind, all in the maintenance of this social order. This is the consistent mistake of reading Asian Americans as "model minorities," for they structurally enact not models for other, less materially successful groups of color, but instead broker the terms through which racial interaction is undertaken, which identities and activities are made legitimate and which are deemed criminal. Brokered societies are older forms of social relations than those based on eighteenth-century Enlightenment modes of universal claims of equality, whether in the imaginary polis or in the substantive realities of subordination to the state. Western liberal states, which look to Greek democracies and Roman republics as ancestral foundations, retain the vestiges of brokering as the means through which power is exerted and felt, and by which people jockey for standing in their bounded communities. But as biblical scholar and first-century Palestine expert John Dominic Crossan warns, "There is a huge difference between a mediator-as-broker who bars or controls the way and a mediator-as-model who exemplifies and opens the way" (*Long Way,* 112).

This huge difference between brokers and models puts into sharp relief the dilemma that troubles a writer like John Edgar Wideman, whose literary career, spanning four decades, is testament to his status as one of American letters' most celebrated writers of Black urban life. The only writer to win the illustrious Pen/Faulkner award twice—once for his painful memoir *Brothers and Keepers* (1984) and then for his equally agonizing novel *Philadelphia Fire* (1990)—Wideman himself has spoken on several occasions to the wrenching anxiety that pervades his extensive oeuvre and to the persistent worry that his work can do little to alleviate the suffering about which he writes so compellingly. In an interview with James Coleman two years before the publication of *Philadelphia Fire,* Wideman turns from personal reflection on his own upbringing in Pittsburgh and later his college and postgraduate tenure at the University of Pennsylvania toward a kind of cultural commentary full of pathos and not a little guilt:

There is a whole issue of what happens when anybody, any black person in
this country, gains a skill, gains an education, gains some sort of power;
whether it's a doctor, lawyer, businessman. How does that individual success relate to the fact that most people are far from successful in those
economic terms, and how does success perpetuate a system that is in fact
oppressing so many black people? (Coleman, 160)

To this Wideman asks even more troubling questions, which uncover,
if only for a moment, the intellectual knot that cannot be unraveled but
is all too visible: "What is our responsibility, to ourselves, to the ones we
left behind? Do we have to leave them behind? Are there ways that we can
be successful without perpetuating the class and racial hierarchy that produced this?" (160). In other words, are Black writers and intellectuals brokers or models? And if they are nothing more than brokers, can members
of the contemporary talented tenth like Wideman escape this prison house
of privilege through a language of liberation?[1] One can feel the palpable
silence in response to these questions, which gives pause in both men, and
sure enough the interview moves on to other topics, with Wideman's inqui-
ries left hanging, unanswered in agonizing suspense.

What words could not express became all the more urgent the day after
Mother's Day in 1985, as the state communicated itself through bullhorns,
bullets, and finally a bomb. On that day, the Philadelphia police and fire
departments converged on 6221 Osage Avenue in West Philadelphia to
evict a radical group called MOVE from their makeshift bunker. MOVE and
the police had engaged in a running war for more than a decade, which occasionally exploded into violent showdowns; MOVE's flagrant violation of
social protocol, their incessant railing at the corruption of modern society,
and their diatribes against the city irked Philadelphia's police into such a
vengeful frenzy that they seemed to embody collectively the rage of their
former boss, Frank Rizzo, notorious for his hatred of radical, particularly
Black, organizations. After a long day of high-powered water cannons and
thousands of rounds of gunfire, a lone police helicopter dropped a satchel
bomb on the rooftop at 5:27 P.M., which exploded and then set the house
ablaze. A whole hour passed before the fire department, which had squirt-
ed water as an offensive weapon in the morning, turned its hoses on again,
but by then the fire was uncontrollable. When firefighters fought the blaze
in earnest at 9:30 P.M., an entire city block—and Philadelphia's blocks are
famously big—was on fire. In the morning, residents, city officials, and
a nation glued to television sets surveyed the damage: fifty-three homes
burnt to the ground, more than two hundred people instantly left homeless
and, above all, eleven people, among them five children, dead from either
fire, smoke, or gunshots as they tried to flee the burning house.

Immediately following this tragedy, scores of journalists and other pundits proclaimed that the event, so singular in its horror and violence, the only time a bomb was used on U.S. civilians by an American institution when the country was not technically at war, would never be forgotten. But within five years, a critical silence would loom over this event. Besides the work of Toni Cade Bambara shortly before her untimely death, the continued struggle for justice on the part of surviving MOVE members, the autobiographical apologia of former Philadelphia mayor Wilson Goode, and a few noted academic scholars, the 1985 bombing of Osage Avenue has quickly and quietly slid into historical obscurity. The blue-ribbon commission that investigated the procedures leading up to the massacre found the police and fire departments, along with city hall, grossly negligent, but no one has been served criminal charges for any part of what transpired. Philadelphia, it seems, has tried hard to move past this darkest of chapters. Thus, the questions mount: what accounts for the kind of forgetfulness that pervades the social trauma, the state violence that devastated this West Philadelphia neighborhood? And what does *this* silence mean, along with the other numerous silences already mentioned? This chapter contends that *Philadelphia Fire* helps us see the conditions under which a group such as MOVE emerged in the 1980s, what social and symbolic work this group performed within the urban terrain of Philadelphia in this era, and how and why a remembrance of these events in the middle of the decade highlights the constraints and choices of those affected, for better or worse, by the forces that made and destroyed MOVE. Despite his repeated admonitions that the novel *not* be read as a commentary on MOVE, Wideman regards the destruction of MOVE as an appropriate metaphor for a larger failure of intellectual will on his part and on the part of others—particularly Black intellectuals like himself—to commit oneself to, if not enable, the liberation of those most dispossessed in Black urban communities.[2] It is, significantly, as the novel's protagonist Cudjoe puts it, a double failure, "about blackness and about being a man."

Cudjoe's journey mirrors Wideman's insofar as both try to write a novel based on the MOVE bombing: one fails to write a novel, while the other writes a novel about failure. Why the failure has something to do with Blackness *and* masculinity is crucial in understanding why *Philadelphia Fire* narrates Wideman's intellectual impasse, which is not simply his own. Cudjoe's main informant at ground zero of the bombing is Margaret Jones, the sole adult survivor of the novel's rendition of the MOVE bombing, and it is from her that we along with Cudjoe learn of the social critique offered by MOVE and the reasons for its destruction. Far from its portrayal as an irrational cult, Margaret provides Cudjoe object lessons in MOVE's radical form of critique against a social structure slowly decimating Black communities. And as a Black *woman,* she extends her critical lens toward the self-destructive forces within the MOVE complex that undermined its oppositional potential as other forces succeeded in destroying it from without. But Cudjoe's (and Wideman's) investment in the conditions that Black men inhabit on either side of the privilege/poverty divide, and the conditioned choices that they make in their particular social positions, forecast the inevitability of each episode in the novel: bound in a particular model of communal liberation whose champion would be the singular figure of the Black male intellectual, Cudjoe can find none, not even in himself. *Philadelphia Fire,* above all, narrates the crisis of Black intellectual life, in the absence or destruction of a visible politics of resistance in the 1980s, as one of structural and instrumental complicity with the reigning structures of racial domination. And to the extent that Wideman identifies his own writerly project with that of Cudjoe's search—both seek to write a narrative that will supplement the legacy of the MOVE martyrs—*Philadelphia Fire* is a novel that chronicles the brokered, mediated, and constrained position of Black intellectuals within the world system of the 1980s, one that makes for difficulty in both resource and representation.

But what is this story of MOVE that Wideman seeks to supplement in *Philadelphia Fire*? The very middle of the novel offers a journalistic account of the bombing; its position in the narrative suggests that, like the eye of a hurricane or Wallace Stevens's famous jar on the hill, the MOVE tragedy is the novel's absent presence, that which gives orbit to swirling social dynamics that crystallized so vividly and terribly in 1985.[3] The conceit of the bulk of *Philadelphia Fire* is in the double search that the protagonist, Cudjoe, takes on in his return to the city after a self-imposed exile on the island of Mykonos: Cudjoe searches for Simba, the sole child survivor, and hopes to write a novel about the bombing after the child has been found. The journey ends in failures; Cudjoe neither finds the boy nor writes his novel. But the MOVE tragedy continues to haunt Cudjoe and others he meets along the way. His conversations, for example, with Timbo, an old friend of the protagonist and attaché to the mayor of Philadelphia, traverse a plethora of topics, including their political work as students in the university, the betrayal of that struggle, the tenuousness of the mayor's administration, the hypocritical position of privileged Blacks in the new urban landscape, and the emergence of a new generation of rebellious, amoral children. But grumbling underneath these discussions, and erupting at moments to punctuate their talk, is, as the narrative puts it, "The fire. The fire" (81). For Cudjoe, the fire and the boy who survived remain the linchpin to the entire meaning of the MOVE tragedy, providing the impetus for his writing (and writer's block) and the emblem for his failure to unveil the truth: "[CUDJOE:] 'Timbo. Has anyone downtown heard anything about the boy who was saved?' [TIMBO:] 'We always talking about the fire, ain't we? No matter what I think we talking about, it comes down to the fire. Well, the answer's no'" (91).

To understand MOVE, then, is to unlock, as Madhu Dubey puts it, the "contemporary crisis in black urban community and a concomitant crisis in literary representation" (580). In part, the representational crisis that Dubey alludes to has to do with the growing skepticism of literature's instrumental role in effecting social change since the high watermarks of the Black Aesthetic era. But how and why representational crisis may in fact be instrumental in the larger social crisis in urban communities demands a framing of this literature in the political economy during which *Philadelphia Fire* was written. To this extent, *Philadelphia Fire,* more than any other narrative in this study, thematizes the ways in which literary work mitigates urban triage. The consequences of Cudjoe's search for Simba and MOVE are, in this sense, enormous: where failure will mark for the writer the deep chasm between representation and reality, language's impotence to transform, it will also signal for the larger community an inexorable movement toward the silence of death. The novel that Cudjoe wants to write, and *Philadelphia Fire* itself, are both narratives struggling to surround the event of the bombing with context, with ethical attention and priority to human lives, and above all to the agency and responsibility of those responsible for and victims of the tragedy. Thus to understand MOVE begs yet another question: How does one narrate communal trauma, as one mediates the minefield of the political economic, racial, and gendered processes that pull on the very meaning of this calamitous event wrapped inside the historical moment and spatial specificity of 1980s Philadelphia?

Wideman marks two narrative tendencies, two aesthetic modes that pervade the novel, which underwrite the tension and the failure to imagine a cohesive community in his exploration. The first narrative mode is ascribed to the modernist artist Alberto Giacometti, best known for his elongated sculptures:

> The more I looked at the model, the more the screen between his reality and mine grew thicker. One starts by seeing the person who poses, but little by little all the possible sculptures of him intervene. The more a real vision of him disappears, the stranger his head becomes. One is no longer sure of his appearance, or of his size, or of anything at all. There were too many sculptures between my model and me. And when there were no more sculptures, there was such a complete stranger that I no longer knew whom I saw or what I was looking at. (103)

The second is voiced through J. B., Wideman's homeless protagonist of part 3, who roams Center City and whose abbreviated namesake is not only that of the soul singer, but also that of the fictionalized leader of MOVE in the first part of the novel. This is his soliloquy:

> J. B., you've got to get up off your ass. World's out there and it's begging for attention. What we need is realism, the naturalistic panorama of a cityscape unfolding. Demographics, statistics, objectivity. Perhaps a view of the city from on high, the fish-eye lens catching everything within its distortion, skyscraper heads together, rising like sucked up through a straw. If we could arrange the building blocks, the rivers, boulevards, bridges, harbor, etc. etc. into some semblance of order, of reality, then we could begin disentangling ourselves from this miasma, this fever of shakes and jitters, of self-defeating selfishness called urbanization. (157)

The first mode of narration prompts a process of defamiliarizing mediation; the narrative act becomes a screen that, in turning a perceived object into material useful for aesthetic practice, makes that object "disappear." In place of the logic of mimesis embedded in the term "model," we are left with the "stranger," but consider why such defamiliarization takes place: the "screen between his reality and mine grew thicker." The artistic task, according to Giacometti, resides in attempting to construct a narrative that attends to, not just represents, reality, the lived experience of the one under investigation by erecting phenomenal layers that compel the artist to challenge his or her own perception.[4] Conversely, the second process puts forth calls for reality as well, but through the stripping away of those layers that prevent one from seeing that reality. This "naturalism" assumes that the artist must wrest herself or himself from the already mediated status of perception, a vision clouded by the built environment (urbanization) and its attendant ideologies (individualism). One mode champions a modernist approach, the other a naturalist vision; one tendency is to get at reality through absolute subjective experience, the other must find reality through exposing objective conditions.[5] Of course, both modes are always at work in narrative, as one is often hidden well inside the other. That Wideman foregrounds the tension produces, in Dubey's view, a "stylistic distress" that undermines his larger desire to imagine community through language. But it is this very distress, this convergence that does not close off worry, that urges us to unravel the relation between modernism and naturalism, subjective and objective accounts, agency and determination, the exertion of pressures—to reiterate Raymond Williams's phrase—and that which exertion bumps against.

Let us, then, for the moment take J. B.'s advice, and fix our sights on

Philadelphia, with the wide-angle lens of political economy. If we were to take this camera on a helicopter and traverse the city's landscape in 1985, we would notice the famous row houses of West Philadelphia, where the Osage community was located; the compacted space of downtown Philadelphia with its office buildings and high-rise apartment buildings never towering over the statue of William Penn atop City Hall; and the industrial parks of South Philadelphia and North Philadelphia. But drop a few thousand feet and we would also notice many of these industries not blowing much smoke, if any at all; many of the row houses, the idyllic emblem of post–World War II urban prosperity, dilapidated and boarded up; those houses left standing and strong pockmarked by empty lots chain-linked with signs that barely read "―――― Realtors" above the uncut grass. Mount the camera on a car and drive and the picture becomes even more stark: police cars stalk through neighborhoods, stopping at corners where Black men are congregating; men, women, and children drive shopping carts on commercial Walnut Street in Center City, looking for a place to go the bathroom as other men and women in suits whiz by them; at sunset, these "suits" pour into train stations and catch the next high-speed commuter rail line to take them to suburban Montgomery, Bucks, or Delaware County, or to southern New Jersey, toward their single-family homes and away from the enclosed office spaces of the only part of Philadelphia that they dare to enter.

No city was immune to the effects of "the Great U-Turn"—deindustrialization, the ballooning of secondary and tertiary labor economies, urban renewal/removal, capital flight to the suburbs—but by 1985 Philadelphia bore an especial brunt of the burden of these changes.[6] Hemorrhage in manufacturing industries affected both white and Black workers, but African Americans did not enjoy the same kind of diversified employment pool as their white counterparts: limited primarily to manufacture, public sector, and low-wage health/domestic service work, Blacks in Philadelphia faced extreme difficulty in the shuttling of industrial work to service-sector employment.[7] And manufacturing was only a microcosm of the economic fatigue and attendant racial difference that Philadelphia was suffering from. Between 1975 and 1985, while unemployment among whites ranged between 6 and 10.7 percent, the unemployment rate among Blacks in Philadelphia was more than double, hovering usually above 20 percent (Stull and Madden, 180). For Black men, this figure was even more grim: by 1982, more than one out of every four Black men looking for work could not find a job.[8]

The story of Black Philadelphia takes on an additional spatial dimension. As Douglas Massey and Nancy Denton have observed, only 7.7 percent of Blacks resided in the outlying suburbs of Philadelphia in 1980; this city carries the dubious honor of remaining one of the most segregated large urban spaces in the United States, a racial separation that has brought about extreme isolation for its Black residents: "In all of these cities [including Philadelphia], at least 80 percent of blacks would have had to move to achieve a desegregated residential pattern" (71–72).[9] We can locate the roots of hypersegregation as far back as the beginning movements of whites into the suburbs—the telltale "white flight"—during the 1950s; between 1950 and 1970, the percentage of blacks in Philadelphia nearly doubled, from 18 percent to 34 percent (45). Accompanying this white flight was the flight of dollars, the siphoning off of financial resources into the city, the aftermath of which would be a fiscal crisis that would plague the ironic emergence of Black mayoral administrations during this era of American Apartheid.

Our discussion of Yamamoto's story highlighted the conditions and consequences of divergent spatial movements of Asian Americans and African Americans in Los Angeles's political economy. So, too, this consideration of the ways in which race affects Philadelphia's Black residents differently shows the *increasing* significance of race in understanding how urban space and identity (collective and individual) work together. Two forces converge on Philadelphia's Black residents, two social processes that help shape their reaction to how their lives must respond to the enervating effects of Philadelphia's economic and spatial decline in the 1980s. These two work in dynamic and sometimes oppositional tension, and while my construction may seem too schematic or temporal, it is important to regard them as concurrent forces; those living on Osage Avenue had to confront the *differential racialization of space* while also coping with the *consolidation of the racial perception*. Differential racialization of space does not mean racial segregation between whites and Blacks, or in the case of contemporary urban areas like Philadelphia, of the hypersegregation experienced by African Americans. This more well known version of how racialization operates spatially within the sphere of housing is well-documented and provides the larger social frame in which differential racialization works. Differential racialization refers rather to the uneven effects of 1980s urban political economies in the development of (segregated) Black communities fractured along, at least, class lines. That is, the political economy of 1980s Philadelphia produced, in the context of the more general and still intransigent racial segregation between Blacks and whites, increasingly visible economic heterogeneity within Black communities.

So far, this is certainly not surprising, nor does this observation seem particularly new; Wilson has argued as much, and much earlier. But emerging from the material fracturing of Black communities is a growing and sharpening debate over notions of Blackness, in questions of both identity and practice, both individual and collective.[10] Race's significance does not decrease in this period; its transformation simply becomes more complex and, therefore, even more important. While competing visions of Blackness, between Black elites and the Black poor, reflect the historical and tenuous (sometimes hidden, sometimes exposed) positions that African Americans held in relation to a given historical formation in U.S. capitalism, the particular valence of the debate as it is shaped in the 1980s must be viewed in its context of Philadelphia's eviscerating economic decline, and for many, material devastation. The emergence of a visible Black middle class, entering not only professional, managerial, corporate, and academic spaces in numbers previously unseen in U.S. history, has taken place during the same time that poverty and joblessness among another segment of African Americans, as we have seen through the numbers above, has ballooned. The irony of the celebration of the new Black middle class and its supposed integration into the American mainstream is that the structural explanation for Black poverty has become more difficult to assert. In the place of this argument—that the Black poor suffer under the weight of economic deprivation and layers of racial discrimination—is the emergent discourse of the behaviorally pathological Black "underclass": no longer "veterans of creative suffering," the Black poor, in the face of the relative economic success of the Black middle class, transmogrify into a dangerous menace, a population lacking basic social skills and values, and requiring even further surveillance and criminal regulation. The production of one community corresponds to the creation of the other; more insidiously, the celebration of one rests upon the regulation of the other.

The economic fracturing between the Black middle class and the Black poor—and as a result, the increasing social and political estrangement between these two groups—leads to a further differentiation within the spaces of the Black poor. Deindustrialization, as we have seen, coinciding with state abandonment of managing the economy to guarantee full employment, has withered the brief gains in blue-collar jobs in the industrial sector to which the Black working class only recently had access.[11] Uneven development in the late-capitalist U.S. political economy has guaranteed not full employment, but definitive and permanent joblessness among a significant portion of the nation's potential workforce, and it should not be surprising which (racialized) communities bear the brunt of structural unemployment.[12] In the face of these material effects on Black communities, a new categorical distinction has emerged—both a structural and experiential delineation—between the "poor" (what some call the Black "working class" or "working poor") and the "destitute" (what primary definers refer to as the "underclass").[13] Both groups share the common fate of receiving and surviving the brutal legacy of racialized economic exploitation; this point cannot be understated: both *poor* and *destitute* are not descriptive words, but relational terms that imply a dynamic of exploitation. The poor are not romanticized workers; the poor are, by definition, *exploited* workers, insofar as the labor they produce contains a surplus that is extracted and unaccounted for in the wage they receive from their employer. The destitute, by extension and in contrast, do not produce labor from which employers extract surplus; the destitute *are* the surplus through which the existing economy can maintain its productivity.[14] The destitute's very body is extracted out of the labor-wage circuit, for it is her or his very non-laboring body that enables the labor-wage dynamic to remain an exploitative one in favor of the employer (the person who determines the wage), to keep the poor just so. The political economy of the 1980s has sharpened the visibility (as well as the demography) of these two groups at the economic bottom of the Black urban community. And it is this increasing notice not only at sociological conferences and within pages of academic journals but also between these two very groups toward one another that the differential racialization of space begets its countersocial process.

The same walls of economic exploitation and hypersegregation that hone the delineation between the figure of the Black destitute and the Black poor, and separate the Black middle class from those two groups who occupy the social and economic bottom, also produce the corollary effect of consolidating racial perception. Thus, while differential racialization has enabled sundry visions of Blackness largely (but not exclusively) determined by the position that one occupies within a political economic structure, these competing versions of Blackness concurrently attempt to form agonistic, and in times of crisis, antagonistic relationships with one another. It is this consolidation of perception that makes the distinction between the Black destitute and the Black poor so critical in teasing out how Philadelphia's Black residents responded to their condition in the 1980s. For this period of economic decline and continued or even increasing segregation engenders an anxiety over these contracting social opportunities and expectations. If the Black poor, those whose working livelihoods faced the prospect of shrinking resources as a result of the deindustrialization and ongoing isolation of residential segregation, suffered the bulk of this material deprivation and loss of political legitimacy, the response to this loss and suffering turns palpable decline into symbolic contest against those who have been shunted completely to the margins: the destitute.[15] That the construction of Black destitution naturalizes what is clearly socially determined by relative positions within a given structure does not make such a paradox any less powerful in this process of consolidating racial perception to build one's own identity. Differential racialization begets conflicting visions of Blackness; consolidation of perception closes the circle of legitimate community by collating and contesting these differing versions against those whom everyone can agree deserve social stigma, the "surplus body" of Black destitution.

In her study of the MOVE bombing, Robin Wagner-Pacifici notes that the vilification of MOVE as a terrorist, even demonic, organization emerged out of a contrast between the group, seen as "bad" neighbors, and the "good neighborhood" of Osage Avenue and, by extension, a contest between the poor and the destitute. This neighborhood, whose residents are all Black, continually staged itself, and were staged by the popular media, as stable, orderly, "house-proud." By most accounts, the Osage residents were exemplars of the "ordinary, middle-class," urban community, whose livelihoods were disrupted by a decidedly unneighborly group. But from the political economy and spatial arrangements of Philadelphia during the 1980s to the relational contestations and mediations of identity and community construction, we see with more clarity the social meaning of the "good neighborhood" of Osage Avenue against the "bad" ones of the MOVE complex. "Good neighbors"—and their corollaries such as "stable community," "working-class neighborhood," "house-proud community"—must be considered as redactions of these larger processes giving visible meaning to this term. What is particularly salient in this construction is the way in which "good neighbors" are staged to certain audiences, special places, namely those readers and listeners lodged in institutional spaces. To whom do they address their implicit disavowal of the destitute in their community? Elijah Anderson points out that this process of abjection by the poor against the destitute allows the poor to "maintain faith in the wider institutions." Given this, it is certainly no surprise that the Osage residents said the following in a letter to the then governor of Pennsylvania, Dick Thornburgh: "Your Honor, we are a small working class block of thirty-nine row houses. We take pride in our homes, and we once cherished the underglow of peace we felt just living here" (quoted in Wagner-Pacifici, 67). The faith that these residents hold seems quite clear, even if the structural bedrock of such faith is indeed becoming more shaky; the residents deserve active and immediate aid from the state because they work (unlike the jobless destitute), hold and cherish property (against the dirty MOVE house), and maintain social relations that do not upset the existing structure (the "underglow of peace"). The claim of being "good neighbors" bears meaning insofar as this assertion is institutionally comprehended and legitimated.

The residents syntactically elucidate Raymond Williams's notion of "residual" cultural practices, those articulations drawn from the past to give meaning to the present, an anachronism that has not yet become a cliché.[16] But the residents' temporal anxiety here exposes a spatial crisis that has left them fearful that they may not be able to reproduce the "underglow of peace." In fact, anxiety has already shattered peace, as the present over-takes the past; the decimating effects of deindustrialization, uneven devel-opment, and increasing racial isolation in the city have already transfigured this neighborhood of poor, yet working stability into a contested terrain of legitimate, even noble poverty and marginalized destitution. The fear that this "working-class" community expresses to the governor, the representa-tive figure of the state, is the fear that they, the residents, are the forgotten casualties of urban triage.[17] The self-representation by the Osage residents as "good neighbors," therefore, places them in perceptual, if not structural, alliance with those of the more affluent Black middle class, those who have followed, in these years of deindustrialization, "white flight" with an at-tendant "Black flight" from the city. Differential racialization and percep-tual consolidation are expressed by the reproduction of what Wahneema Lubiano calls the "metaphors for deviance," imaged as Black destitution not only visible to a mediated non-Black audience via the media, but also visible to Blacks themselves ("Mugged," 74). Robin Kelley puts it this way: "The very existence of the 'nice-Negro,' like the model-minority myth pinned on Asian Americans, renders the war on those 'other,' hardcore niggas justifiable and even palatable" ("Confessions," 20).[18]

Much has been written about the ambiguity of MOVE's philosophy and ideology, whether, for instance, the organization based itself on political or religious ideals. Wagner-Pacifici's argument is premised on the notion that the meaning of MOVE ultimately cannot be fully known, neither its origins nor its definitive development. The cluster of newspaper articles concerning MOVE before, during, and after the 1985 bombing exemplifies this inability and even unwillingness to identify the group's stated purpose; consistently, the *Philadelphia Inquirer* reported that "the origins of the name 'MOVE' are unclear: It apparently does not stand for anything." Subsequent book studies, besides Wagner-Pacifici's, spend at least one chapter speculating on MOVE founder Vincent Leaphart/John Africa's tumultuous past: his initial failures at public education (and his supposed low IQ), his foray into other religious movements like the Phoenix-based "Kingdom of Yahweh" sect, and his eventual rejection of all things "civilized" and worldly ("man-made," to use the term popular in MOVE tracts).[19]

But it is the group's deeds—their strict vegetarianism (and occasional eat-ing of raw meat), their simple clothing (or, in case of the MOVE children, lack of clothing), their refusal to bathe with soap, their lambasting of modern technology (electricity and plumbing), their keeping of dogs and welcoming of the city's vermin—that at once horrified those who reported on MOVE and also obscured their coverage. For MOVE's actions, and even harsher rhetoric, find a definitive corollary in the Greek Cynics, a movement that emerged during the time of imperial Rome. Much of the Cynics' religio-political critique of Roman political society and Greek cultural hegemony manifested itself in almost exactly the same kind of social practice that the MOVE followers espoused: a Cynic's "uniform" consisted of a simple triadic cloak, a wallet, and a staff to signify personal self-sufficiency and disdain for normative, conventional life; the Cynic's diet amounted to eating raw vegetables and, in the case of its symbolic founder Diogenes of Sinope, raw meat; finally, the rhetoric of Greek Cynicism employed frequently polemi-cal diatribes against the ethos of conventional Aristotelian rhetoric, moral-izing harshly against social injustice, war, rampant material luxury, even landed property.[20]

The connections here warrant much further investigation, but I will add only two more comments from the relationship between this "Black terror-ist" group and a band of Greek subversives. First, both Cynic and MOVE followers were decidedly *not* apocalyptic and escapist. Neither movement fled to mountains, the desert, or other isolated regions to be free from so-cietal evil; both groups practiced their subversive and ethical radicalism in the city, in the seat of social, economic, and political power, and sought to scandalize those who regarded themselves as "normal." Second, Cynics and MOVE members recognized their visual relation or proximity to the destitute, the expendables of their respective communities, and actively took on these characteristics (clothing and hygienic practice especially) to put forth an alternative way of life. Theirs was what I would call a *willful destitution,* an intentional practice of foregrounding through bodily scan-dal their surplus status in the political economy. By using their very bodies as emblems of their abandonment of normative exploitation, both Cynics and MOVE members highlighted a radical critique of a system that produces economic, psychic, emotional, and spiritual loss.

We have, then, a partial answer to why the Osage residents viewed them-selves as "good" (read: normal) neighbors against the latter-day Cynics in their midst. The rest of the answer resides in *Philadelphia Fire,* most im-mediately addressed in the encounter between Cudjoe and Margaret Jones. Margaret stands in as the only character in the novel who is part of that social space I have called the Black poor, or the working poor (and the only autonomous female character). All the other (male) characters are figured as either outside the sphere of urban poverty, and therefore on the side of economic and social privilege (Sam, Timbo, Richard Corey, even Cudjoe), or embody the spaces of Black destitution (J. B.), the surplus population left behind. Ostensibly, Margaret represents the epitome of the good neighbor on Osage, and initially she is that kind of neighbor, her daily commute to and from an office job a twelve-year routine to maintain a house that she owns. She works and owns property; her reaction to the infamy of King's smell and sight would not surprise us. But she also personifies the forces and structures that have squeezed Black communities into ever more contracted social and economic space and into declining life choices: her college education, that "little piece of degree," only affords her an entry-level office job, a place on the bottom rung of a service-sector economy just beginning to burgeon in Philadelphia when she graduated from school. Margaret's frustrations about work, which extend into an existential crisis about her life ("Who I been all the days of my life?" [14]), make manifest the flimsy hold that she has on keeping herself from slipping into the other side of the structural divide of Black poverty, destitution. She is, Wideman would say, hanging on to the "bottom rung of the ladder of opportunity," just barely above "the space beneath the bottom rung" ("The Night," 25). And it is not surprising that the narrative codes Margaret's reified condition in both racial and bodily terms: "Working like you for some white man or black man don't make no difference cause all they pay you is *nigger wages,* enough to keep you guessing, keep you hungry, keep you coming back. Piece a job so you don't never learn nothing, just keep you busy and too tired to think. But your *feet think*. They tell you every day God sends, stop this foolishness. Stop wearing me down to the nubs" (15; my emphases). Here Margaret offers a sharp rebuke to Wilson's notion that structural changes in the American economy go beyond the parameters of racial discrimination; she reads her economic survival as definitively racially bound, her "nigger wages" a sign of the consequences of differential racialization. And her visceral, bodily response to enervating labor tells us two consequences of her position of exploitation in this racialized political economy: first, her feet, her body informs her that she will lose this battle, her fatigue a symptom of a larger structural fatigue; second, her struggle is atomized, individualized, and alienated, and lacks the possibility of an earlier collective agency that manufacturing-based unions might have been able to harness and that she seeks in her brief membership in MOVE. Margaret does not mention anyone else who shares her suffering, but remains alone to battle her psychic bitterness, physical exhaustion, and financial instability. She can only place herself in a vertical line of descent of similar solipsistic labor, the antecedent figure of her own mother: "What I got to show for it but sore feet, feet bad as my mama's . . . after fifty years cleaning up white folks' mess" (14). Margaret situates and makes meaningful her agency in terms of the differing same of Black labor history, from domestic work to office servitude, a debilitating legacy of being paid "nigger wages" to clean up other people's mess.

Margaret's critique of her relative poverty therefore makes her decision to cross over into the willful destitution of King's organization and ideology a perfectly rational response to an irrational system that calls "thirty kinds of soda pop, twelve different colors of toilet paper . . . progress" (14). Wideman's reconsideration of MOVE through this character makes Margaret's decision to move beyond the "progress" of late capitalist commercialization and exploitation as logical a mode of social, albeit scandalous, resistance as that of the Cynics shedding the oppressive garb of Roman imperialism. That Margaret's movement from tenuous poverty to willful destitution, from a vertical legacy of languishing labor to a horizontal community of freedom and "Life," takes place in the same urban space reminds us that this utopian group is not escapist, nor is this rejection of all things societal and civilized brewed from unfathomable places. Rather, MOVE's ideology represented in King's philosophies in *Philadelphia Fire* are homegrown, an organic emergence of practical critique that exposes the compromised and compromising relationship between the exploited, whose labor maintains the prosperity and "progress" of the exploiters, and those who benefit from this landscape. In the normalized political economy of the 1980s, the state assumes the capacity and responsibility of managing, through police containment and criminalization, the social surplus of Black joblessness, destitution so very visible in the community. But Margaret's move into destitution is a conscious refusal, a repudiation given legitimacy by communal, practical actions that, in taking herself out of the sphere of capitalist relations, makes destitution no longer the constitutive by-product of a postindustrial political economy, but an agency that deems the management of Black destitution illegitimate. The backlash to MOVE's alternative ethic to normative social relations in urban space makes Margaret a bad neighbor, even a bad mother, in the eyes of those in the community and in her family, and turns her into a social pariah: Margaret hates her sister Anita for "taking care of Karen and Billy," her children, and resents Anita's economic privilege "up there in their dicty Detroit suburb living the so-called *good life*" (16). In its larger context, however, such social reaction is always political in its reliance on the neighborhood's "legitimate" complaint to the state to maintain and reproduce, even reclaim, the "underglow of peace" so under attack by a group whose actions are such a travesty to the values upon which such peace rests. Regulation of willful destitution is, then, a confrontation with terrorists, not only the management of the criminals of those structurally destitute.[21]

But if Wideman's emblematic figure of willful destitution foregrounds MOVE's critical capacities and protest against the forces of U.S. economic readjustment, Margaret's construction of her brief time in the MOVE organization is crafted in the aftermath of the bombing, and by extension her return to a normalized community. And immediately, when we take notice of this shift from willful destitution back to ostensibly good neighborliness and her resigned poverty, we find that Margaret's allegiance has once again turned vertical: she is concerned solely for her two children. The brief horizontal community proposed by MOVE has once again been supplanted by the vertical community of descent, just as prior to her joining the group, she sought identification through her motherhood: "I knew I couldn't put nobody, not even King, before my kids" (19). Putting nobody before herself or her children is both a return to normative constructions of community—vertical blood kinship, the family—and a simultaneous isolation, as a result of making the vertical community exceptional, from finding capacities for community among those whom she might have regarded, had MOVE continued, as fictive kin. And if Margaret's frustration with her intractable social position compelled her to find in the MOVE group a form of Cynical protest against the very system that keeps her earning "nigger wages," her egress from the organization leaves her with a worldview even more cynical than before, even nihilistic.

This shift from intellectual Cynicism to cynical intellectualism, from visible communal protest to individual resentment, highlights the difficulty of turning social anger into political resistance in the absence of communal, collective formations within those urban spaces whose inhabitants feel the effects of deprivation, repression, and isolation most viscerally. In addition, the movement into personal rage against the system becomes important insofar as the narrative hints at three other possible explanations for Margaret's newly wrought, post-MOVE cynicism, three interpretations that become for Wideman the basis for exploring narratively the troubled coupling of personal failure and political immobility, of shattered commitments and compromised resistance, and the turn from a model community to brokered relations.

What we glean from Margaret's triadic ressentiment is the taut anxiety that Wideman continually but agonizingly explores to uncover the ways in which a brokered masculinity corresponds with the political compromises in Philadelphia racial politics out of which a sacrifice must be made: immediately, MOVE, but more generally its structural correlative, the Black destitute. First, we find Margaret's post-MOVE cynicism in her consideration of the state of the neighborhood after the bombing. Although she once brought her children to the playground at the local park, she now disparages those who congregate at Clark Park, particularly the men at the basketball courts. In a moment that might have been a spark of connection between her and Cudjoe, since he had also once lived on Osage and played ball at the very same park, Margaret immediately dashes that potential commonality of frequenting this public space, the little afforded to the Black poor. Instead, the park becomes a space at once criminalized, racialized, and gendered:

> Well, I might have seen you then. I lived on Osage. Spent half my life in the park. Played a lot of ball here.
> They still play. Or call themselves playing. More drinking and snorting and smoking reefer than ball playing. A rowdy bunch now.
> Used to be good hoop.
> I wouldn't know anything about that, but I'd skin Billy or Karen alive if I caught them hanging around here. Pimpmobiles and dopemobiles. See you anything you big enough to ask for. And if I know what they're doing, the cops got to know. You think the police do anything about it? Hell no. Not till one these little white chicks slinking around here ODs and turns up dead, then they'll come down on that corner like gangbusters.
> So the park's not what it used to be.
> What is? Tell me if you know what is. (32)

The park has been marked, and this mark is a sign of damage, like the mangled bench Cudjoe notices right before this conversation (29). Whereas before Margaret found the park a refuge to escape the isolation of nurturing children, now the park signifies gendered space; only men gather. And these are Black men, for the management of the park is determined also by its racial composition; if whites (women) are threatened, the (police) state responds, but Blacks (men) alone do not constitute an emergency. And finally, these are Black men committing petty crimes, which in Margaret's imagination are harbingers for more dangerous acts, the individual acts of "drinking and snorting and smoking reefer" escalating into a veritable sex and drug industry of "pimpmobiles and dopemobiles." Margaret extends her invective of the park and those who occupy that space into a general cynicism of everything social, a remark that is more full of bathos than of futility as she responds to Cudjoe's question: "What is [what it used to be]? Tell me if you know what is."

So effective are the forces of differential racialization and consolidated perception in the regulation of people's attitudes and behaviors that even Margaret, once a sharp cynical critic of the state and economy she regarded as responsible for such deprivation of public space, places herself in opposition to those who are relegated to the social space of destitution.

She is, once again, a member of the Black poor, creating social (and spatial) distance from those whose position of structural excess emerges common-sensically as excessive criminality and uncontrollability. Critical here is the way that Margaret finds no other means to respond to these Black men except resorting to state action by the police; she consents to the policing of the Black destitute not as a desired response to this loss of public space, but as the only response. As a person now individuated, isolated, and alienated from a horizontal community, her capacity to enact any kind of social agency can only be exercised through the admission of state power to police, criminalize, and eventually remove these men. Margaret's vision of the park depends on the state's policing of space, both materially and ideologically. Her cynicism, then, relies on the intractable narrative of Black (male) destitution as a main reason, if not the primary means, for understanding the declining opportunities and qualities of Black life within urban space.

Margaret's second moment of cynical resignation lays further political waste to the possibility of help from "above." More specifically, she reveals a profound skepticism of those who control the institutional spaces of social knowledge, those in the academy and in the city government who amass information about urban communities. She mistakenly, but not incorrectly, conflates both academic and bureaucratic knowledge and views Cudjoe as an embodiment of both. Cudjoe's attempts to tell Simba's story are viewed by Margaret with extreme skepticism, as such knowledge gathering is immediately absorbed and diffused once it is articulated within institutional space: "You mean you'll do your thing and forget Simmie. Write your book and gone. Just like the social workers and those busybodies from the University. They been studying us for years. Reports on top of reports. A whole basement full of files in the building where I work. We're famous" (20). Later, Margaret forecloses any possibility of assisting Cudjoe in his search for Simba as she relates to him the consequences of those who collect such information to "help" this struggling neighborhood: "We're not looking for help from you or nobody else. Help is what started this mess. Somebody called himself helping is the one lit the fire" (34).

This somebody "helping" is the city's Black mayor, Wilson Goode, and what is suggested in Margaret's devastating polemic against academic and bureaucratic information-gathering is the implicit self-interest that undergirds any project of assistance. Met with recalcitrant and resistant silence, Cudjoe's ethnographic foray to write a story is severely compromised, his authority as a writer undermined by those who expose what he consistently fears throughout the novel: his attempt to make his narrative socially and even politically productive is *not* the desire of the community that he ostensibly hopes to serve and save. For what has such narration accomplished except to further pathologize the very community it purports to assist? The "University" studies its surrounding neighborhood, makes the residents of West Philadelphia "famous" by constructing them in a way that leads directly to the regulation and containment made visible by Margaret in her envisioning of the "dangerous" park. The very rhetoric of "help" becomes the means of reproducing notions of Black destitution that further create the social divide between working and workless residents within poor Black communities. To Margaret, Cudjoe's impulse to tell Simba's story is not the altruistic or even politically engaged impulse of Du Bois's "talented tenth," but the instrumental compromise of the Black privileged, who serve and legitimize the maintenance of economic, social, and political disparity.

From the vantage of someone who consciously removed herself from the circuit of "progress," Margaret exposes the troubled affinities between those on the two sides of the political and economic divide, those who are regulated by the state's repressive forces and those who help manage the repression. But perhaps most damaging and most cynical, Wideman insinuates, is Margaret's third movement from Cynic protest to cynical resentment, one that takes place during Margaret's testimony about King, the fictionalized leader of MOVE. By the time Margaret talks to Cudjoe, she acknowledges that King's practices undermined the larger project of MOVE's antisystemic critique, that "he did it wrong," even though "he was right" (14). In essence, King reinforced new hierarchies of control toward his followers, the ideal of a horizontal egalitarian community disintegrating into the most basic of inequalities: "And he was king because we was slaves and we made him our master" (11). And Margaret locates this master/slave relation in the sexual relation: "[W]asn't more than a couple months later I'm holding my breath and praying I can get past the stink when he's raising the covers off his mattress and telling me lie down with him. . . . crawled up under the covers with King cause he's right even if he did things wrong sometimes" (15). Reminiscent of Stokeley Carmichael's now infamous statement on the position of women in the Black liberation struggle, King's assumption of heterosexist prerogative not only reinforces the visible workings of power in the construction of sexual hierarchy, but also undermines the very ethic of horizontal community that first attracted Margaret to the organization. The "wrong" of masculinist reassertion over women overtakes the "right" of its social critique.[22]

Wideman ends this encounter between Margaret and Cudjoe, the one extended conversation between a man and woman, with these cynical failures, and in doing so limits the possibility of forming a "beloved," women-centered Black community established by Toni Morrison in her most celebrated novel in the 1980s, *Beloved*. Sethe's liberation from the repetition of guilt's ghost—Beloved—comes in Morrison's narrative when organic bonds of community restore, through difficulty and necessity, the fragile relational dependency of each person in the community, the sum far more significant than its parts added. Such interdependency can only be re-created through Morrison's metaphorical action of "rememory," the working through of unredeeemed, isolating guilt through communal redemption, brought about largely by the community's women "gathering" the collective, psychic ethic of survival in the aftermath of emancipation's dashed hopes. But Wideman's narrative never illumines this possibility; Margaret's relation to women is vertical and therefore lost, and leaves only the repetitive legacy of poverty and fatigue—tired feet and "nigger wages"—and her one experiment with horizontal community goes down, literally and metaphorically, in flames. Why Wideman's narrative focuses much more on the social solipsism within racialized urban space while Morrison's vision moves toward at least a tentative imagination of calculated community might be explained, at first glance, by Wideman's attention to the predicament of Black men as opposed to Morrison's centering of her narrative in the "intersectional" experience of Black women, both raced and gendered.[23] Yet such an ostensible difference in focus still leaves open the issue of why Wideman focuses on the men, and why that (masculinist) vision does not look toward a redeemed garden (where the women gather to liberate Sethe in *Beloved*) but toward an urban plot burnt to the ground, whose ashy mixture of flesh and edifice, bone and wood, engenders that most desperate counsel of narrative survival, "Hold on" (151).[24]

More suggestive, but not supplementary to the divergent gendered approaches in the two novels, is, according to Charles Scruggs, Morrison's willingness to imagine in the 1980s the "discovery" of bonds of fictive kinship that testify to the longer legacy of the bonds of what he calls the "invisible city" in Black literature and culture. Turning attention away from the street and toward the home, *Beloved* replaces the alienation of the city with domestic intimacy and offers the home—still certainly fraught with the vampiric past of slavery—as a momentary recuperative place from which to model urban space differently. "[T]he conclusion of *Beloved*," Scruggs closes, "seems to offer an escape, however ambiguous, from a hopeless repetition of action and memory" (204). To this, however, we might add that Sethe's home provides not only ambiguous escape, but *temporary* refuge. Against all odds, home in *Beloved* is community imagined into existence. But forces on the other side of the door begin immediately to reconfigure the space of sanctity made possible by the women (and man) holding on to one another. Sanctuary inside always means danger outside;

temporary and ambivalent escape signals that you are still being chased, hunted down. It is not simply that Wideman's failure to imagine a beloved community, a city within a city, has to do with his persistent attention to men and neglect of Black women—although it is that, too—but also with a certain cultural unease in the synecdoche of the home, Morrison's Giacomettian sculpture of liberation, which must be temporally arrested and spatially set aside from the bombs dropped and bullets fired on other homes. Wideman's skepticisms are in fact constitutive of the larger anxiety that marks the historical conditions of the Black writer trying to narrate Black urban space and crisis in the 1980s.

Where Morrison's novel enters and finds relief in 1987, Wideman's must leave in 1990, furrowed with the worry that those who did not die in the home in 1985 struggle in desperation with fewer spaces to give quarter. And in trying to narrate about and through this anxiety while at the same time struggling to remain attentive to those spaces and people, Wideman does not simply jettison Margaret in her fall from radical Cynicism to enraged cynicism but instead uses her failure as a template for Cudjoe to follow specific journeys of race, gender, and social privilege in urban space. What we learn from Margaret's encounter with Cudjoe becomes the visible paths by which the failure of wholeness narratively or community politically can be understood. We can read, therefore, Margaret's narrative disappearance as also a sublimation of her vision into a ghostly presence throughout the novel. The anxiety of failure and the anxiety in failure that permeate this novel both effect and enable Wideman's exploration of the failed urban community, as seen through men's eyes, but whose source, if not origin, is the vision of the ex-MOVE member.[25]

Thus Margaret helps us to comprehend Cudjoe's turn to the compromised spaces of brokered masculinity. The three arenas that prompt her cynical resignation and rage at a system that murders Black children and forces those in the areas of Black poverty to make "some rich man richer" (19) serve as useful models from which to examine Cudjoe's encounters with others as he searches for Simba, meetings that foreground the process by which models become strangers and objective "realism" becomes mediated, tainted.[26] As we follow Cudjoe's encounter with other men, Margaret's first two modes of cynicism become narrative guides. And as Cudjoe journeys, we might shift the troublesome question that Cudjoe asks and for which so many critics have taken Wideman to task—"What was he looking for in women's bodies? (27)—and ask that question of the men as well. What is Cudjoe, and by extension, Wideman, looking for in men's bodies?

Margaret, in her meeting with Cudjoe at Clark Park, views the park as space inhabited by dangerous Black men, the criminalized destitute, whose

occupation is not, but should be regulated by police force. Immediately following this encounter, Cudjoe plays basketball with these men and through
this episode Wideman rehearses what Darryl Pinckney regards as perhaps
the best, most "authentic" depiction of the cultural space of poor Black
men.[27] Questions of authenticity notwithstanding, Cudjoe encounters in
this scene a group of men who not only come together, however provisionally, in the course of the game, but also offer their own critical insights into
the MOVE bombing, the limitations of a Black-led mayoral administration,
and the consistent "nigger control" exacted on those in the neighborhood
(41–42). These players produce a trenchant critique of the built environment that has produced the differential effects of racial realignment, a simultaneous assignment of Black privilege and Black poverty: "Downtown
chumps all eating out the same bowl. They come in where I work" (42).
Casting skeptical light on Margaret's wholesale dismissal of the Clark
Park players, Cudjoe finds these men perceptive in their social vision and
incisive in their reading of how park space is viewed and regulated by those
downtown.

Yet even as the men highlight sharp, critical capacities, Cudjoe finds
inescapable the cynicism that Margaret conveys, and the mediating perception of Black destitution transforms this group testimony into Giacomettian
"sculptures" that turn the familiarity of playing basketball into something
much more strange. As the men continue to talk, drink, and smoke into
the night, Cudjoe observes that they become increasingly strangers, their
bonds increasingly broken: "Faces around him are masks. Would he recognize any of these guys if he saw them in clothes on the street tomorrow?"
(43). These "masks," which occlude recognition, do not prevent Cudjoe
from making judgment; in fact, it is precisely these "masks"—those produced by consolidated perception and differential racialization—that enable him to view the park as a rite of Black destitution. During the game,
Cudjoe meets his former friend's brother, O.T., who relates to Cudjoe both
Darnell's life tragedy (in prison for being "into the dope shit") and his own
troubles and struggles to "get myself together." O.T. mirrors all the qualities of Darnell's that Cudjoe admires, but it is precisely the brothers' simi-
larities that compel Cudjoe to place on O.T. the "mask" of his brother:

> Cudjoe watches O.T. move off. Darnell Thompson all over again. Big,
> black, graceful. Broad shoulders, narrow waist, short, bouncy, almost
> delicate steps. Darnell's soft, easy manner. Eagerness in his voice as he
> leans into a conversation. Enjoying what he's saying, what you have to say.
> Taller by inches than his brother. O.T. had grown a body to fit Darnell's
> enormous hands. Ten years. Did anything get better instead of worse?

Why couldn't he believe Darnell's brother? Why did he hear ice cracking as O.T. spoke of his plans? Why did he see Darnell's rusty hard hand
wrapped around his brother's dragging him down? (37–38)

If the sight of idealized masculinity enables the sound of men talking to one
another, the sound of "ice cracking" engenders a new vision that breaks into
Cudjoe's fantasy and turns O.T. into a "stranger."[28] What interrupts the first
vision and produces this chiasmic structure in the narrative—from sight to
sound, sound to sight—is coded first as the ambiguous term "anything,"
later specified in the sensory image and sound, "ice cracking," and finally in
the unnerving, ghostly repetition of Darnell's hand synecdochically "dragging" not only O.T. down, but also pulling down Cudjoe's vision. Darnell
"triangulates" between Cudjoe and O.T., not to mediate homosociality.
Instead, triangulation occludes the fantasy. The initial "anything" that
only seems to get worse is as vague as Margaret's resigned remark that
"nothing, nowhere any better," an understood assent to normalized social
decline. The fragility of O.T.'s life chances in 1980s Philadelphia, with all
of its attendant economic, political, and social decline, is as tenuous as
the brief joy of skating on thin ice before he literally slips through into the
deathly water underneath, the cage of prison in which Darnell is already
locked. Cudjoe views with skepticism O.T.'s attempts to "make something
of [him]self" by reentering the university; the "pull" of Black destitution
that enervates Margaret's political desires is echoed here by the broken and
brokered masculinity whose efforts, even the most heroic attempts of individual agency and entry into legitimate forms of social mobility (education), seem futile in the eyes and ears of Cudjoe. A "stranger" is produced
from a friend's brother, the intervening "sculptures" created by the default,
inevitable narrative of Black destitution and imprisonment scripting O.T.'s
life to a tragic denouement. Such dependence on this racial narrative seems
automatic, shameful yet as irresistible as Cudjoe's filmic fantasy when he
first enters the basketball court as both actor and director: "Cudjoe is an
actor embarrassed by the clichéd shot, a director who can't resist filming it
this way" (31).

The ten years that separate Darnell's shot at social mobility and O.T.'s
attempts to return to school have further consolidated the maintenance of
the dual exploitation of Black poverty and destitution, in which those who
are not struggling to just "make a living," as Margaret remarks, are cordoned off "in the slam" like Darnell. Caught in the ongoing malign neglect
on the part of the state to absorb the surplus labor population produced by
capital abandonment of Black communities in Philadelphia—once industrial centers and now fallow zones of gentrification and isolation—O.T.

struggles at the end of a period during which Darnell was one of the first victims. These are the ten years of the Reagan-Bush onslaught against Keynesian full employment, the relinquishing of funding for community organizations and educational expenses, the governmental incentives for capital flight out of the city, and the criminalization of those left behind, with few if any social or political alternatives from which to challenge these trends.[29] Such is the environment that enabled the emergence of the radically critical vision of MOVE in the middle of this decade. That the survivors of the bombing (the remnant of the willfully destitute) and Darnell (falling into destitution and rendered criminal) both end up in prison provides insight into the larger narrative fixing Cudjoe's vision of O.T.'s eventual failure. Darnell may "pull" O.T. down, the "ice cracking" may be the emblem of the fragile state of Philadelphia's political economy, but the "push" factors, although not made visible in this passage, have become all the more strong in these intervening years. If Cudjoe's image of Darnell's hand depends on the dual processes of differential racialization and consolidated perception to *define* how and why O.T. will eventually fall, the larger frame around which this vision is imagined *determines* this failure. In other words, what is considered here a "pull" into destitution by the time Cudjoe imagines O.T.'s struggle is the normalized and calculated "push" into destitution that began at least ten years earlier.

The "push" factor remains unnarrated at this moment of the novel: Cudjoe's somber epiphanies of O.T.'s tragic, eventual modeling of his brother's life lead to a certain blindness that pervades his perception of many of those within this particular neighborhood. Why the "push" forces that make the ice so thin and the narrative of Black male destitution seem so inevitable that they look very like the "pull" from below has in large part to do with, as I mentioned in chapter 1, the emboldened discourse around Wilson's continued prognosis of the "declining significance of race." For alongside the ways in which communities are organized, resources are distributed, and justice adjudicated rides the increasingly visible presence and attendant discourse of multicultural celebration from above, those in power who have ostensibly benefited from this discursive declining significance of race. During the ten years between Darnell's struggle and O.T.'s, Philadelphia saw its first Black man assume the helm of the city government, part of a larger trend of seemingly successful Black politicians making their way into the seat of municipal, and sometimes state, power. The rise of this small cadre of bureaucratic Black power, when coupled with the "sculpture"-producing mediations that script poor Black men within the spaces of destitution, allows us to understand the processes by which the forces that push someone like O.T. through thin ice arise out of calculated, even if not intentional, practices rendered invisible but made legitimate by this new Black power. And as Cudjoe's basketball buddies point out during their conversation, the fiction of race's declining significance belies race's prominence in these practices: "Mayor's not in office to whip on white folks. Nigger control. That's what he's about" (41–42).

If Cudjoe encounters one vision of Black masculinity cordoned into a narrative of criminalized destitution, then the novel's protagonist also enters the spaces in which the vision of brokered masculinity becomes visible, those whom Margaret sardonically calls "help." To meet O.T. and the other men who seem to Cudjoe destined to live the narrative of Black destitution, Cudjoe travels to the park and plays basketball. As we follow Cudjoe to meet Timbo, the "cultural attaché" to the mayor, we must put on nicer clothes to enter a five-star restaurant in Center City Philadelphia, which caters to the Black and white elite of the city. This is the space of multicultural oasis, the privileged site in which wealth makes racial slurs impotent, even complementary. "Who's zooming who," Cudjoe wonders. "A new language. New license. Niggers and dagos. Cityspeak. No secrets, no history, what you see is what you say" (76). Cudjoe is more than confused, as the narrative relates here, at the changes in race relations; the ease with which Timbo associates with Maurice, the Italian restaurant owner, disturbs and unnerves Cudjoe in a manner that forces a disjunction between what he sees viscerally and what he knows, the seeming racial paradise of the moneyed and powerful and the fractured history of tension, violence, and segregation that the restaurant appears to cover over. Wideman reminds us through Cudjoe's anxiety about "who's zooming who" that prior to the administration of Wilson Goode and the promise of a "Black Camelot" (Timbo's words), Philadelphia was Frank Rizzo's town, the infamous Italian American mayor whose legacy in both that office and in his prior job as the city's police chief left lasting scars within Philadelphia's communities of color.[30]

That Timbo's usage of "dago" generates not an association with this long and bitter history between Blacks and Italians personified in Rizzo but a new "cityspeak" compels us to ask what enables the mayor's assistant to move so easily from a bitter racial history to an Edenic multicultural present, how a new language can emerge in the disjunction between word and its historical reference. What intervenes in order to make racial epithets safe and for former enemies to look like friends? Cudjoe provides the most obvious answer when, after finishing his meal with Timbo, he feels overwhelmed by the guilt of racial betrayal brought about by economic privilege. Described as a "wave of shame and humiliation" over the "time and trouble required to fill the stomachs of two black men," the shift from racial to class allegiance and the concomitant unease produced by that all-too-easy move on the part of Cudjoe is seen through its effects, the after-math of a simple lunch in a luxury restaurant: "Why did he sit still for it? Accumulating. Bloating. Smiling and chattering while piles of bones, hunks of fat, discarded gristle and cores, skins and decorative greens and sculpted peels, corks, cans, bottles, grease, soiled linen, soggy napkins, crumbs on the floor, shells, what was unconsumed and unconsumable, waste and rot and persiflage heaped up, the garbage outweighing him, taller than he was, usurping his place" (92). This litany of refuse overwhelms, a mate-rial manifestation of his inward guilt, but Cudjoe's sense of complicity in his participation in such "excess" is double: first, his "bloating" and "ac-cumulating" is possible because he is willing to "sit still" as he consumes what others labor over, each piece of once useful product rendered useless and transformed into "waste and rot." And, second, just as Cudjoe and Timbo consume the surplus of the labor that provides them with food and presentation, so the surplus of their consumption—the garbage—is visible for all, especially Cudjoe. There is no avoiding that garbage is the unwanted archaeology of both its productive labor and its unproductive consumer. And that the accumulation of food surplus parallels the excess of language occurring at the same time—"smiling and chattering" likened to "persiflage"—suggesting that the ease of the "cityspeak" of "niggers" and "dagos" is the surplus, the remainder and reminder, of an urban racial history consumed but not digested.

But like the rot of the unconsumed parts of the meal "heaped up," the seeming ease of racial language also reminds us of the unwanted history continuing to accrue, even if those like Timbo and Maurice wish that his-tory was smoothed over by the ceremony of a luxurious meal. In other words, garbage does not disappear: it has to go somewhere; likewise, the racial history of Philadelphia bears its debilitating effects somewhere in the city, no matter how much that history is "zoomed," rendered invisi-ble, in the privileged spaces of Maurice's restaurant. The archaeology of garbage and the history of racial talk is not lost on Timbo; he likens the "garbage" that many residents of the city must live off to an image we en-countered earlier, "thin ice . . . [d]amn thin ice and we all dancing on it" (80). Timbo's echoing of Cudjoe's sound image of "ice cracking" reminds us of the tenuousness of countless lives in the city, people slipping into so-cial invisibility with, and as the refuse of, downtown consumption, but it is important to note the difference between Timbo's reference to "thin ice" and Cudjoe's invocation of the same metaphor. Whereas Cudjoe sees, from relative safety, O.T.'s falling through the cracked ice, Timbo implicates himself (and Cudjoe, and the entire city) in the eventual slippage underneath the ice: "we all dancing on it." The multicultural oasis enabled by the restaurant not only will not keep its patrons from confronting the reality of the garbage in the city, but, as Timbo suggests, this island of seeming racial harmony upon which the privileged of the city dance is precisely the place that engenders such doom.

Perhaps because of his understanding that his opportunities and opportunism are fleeting, and perhaps because his official position in the city government requires his traversing the urban space of uneven development, Timbo sees the "thin ice" structurally, while Cudjoe initially can only consider it instrumentally. Cudjoe envisions O.T.'s fall as the "pull" from Darnell, the downward mobility of Black men into the narrative of destitution, what so many conservative revisionists encode racially as the "culture of poverty." Timbo, on the other hand, even in his most greedy, status-conscious moments, clearly understands the extent to which the city maintains a complicity in the production of social destitution, making expendable (surplus) whole communities as a logical outcome of contemporary urban "renewal." As the two men drive throughout the city, Timbo "sketches" for Cudjoe a map of the city that will turn "every square foot into solid gold," the project of revitalizing Philadelphia to new urban glory:

> All this mess around here, warehouses, garages, shanties, all these eyesores got to go. When redevelopment's finished, a nice, uncluttered view of the art museum. That's the idea. Open up the view. With universities just a hop skip down the way what we're trying to create here is our little version of Athens, you dig? (78)

But Timbo juxtaposes present-day Hellenistic glory with its necessary social consequence: "We still got sections of this great metropolis where nobody don't love nobody. Too ugly. Too mean. No time for love. Niggers scuffling and scheming twenty-four hours a day to survive. . . . them that ain't got and never had, they worse off than ever. . . . Some these pitiful bloods off the map, bro. And they know it" (79). Here is Timbo's rendition of the process of "remapping" the city through redevelopment, what Joseph Schumpeter coined more than fifty years ago as "creative destruction," or what I have been calling urban triage. Moving out into the cityscape from the restaurant, we see how Timbo's "map" reenacts the same dynamic of development and demolition, profit and destruction, consumption and garbagemaking in the urban space of which Maurice's restaurant served as both manifestation and metonymy. Attending to the demands that deindustrialization and capital flight have produced, urban triage through a partnership of private business interests and the city government has leveled the old physical markers of industrial capitalism to pave the way for capitalism's postindustrial, service-driven future. By extension, demolishing old landmarks of one economy (the infrastructure) in order to make room for the new (gentrification) also required the removal of those who labored within that economy: these are the "pitiful bloods off the map" whose apparent unsightliness in the project to build "Athens" are shunted off even further and deeper into the most underdeveloped, neglected sections of the city.[31] And yet, as implicated as Timbo is and as guilty as Cudjoe feels about his own participation in consumptive garbage making, Timbo's mapping suggests that urban triage is a necessary, even logical step to maintain the machinations of capital's march, despite and through destruction, toward further growth.

Timbo's comments make clear that one unholy alliance produces another: the trinitarian convergence of economic, political, and cultural institutions—private interests (real estate speculation, gentrification), public sanction (eminent domain, deregulation, financial incentives), and university repriority (research over service, theory over practice)—helps to reshape Philadelphia as a new "Athens" in the 1980s. Yet also embedded in such confluence of redevelopment are the social costs, affecting all of Philadelphia's poor, but especially its Black communities—displacement and removal (the destruction of low-income housing and rental units, the leveling of industrial sites), destitution (unemployment and underemployment, homelessness, educational disparity), and criminalization (increased policing, extralegal activity).[32] In other words, if Timbo's map casts Philadelphia as a new Athenian oasis, then this built environment also seeds its correlative geography of Cynicism's island, of which MOVE represents its logical formation. For if urban growth necessarily leaves a substantial number of the city's population behind, and if those who bear this brunt know it, then the protest of Cynicism must emerge to interrupt, if not disrupt, the otherwise unrelenting push toward Athens. Wideman bumps corresponding images together—racial oasis and islands of destitution, food and garbage, the new language of cityspeak and its contentious history, Athens and Cynicism—not only to give fuller witness to Margaret's critique of "help" from above, but also to demonstrate that the structural imperatives requiring the sacrifice of one space for the salvation of another determines and is lubricated by the cultural practice defining the map of redevelopment (who is made visible, who is off the map).

This fuller exposition of Margaret's first and second critiques of both policing those "below" by the help from "above," differential yet constitutive islands of both privilege and poverty, implicates Black masculinities as profoundly brokered, compromised, and mediated. The vision of unbroken agency that Cudjoe longs to find in the figure of, and in community with,

Simba cannot be approached, for what remains culturally available to construct a Black masculinity are identities inextricably bound together in a circuit in which two Black men enjoy the desserts of social privilege at the expense of others falling through "thin ice." One man's movement toward Athens, Wideman suggests, is another's journey away from this idyllic city, toward the space of Cynicism or, worse, the unmarked state of cynicism. And those who occupy these spaces of institutional privilege must invariably participate, even if against their own intentions, in a master plan to regulate one form of Black masculinity in the maintenance of that other one. What is then left for those still left standing on, and not drowning underneath, the social "thin ice" of the 1980s, the narrative describes through Timbo as individualistic opportunism—"Looking out for number one" (84)—and through Cudjoe as self-selected escapism—"I lived on an island. . . . Wound up staying away ten years" (86).[33] The necessary complicity of Black men holding bureaucratic, political positions in the creatively destructive processes of urban redevelopment, spatial triage, and the reproduction of Black destitution forecloses the possibility of being much more than crisis managers of those who are "ground up underneath" (84) the new enclosures of Philadelphia's urban political economy. In his autobiography, former mayor of Philadelphia Wilson Goode crafts his narrative as a model for a "generation of African American males," in the face of his observation that "responsible black men in our society seem to be vanishing" (xv, xvi). But when confronted by the bureaucratic role he must play in ensuring private accumulation of public lands in the postindustrial age, and when coming to terms with his own passive participation in the eradication of MOVE's willful destitution that exposed his instrumental complicity, Goode must cede his social desires to his administrative script: "That's not within my jurisdiction" (164). On this side of thin ice, moving beyond this instrumental *and* structural agency of Black (male) privilege is, if not impossible, not yet imaginable.[34]

The masculinities explored in this novel, constituted and challenged in Cudjoe's encounter with other Black men, reveal relationships that expose how these identities work to reproduce larger social relations structured in the particular formations of dominance of its era. Each vision of masculinity constructed in relation to, constitutive of, even if antagonistic toward one another, produces both a crisis in other constructions of masculinity and a crisis in itself. But such crisis does not entail a failure to act, to produce effects or results; on the contrary, as Timbo elucidates for us, his brief ambivalence toward his instrumentality still enables him to map out the city with a social vision that generates, and will continue to generate, terrific effects of social dislocation for many, and exorbitant wealth for a few.

Cudjoe's sorrowful fantasy of O.T. and his guilty enjoyment of Timbo's company betrays his own anxiety about his privileged if tenuous status as a Black man enjoying the fruits of another's unrequited labor, a masculinity that in its crisis-in-prosperity reveals the larger consequence of brokered masculinity in the compromised space of urban racial politics. The absence of a language of resistant masculinity is the presence of a crisis identity, one that Wideman frames in terms of its quiescence to, and not challenge of, the particular racial order from which it emerges and helps to sustain. If we remember the tension between "modernist" and "naturalist" visions of the narrative act that undergirds Wideman's artistic dialectic and whose effect is one always of failure, we see that the failure of Cudjoe's masculinity marks a crisis in which one social narrative is foreclosed (O.T. falls through thin ice) by the constitutive opening of another (Timbo works to displace and gentrify another Black neighborhood). Simply put, crisis does not preclude action; crisis enables the routing and detouring of struggle and agency.

We have thus far seen Margaret's first two modes of cynical resentment in play, working together to demonstrate the intimate connection between the construction of the criminalized masculinity of Black destitution and the instrumental, brokered masculinity of Black prosperity. Now we return to Margaret's third critique, this one against King's heterosexism. What we have learned from Cudjoe's exploration of men brings us back to his dismissal of Margaret as we investigate what he looks for "in women's bodies" (27). The homosocial triangulation that Cudjoe imagines between himself, Margaret, and King occasions one of the only moments in the novel that Cudjoe feels sexual desire for a Black woman (albeit a mediated one, since he is more interested in the "sacred residue" of King on Margaret's body than he is in Margaret herself). The only other time that Cudjoe shows concern for a woman of color is when he watches children playing in the fountain and focuses on one teenage girl he notices is at the beginning of her pubescent development (48). In this scene, the girl's entry into the world of sexual relations is framed in terms of predation, of suddenly curious boys "swarming" (48) around her. In both cases, the narrative frames Cudjoe watching someone else's desire, not his; *his* sexual interest is in observation, a seemingly detached spectatorship that, as I have mentioned earlier, enables a safe reconstitution of a heterosexist sexual economy.

In *every* other encounter with women, Cudjoe expresses sexual desire for *white* women. What is Cudjoe looking for, to repeat and qualify the question, in *white* women's bodies?[35] What is Wideman suggesting in male characters who continually look to white women as figures of desire? A key phrase that helps unlock this puzzle is repeated when Cudjoe, early in the novel, wonders about the woman in the apartment across the way, and thinks about his marital conflicts. Reading with the grain of the narrative, one explanation to the question emerges as Cudjoe describes this unnamed woman: "No name. No history. She was the body of woman. No beginning, middle, end to her life. All women. Any woman" (54). Later, Cudjoe reflects on this woman again and repeats the phrase, "All women" (55). The logic of Cudjoe's desire here is both inductive and deductive, more specifically inductive, *then* deductive; the unnamed woman becomes a representation of "all women," and therefore her generality can stand in for his specific object of desire: his estranged white wife, Caroline. All white women—in fact, white women's bodies—become metonymies, all like "the woman he'd married" (54). In this version, Cudjoe's constant return to Caroline has as much to do with his failed marriage with her as it does with her whiteness, of which Cudjoe is constantly aware and concerned. For, as he puts it when he imagines Margaret's silent judgment of him, his is a double failure: "How did they [Margaret and her sisters] know he'd failed his wife and failed those kids, that his betrayal was double, about blackness and about being a man?" (9–10). Casting himself as a "half-black someone, a half man" (10), Cudjoe makes explicit that his double failure, the sins of racial betrayal and masculine desertion, will continue to haunt him in the constant repetition of a white Everywoman. And that these neurotic returns to white womanhood result not in a recalibration of his masculinity, but rather in lapses into silence that suggest that his abandonment of Caroline and his "half-white" (notice, not half-Black) sons figure as the source, if not the origins, of his obsession. In this reading, it is, therefore, not insignificant or coincidental that Cudjoe's search for the mythic paternity of Simba also involves his constant fantasies of white women's bodies, for both reflect acts of contrition to somehow overcome his two familial betrayals that signify racial and conjugal failure.

It is difficult, however, not to read this desire for white womanhood the other way around, since much of the discourse around interracial sexual (primarily heterosexual) relationships testifies to the implicit racial power embedded within the sexual relations of Black men and white women. One cannot view the narrative's fascination with white women without recalling Fanon's chapter, "The Man of Color and the White Woman," in his classic study of Black psychology, *Black Skin, White Masks* (1952). Not unproblematically, Fanon would locate the Black man's desire for the white woman, coded as "white flesh" and "white whiteness," as the externalizing of his desire to be "worthy" of white love, to be "loved like a white man," and to be "a white man." For Fanon, the white woman remains the external object of the Black man's fundamental neurosis, a fundamental insecurity produced by a built environment of racism: "The neurotic structure of an individual is simply the elaboration, the formation, the eruption within the ego, of conflictual clusters arising in part out of the environment and in part out of the purely personal way in which that individual reacts to these influences" (81). But this deep neurotic structure within the Black man's psyche—the "purely personal way" of his adjustment to racial and sexual hierarchies—can only be overcome through collective, not individualist, endeavors, what Fanon refers to as a "restructuring of the world" (82). In this vision, Caroline and the other white women in the novel disappear into the abstracted figure of White Woman—"Any woman," as Cudjoe puts it—and serve as the object relation that signifies Cudjoe's Blackness and reminds him of an intrinsically damaged masculinity only reparable by a complete overturning of racial protocols.[36]

This repetition of a white Everywoman is most pronounced in Cudjoe's work to stage a production of *The Tempest* using local adolescents from the West Philadelphia neighborhood as the play's participants. His rendition of *The Tempest*—which the narrative describes as a tale of "colonialism, imperialism, recidivism, the royal fucking over of weak by strong, colored by white, many by few" (127)—is reminiscent of another anticolonial revision of Shakespeare's play, namely Aimé Césaire's *Une Tempête* (1969). Both redactions of the original play make act 1, scene 2, of vital importance in the development of the relations of power between Caliban, Prospero, and Miranda, for it is in this moment of Shakespeare's version that the characters' relationships expose most visibly the undercurrents of language, history, sexuality, exploitation, education, geography, and power. Clearly, both Cudjoe's and Césaire's versions make Caliban's desire to reclaim language of prime importance, whether it is Césaire's Caliban exclamation, "Uhuru!" during his initial entrance into the play, or Cudjoe's attempts to "derail the tale . . . that Mr. Caliban's behind is clean and unencumbered, good as anybody else's" (79).

But clearer still in placing the two revisions next to one another are the divergences in how the relations of power and the battle over language are exercised. And it is over the question of sexuality that the interpretations part company. Césaire's redaction first excises entirely the "abhorréd slave" speech, but more importantly turns Prospero's accusation of Caliban's attempted rape of Miranda into pure hoax. Rather than Shakespeare's Caliban responding with the taunting "O ho, O ho! Would't had been done!" Césaire's answers Prospero this way:

> Rape! Rape! Listen, you old goat, you're the one that put those dirty thoughts in my head. Let me tell you something: I couldn't care less about

your daughter, or about your cave, for that matter. If I gripe, it's on principle, because I didn't like living with you at all, as a matter of fact. (13)

Caliban's disavowal of Prospero's accusation demonstrates two elements
that Césaire wishes to highlight. First, the fact that Prospero is "the one
that put those dirty thoughts" in Caliban's mind recalls the critique of
the myth of the Black male rapist, certainly not an exclusively American
phenomenon (but readily prevalent in the United States), who threatens the
"sanctity" of white womanhood. Second, Caliban is simply not interested
in Miranda, as he has more important struggles to undertake—his freedom
from Prospero's oppression. Caliban's antagonism is not carnal at all, but
ideological ("it's on principle"); Césaire politicizes Caliban's sexuality by
submerging it, burying it so that the more pressing issue of emancipation
remains uncomplicated. For Césaire, the sexual dynamic in this triangulation between two men and one woman would obscure his overriding protest of colonial and racial exploitation by a white man over a Black man. So
he simply cites Caliban's sexuality but ignores it.

Cudjoe, on the other hand, hones in on the very thing that Césaire
wishes to avoid. The initial characterization of Caliban as a dreadlocked,
Rastafarian revolutionary railing against Prospero's gentrification of the
island gives way to the central attention of the play, Miranda's "abhorréd
slave" speech, and Caliban's commentary. Miranda does not, in Cudjoe's
dramaturgy, direct her speech to Caliban directly, but rather faces the audience, her speech turned into soliloquy: as Cudjoe advises, "Prospero and
Caliban should become as insubstantial as possible without actually exiting
the platform" (139). Such stage direction seeks to make her speech "unencumbered" (141) and reverse the prevailing construction of Miranda as the
projection of male desire onto a female body. By staging her speech "clear
of the shadow of their [Prospero's and Caliban's] lusting, Cudjoe seems to
suggest that it is in fact Miranda's racialized femininity that becomes the
basis upon which the two men articulate and frame their competing visions
of masculinity. Thus, Miranda's exclamation, "I endowed thy purposes,"
foregrounds that her white womanhood constitutes not only the language
by which Caliban can make himself known, but also the terms through
which Prospero has been able to assert his dominion over the island and
its inhabitants. Within the triangulated frame that Cudjoe has established,
with Miranda highlighted, stage front, and Prospero and Caliban receded
on opposite ends of the stage, Miranda determines, at least in this specific
moment, the contours of the struggle between the two men and their eternal
fight. Miranda is, as the narrative suggests, "their excuse" (141) for fighting, and she thus becomes of prime importance in how that fight is framed.

But Cudjoe is also clear in making the terms of this fight a sexual one, one that casts the definition of victory in terms of sexual conquest over Miranda. If Miranda's womanhood is "their excuse," phallic domination marks the language of the debate, the struggle to discover "what's secreted between her thighs" (141). Sandra Gilbert and Susan Gubar once likened the pen to a literary phallus; here, Prospero and Caliban reverse that comparison, as phallic symbols become, in effect, their instruments for deploying their power and control over the terms of identity and legitimacy:

> So it's Caliban who gets moved out, exiled, dispossessed, stranger in his own land, who gets named just about every beast in the ark, the bestiary, called out his name so often it's a wonder anybody remembers it and maybe nobody does. But is Caliban the snake on this island paradise or is the serpent wound round old Prospero's wand? Or is it Caliban's magic twanger, his Mr. William Wigglestaff he waggled at Miss Miranda and said: C'mere, fine bitch. Make this talk. (140)

The serpent in the Genesis myth is, of course, the figure of virility who makes available to Adam and Eve the capacity to see the world anew apart from God's eyes, to view the world with "knowledge," particularly sexual knowledge. In essence, the serpent joins sexuality with identity, since after acquiescing to the serpent's urge to eat the fruit, Adam and Eve "discover" themselves through one another: "Then the eyes of both were opened, and they knew that they were naked" (Genesis 3:7). Both Caliban and Prospero are aligned with the serpent metaphor, an assignment that ascribes to phallic virility the capacity to name, to give utterance to language and therefore identity to oneself and to another. The narrative here subtly shifts the terms by which both men define their masculinity, how they are "named." Initially, it is Prospero who creates the vocabulary by which we understand Caliban: he is a beast, figured as the mythic serpent. Caliban is the serpent, named by Prospero. Antagonistic masculinity, framed according to historic terms of opposition that establish separate arenas for U.S. white and Black men—most notably the racial divide between white humanity and black bestiality—shapes the relations between Prospero and Caliban, but it is clear that Prospero holds the cards of the lexicon of masculine identity. But enter Miranda, and the story shifts. No longer does the narrative pose Caliban *as* the serpent, but rather as *having* a serpent. This sudden yet subtle movement from being to having, from being a phallic symbol to owning one, transforms a prior antagonistic masculinity into complementary, even if competing, positions in which both Prospero and Caliban now wield the instrument to define. If Prospero asserts power through his "wand" over Caliban, Caliban uses his "magic twanger" over

Miranda. Prospero's serpent-wound wand grants him the capacity to name Caliban; but likewise, Caliban asserts his desire to control through his ambitions to rape Miranda, to make his penis talk.

Cudjoe does mention that Miranda's struggle to speak for herself is already travestied by Prospero's imprisoning domination, but more attention is paid to Caliban's fantasy of rape in order to weave through the complicated dynamics of this heterosexist and homosocial triangle. The connection between sexual violence and the reclamation of an oppositional, masculinist identity is made clear a few passages later, when Caliban offers his "blueprint for the future": "First, gimme. Then I'll be much obliged, he says. Flesh today. Word tomorrow is the proper order of business. Later, afterwards, we'll rap in that postcoital snuggle . . . [a]ll the talk we'll ever need" (142). Caliban's vision of liberation from his oppression by Prospero through Miranda conflates two contesting desires. On the one hand, Caliban wants to use sexual coercion to engender power over Miranda, to highlight the capacity of violence that he wields through his rape fantasy. On the other hand, Caliban tries to view this act as a consensual one, a conjugal encounter that will establish an interracial, sexual alliance of sorts between two people whose lives have been shaped by the figure of dominance, Prospero. The relationship between sexual coercion ("gimme") and alliance ("postcoital snuggle"), and the linking of this conflicting project to one of gaining mastery over the terms of identity and freedom for Caliban (and, in his view, Miranda), recalls Eldridge Cleaver's infamous section in *Soul on Ice,* in which Cleaver recounts how his definition of his robbed, Black "manhood" is crafted in the context of his inaccessibility—because of the U.S. history of mythologizing Black male rapists, the white sanctioning of lynching as a form of sexual control—to white women's bodies. Confronted by a combination of hatred and desire for white women, Cleaver articulates a demand, "We shall have our manhood," that invests sexual access to white women as a primary index of that will to Black masculinist power. Caliban's model, "flesh today word tomorrow," distills the process that Cleaver argues is the strategy for achieving this "manhood": sexual coercion will radically transform relations of power between white men, white women, and Black men. Flesh today, word tomorrow, Caliban asserts, and cancels out the antecedent "word" of a Black masculinity shaped by emasculated virility and unrealized power, and will engender a "word tomorrow" that develops a world tomorrow in which "liberated" Black men, with their white female bedfellows, rule.

Left out of this triangle, glaringly, are Black women.[37] Michele Wallace, more than a decade before Wideman crafted Cudjoe's revision of *The Tempest,* demystified this logic of Black masculinity—which she coined

"Black Macho"—by attacking the proponents of those like Cleaver who sought to construct their "manhood" through coercion and "access" to white women (not to mention homophobic diatribes against gay Black men as race and gender traitors). Arguing that the "Black Macho" reaffirmed the ideological conventions of American masculinist constructions of heroism and violence (including a sanctioned violence against women), Wallace makes especial note of the position Black women occupy in the logic of revolutionary macho:

> Black Macho allowed for only the most primitive notion of women— women as possessions, women as the spoils of war, leaving black women with no resale value. As a possession, the black woman was a symbol of defeat, and therefore of little use to the revolution except as the performer of drudgery (not unlike her role in slavery).
>
> The white man had offered white women privilege and prestige as accompaniments to his power. Black women were offered no such deal, just the same old hard labor, a new silence, and more loneliness. (68)

For Wallace, Black revolution against white oppression disintegrated when Black men focused their attention on "their genitals" (69) and aimed their "weapons"—guns and penises—at, respectively, white men and white women, while relegating Black women, "symbols of defeat," to the sidelines of the struggle for power. Cudjoe's Caliban follows this logic of the Black Macho, his fantasy of a new world order invested in the propagation of the interracial descendants of himself and Miranda. As he claims, these "generations of Calibans will grow up to be a full-fledged voting member of the United League of languages" (142).

Perhaps attuned to the critique that Wallace offers, Cudjoe tweaks the play even further, and proposes that a Black teenager play the part of Miranda. This substitution conflicts with Caliban's sexual fantasy of liberation, so it is most likely the case that, sensitive to the fact that his interpretation of *The Tempest* has all but left Black women out of the picture of this "revolution," Cudjoe is willing to sacrifice the dimensions of Black Macho that he has built up so extensively in the prior passages. But recalling the earlier detached spectatorship that he employs as he imagines both Margaret's affair with King and the young Black girl's entry into a predatory sexual world at the museum, we should regard the assumptions underlying Cudjoe's vision of the girl who will play Miranda. Like his recounting of the girl at the museum, Cudjoe focuses on the emerging, pubescent sexuality of this young woman and tries to relate this budding desire to Miranda's character: he analogizes Miranda to the unnamed girl's sister, who has "boys on her mind all the time" (143), and then prompts her:

"You're smiling. You know what I mean" (143). Gone are the references to Miranda as the object of sexual aggression. But then, as the narrative continues with Cudjoe discussing how women married and started families at a much younger age than today, the passage ends with a surprise, a shift that is accompanied by a change in the tone:

> Boys and girls fall in love. Right. Your sister likes boys and Miranda likes boys. Some things will be different, of course. In Shakespeare's day, when he wrote *The Tempest,* girls were married very young. Much younger than usual today. They started families at an age when we'd still consider them children.
>   Oh. Your sister does? Twins? (143)

The irony in the last line is unstable: at first glance, Cudjoe's incredulity reflects the extent to which he assumes anachronism between the play's setting and the actors' approach to Shakespeare's story. The girl knows much more of Miranda's experience than Cudjoe realizes, which signals to the reader how little he actually knows of the community and its teenagers, whom he wishes to help. But the more important irony is suggested in Cudjoe's exclamation, "Oh." This small outburst indicates a recognition of the girl's sister's experience, a familiarity that makes the following questions satirical, even cynical, reminders of the larger narrative's apparent knowledge of a social fact from which the last line makes perfect sense. We are, it seems, meant to respond with complex, conflicting emotions, the choked laughter at Cudjoe's ignorance and the resigned sigh of its familiar knowledge.

Wideman here undercuts Cudjoe's attempts to recuperate the agency of Black women in this rendition of *The Tempest* by lambasting satirically Cudjoe's ethos, and highlighting his distance from those in the neighborhood. Yet how the narrative achieves this makes for a more troubling satire, one that depends on the acceptance of another social narrative undergirding the identity of Black women throughout the novel. Certainly, we are meant to note with humor and sadness the fact that the girl's sister knows quite well Miranda's situation, of having children at such an early age, something that Cudjoe claims does not or is not supposed to happen today. (We can infer from earlier in the novel that the girl is eleven, her sister with twins therefore thirteen years old.) There's the ironic rub that turns the passage satirical: children who aren't supposed to "get" Miranda indeed seem to understand, because these same children are already living that life. But the irony created by Cudjoe's sudden recognition "Oh" necessitates an acceptance of this "fact"—the "fact" of Black, teenage, unwed mothers who are "abnormally" bearing children at younger and younger ages.

We know how Charles Murray would react to this passage: he would cast this scene in the light of what he perceives to be the social legacy of the Great Society initiatives of the late 1960s, whose welfare programs not only erode the work ethic, traditional nuclear family structure, and therapeutic self-reliance, but more important for Murray produce the much-touted "culture of dependency," which fosters out-of-wedlock motherhood for young, urban women. Like the seeming clarity and authority of journalism, Wideman's commentary on this young girl's sister grants Murray's neoconservative thesis the capacity to personify this young mother's situation as a communal emblem of that which is articulated in *Losing Ground*. The ironic humor of the passage works *only* if we accept the narrative that gives impetus to Wideman's depiction, that the young mother is indeed a social "fact" that needs no further response, just the grudging acknowledgment of the existence of this societal problem. It is, therefore, not coincidental that the passage breaks off after Cudjoe asks these apparently rhetorical questions, "Your sister does? Twins?" Murray has already put into place the convention, the argument that makes further inquiry into this scene appear unnecessary.

But if we are skeptical of Murray's claims as well as his assumptions and conclusions, then Wideman's passage leaves us with the quandary of explaining this sudden emergence of this young girl's sister, what this passage is doing, particularly since this is a rare moment in which Cudjoe encounters Black women. Even if we provisionally assume that this young mother may stand in as Wideman's communal symbol of the status of urban Black women, we might provide another context from which to wrest this passage against the grain of its ironic depiction of a "culture of dependency." Black women in deindustrialized, hypersegregated spaces are no less immune from conditions of destitution than their male counterparts, sites of exploitation that structure agencies whose life choices neoconservatives like Murray profoundly misunderstand at best, and at worst pathologize and discredit. As Stephanie Coontz argues, the rising proportion of single-parent, mostly female-headed households is the *effect*, not the cause of the protracted crisis in urban, Black communities.[38] Within the social context of heterosexual relationships, Coontz cites the social costs of the restructured political economy of the 1980s—hypersegregation, deindustrialization, capital and white flight, chronic unemployment, hemorrhaging of public coffers, abandonment of public infrastructure—as the main culprit driving the rising numbers of single-parent households during this decade. Asserting that familial decisions cannot be understood unless considered in view of the structured availability of economic choices, Coontz offers the following report: "Much growth in black female-headed family poverty is merely a 'reshuffling' of economic distress. . . . Two out of every three poor blacks living in single-parent families were poor *before* their families split up. . . . [T]he poverty of female-headed families is due more to job structure than to family structure" (251). The "facts" of a teenager bearing children and single motherhood, in Coontz's view, bear witness to political economic conditions that produce specific, gendered responses by Black women to widespread impoverishment felt by both men and women. To focus our eyes on the young girl would be a mistake, according to Coontz, for single-parent households direct us instead to the general illness of the contemporary political economy and its attendant urban landscape.

Coontz's counterreading enables us to reconsider how this short passage operates in the narrative *and* to reject the seeming "truth" of this young mother. Cudjoe's encounter with this mother's sister, who is to play Miranda, forces him out of his reverie of a Caliban enacting sexual vengeance on white women to assert a masculinist response to white (male) dispossession of Black territory. His rewriting of *The Tempest* simply ends, and the production's failure is finalized by a rain that washes out all the work that Cudjoe had put into this project (149). Cudjoe's fantasy has offered a paradigm of rebellion and resistance that would only work for the possible recuperation of Black men into the circuit of normative masculinity, that would only succeed if power were exercised through the bodies of white women. But his vision of *The Tempest* does not grant space to Black women, indeed it does not even begin to grasp the profundity of the conditions and the complexity of solutions necessary to confront the situation of Black men *and* women. Caliban's liberation from Prospero through his rape of Miranda, far from being an attack on systemic forces that have produced the prevailing destitution and dispossession of the landscape, can never achieve its goal, nor can it offer programmatic gestures toward this freedom: locked in this paradigm, the play always ends up with Caliban defeated, further shunted to the margins of the island: "Play got to end the way it always does. Prospero still the boss" (144). So momentary in the narrative, it is the figure of the young mother—not even present, but only traced by her sister—who compels Cudjoe to exclaim "oh" and shatters the model of resistance that leaves Black women out, even if, and especially if, the sister is to play the part of Miranda.

Cudjoe's fantasy of Caliban asserting freedom through white women clearly stems from his own experience with women, most of whom have been white. To this extent, his fantasy of using *The Tempest* and rewriting that story as a template, an allegory, to explain the conditions within Black communities in the wake of the MOVE disaster seem almost logical. But then Cudjoe would not be Caliban; he would be Ariel, and indeed an Ariel studying how to be a Prospero. As the "airy spirit" who serves Prospero, whom Cudjoe describes as "that evil little CIA covert operations motherfucker" (144), and who in *The Tempest* performs all the work that Prospero requires to maintain power on the island, Ariel plays the role of collaborator, the one for whom power and freedom are promised if he provides service to the one who wields power and authority. Ariel gains freedom, not by active and visible rebellion against Prospero, but by his willingness to do all that Prospero commands. Following this road to success, Ariel maps out in the play what Cudjoe eventually does in his own life: after the failure of the play, Cudjoe abandons his commitments to the children and goes to graduate school, to enter institutional halls to escape what he ultimately views as a hopeless affair. Though full of guilt, Cudjoe decides that he cannot stomach the conditions of the community that he serves, and that this reality cannot be undone or transformed by the performance of another, the play: "When I was teaching, every day I'd go home with a sad feeling, a guilty feeling, knowing I should have done so much more. And that's what kept me coming back. It's also what finally drove me away. Running, talking to myself. Tail between my legs" (150). Although the reference to his "tail" aligns him with Caliban from earlier in the narrative (Cudjoe's project is, as he claims, to "Derail the tale" that "Mr. Caliban's behind is clean and unencumbered" [131]), Cudjoe regards his decision to pursue his own ambitions as a calculated act of betrayal and a sign of cowardice: these are not the characteristics of his Caliban, but of his vision of Ariel. In fact, Cudjoe may even regard his Ariel-like decision as a step toward becoming a proto-Prospero, as it is Prospero who is, according to Cudjoe, the "one with the tail" (131).

It is here that we see most clearly how Wideman's narrative employs Cudjoe to speak a language of rebellion and resistance, to "derail de tale" of Black pathology and expose the underpinnings of Black destitution, but whose language remains inadequate to effect anything more than the felt contradictions of a guilty soul who has left the scene of a social crime. Cudjoe's guilt acts out the profound limitation, even failure, of his narrative powers to do what Giacometti argues can be done: that the work of narrating through the lens of experience, to turn that experience into aesthetic practice, and then to enable that perceived reality of the artist to become, not just mimic, known reality (the "realism" and "naturalism" to which J. B. refers in the last section of the novel) cannot attend to the historic immensity of Black communities in the throes of economic devastation and desperate survival. It is in this act of waking up to the realization that Cudjoe can never be Caliban, but must always play Ariel, that Wideman's voice erupts most poignantly in the narrative: "Why this

Cudjoe, then? This *airy other* floating into the shape of my story. Why am I him when I tell certain parts? Why am I hiding from myself? Is he mirror or black hole?" (122; my emphasis). Psychoanalysis teaches us that the "mirror" that Wideman considers Cudjoe to be is *also* his "black hole"; Cudjoe occupies a certain lack, an incompleteness or absence, that engenders the construction, through language, of a mirror image through which Wideman attains his identity, his subjectivity. Likening this incomplete mirror to Ariel, Wideman ascribes to himself the very same self-conscious anxiety that he narrates in the figure of Cudjoe. Confronted by the realization that his narrative is powerless to depict and transform the present condition of Black Philadelphia, even unable to attend to his own son's condition in prison—and thus implying the connection in both—Wideman demonstrates in this identification with Cudjoe-cum-Ariel that his is a narrative locked in the prison house of complicity. This narrative collaboration is upheld by the historic forces of the decade, which enable Wideman's creation of Cudjoe and the character's attendant explorations of masculinity, yet which also preclude this masculinity from reaching beyond its specific, brokered state, and result in its eventual alienation from that language of resistance so sought after by Cudjoe's fantasy as Caliban.

We are a long way from Margaret's Cynicism and MOVE's willful destitution. And perhaps this is the point: Cudjoe listens to Margaret but cannot hear her; Wideman sees Cudjoe's failure, but can imagine no other vision to replace this failed one. Cudjoe's response to the MOVE tragedy and to Margaret's testimony revolves around the recuperation of a mythic paternity and salvific figure whose exceptional masculinity would bring messianic promise in the wake of the low-intensity genocide of Black communities in Philadelphia. Likewise, Wideman ultimately turns Cudjoe's journey not into a *bildung* of new capacities for struggle, but into a search whose path already returns to the character's own implication in the resigned, guilt-ridden vocabulary of failure. Both Wideman and his "airy other" are committed writers, struggling to create that exceptional sculpture of liberation's promise, whose solitary act of narration leads them to confront the political economic and racial conditions of Black communities with the resignation of their own paucity. But Cudjoe never finishes his novel and never finds Simba; Wideman does craft a narrative, but finds no redemption by its end or through its completion. By the end of the two men's travails, we, the readers of Cudjoe's journey and Wideman's exploration of Black masculinities in Philadelphia during the 1980s, are far off from Margaret and MOVE, because what they offer instead—the alternative vision of Cynical, willfully destitute, communal resistance, not encumbered by the myths of Black paternity or violent, even sexual, entry into the white world—cannot be shared by the two men. For to attend to Margaret, to MOVE, to the foreclosed space of Black women's agency in the constructed world of *The Tempest* in West Philadelphia, would challenge the primacy of the writer's agency in mitigating urban triage, even if his narrative, determined by its necessary negotiation with the larger historical "naturalism" of Black Philadelphia in the 1980s, exposes its anxieties and the failures of this very agency, the mirror actually a Black hole.

Not surprisingly, the consequences of brokered masculinity—that which bars and controls, rather than models and leads the way—become clear in the final scene of the novel, in which Cudjoe attends a rally commemorating the anniversary of the MOVE bombing. Sparsely attended, Cudjoe considers the event a failure. In fact, the various facets that the narrative has explored with regard to Cudjoe's masculinist journey weigh heavily on how he perceives the rally, as well as its participants. Cudjoe is filled, not with the energy that comes from a public gathering, but with the cynicism that stems from the felt powerlessness of one who ascribes to himself a certain capacity or agency. A white woman gives him a candle for the vigil portion of the event, and Cudjoe judges her appearance and denigrates her good intentions: "She is his mother's age. She's overdressed for the heat. Cudjoe doesn't want to feel sorry for her. A faint mustache he tries to ignore above her determined lip" (194–95). Viewing her through the same sexualized lens with which he has viewed and judged and constructed elaborate fantasies of other women, Cudjoe feels no attraction to her, loses interest in her presence, and moves on to look at others. Later, during the actual vigil, some Black men share candlelight with Cudjoe, causing him to sardonically think to himself, "Clever, clever" (196). Casting the sharing of flame in drug vocabulary, Cudjoe views this ceremonial lighting as isolated points of feeble light, not the incandescence of a growing community: "Another man gets a hit from Cudjoe" (196). And while he finds no sentiment to share with the others in Independence Square, Cudjoe does revel in the revolutionary chant of one "dreadlocked priest," whose performance ritually resembles the energy of Cudjoe's fantasy of Caliban; yet while he fixates on this man who pounds, through voice and drum, "Fire fire fire" (196), Cudjoe cites and then all but ignores the work of Black women on the stage: "Two black women read short poems" (196).

These communal acts of commemoration, the rituals and artistic production of remembrance, however scattered and paltry, gesture to a different mode of making a "model," a sculpture of the city that maps out social relations not in terms of a singular figure fighting against his own complicity, but in the creation of a collective vocabulary struggling to hold accountable the state's repression of another group—MOVE—who created an alternative vision of community. As with MOVE, this gathering is messy, and only modestly effective in articulating its protest voice. Wideman narrates this scene through the embittered eyes of Cudjoe, who only sees a legacy of defeat: unable to take seriously the possibility of horizontal relationship with others in the gathering, the basis for a willed, intentional community, Cudjoe opts to compare the apparent impotence of this rally with another vertical, historical moment of Black defeat: the driving out of Blacks from Independence Square during the Fourth of July celebration in 1805. For Wideman's character, the commemoration of the MOVE tragedy can lead only to cynical reflection that mirrors his own sense of complicity: "The victors repossess the square." And for those now in the square, he hears not the articulate, if provisional, cry for justice, but imagines those around him from a perspective not unlike the eyes and ears of an agent of the state: "Cudjoe hears footsteps behind him. A mob howling his name. Screaming for blood. Words come to him, cool him, stop him in his tracks. He'd known them all his life. *Never again. Never again.* He turns to face whatever it is rumbling over the stones of Independence Square" (199). Looking to history as the story of defeat, and hearing little more than the sound and fury of those in the present, Cudjoe turns to face those who will, despite his cynical abandonment, continue to voice the sounds of Cynicism, to rail against the institutions that wish to forget atrocity and continue to alienate and abandon destitute communities its has helped to produce. Whether the sounds of a mob will force our figure of the contemporary talented tenth to not only turn around to look, but also to walk in the other direction remains unclear. It is the ambivalence of Cudjoe's posture, looking back at a struggling community but still walking ahead on his own, that is Wideman's own troubled, brokered, even broken, sculpture, a model of himself writing in a world "begging for attention," and finding that the finished product is the unnerving portrait of a stranger.

5

Whiteness, Virile Masculinity, and Viral Satire

> Forget that I'm white. Never forget that I'm white.
> —Mary Foulke

Where the city yields in its layered histories buried lives, those who, like the MOVE dead, warrant novels of lamentation from a writer like Wideman, it also offers urban graves upon which Tom Wolfe dances with glee. But if Black grief provokes white laughter, racial grievance of the dispossessed foments the anger—and fear—of the privileged. The richest of New York's boroughs, Manhattan, is an island surrounded by what Saskia Sassen calls a ring of poverty, and the natural barriers of the East and Hudson Rivers can only filter, but not prevent, the wretched of the earth, who have made homes in this global city, from dissimulating the fantasy of unbounded prosperity *after* they have been disaggregated from Gotham's globalizing economy and excess state capacity. The truly advantaged awaken from reveries of great white ways and confront borne social fruit, that in repressing the delayed promise of urban unrest they must enclose themselves into ever more obsessive containers of security in this same space. And as perverse smiles wither into hardened grimaces, there is a felt loss in the realization that white privilege does not necessarily mean protection. In the 1980s, New York regained its status as a world city, the de facto broker of global finance, but even as money poured into the city and infused the affluent (though not necessarily talented) tenth with unimaginable wealth, one could not help but feel that something was lost in the way of white assumptions of power, that there was something anxious that made people hold on

144

ever more dearly to their racial possessive investment. We are left to wonder, then, if this loss that turns to racial anxiety is different from the others explored in this study, whether white anxiety in the 1980s qualitatively differs from that of cultural workers of color, or if it is simply a difference in degree.

Usually, Tom Wolfe shakes his anxiety off with Nietzschean laughter, but there are days—and moments in his work—when his shrugs reveal a dead seriousness and incredulity. Not taken to the kind of casuistry that others opine about the disuniting of America, Wolfe nevertheless reckons with the fact that he is a citizen of a nation turning brown and a resident of a city leading the way. In this regard, and perhaps in this regard only, he and June Jordan, whom we encountered at the beginning of this study, agree. And when that day comes, that demographic tipping point in the United States, Jordan and Wolfe may both be laughing, but his will be forced, widened eyes betraying latent worry about his future. Wolfe's oft-cited "literary manifesto for the new social novel," really an apologia for his massive novel published two years earlier, locates one of the main impetuses of writing *Bonfire of the Vanities* (1987) in the tectonic shifts of New York's contemporary racial and ethnic demography: "New York and practically every other large city in the United States are undergoing a profound change. The fourth great wave of immigrants—this one from Asia, North Africa, Latin America, and the Caribbean—is now pouring in. Within ten years political power in most major American cities will have passed to the nonwhite majorities" ("Stalking," 51–52). Wolfe is wrong on this final point. Ten years later, the two most immigrant-rich, culturally diverse cities in the United States, Los Angeles and New York, were helmed by white Republicans who led a palpably nonwhite, urban plurality. But notwithstanding his error in prophecy, Wolfe reveals in this passage a rare moment of tonal earnestness. His trademark posture of the anachronistic, urbane dandy—most obvious in photo shoots, but evident also in the audacity (vanity?) of his use of "manifesto"—melts when he narrates his own reaction to the changing face of the city in which he lives and about which he writes. "Does that," Wolfe asks about this new, nonwhite immigration, "render these cities incomprehensible, fragmented beyond the grasp of all logic, absurd, meaningless to gaze upon in a literary sense? Not in my opinion" (52).

Wolfe is also mistaken that this last great wave of immigration signals a qualitatively different shift in racial tolerance of "nonwhite" newcomers to the United States. Although the criterion of national origin was firmly abolished with the Immigration Act of 1965, the United States has almost always regarded each successive wave of immigration as perfunctory influxes of nonwhites, as potential threats to established understandings of whiteness. As Noel Ignatiev, David Roediger, and Karen Brodkin have assessed, Irish and Jewish immigration from the late nineteenth and early twentieth centuries were seen by American nativists to threaten the ground of white supremacy upon which the United States was founded. That slavery could no longer serve as the basis through which the category of "free white men" would be determined to mark U.S. citizenship produced new state reassertions of what constituted whiteness in the wake of U.S. cities' growing heterogeneity. The power of white supremacy has always been in crisis; and this crisis has compelled the architects of whiteness to work feverishly to transform its boundaries in order to maintain its power. "In the closing decades of the nineteenth century," David Theo Goldberg observes, "heterogeneity in the metropoles—including American towns and cities—was becoming palpable, and so undeniable. Thus emerged a shift to reestablishing and reimposing the artifice of homogeneity in the name of whiteness" (177). In the latter half of the twentieth century, we have become so used to particular ideas about racial identities and groups that we forget that the contours of race have always been in flux, that definitions of whiteness have been much more elastic than its rhetoric of sameness asserts. Immigration has been viewed almost always as a movement of nonwhite people into the United States; whites have simply embraced, not without contention, some of these new groups as their own. What makes this "fourth wave" different is not Wolfe's rendering of its demographic nonwhite so much as it is the response to this newest threat to whiteness. If the cultural imperative, thanks to multiculturalism, no longer rests in the strident adoption of nonwhites into the orbit of whiteness, and palatable strands of "ethnic" identity are now celebrated to smooth over the machinations of urban triage, then what changes are in store for whiteness and, by extension, for "white" people, to avoid their racial obsolescence? If civil rights and liberation movements compelled whites to accept, however grudgingly, the seizure and uneven expansion of social rights, then what are white people, living in urban spaces of racial heterogeneity, to do in order to survive? What does whiteness mean in the age of multiculturalism, and how does urban triage mitigate this crisis in meaning?

For Wolfe, writing about New York City bears this historical and cultural—and most importantly, ethical—profundity. His reference to the "fourth wave" of immigration of the late twentieth century enables him to hearken back to the era of the first great migration of people into the United States, a century and a half earlier. Back then, Wolfe recounts, the immigrants hailed from Germany and Ireland.[1] The decades of the mid-nineteenth century seemed no less apocalyptic than the sense of time and space disjointed in *Bonfire*'s age: the moral pacifism of abolitionism would see its hopes for emancipation by rational persuasion and spiritual revival dashed in the infamous Compromise of 1850; crestfallen abolitionists would ultimately find their model of liberation in the 1859 attack on Harper's Ferry by the militant race traitor John Brown, who, at his execution, prophetically exclaimed, "The crimes of this *guilty, land will* never be purged *away*; but with Blood" (quoted in Erkkila, 124). With the country edging ever closer to war over these enslaved inhabitants within its borders, U.S. cities, particularly New York, were absorbing thousands of migrants from non-Protestant nations, an influx of people who electrified nativist, xenophobic sensibilities and generated anti-immigrant societies such as the Know-Nothings. Divinity's Judgment Day, it appeared, was coming as an earthy mass of the Black and the catholic, the Celestial and the swarthy, to topple the idolatry of white supremacy.

Slavery and immigration served as the flashpoints for delineating U.S. destiny, the seething conversation bubbling into pitched battles that formed the tableau for the New York writer of his day, Walt Whitman. And although he is best known for revolutionizing the poetic line—that formal break from the tyranny of eighteenth-century modes to which American writers remained captive—Whitman's innovations in his 1855 *Leaves of Grass* were evidence that New York's changing demography and the political turbulence in the United States demanded new poetry.[2] The era in which he lived did not just determine his work, but enabled his writing to make poetic stuff from what seemed to be otherwise disjointed meaninglessness. And for this reason, Betsy Erkkila submits, "[W]hat makes Whitman unique as an artist . . . is his embeddedness in his time rather than his transcendence of it" (10). The ways Whitman made this embeddedness manifest in *Leaves of Grass* have become trademarks: the encyclopedic catalog of images, people, landscapes; the juxtaposition of contradictions in order to "contain multitudes"; the absorption of different personae into the ever-present "I."[3]

But the containment of ethnic multitudes, their assimilation, has demanded of them strict allegiance to the prerogatives of whiteness. Twentieth-century immigration history, and indeed the appeals to U.S. law to expand civil rights to heretofore marginalized groups, reveals the extent to which those considered nonwhite were compelled to use the logic of white supremacy to yield material gain. The previous chapters in this study have underscored the power of this logic: Asian American mobility in "A Fire in Fontana" depends on structural alignment with whiteness alongside rhetorical affiliation with Blackness; but Blackness itself is broken open by the instrumental complicity of its contemporary talented tenth; even the Chicana/o space of resistance must accede to the imperatives of private property that first benefit whites before offering its Brown neighbors shelter. If contemporary multiculturalism has done anything, it has rendered visible the power of whiteness, for all to see and for some to enter, but it has not prevented or diminished the power upon which interrogations of whiteness rest: white supremacy. The flexibility of whiteness to embrace the colored few forces open a split between a cultural whiteness that demands a fascism of homogeneity and a structural whiteness that accepts ethnic difference into racial similarity, as long as order is maintained, the Law protected, and the dynamic map of urban triage unfettered. But even flexible whiteness still begets anxiety; the history of white absorption of immigrant ethnics has been nothing but contentious. Whitman's embracing "I" may signify the tenuous acceptance of the U.S. body politic reconstituted along ever expanding ethnic pools, but it cannot hold together the multitudes without the larger sense that flexible whiteness's gain also entails cultural loss in whiteness. In each case of a group "becoming" white, there has always been the threat, even if ultimately placated, that white supremacy's belt might snap as it consumes and claims yet another community as one of its own.

Such is the debt to whiteness, that its wage or possessive investment demands of its beneficiaries allegiance and action that they can never fully repay. Nor is whiteness an imperative that we can refuse to acknowledge, even if that acknowledgment takes on the stance of refusal or rejection. It is, of course, neither natural nor biological—even neoconservatives argue this much. But it is a real social currency, as much a status of truth as money is, as Marx wrote, at bottom, a sign of real social relations. But if whiteness and material accumulation are like each other insofar as they depend on the surplusing of others' power and labor—and toward the end of this chapter, I will suggest that there is more than simply a metaphoric relation—that surplus is not sustainable. Marx's valuable insight into the commodity does not turn on, as some postmodernists have argued, the commodification of everything, the replacement of simulacra for real social relations, or, as mechanistic Marxism might put it, that everything, every interaction can and should be distilled into economic terms. His real contribution to the commodity lies in his analysis of the *kind* of social relation the commodity, most visible in money, produces: commodities, like whiteness, depend on the expropriation and therefore *exploitation* of value—and people—for its sustenance. Eventually, the insatiable logic of money, the valorization of capital, turns the earth into a "universal means of production" (Smith, *New Urban,* 78), the roundness of the world flattened to create differentiations of value and the extraction of profit.[4] Whiteness demands of its adherents more bodies to break, more faces to ridicule, more cultures to negate so that its power retains the fiction of its omnipotence. But the tendency is for the rate of profit to decline, for accumulation to slow, for the machine to come to a halt; as this chapter argues through a reading of *The Bonfire of the Vanities,* whiteness's historical hoarding of the social wage—what some call democracy, or what others might call public space or the public sphere—cannot continue indefinitely. Eventually, it feeds on itself, eats up its own children, its embrace of others into its gated community tightening to become a grip of death.

Whereas Whitman's metaphorical vehicle of immigrant bodies yields a tenor of social embrace[5] and a will to produce a larger poetics of material and spiritual abundance, Wolfe deploys in his prologue to *Bonfire* a similar image of clamoring outsiders, but for an altogether different narrative of fear and scarcity. Like Whitman's challenge to his reader, Wolfe's tone—in the persona of the besieged mayor of New York in a Harlem town meeting—is sarcastic toward a white audience. But Whitman's satirical portrait of his reader is meant to enlarge the social arena to encompass all bodies; the mayor's audience in *Bonfire* is complacent with the onslaught of a mob verging on the chaotic potential of a riot. Consider the parodic inflection of this Whitmanian passage, monologued internally by the mayor:

Come down from your swell co-ops, you general partners and merger lawyers! It's the Third World down there! Puerto Ricans, West Indians, Haitians, Dominicans, Cubans, Colombians, Hondurans, Koreans, Chinese, Thais, Vietnamese, Ecuadorians, Panamanians, Filipinos, Albanians, Senegalese, and Afro-Americans! Go visit the frontiers, you gutless wonders! Morningside Heights, St. Nicholas Park, Washington Heights, Fort Tryon—*por qué pagar más*! The Bronx—the Bronx is finished for you! Riverdale is just a little freeport up there! Pelham Parkway—keep the corridor open to Westchester! Brooklyn—*your* Brooklyn is no more! Brooklyn Heights, Park Slope—little Hong Kongs, that's all! And Queens! Jackson Heights, Elmhurst, Hollis, Jamaica, Ozone Park—whose is it? Do you know? . . . You don't think the future knows how to cross a *bridge*? And you, you Wasp charity-ballers sitting on mounds of money up in your co-ops with the twelve-foot ceilings and the two wings, one for you and one for the help, do you really think you're impregnable? And you German-Jewish financiers who have finally made it into the same buildings, the better to insulate yourselves from the *shtetl* hordes, do you really think you're insulated from the *Third World*? (7)

Whitman's poetic embrace of his New York landscape gives way to Wolfe's discombobulating litany of a city fragmented, but the anxiety evident in this passage yields three points through which Wolfe's narrative vision tries to render meaning from this fragmentation and save it from "absurd, meaningless" panic. First, a consistent thread throughout this study is the racial mapping of urban space, which in the mayor's musings is staged in terms of neighborhood and borough—whites occupy only portions of Manhattan, Staten Island, upstate New York counties, and Long Island suburbs, while people of color reside in every other section of the city. Brooklyn, Queens, the Bronx, Harlem, once the workhorse boroughs of industrial New York are now aligned with the "Third World" and have become frontier spaces, no longer inhabitable or passable by white New York without fear. Second, with the contraction of traversable space for whites in New York, the historical privilege granted to whites through their whiteness—those who reside in the "swell co-ops" with even segregated wings—has become a social handicap. Social insulation, material over-abundance, and presumed power, hoarded through the possessive invest-ment of whites in the political economy of the 1980s, have produced the contradictory result of a white identity enervated and ultimately doomed to face the apocalyptic onslaught of a colored invasion crossing the bridge into Manhattan. Third, Wolfe narrates this multicultural confrontation between complacent whites and seething others through a satirical mode that offers a terrain, if not the pathway, toward a corrective to save white-ness from its debilitating destiny. But this satire is double-layered: the first, the mayor's harsh critique of his white audience, demands that white New York wake up from its privileged slumber; the second involves Wolfe's sat-ire of the mayor's strident admonition, which blankets the mayor's anger to evince a "token fantasy" of a restored whiteness, one that enables white New York to once again take over the streets that have been supposedly ceded to the members of the great "fourth wave."[6]

Wolfe's parody of a Whitmanian geography poses for us the historical limit of the expansive horizon posed 150 years earlier, a boundary I sieve through the multicultural filter of this study. Whitman may not have imagined his New York so Brown, Black, and Tan, but the logic of his poetics—and Wolfe recognizes this—demands that a white writer must not only share space with, but engage the symbolic and cultural signifi-cance of these demographic shifts. What is finally ironic, if not consciously satirical, about Wolfe's passage and his claims of mapping the "billion-footed beast" of New York in this present age is the discontinuity that Liam Kennedy has noted: despite his supposed intentions to narrate mean-ing out of a city so diverse, Wolfe's novel falls far short of representing a "polyglot metropolis" and opts instead to "construct a narrative of two cities—represented by the black Bronx and white Wall Street/Park Avenue—and focalizes [sic] all the action through the consciousness of the white protagonists" ("It's the Third World," 96). Moreover, the novel rehearses the dual city paradigm through the consciousness of its white *male* protagonists, white men living in the aftermath of the heyday of militant civil rights, Black power, and feminist movements. Distilling the experiences of the new immigrants of New York through the crucible of a Black/white historical landscape—note how the litany of immigrant groups ends with U.S.-born "Afro-Americans"—Wolfe's novel anachronistically but tellingly enacts the racial story of New York City in the 1980s of how white men, wading in their assumed privilege, slowly lose their power to everyone else. Crucial to understanding the narrative's critique of white male blindness and insulation is the satirical mode that Wolfe employs, for it is through satire that whiteness can be both lambasted and reconstituted. Moreover, and more importantly, satire acts as both a sword and a shield; incisively attacking the social tableau and political economic terrain on which white male identity rests, Wolfe is also able to cushion his pedantic vision of what whiteness must become in order to survive in New York City in the 1980s. Satire works to assert a militant whiteness in the urban context of *Bonfire*'s "Third World" New York, a racial will to power adequate enough to struggle in the increasingly Manichaean and Machiavellian world of New York's "real" social relations.

For Wolfe, two groups of people ostensibly control New York: the "Masters of the Universe," those who trade bonds on Wall Street, and those who work for "the Power," the judicial system of which we see most in "Gibraltar," the Bronx courthouse. Notwithstanding the unholy alliance between the opportunistic black minister, Reverend Bacon, and the alcoholic British tabloid reporter and sole immigrant in the novel, Peter Fallow, *Bonfire* stages those who control the money and manage the law as the city's wielders of power. Both groups are white and for Wolfe, the whiteness of the social and political elite of the city is of prime importance. Whiteness, early on in the novel, is equated with privilege, a privilege more imbued by the legacy of inheritance than by the member's individual diligence. And it is this inherited status of whiteness that Wolfe will continually ridicule throughout the novel, as the main reason for the enervation of whiteness in an age of conspicuous white privilege.

Inherited privilege is most visible through the spaces that gird those within. Just as a poor white man donning a police uniform grants that person, otherwise powerless in society, the authority of the state and the capacity of state violence, so does Kramer, otherwise a frumpy, overworked lawyer, feel the thrill of being part of the Power whenever he walks in Gibraltar. And as much as Sherman, the novel's model Master of the Universe, would like to believe that his company is "a respecter only of performance" (62), the fact that not one woman or person of color is a bond trader in his company belies Sherman's capacity to hold such a job as having more to do with the space in which he works. Space, like language, determines agency. Space, also like language, attains its meaning through its changing history, which in turn recalibrates a person's identity within that temporally specific spatial meaning. Both Kramer's and Sherman's white privilege emerge as products of the particular sites of authority, not only the space's particular geography, but also each space's history. And it is through this history that Wolfe establishes the specific brand of whiteness that the two characters occupy and for which they deserve satirical ribbing.

In describing the place in which Kramer works, Gibraltar, or the Bronx County Building, Wolfe notes not only the edifice's architecture, but the origins of the building's construction. Kramer's narrative of nostalgia for "poor sad Jewish Bronx," this recounting of the transformation of the Bronx County Building into Gibraltar reveals the changing meaning of the structure within the larger urban landscape. Once a symbol of the democratic vista open to European immigrants of the early twentieth century, Gibraltar now appears anachronistic in its setting: "The building was a prodigious limestone pantheon done in the early thirties in the Civic Moderne style. It was nine stories high and covered three city blocks, from 161st Street to 158th Street. Such open-faced optimism they had, whoever dreamed up that building back then!" (38). Clearly a building designed to represent monumental stature beyond functional use, Gibraltar's imposing structure stirs a wellspring of nostalgia within Kramer, who still feels its symbolic power as he walks to work. But such romantic visions of the building and of its builders' "open-faced optimism" are replete with the irony of Gibraltar's history. Its moment of construction (the 1930s) and its architectural style (Civic Moderne) definitely place Gibraltar's origins during the depression, a moment in U.S. history not usually known for open-faced optimism.[7] The 1930s marked a unique moment in U.S. history in which massive unemployment reached not only its usual victims (the working class, both industrial and rural) but also pulled down many from presumably "professional" echelons, architects included. The construction of Gibraltar coincides with the massive public works projects instituted by the Roosevelt administration to mitigate what was turning out to be a crisis decade for not only the United States, but world capitalism. Alongside better-known acronyms such as the WPA, the depression-instigated public works programs enabled the construction of hundreds of federal buildings, all of which enjoyed artistically innovative, modern stylistics as a result of the architectural creativity of out-of-work designers. It would be, for all intents and purposes, the first and last time that the United States would dabble in a national project to state-sponsor a cultural vision, a nascent socialist aesthetics on American soil.

The "optimism" to which Kramer ascribes the building therefore takes on new meaning if we consider more closely these historical specificities. The details of the building that Kramer notices—"classical figures at every corner . . . noble Romans wearing togas in the Bronx!" (38)—have less to do with the builders' "golden dream of an Apollonian future" (38) than with the architects' relation to a political economy in the 1930s whose ethos was to lift up an entire nation, not just perpetuate its wealthy elite (who were seen as having brought the country into this deplorable situation). The Bronx County Building was a monument meant to remind the surrounding residents that the state could sustain when capitalism could or would not, that the building was a sign of much more that the state would provide its citizens.[8] In an era of crisis, austerity, and decline, this building stood on the edge of a social hope built on the grounds of a political economy designed to expand resources in a decade of sheer survival and material desperation.

Kramer looks upon Gibraltar fifty years later, in an age of unsurpassed wealth and abundance, and sees the building not as a monument, but as a fortress. Where once the architecture and place of Gibraltar on top of a hill implied innovative capacity and symbolic hope, now the building's designs serve as a useful model to protect its workers from those it is meant to regulate, survey, and incarcerate. The space outlying the building, Franz Sigel Park, which was revitalized and landscaped in the early 1970s for the surrounding Bronx community, bears the characteristics of a moat, rather than a shared public arena. Buffered by a perceived "no-man's land" park, those ensconced in the county building fear going outside even for a midday lunch ostensibly because of brazen criminality, but actually because the criminals are not white.[9] Wolfe makes clear that the landscape around Gibraltar, seen through the eyes of the white workers, is racialized and therefore regarded as dangerous, criminalized space and not as the site of public commensality: "They stayed inside the building, this island fortress of the Power, of the white people, like himself [Kramer], this Gibraltar in the poor sad Sargasso Sea of the Bronx" (39). This passage is doubly ironic: the building formerly considered a bastion of public works and space is reduced to a beleaguered fort; and a group of white people, the "Power" able to determine the destinies of those in the adjacent communities, are terrified of sitting on a bench only ten feet into the park. The mixed metaphors finishing this sentence, of a Gibraltar in Sargasso Sea, give the irony a racial focus, as both places make historical reference to a white defense against encroaching invasion by darker peoples. Gibraltar, a consistent source of pride for the remnants of the British Empire, bears the legacy of European rule since the fifteenth century, when the Moors were driven out of the region. On the other hand, Sargasso Sea signifies to Anglophiles of Britain's imperial past a history of the constant insurrection of its mostly African slaves in its former Caribbean colonies. Brought together in the Bronx, this anachronistic vehicle of Gibraltar in Sargasso Sea produces a tenor of racial paranoia created by a perceived combination of guilt (that, as colonizers, they do not belong in this community) and fear (that the residents will someday throw them out) that casts the actions of the Power in the role quite differently from the story told through the building's architectural history. Whereas in the 1930s the county building would serve as an edifice signaling the people's consent to state mitigation of larger social ills (like an economic depression), in the 1980s Gibraltar signifies the maintenance of white supremacy through state repression and regulation, the people filtered through the doors of the courthouse to be monitored, rather than to be welcomed as participants in a public space.[10]

Likewise, racial paranoia of public space determines the everyday decisions that Wolfe's Master of the Universe, Sherman McCoy, makes in order to sustain his overabundant, sheltered life. Not hampered by the pretense of public service to which Kramer remains at least nominally bound, McCoy crafts his social choices, as Liam Kennedy puts it, "by two closely-linked factors, conspicuous wealth and social insulation" ("It's the Third World," 98). McCoy's exorbitant wealth (actually more fictitious than real, since much of his earnings are used to pay off a massive loan) enables a special kind of insulation from the public: his co-op contains two wings in order to accommodate, but segregate himself and his family from, the "help," and his front door is really a private elevator stop controlled by the apartment doorman. McCoy's Fortress Manhattan sensibility extends outside his domestic space, prompting him to send his daughter, Campbell, to the exclusive Taliaferro school, a private institution that employs its own bus service for its children, despite the fact that most of the students and their families live within walking distance (48). Segregated wings, hired guards, private schools—each of these are familiar social practices barely concealing their racial semiotic: to keep white skin from being too close to others.[11]

Wolfe displays Sherman's siege mentality most vividly in the bond trader's daily commute downtown to Wall Street from his midtown apartment. Rather than taking the subway, like his father did and continues to do, Sherman opts to pay the hefty fare of ten dollars and take a taxi, thus avoiding congregating even for a brief moment with those whom he continually casts as "those people" (55). The satirical portrait that Wolfe paints of Sherman is first made by the very route that the taxi takes to arrive at the brokerage firm, "down along the East River on the highway, the FDR, the Franklin Delano Roosevelt Drive" (54). A reference to the president (and to the depression era) who set into motion public policy that strove, at least in theory, to bring accessibility to public resources, the highway with Roosevelt's name now traffics the white elite up and down Manhattan and shields Sherman and his colleagues from the people who are seen to benefit most from Roosevelt's policies. We are left to wonder why Sherman's father remains adamant about taking public transportation—the narrative mentioning only that John Campbell McCoy would on "principle" not allow others to "drive him out off the New York City subways"—the explicit reference to FDR suggesting that Sherman's father, who in all likelihood lived through the depression, fashioned his daily routine in a New Deal era ethos of shared struggle and frugality. In fact, John McCoy's commute on public transportation was made possible by the funneling of transit money into the construction of a subsurface subway line (and the ensuing creative destruction of the Pearl Street El), one that directly connected the east side of midtown Manhattan to Wall Street. Given highest priority in the 1960s, the Water Street subway, an extension of the Second Avenue line, exemplified a redistribution of public funds for the benefit of office developers and other downtown business interests (Fitch, 139). What the narrative makes clear, notwithstanding this governmental assistance, is that Sherman's father is of a generation whose ethos remains one of struggle—the "principle" of "determination"—in belonging within the most public of arenas.

Sherman, on the other hand, harbors historical relation neither to the time of economic scarcity of the Roosevelt era, nor to the fact that the subway has been tailored specifically for his use. Instead, Sherman's principle is of even greater social expedience and convenience, the consumerist means of purchasing protection; his "principle" is not one of determination but of "insulation":

> But to the new breed, the young breed, the masterful breed, Sherman's breed, there was no such principle [like his father's]. *Insulation!* That was the ticket. That was the term Rawlie Thorpe used. "If you want to live in New York . . . you've got to insulate, insulate, insulate," meaning insulate yourself from those people. The cynicism and smugness of the idea struck Sherman as very *au courant*. If you could go breezing down the FDR Drive in a taxi, then why file into the trenches of the urban wars? (55)

Despite his claim to a hyperabundance of wealth and thus his self-proclaimed social niche as a "Master of the Universe," Sherman's economic status actually differs little from his father's. Both son and father enjoy substantial incomes, and while purportedly making more money than his father, Sherman's indebtedness is much greater as well. But Sherman *expresses* his wealth in a manner much more flagrant than John McCoy; no longer wedded to a fiction of egalitarianism in public space, Sherman pays for a spatial apartheid that, in his attempts to "insulate" the exceedingly rich from the poor and the colored, marks both the final logic and a perceived break from the "determination" of the older generation.

Yet the ethos of insulation carries two social costs, limits that provoke continual anxiety in Sherman and become moments for Wolfe to enact a trenchant satire of Sherman's identity. First, Sherman's life is dependent on and devoted to the idea of credit. Owing almost $2 million for his $2.6 million co-op, the bond trader worries constantly about making his $21,000-a-month payments. His reckless financing, contrasted with his parents' frugality and diligence in buying and renovating "an old wreck in a down-at-the-heels block" (55), tellingly compels a life led catching up with his bills, rather than having true command over his money. For all of his supposed economic mastery, Sherman remains a servant to indebtedness. Likewise, as a bond trader, Sherman actually exchanges no real money and sees no results of his frenetic attempts at overvaluation. Instead, as his wife, Judy, so deftly puts it as she explains her husband's job to their daughter, "Just imagine that a bond is a slice of cake, and you don't bake the cake, but every time you hand somebody a slice of the cake, a tiny little bit comes off, like a little crumb, and you keep that" (229). Sherman, as Judy extends this metaphor, "collects millions of marvelous . . . golden crumbs" (230). Like the enormous loan that undergirds and structures his own life, Sherman engages in work that facilitates and extends an economy of debt and that masks the deep scarcity at the root of seeming monetary abundance. Second, to further exemplify this borrowed life that Sherman leads, the narrative contrasts the bond trader's masculinity with that of his father. John McCoy lives with "determination" and with a "spirit of adventure" (223) to carve out a space for himself and his family; like the mythology of the frontier, Sherman's father, at least in the eyes of his son, is an urban pioneer who has laid a foundation of familial stability and financial constancy through a combination of audacity and diligence. Sherman views himself as having none of these qualities. Instead, he gropes for signs of his masculinity that, if not modeled after his father, use John McCoy as a reference point from which to measure. As he whisks down the FDR Drive in the taxi taking him to Wall Street, Sherman imagines his father's reaction to a livelihood based on borrowed money: "The Lion of Dunning Sponget would be appalled . . . and, worse than appalled, wounded . . . wounded at the thought of how his endlessly repeated lessons concerning duty, debt, ostentation, and proportion had whistled straight through his son's skull" (56). Although Sherman constantly proclaims his status as Master of the Universe, his anxiety over his failure to live up to his father's sense of manhood betrays the bond trader's confidence. Sherman overcompensates for his sense of a lost masculinity throughout the novel, as he fantasizes about his own sexual capacities (54), turns the trading room into vibrant and virile space (70), and celebrates his supposed heroism in the Bronx (95). A simple taxi ride, it seems, not only costs much more than a subway commute, but it also invokes a symbolic network that both confines and defines Sherman's anxious, privatized identity.

Wolfe places Kramer and Sherman in radically different social spaces, one a struggling assistant district attorney who cannot afford to take anything but a subway to his militarized workplace, the other an over-accumulating bond trader who can afford not to take the train to a glass citadel that simultaneously "survey[s] and shut[s] out the surrounding city space" (Kennedy, "It's the Third World," 99). Both characters, however, regard the public settings separating their homes from work (and in the case of Kramer, even work space) as fraught with danger. In fact, what has been considered in intellectual circles as public space or the "bourgeois public sphere" (Jürgen Habermas's phrase) has largely disappeared as a result of the ever-increasing contestation of competing private interests in a late-capitalist society; public space in an urban setting like New York, as the characters see it through the arenas of the subway and the courthouse, are places where "criminals" congregate. And these "criminals" are, significantly and stereotypically, "blacks and Latins" (105), most of whom are, as Kramer puts it, "truly guilty" (105) of their crimes. This *racial* difference between Kramer and Sherman and the criminalized whom Wolfe's main characters fear thus helps define in the novel the kinds of spaces safe for whites to traverse and those places that must be avoided at all costs. Wolfe's white characters, if not armed police officers, meet in privatized enclosures safe from the dangerous trenches of the urban, public landscape—elite bars and restaurants, office buildings, and gated apartments make up the gentrified oases of New York's white residents, while summer and vacation homes on the eastern tip of Long Island provide non-urban getaways. If the subway and courthouse are figured as the apposite spatial markers of colored turf, then those regarded as private property barrack the city's besieged whites, whose fear and loathing of urban public space barely mask the imagined racial undertones of these arenas.

Thus the spatial divide between public and private maps the ways in which Kramer and Sherman manifest their whiteness. The only safe space, in the characters' vision, is one either heavily guarded or enclosed from the more sinister places that people of color have taken over. This analogue between whiteness and privatized space, or as it is better known, private property, becomes heightened if we consider the aptly titled essay written in 1993 by Cheryl Harris, "Whiteness as Property." Arguing that the historical construction of whiteness sedimented on U.S. soil as a form of property (with all of property's legal sanction), Harris, in order to establish how modern views of property buttress white privilege and maintain a system of white supremacy, borrows at one point from Jeremy Bentham's famous definition of property: "Property is nothing but the basis of expectation consist[ing] in an established expectation, in the persuasion of being able to draw such and such advantage from the thing possessed" (qtd. in Harris, 1729). This understanding of the potential "advantage" derived from an assumed legacy or "expectation" structures socially and especially legally the correlation between whiteness and property; in other words, "[W]hiteness became the quintessential property for personhood. . . . Whiteness was an 'object' over which continued control was—and is—expected" (1729). If white people in the United States harness the capacity to exert their whiteness as a form of social privilege, then such expectation can be expressed, acted upon—just like other forms of property possessed—in social practice. Potential expectation, as Harris notes, is transformed into actual "use and enjoyment": "As whiteness is simultaneously an aspect of identity and a property interest, it is something that can be experienced and deployed as a resource. Whiteness can move from being a passive characteristic as an aspect of identity to an active entity that—like other types of property—is used to fulfill the will and to exercise power" (1734). The movement of a white person from "settled expectation" to "deployable resource" in the exercise of his/her whiteness is historically entrenched in the social history of U.S. white supremacy, and has constituted, in Harris's view, the cornerstone of white identity as a specific, insidious, and intractable form of privilege.

Central to this understanding of whiteness as property is the idea that property in its generic formulation precedes and therefore determines the ways in which whiteness is defined. Even as the whiteness inherent in Kramer's and Sherman's vision of public space in the city provides the lens through which they view New York's inhabitants, it is the primary notion of space not as public but as private that provides the basis by which to racialize the landscape. Thus, for our purposes, Harris's thesis might be best prefaced by Neil Smith's formulation of U.S. urban space: "The basic building block of urban space is the individual absolute space of private property" (*Uneven Development*, 138). For Smith, the construction of the "public" is nothing more, as a result of the embedded history of modern capitalism, than an aggregation of atomized units of private property, sections of land through which a person is authorized to say, "this is me, this is who I am." Private, or more specifically privatized, property fashions our modern concepts of individual identity. Just as ownership of a piece of external space affords a person the fiction that she/he can do what she/he wills within those borders, so, too, does this logic of possessing an individual identity enable a person to turn her/his potential, internalized individual power into the expression of individualism *against* others. And this confluence of private property and individualism is harnessed most powerfully through the notion of whiteness—the sign of racial supremacy in the United States—and confers onto this triumvirate of property, individualism, and whiteness such social significance that this racial formula becomes naturalized, the assumption of "ownership, control, and dominion" (Harris, 1735).

Thus the fear that Kramer and Sherman map onto public space is as much an index of a perceived crisis in their whiteness as it is a concomitant conferral of racial and criminal characteristics on the nonwhite bodies they envision. What generates their anxiety is precisely the sense that they have lost their property as white men. Unable to consider their whiteness as their means to assume power and protection, they must enact practices that shore up security in an urban world no longer secure. For Kramer, this means that he must depend on the repressive capacities of the state to regulate and imprison those whom he prosecutes and yet still encounters on the subway and at the entrance of Gibraltar; for Sherman, the perceived loss of white privilege compels him to purchase social insulation, to forge ever more privatized circuits of mobility in order to traverse the city safely. Paradoxically, the whiteness that has enabled a group of people to take their enjoyment and use of racial privilege for granted—and therefore enabled the semblance of individualism—becomes in its mode of crisis the rallying call for white people to reassert their shared racial characteristic. If whiteness is most powerful when its property and its vision of urban space as privately owned can be assumed, then whiteness is most visible when those expectations are regarded as under threat and thus must be reinforced.

"Race," Michael Keith and Malcolm Cross argue, "is a privileged metaphor through which the confused text of the city is rendered comprehensible" (qtd. in Kennedy, "It's the Third World," 104); the white characters of *Bonfire* make semiotic stuff of this primary metaphor in their attempts to fortify their safety. A most telling example in the narrative takes place in the evening at the "besieged" Gibraltar, the practice of "wagon-training." In this moment of ostensible protection from violent criminals lurking around the courthouse at night, class and status pretensions yield to white racial solidarity: all the workers of the courthouse, not excluding even the judges like Kovitsky or the district attorney Abe Weiss, assemble their cars in a semicircle closer to the building, and thus create an automotive barrier for the workers of Gibraltar. A pseudo-historical reference to popular TV and film westerns, understood both by the characters and made explicit by the narrative, "wagon-training" transforms the already policed "public" space of the courthouse into a cordoned area further buttressed for white safety, this time using privately owned vehicles: "The wagon train. 'Yo-ohhhhhhh' was the cry of John Wayne, the hero and chief scout, signaling the pioneers to move the wagons. This was Indian country and bandit country, and it was time to put the wagons in a circle for the night" (173–74). The courthouse workers, here likened to "pioneers" of an earlier century, construct a spatiality of siege against the seeming wilderness of the Bronx urban landscape. And like the nineteenth-century colonizers of native land who regarded "safe space" as private property expropriated and cultivated from the "wild" plains, those sanctuaried in Gibraltar look to the public space surrounding the courthouse as dangerous, because not privately controlled. The incredible racial fantasy built into this practice—not only that whites in the Bronx are "under siege," but also that state power is so weak that it must be supplemented by the strength and comfort of mobile private property (one's car)—demonstrates the profound contradictions that must be elided to maintain the sanctity of white safety. Kaminsky, the fat white court officer, may play the role of John Wayne in this parodic rendition of the white settler/Native aggressor movie, but what makes this apparently humorous scene still powerful is the extent to which even the most unattractive of white characters—those whom Wolfe's narrative lambastes in terms of appearance and status—are able to rally white people into a singular racial consciousness.

This is one of numerous instances in which Wolfe narrates the "vanity" of his white characters, a moment to plumb a satirical line. As in the description of the Bronx County Courthouse, a favored strategy of Wolfe's for entering into his satirical world is the ironic staging of anachronistic references. Aligning the white workers of the courthouse with nineteenth-century white settlers of the frontier, the narrative compels the reader to make concurrent associations between the relatively new inhabitants of the South Bronx (those whom Wolfe in "Stalking" says are part of the last wave of immigration of the past thirty years) and the original Natives of the lands stolen by the "pioneers." Such correlation would only be possible if one were completely ignorant of such profound social differences and thus made a racial alignment between otherwise divergent nonwhite people. Assuming that Wolfe's readers demonstrate at least nominal understanding of U.S. social history, the contradiction would invite such a dis-junction to disrupt the mimetic function of the reference to "Indian and bandit country," and thus provoke the satirical moment. Moreover, that such a construction of whiteness championing a protective siege mentality emerges from the popular mythology of John Wayne movies would make even the prior anachronism to the whites versus Natives model ludicrous, turning ironic even the irony set forth by the image of the wagon train. We are in deeply fantastic territory by this point. And Wolfe's readers therefore might be invited to poke holes into the facade of this narrative of whites terrorized who project their racial fears onto the urban landscape they must reputedly share with people of color.

Yet critical regard of *Bonfire* does not follow this logic. A brief survey of Wolfe's readers directs us toward two camps, one effusive in its praise for the novel's balanced even if satiric realism, and the other damning Wolfe's dependence on the most degrading of falsity and stereotypes. Most of those who praise *Bonfire* take a cue from Wolfe's own "Stalking the Billion-Footed Beast" and celebrate the fact that the novel is, first, big and fat and realistic, not of the "short-winded and . . . anti-social fic-tion" (quoted in Bloom, *Tom Wolfe,* 185) that Wolfe himself excoriates in "Stalking." James Andrews's review of the novel exemplifies the spirit of those who consider the novel to be a feat of Dickensian proportions (a comparison made by at least three different critics). And while Andrews acknowledges the satire seething throughout the novel, he marvels more at the capacity of Wolfe to show *Bonfire*'s readers a tableau of New York almost perfectly matched to the real city, the "*real* New York" (183). And not wedded to any political persuasion, Andrews asserts, the book's satiri-cal vision remains "evenhanded . . . wide in its wide canvas, vivid charac-ters who stop just short of being caricatures, stinging humor that betrays the underlying anger of the idealist, and perfect rendering of a specific city in a specific time" (184). Satire, for Wolfe's supporters, only punctuates and sharpens what is otherwise a hefty novel that displays for the readers a story full of knowledge and truth (188).

Wolfe's detractors, on the other hand, ridicule the cartoonish depic-tion of the novel's characters and find fault, especially with the novel's nonwhite, nonmale characters. The offense of *Bonfire,* for these critics, is greatest when Wolfe depicts the Bronx and its inhabitants of color. Kennedy rails against Wolfe's ignorance of anything outside of white Manhattan, the racial stereotyping of the people of the Bronx displaying a fundamental misanthropy toward those on the other side of the bridge: "[I]t is clear that [Wolfe] has little or no knowledge of either the social or the interior worlds of the people occupying the blighted spaces of poverty.

Rather than document their lives he constructs scenes of contrast and juxtaposition in which the urban poor . . . function as symbolic projections of
the fears and prejudices of his white protagonists" ("It's the Third World,"
101). The key term here, "document," underscores Kennedy's claim that
Bonfire fails as a "classic realist novel" to capture the city accurately (95).
Even as he acknowledges that Wolfe's mode of narration falls within a
"satirical perspective" (96), Kennedy (with others concurring) expresses
profound dissatisfaction with the novel's treatment of race, a narrative approach that never fully attains a vision worthy of true realism. Curiously,
writers on both sides of the critical fence affirm or disapprove of the novel
by measuring the narrative's "realism" against what they believe to be the
"true New York," all the while conceding, yet sidestepping the marginal
but constant mention of Wolfe's satirical style, the trademark for which he
is most well-known.

It is not surprising that critical attention to *Bonfire* has largely avoided
tackling the satire embedded in the novel. Satire remains, after centuries of
commentary, an elusive topic on which to pronounce judgment, especially
because that judgment usually strikes exposed political nerves. In its most
generic definition, satirical writing depends on the creation of multiple
communities of readers who help produce a disjunction that ultimately
leads to its general attack on some fundamental error in society. Deriving
from the Latin "laux satura" (mixed fruits), satire assumes not only a mix-
ing of contradictory, contingent elements and values within its narrative,
but also the mixed audience receiving the satirical message. To put it most
bluntly: if satire is a kind of joke, then that satire works only if one can
imagine that one group of readers "gets the joke," while others remain
oblivious. Even if everyone can see where and how the satire is done, one
must at least fantasize that someone else has fallen dupe to the joke. In
other words, in order for satire to be funny (and thus effective), another
person must take it in all seriousness. This construction of at least two
imagined readerly communities produces an interpretive ambivalence that
is evident in Wolfe criticism, particularly commentary on *Bonfire*. Thus
circumvention of satire and direct interpretation of the novel as some kind
of realism predominates; Wolfe's depiction of New York *must* be utterly
true or utterly false, for to be unsure and indecisive would place a reader
definitely on the wrong end of the laugh.

Such overdetermined certainty on the part of *Bonfire*'s readers on the
truth or falsity of his fiction belies the fundamentally unstable quality of
satire, one that Steven Weisenburger, in his study of twentieth-century
American satire, describes as the "parasitic" nature of satire onto any
mode of narration (147). Instability, however, does not mean inaccessibili-

ty or impenetrability. The conundrum is therefore this: satire demands that its reader render meaning and judgment, yet it retains the capability to escape from that provisionally placed interpretation. It is perhaps for this reason that when put into a political context, satire arouses ire and celebration from readers both left and right. The example of Wolfe is no exception. While *Bonfire* has in the popular press been touted as the political right's novel celebré, a veritable guidebook to the 1980s for neo-conservatives, not a few critics look to Wolfe as a writer whose multivoiced narratives eschew and even undermine any attempts at appropriating the novel for conservative purposes.[12] Yet such flexibility in point of view still begs the question not of whether Wolfe "succeeds" or "fails" in his satire or realism, but what the very stakes are in Wolfe's use of satire. If satire, in the final instance, remains difficult to pinpoint, "lack[ing] a steady narrative voice, specific 'targets,' and fixed norms or corrective goals" (Weisenburger, 14), then attempting to fixate on the political persuasion of the narrative leads at best to an educated guess from which the writer's supposed meanings could always slip away. At worst, such an interpretive journey would miss the point of satire. Linda Hutcheon's comments on the "transideological nature of irony" are no less true for satire, one of irony's delivery systems: "[I]rony [and satire] can and does function tactically in the service of a wide range of political positions, legitimating or under-cutting a wide variety of interests" (10). More important is the ground upon which such a satire is deployed, the history undergirding the impetus for Wolfe's satirical impulse. For it is this cultural ground—the racialized landscape produced in the 1980s—that is the soil of *Bonfire*'s satire, the conditions through which the novel generates its narrative vision of white-ness. For, to recalibrate Hutcheon again, "It is less that irony [read: satire] creates communities, then that discursive communities make irony [satire] possible in the first place" (18).

A brief scene in the novel serves as an apt example. Peter Fallow, the novel's immigrant reporter, has resuscitated himself from his alcoholic stupor to break the story of Henry Lamb for the local tabloid paper *City Light*. Wanting to paint Henry Lamb as an exemplary young man grow-ing up in the roughest section of the city, Fallow interviews Lamb's junior high school teacher, Mr. Rifkind. Rifkind betrays in this conversation his racist feelings toward those he teaches at the local Bronx junior high school, noting that the students' range of performance "runs more from cooperative to life-threatening," but never outstanding (219). Talking from his Long Island home, Rifkind exhibits all of the projections of white fear onto his black students: Fallow asks about Henry Lamb, and Rifkind replies immediately, "Doesn't ring a bell. What's he done?" But even more insidious than Rifkind's assumption of Henry Lamb's criminality is the closeting of his racism to protect his job: "Seems like a nice boy. We're not supposed to call them boys, but that's what they are, poor sad confused boys with a whole lotta problems. Don't quote me, for Christ's sake, or *I'll* have a whole lotta problems. Hey, listen. You sure you couldn't use a 1981 Thunderbird?" (221). The narrative layers a series of ironies, each meant to serve as a moment of narrative pause to force Wolfe's reader to uncover Rifkind's intractable racism. First, Rifkind's use of the term "boy" to describe Henry and other Black teenagers harkens to the racist language of the more visible racism and racial violence earlier in the century. Parroting this language, Rifkind is cast in a light reserved for the likes of Bull Connor. Second, Rifkind's injunction not to quote him and thus to hide his racism underscores both the ludicrousness and selfishness of a teacher who holds such damning views fearing exposure to keep his job, and the fundamental flaw in a school system that allows such a person to be in such a position. And finally, the narrative hammers home Rifkind's already suspect opinions by turning him into a weekend used-car salesman, as someone whose attempts to sell his 1981 Thunderbird remain higher on his list of priorities than the life of one of his students. This final line moves us beyond irony and turns Rifkind into a grotesque figure, only barely on this side of the threshold of what constitutes humanity.

According to Weisenburger, a formalist approach to a satire of this kind would involve looking for four elements. Distilling the theoretical tradition of satire put forth most notably by Northrop Frye, Weisenburger locates the following:

> First of all, satire in its purest forms was held to be a profoundly *rhetorical* mode, a persuasive literature at least and at most an openly polemical discourse. Second, it followed that satire would be unthinkable without some *target of attack* in the "real world." Third, in opposition to that target, satire was defined as proposing a *corrective* or ameliorative course of action. Finally, this course was unthinkable without reference to some absolute moral code; in short, satire had to be universally *normative*, for this last element would legitimize the unleashing of aggressions that followed from the other three. (15)

Neither Weisenburger nor I consider strictly formalist attempts at understanding a passage such as the Rifkind scene in *Bonfire* sufficient for unearthing the force of satire, but this New Critical model of satire serves as a useful paradigmatic point from which to begin, if only to point out the necessity of historicizing such a scene. A generative if rather bland interpretation of this scene using the formalist model would go something like this:

Wolfe's narrative launches an aggression against racists (rhetorical argument against irrational racism) like Rifkind, whose positions of influence belie and actually reinforce (instrumental target of attack) the fundamental problems of the public school system. Getting rid of such racists (corrective) would enable nonracists to bring hope to the schools, empower the students, and ultimately benefit a society that doesn't reward such bigotry (normative vision of the world).

Yet the invective here threatens much more than the idiocy of one school teacher, or even the effects of such a bigot on the New York public school system. The narrative's quick but essential glossing of Rifkind's residence—the town of Hewlett, located in Nassau County on Long Island (218)—may be news for Fallow, but this signal of where Rifkind lives crucially triggers the nexus of privatized space and whiteness. It would be easy to castigate a racist like Rifkind, and Wolfe's readers would be hard-pressed not to. But the satiric moment in this passage, of turning Rifkind into such a grotesque and therefore damning figure, has its foundation in the historical movement of white New Yorkers from an increasingly diverse city to the outlying suburban towns still resolutely white and segregated. The story of white flight is, at this point in this project, well-rehearsed, almost knee-jerk in the literature that we have attended to, but it is this very endemic quality of white flight in the contemporary era that forms the linchpin of racial politics, and New York is not an exception to this historical rule. Rifkind's bigotry is nurtured on segregated soil, planted during the late 1960s when then Mayor Lindsay undertook major public-sector housing projects to help facilitate the integration of the city's black and poor residents into the white enclaves of New York's boroughs. It was also Lindsay who, according to Roger Sanjek, sought to establish a coalition with the city's unions and increased the wages and benefits of city employees (police, fire, and educational); ironically, this better-paid municipal white workforce enabled the mass migration of whites into racially exclusive suburbs (85–86). The emergence of a commuter New York and its attendant ideology, the protection of white spatial sanctity through the ever-increasing spiral of privatization and suburbanization, qualifies the vituperative portrait of Rifkind, for his racism is no longer singular but endemic, not individual but structural. The narrative may launch its anger toward what Rifkind says and thinks, but its target of attack spills over to where he and the hundreds of thousands of other ex-New Yorkers he represents live. The critique of the projection of white fear over Black criminality only gestures to the tip of the spatial history upon which the satire depends, and the parasitic narrative aggression against one man is in danger of infecting and exposing the more general apartheid that frames Wolfe's satirical vision.

It is therefore less the case that *Bonfire*'s satire fails to accomplish for its characters of color what Wolfe succeeds at doing for the white "Masters" and "Powers" of New York—to "transcend through satire the racialized images and discourses [Wolfe] evokes through stereotyping" (Kennedy, "It's the Third World," 104)—and even less the case that Wolfe's novel is able to lampoon the pretensions of the upper class and the whites who strive to hang out in those elite corridors. Both accounts are, in fact, correct, but they tell us little about the kind of cultural work *Bonfire* is doing not only through, but also *as* satire. Wolfe's satire more importantly follows the trajectory of white privilege that is wedded to an urban political economy whose history bears the effects of this privilege in the increasing privatization of space and the evisceration of communities of color. Satire in the novel not only serves to comment on the privilege of its white characters; it is also, for Wolfe, the historical narrative mode by which whiteness is maintained.

The novel's infamous scene of Sherman's and Maria's "descent" into the "urban jungle" of the Bronx exemplifies the circumscribed history that engenders Wolfe's satire of the racial landscape. Wolfe narrates Sherman's racial paranoia through phantasmagoric imagery, as the bond trader mistakes a broken chair for a woman's head and trash cans for dead bodies (79, 85). Sherman also expresses his racial panic through the more mundane act of locking his car doors as he passes by "dark faces," who, fully understanding the racialized nature of this action, smile back at him (83–84). Without the familiar grid pattern of downtown and midtown Manhattan streets, the landscape of the Bronx "no longer," in Sherman's eyes, "looked like New York" (83). Already we are in satirical terrain, Sherman's supposed mastery of the universe apparently useless in the most powerless of urban spaces. And while the narrative of racial paranoia reaches its crescendo in the dramatic folly with the two young men whom we later discover are Henry Lamb and Roland Auburn, what produces in Sherman a more generalized fear even before anyone steps on the scene to "threaten" him is the landscape itself:

> —*astonishing*. Utterly empty, a vast open terrain. Block after block—how many? six? eight? a dozen?—entire blocks of the city without a building left standing. There were streets and curbing and sidewalks and light poles and nothing else. The eerie grid of a city was spread out before him, lit by the chemical yellow of the street lamps. Here and there were traces of rubble and slag. The earth looked like concrete, except that it rolled down this way . . . and up that way . . . the hills and dales of the Bronx . . . reduced to asphalt, concrete, and cinders . . . in a ghastly yellow gloaming. (82)

The seemingly featureless terrain of the southern portion of the Bronx is punctuated only by skeletons of buildings "ready to keel over at any moment" (82) or old billboards ("Meat Warehouse," [80]) that have long since lost their signifieds. For Kennedy, this scene rehearses Wolfe's failure to satirize fully the stereotypes that underpin this portrait of the Bronx landscape and its inhabitants. Rather than focusing on "black poverty," Kennedy asserts, Wolfe's depiction of Sherman's and Maria's visit to the Bronx manifests and "dramatizes the white middle class New Yorker's worst nightmare, to be lost in the degraded city spaces of the other, the black underclass" (102). Reliant on what Mike Davis regards as a racialized "paranoid spatiality," Wolfe in Kennedy's view maps white fear onto the urban spaces that help facilitate the discursive construction of the dual city—one white, rich, and in Manhattan, the other poor, colored, criminal, located in the Bronx.

But this critique of Wolfe's use of racial paranoia does not account for the reasons why this scene should then be taken as a moment of satire. The ghostly quality of this scene, a tableau of an "eerie" wasteland viewed in chemical twilight, not only corresponds to the troublesome racial discourse of urban nightmares, but unveils an even deeper, more material economy that undergirds this symbolic one. As Weisenburger suggests, "[T]he narrative style [of satire] soon breaks through to more chilling, actual violence" (148). The satire in this scene leaves critics wondering about its intentions—does it recapitulate racial stereotypes or reveal these stereotypes to be fantastic projections?—but it is the material ground of the political economic history on which this portrait of the Bronx's streets depends that seeps in to form even more infectious implications. For this scene crystallizes much of what I have been arguing throughout this study, that a vision of an urban wasteland made racial is fundamentally the anxious expression of the eviscerating forces of the 1980s U.S. political economy. And Wolfe's satirical vision, a "vast open terrain" hollowed out with nothing but the barest of infrastructure—"streets and curbing and sidewalks and light poles and nothing else"—reflects specifically in the narrative the uneven development of urban space largely responsible for the racial realignment that has brought about such racial anxiety, in this case, in the form of white fear. To reiterate Neil Smith's axiom about the "spatial fix" of capitalist processes and its inevitable crisis: "As uneven development becomes an increasing necessity in order to stave off crises, geographical differentiation becomes less and less a by-product, more an inner necessity for capital" (*Uneven Development,* 153). The ever-increasing and frantic cycle of accumulation and crisis demands its spatial expression by the overdevelopment of some sections of New York and an attendant underdevelopment, even complete destruction, of other spaces. Sherman's "descent" into his racial nightmare is our entry into the visible signs of this history of creative destruction, one that has mapped the glaring social, economic, and political contradictions of the past two decades onto the streets of the Bronx that compels its viewer to remark, "astonishing."

The billboard pronouncing "Tops in the Bronx/Meat Warehouse" and the sole building barely standing on otherwise vacant space is a testament to the industrial past of the Bronx, indeed of New York, laid waste by the calculated coordination of Manhattan's white corporate elite (those whom Wolfe charges will not come down from their midtown co-ops) and the city government that has created what Roger Sanjek refers to as the "permanent government" of New York City. And unlike other cities struggling to stave off their own downward turns during the 1970s and 1980s as a result of the hemorrhaging of manufacture-based industry, this permanent government in New York worked to usher in and maximize the postindustrial transformation of the city sparked by the crisis in capital starting in the early 1970s. This new economic structure, based primarily on the aptly acronymed FIRE sector—Robert Fitch's term for the trinitarian economy of "finance, insurance and real estate"—sought to accelerate the trend not only to redevelop New York through new building projects, but more importantly to privatize the land itself on which construction would take place. Like the fictitious capital produced by the likes of Sherman McCoy, whose bond trading exacerbates an economy serviced entirely by debt and credit (and not real production), the permanent government in New York built its public policy to maximize real estate value in New York by diverting almost all of its resources into the overvaluation of Manhattan's office buildings (Fitch, 30).

The funneling of a once economically diverse city into the "monoculture" of a feverish edifice complex of the city's elite has been, according to Fitch, the main reason why the indices of New York's real economy—unemployment, job loss, income depreciation, housing shortage—have remained, even in the economic upswings of recent times, intractably down. The unspoken maxim of the permanent government, "public policy for private gain" (Sanjek, 34) has left a New York, coined a "world city" by each of its mayors since Ed Koch began these policies, glittering at the center and gasping at the edges, a political and economic story that Sanjek summarizes and which I quote at length:

> Throughout the city's history the expansion of these highest-return uses in Manhattan's core has squeezed outward such other uses as manufacturing, shipping, warehouse, mass-market shopping, and housing for neighbor-

hood New Yorkers. Openly or behind the scenes, members of the permanent government direct public policy to support and speed up this process. As a result, public expenditures are championed that make Manhattan office buildings and luxury housing more feasible and more profitable—mass transportation connections, tax exemptions, park and landfill creation, subsidies for "high culture" institutions, and removal (rather than in-place upgrading) of "slum" housing and "unsightly" manufacturing. This process sends ripples and waves across neighborhood New York, spinning working- and lower-middle-class jobs farther outward, relocating masses of ordinary people, transforming the nature of existing neighborhoods (if not eliminating them), and providing only minimal transportation and quality-of-life services to the outer boroughs. (32)

Permanent government policies only intensified throughout the 1980s, solidifying a profound bifurcation so evident that New York became for the popular media the exemplar "dual city" (Mollenkopf and Castells, 4–5).[13] Thus, even in the midst of the 1975 crisis that precipitated the city's fiscal bankruptcy and even though by this time 32 million square feet of Manhattan office space remained unused, plans were already underway to use public money to subsidize private development of numerous projects around the borough, with Battery Park City being the most notable (Sanjek, 88; Boyer, 120). For neighborhood New York in the 1970s and 1980s, especially under the leadership of Ed Koch, the fiscal crisis was used as an excuse to slash social services in the name of planned austerity, leaving behind a faltering education system, collapsing infrastructure, contracting public employment, and a burgeoning underground economy (Sanjek, 93–96). New York's neighborhood boroughs—Queens, Brooklyn, and the Bronx—which housed most of the city's communities of color, were in essence sacrificed at the altar of what Christine Boyer calls the "city of illusion": the permanent government's spatial fix to facilitate the new political economy of FIRE masked privatization as public policy, and ensured that the growing army of under- and unemployed people outside of Manhattan's core would remain frozen out of this spending spree of real estate speculation (115–16).

There is nothing "natural" about the kind of urban transformation that New York underwent before and during the 1980s; Sanjek echoes Fitch's assertion that the disinvestment from outlying boroughs is not even the consequence of "market forces" (Fitch, 30, 52): "Neighborhood change is the result of deliberate action by persons and networks within the social order that seek to maintain or increase the value of their investments in land" (Sanjek, 34). It is therefore this "deliberate action" that facilitated the voiding of economic potential in areas like the Bronx, and engendered the kind of landscape that Sherman views when he takes his wrong turn off the Triborough Bridge. If Cudjoe's friend Timbo in the previous chapter on Wideman's novel imagines how Philadelphia would "revitalize" its economy by razing the remnants of the city's industrial past and displacing its unemployed workers ("all this got to go"), then the "utterly empty" space of the Bronx in Wolfe's narrative displays the logical effects of this vision of redevelopment.[14] Of course, Sherman *does* define the Bronx in terms of racial criminality; more crucial, however, is that this landscape of "rubble and slag" also serves as a spatial testament to the forces that have largely determined this racialized vision. And it is this story of the assassination of New York on which this grotesque scene depends that Wolfe's narrative encounters its own implication in the creation of such monstrosity. The exclamation that precedes the description of the Bronx landscape—"astonishing"—lays bare that the ground on which Wolfe works his satirical narrative belies satire or rationalization. It is simply shocking, refusing ironic mediation. To confront this terrain is to come to terms with one's complicity in its maintenance; and to displace complicity demands that one turn to satire. But, conversely, satire leads the unwilling back to the place of its original sin.

Thus the calculated effort to mask private control of Manhattan's land as "public" and to decimate and criminalize the outlying terrain of the outer boroughs forms the material ground of Wolfe's satire of his characters, whose social choices are largely scripted by these changes. And we might view Sherman's and Maria's hit-and-run crime against Henry Lamb and the ensuing investigation and trial as the satirical denouement of those wedded to an ideology of whiteness—individualist privilege enabled by state-sanctioned and subsidized privatized space—who are largely responsible for this "dual city" teetering on the brink of racial warfare. Indeed, Wolfe's satire is most pointed if we regard the criminalization of Sherman—Abe Weiss's "Great White Defendant"—as the ironic moment in which white projection of criminality onto Black and Brown people comes home to roost in Waspish garb. That Sherman, the symbolic pinnacle of white success in the 1980s, becomes the sacrificial lamb in order to maintain the fiction of equal justice in New York enables Wolfe to make that most ironic of statements in the middle of the novel: "A liberal is a conservative who's been arrested."

More specifically, as Maria points out to Sherman in one of their exchanges about their crime, a "liberal" is someone who recognizes that the law protects a white citizenry, and yet is willing to take away that racial privilege in order to maintain its operations. She says of and to Sherman,

"You had a good upbringing. Laws weren't any kind of threat to you. They were *your laws*, Sherman, people like you and your family's" (264). And as the novel's ending bears out, Wolfe's barb initially may have been directed at Sherman's foibles (toward the end of the novel, the narrative sighs at Sherman's pathetic fall, "Oh, Master of the Universe" [601]), but the narrative's epilogue indicts the other white characters for somehow benefiting from Sherman's case. White privilege reconstitutes itself as Sherman's downfall smooths the larger structural machinations that enable the most powerful characters to attain even greater power: Abe Weiss wins reelection as the Bronx district attorney, Tom Killian moves to Long Island, Sally Rawthrote sues McCoy to receive an unearned commission (not unlike the procedures of bond trading), Maria inherits the Ruskin fortune and marries her Italian lover, and even the once down-and-out Fallow wins a Pulitzer Prize and marries his boss's daughter, Lady Evelyn Steiner (65–69). The white characters of *Bonfire* accrue more wealth, property, and status for their own personal, private "use and enjoyment." And that each of their own fortunes is sanctioned by the law indicates that the property interest of and as whiteness has been enhanced by the prosecution of Sherman, the Great White Defendant. Satirical aim no longer pointed at Sherman, the narrative gestures to the even larger horror of the greater injustice of social privilege through which the white characters use and enjoy their new accumulations. By the novel's end, Wolfe leads his audience to laugh sickeningly at the realization that whiteness is, as David Roediger puts it in a more emphatic tone, "not merely . . . oppressive and false . . . whiteness is *nothing but* oppressive and false" (13).

If his first "descent" into the decimated spaces of New York, his foray into the Bronx, shakes and yet reinforces Sherman's commitment to whiteness, it is his second fall, this time into the depths of the criminal justice system, that signals what he has lost: the nothing and everything of whiteness. Wolfe's satire exposes the tenuousness of whiteness, its foundations grounded in the political economy of a New York privatizing everything and then naturalizing those economic processes as inevitable and even favorable occurrences. And yet the novel's characters remain firmly aligned with the power accorded to the historical and spatial constitution of whiteness upon which the racialized characteristics of New York's boroughs (Manhattan as "civilization"; the Bronx as urban jungle) and its people are layered. But Sherman's adherence to this circuit of racial, social, and economic power—whiteness, unencumbered individualist ambition, private property—is broken by his arrest and his detention in the Bronx county jail. After this traumatic event, not only does he lose his social connections to his colleagues at work, his elite neighbors at his co-op, his and Judy's circle of acquaintances in New York's socialite world, he also loses the pretension of the protective capacity of whiteness. For all of the previous assumptions that he held, of his individual diligence and struggle to "earn" the self-named title of Master of the Universe, Sherman's identity depended on the potential advantage—Bentham's "basis of expectation"—that his whiteness afforded him. Indeed, this is what is hinted at early in the novel, when Wolfe pokes fun at Sherman's "need" to take a taxi to work for fear of descending into the subway, the public space of the "urban wars." Sherman's very masculinity is built on a construction of whiteness totally dependent on a network of goods and services provided to protect whiteness and the sanctity of private property; thus, his constant need to compare himself with his father, the "Lion" for whom masculinity and confidence seem born out of struggle, not bought.

Indeed, it is in Sherman's constant need to claim his masculinity that we see Wolfe making a directed point about the specific mode of whiteness that his satire follows and seeks to attack. Sherman must constantly and vigorously reaffirm and redeem his manhood, first by finding virile energy at his workplace, a kind of reverse sublimation through which economic mastery and competitiveness is taken as a sign of masculine aggression (Kennedy, "It's the Third World," 105). The second instance takes place as Sherman recounts his and Maria's adventure in the Bronx and revise their crime into a story of peril and rescue of his mistress: "He had saved a woman. . . . He was not merely a Master of the Universe; he was more; he was a man" (98–99). This passage exemplifies "Sherman's sense that there is more to manhood than economic mastery" (Kennedy, 106). This distinction made, between *homo economicus* and a real "man," forms a crucial marker of identity that Wolfe exploits to satirize the "nothingness" of whiteness constructed in the 1980s: although whiteness enables white New York to accumulate ever-increasing amounts of wealth and power and enjoy accelerating privatization, such social expectation and its display (through status, property, position) remain at best a protective bubble ready to burst at the moment the fiction of whiteness is exposed—thus the need for constant protection and insulation. For Wolfe, the irony of whiteness—that which would be regarded as the pinnacle of individualism—is that it is, at its height of social power and privilege, an enervating culture, one that prevents Sherman from being a truly real man.

As a result of his arrest and detention, Sherman's "Wasp identity crumbles" (Kennedy, 107), and the accoutrements of inherited whiteness disappear: he loses his job, his midtown co-op, his friends and family. He is, in essence, totally alone, finally a true individual in the existential sense; his loss of whiteness is simultaneously a loss of his private property, and paradoxically his sense of individualism. After his temporary release from jail, Sherman reports to Killian this transformation, one that is recorded as a loss but also as the birth of a new identity:

> [S]omething's gradually dawned on me over the past few days. I'm not Sherman McCoy anymore. I'm somebody else without a proper name. I've been that other person ever since the day I was arrested. I knew something . . . something fundamental had happened that day, but I didn't know what it was at first. At first I thought I was still Sherman McCoy, and Sherman McCoy was going through a period of very bad luck. Over the last couple of days, though, I've begun to face up to the truth. I'm somebody else. I have nothing to do with Wall Street or Park Avenue or Yale or St. Paul's or Buckley or the Lion of Dunning Sponget. (625)

Sherman's loss of his "proper name," the name that signifies his connectedness to the permanent government buttressing the ideological power of whiteness, turns him into someone who is merely "standard issue" (625). Whiteness had once given him his "proper name," the pedigree of his social access to a network that bound him to privilege; now, having lost his whiteness, his privilege, his assumptions of insulation, Sherman also loses the capacity to align his already fragile masculinity to the circuit of private property, individualism, and whiteness. He is now part of, not insulated from, the urban trenches that he so eschewed during his taxi-cab days.

"Arrest," Allen Feldman has written, "is the political art of individualizing disorder" (109). Sherman's loss of his white community makes his arrest look like and hide as a classic confrontation between the individual and the state. But what makes Sherman's arrest and trial different from the incarceration of nonwhite persons revolves around what types of disorders the arrest individualizes. Whereas the arrest of Black and Brown men, in the eyes of primary definers, is rationalized as the social disorder of violent crime, gang activity, and drug epidemics, Sherman's case suggests that the disorder is the pathology of a metastatic state itself. Abe Weiss wants to convict Sherman simply to increase the district attorney's chances of winning reelection, to put away a "Great White Defendant" and thus protect both himself and the institution for which he works from the charge that the state's reproduction and legitimacy depend on the racial criminalization of communities of color. White supremacy, simply put, must sacrifice one of its own. And in this regard, Sherman's loss of a white identity once tied to property, individualism, and protection ties him to a racial identity not unlike that of Blackness: Sherman joins the ranks of O'Day Short, whom we met in Yamamoto's story in chapter 3 and Darnell of *Philadelphia Fire*. He has become the victim of the very urban triage that supported his prior conception of identity in whiteness. Sherman has encountered what Ruth Wilson Gilmore, following from Orlando Patterson, refers to as "social death," the physical removal into cages of those deemed ideologically and socially deviant, "criminal," and therefore beyond the possibility of rehabilitation. Larger disorder individualized has caught up with the very person it was meant to protect, and although the political project of incarceration is intended to naturalize the social death of prisoners of color and the death that inheres in urban triage, the *effect* of this logic requires that, for multicultural legitimacy's sake, some white people must die, too. From the moment of his arrest, and throughout the trial, Sherman repeats this refrain of death. It is the theme of the chapter when he is finally taken away into custody: "And then he was dead, so dead he couldn't even die" (455); "It was *not* an ordinary arrest. It was *death*" (455); "His thoughts told him it was something dreadful, but he didn't feel it. *Since I'm already dead*" (480). Wolfe's satire, then, is complete: Sherman's arrest and "death" establish the "oppressive and false" nature of whiteness (Roediger, *Toward the Abolition of Whiteness*) writ large in the maintenance of the state that manages urban triage, and approaches what Gilmore, repeating Keynes with a difference, considers the cultural axiom of the protection of private property, state power, and redevelopment's decimation: "[I]n the long run, we're all dead" ("From Military Keynesianism," 185).

But the "death" of Sherman McCoy, as the pampered son of the "Lion," as the product of elite private institutions, and as a bond trading Master of the Universe, has also catalyzed the "birth" of another Sherman, a "somebody else" who emerges from the depths of the jail to don the clothing of a new man. Not wedded to the network of whiteness through which he can purchase his individualist identity, Sherman is alone, alone to fashion a new identity through which he can still survive in an urban landscape that he once sought to escape during his days as a white man. Having lost his protective whiteness, Sherman gains manhood. It is the narrative logic of this distinction—the loss of whiteness produces the resurrection of a virile masculinity—that forms the crux of Wolfe's corrective pedantry, the cautious rebuilding of the social world brought down by his satire.[15] This is, for Kennedy, Wolfe's final and most profound failure, if only because Sherman's transformation could have been a moment in which the racial "vanities" of those living in late-capitalist New York are exposed for their true insidiousness and fantasy. Sherman's rebirth as the emblem of "imperial white manhood" instead provides the corrective or polemical gesture that satire seems to demand, and which Kennedy argues is Wolfe's disappointing dependence on the maintenance of white masculinity, albeit an insecure and anxious one. Indeed, Sherman's newfound violence and aggressivity suggest that he has been racialized anew: if whiteness, as we have been discussing thus far, is so deeply entrenched that its mode takes on universal and therefore nonracial attributes, then Sherman's rebirth is the simultaneous self-consciousness and denaturalization of a racial whiteness, a mode of identity that necessitates as much assertion as the racial identities of others (people of color). Sherman, in losing his whiteness as racial privilege, must struggle to become white as ethnic codefendant. That Sherman's discovery of his violent streak enables him not only to win the brief melees against the "rioters" in the final scene, but also to survive as a "career defendant" in and out of the judicial system (including the holding jails) does at first appear to turn the once butt of Wolfe's jokes into a victimized and therefore redeemed hero. Sherman's assertive whiteness, no longer an assumed privilege, appears to garner a certain pathos as the narrative suggests that sympathy is possible because he is now on the other side of a contemporary politics of ressentiment. In other words (and in Frye's terms), his redemption and resurrection as what Kennedy describes as the "new (old) man" turns the satire directed against him into a classically tragic finale.

Crisis, to reiterate Stuart Hall, is not in and of itself a good or bad thing; crisis simply signals the interruption of social reproduction, that new forms of action must be taken because prior ones have been shut down. In the case of Sherman's identity, the crisis generated by his crime, arrest, and trial precludes him from ever recognizing in himself his prior life of whiteness. His social death forces him to jettison whiteness's pretensions to imagine insulation by the state and private property as normative conditions through which to live his life. That Sherman's crime and subsequent travails allegorize the social disorder of New York, implicate unwitting white privilege in the organized killing of Black communities, and demonstrate the capacity of white supremacy to sacrifice its own, bring together the satirical and pedantic strains of *Bonfire* and highlight Wolfe's greatest racial anxiety about the 1980s. If Sherman's crisis in social death leaves him orphaned from whiteness, to whom does he now turn? For white people who have been sacrificed at the altar of whiteness for the maintenance of urban triage, and who awaken to the realization that the little that works for them as white people cannot mitigate the social forces that work against them—like those abandoned in urban triage—what recourse of recognition is left for them? The tentative answer to this question, in Sherman's case, is a reconstituted virile white masculinity. But whom does this resurrected whiteness serve, and to what end?

Around this celebration of a resuscitated white masculinity built on a "precapitalist model" circles what Wayne Booth calls the "kindred spirits" of Wolfe's readers, who reach an implied catharsis with Sherman. And thus Wolfe's satire, enabling his readers to feel a final sympathy with Sherman's victimization, can create an "amiable community" by foregrounding Sherman's plight as a more general truth of whiteness's status in the contemporary American scene of social relations (qtd. in Hutcheon, 93). Yet both this positive reading of Wolfe's polemic and the more negative consideration of Wolfe's failure to go further with his satirical scalpel (Kennedy's assertion) are built on the premise that it is Wolfe who wields the power and capacity to create a satirical consensus around his narrative. It is Wolfe who then looks like the one calibrating the measure of normative value through which his knowing educated reader would be welcome and his narrow-minded detractor remains outside this colluding community. As Linda Hutcheon suggests, however, satire does not build its elitist community of readers who "get the joke" as much as it reaffirms an already existing community of readers whose values and assumptions form a "discursive community" in which a well-received satire finds a vein: "But what if the discursive community *precedes* and *makes possible* the comprehension of irony? . . . *it is discursive communities that are simultaneously inclusive and exclusive—not ironies*" (94, 97; original emphasis). Hutcheon's interpretive reversal, that a given community of readers historically (and geographically) situated determines the viability or accessibility of a purported satire, helps us once again displace the question of whether Wolfe's satire fails or succeeds; instead, we are left to consider what makes Wolfe's satirical agency possible and, more specifically, what necessitates this final resurrection of Sherman as the narrative's victimized champion.

Thus, rather than viewing Wolfe's recuperation of Sherman as a failure of satirical will, we should set in motion this "precapitalist model of masculinity" with the late capitalist political economy against which Sherman purportedly stands. And set into motion, Wolfe's vision of an enervated whiteness—one based on the correspondence of private property, individualism, and the privilege of social insulation—requiring and resurrecting into a more assertive, even violent white masculinity poses the historical limit of the color-blind ideology put forth during this decade. Sherman's identity-in-crisis made evident in his assertive masculinity bears witness to the logical response to a more general crisis in whiteness perceived in the social relations of the 1980s. To put it bluntly: when the naturalized hegemony of whiteness is seen to be under attack, whiteness must reemerge as a bloc to reassert its will to power in the urban landscape of competing racial interests. Sherman captures this vision of whiteness shorn of its normative power in animalistic terms that bear an almost Hobbesian imprint: "The dog doesn't cling to the notion that he's a fabulous house pet in some terrific dog show, the way the man does. The dog gets the idea. The dog knows when it's time to turn into an animal and fight" (626). Like the reawakened self-consciousness of a house dog's more base instincts of violence and survival, Sherman's reaction to his loss of status, privacy, and protection is to reassert a masculinity that exposes the circuits of violence and power used to maintain the social order.

Although this formulation of Sherman's virile whiteness bears much similarity to Kennedy's treatment of Sherman's newfound aggression as the expression of "imperial white manhood," there remains one profound difference: whereas Kennedy regards Sherman as a throwback to a pre-capitalist model, I consider Wolfe's construction of Sherman as showcasing the double nature of whiteness wedded to a political economy that also requires both normative and "primitive" modes to further its march toward increasing accumulation and privatization. Sherman's new/old identity is not anachronistic; rather, he embodies in his transformation the necessity of late capital in the United States to employ both the seemingly automatic, "free-market" processes of accumulation and the highly visible but necessary violent forces that coerce the accumulation process in places where there were none. Capitalist development, as Toni Negri has shown, necessitates the creation and expansion of a "warfare state"; capital cannot infinitely valorize itself, as much as the once bond trader Sherman would have liked to believe. The accumulating capacity of capital is always fettered by the generation of its own crises, and thus capital needs an external agent—and for Negri this agent is the state recalibrated not to provide welfare, but to realize its increasingly violent and repressive (both military and financial) capacities to ensure the maintenance of capital's success.

Negri's formulation of this "crisis-state" or "warfare state" is a contemporary reenactment of Marx's distinction between "capitalist" and "primitive" accumulation, an observation he made as he considered the British state's role in moving that nation more quickly into its industrializing economy. For Marx, primitive accumulation was the necessary historical process of "divorcing the producer from the means of production" (874–75). It involved the dissolution of feudal society, which in turn transformed former laborers of the soil into "free" labor; in turn, this emergence of "free," propertyless wage labor was made possible through a series of "bloody legislation" forcing former workers of the soil off the land (Enclosure Acts), creating home markets, controlling wages and prices, producing a national debt, and establishing international credit systems. Marx implies that the capitalist mode of production did not emerge magically, or through the hard work or frugal savings of the capitalist class, but through the use of a coercive state, with its parliamentary acts of "expropriation," to induce the transformation toward a capitalist mode. Marx describes the state's role in actively facilitating the development of capital quite explicitly: "But they [the methods of primitive accumulation] all employ the power of the state, the concentrated and organized force of society, to hasten, as in a hothouse, the process of transformation of the feudal mode of production into the capitalist mode, and to shorten the transition. Force is the midwife of every old society which is pregnant with a new one. It is itself an economic power" (915–16). The state does not merely reflect the historical changes taking place in the transition from a feudal mode to a capitalist one; for Marx, the state undertakes the role of instigating these very changes, utilizing its political authority to initiate and fuel the historical process. Capital's birth is an economic transformation predicated on the politicizing of the economy by the direct control and transformation of the state's power. The economic, within primitive accumulation, becomes an exercise of power through violence.

The simultaneity of capitalist and primitive accumulation continues in the late capitalist era, most visibly for our purposes in the state (the city government in this case) deploying policies designed to accelerate and extend real estate valorization during the 1980s. And just as whiteness is tied to the speculative economy that enabled Sherman to accumulate his vast even if fictitious wealth in the beginning of *Bonfire*, so, too, does his virile whiteness reflect the violence inherent in the "primitive" underbelly of late capitalism and the state that sanctions it. Sherman, we must remember, goes on the offensive and pummels demonstrators and bystanders alike (both men attacked are nonwhite) while Kovitsky, the presiding judge lamenting his loss of courtroom control, balks at addressing the crowd. Just as Kovitsky decides reluctantly to retreat with his gun-toting court officers, Sherman admonishes the judge to stand his ground:

> "Their only friend, their only fucking friend." [Kovitsky] looked at the court officer. "Okay Brucie, let's go."
> *No! Now!* Sherman yelled out: "No Judge! Do it! I'll go with you!" (656)

Sherman's aggression takes over as institutional power feels its temporary loss of power. A provisional moment of reversal, it is Sherman whose maniacal violence staves off the "mob" and enables the "little band [to] beat a retreat down the marble halls" (656). Wolfe here is drawing an ironic parallel between Sherman's "accidental" assault on Henry Lamb and the more intentional attacks on two other Black men: Sherman's sense of his own liberation and innocence comes about as a result of his deliberate violence. But the satire imbedded in this irony, that in the final instance Sherman's demonstration of his potential to resort to such brute force actually saves this little white band, does not engender his juridical freedom, but rather prolongs his litigation, his new job as a "career defendant." Sherman, tellingly, is not charged for these new assaults in the retrial. For it is this man, who has lost his privileged yet enervating whiteness, whose individual actions provide safe harbor for those aligned with the state, whose safety ultimately allows the other white people associated with the case to benefit materially, to become more ensconced in the circuit of whiteness. Sherman's violence may be at once primitive and astonishing to others, as well as liberating for himself (from the whiteness to which he was once wed), but his newfound expression through fists and fights rather than insulation and money mitigates the crisis that threatened the legitimacy and even the safety of the state.

The contradictory trajectories that Wolfe marks in this final scene of Sherman's virile whiteness protecting and actually perpetuating ensconced, enervated whiteness and its institutions signal if not the success of his satire, then the anxiety fomenting this narrative mode. For as much as Sherman's identity is remolded into one that feels like his is a life that will fight the power (signified in a barely ironic parody of the Black Power salute), what is evident in the epilogue is the undercurrent of rage that Wolfe tries to express with humor as the mock newspaper article recounts the apparent successes of the other white characters. Wolfe's epilogue dramatizes what Thomas Nakayama and Robert Krizek argue is the capacity of whiteness to realign seeming contradictions in its ideologies to retain its social and political power: "[T]hese contradictions are central to the dynamic lines of power that resecure the strategic, not tactical space of whiteness." (102). Sherman's transformation, rather than signaling an alternative identity that is distanced from the whiteness to which he once adhered, serves to suture the circuits of power that enable the continuation of whiteness through the hegemony of property, privatization, and state sanction. And that Sherman's restored masculinity and lost whiteness serve also to restore the larger map of white racial power in New York suggests that Wolfe's satire reflects the paucity of possibility in moving beyond the scope of whiteness as a force that, like capital's capacity and need to destroy, create, and accumulate, deploys contradictory modes to enable its survival in ever more enclosed, privatized spaces. Wolfe's novel must remain satire, since what is consistently satirized—whiteness—cannot move beyond its historical horizons of limitation.

"One moral of this story," Claire Jean Kim has written in a different context, "is that racial power cleans up after itself. It inevitably generates protest by subordinated groups, but it also names, interprets, and ultimately silences that protest" (219–20). To render whiteness comprehensible in the era of multiculturalism, white people, who lose state protection and private property and who still remain wedded to their whiteness *as* property, have no recourse but to defend a structure of white supremacy that may in fact push them outside the comforts of privatized urban spaces and into triaged places. But Wolfe's example of Sherman gestures to even greater consequences of whiteness's defense: alongside the privatization of space is the *socialization* of punishment. In order for urban triage to expropriate land to facilitate and fuel its drive to garner greater spatial enclosures, it must, by way of the state, expropriate people and send them to early social death, to silence them, and to prevent them from recognizing their shared condition of death so that capital may live. This dual process of urban triage, as we have seen, depends on a racial logic that surpluses people of color first, but those who have occupied whiteness's deathly embrace are not exempt either. They must sometimes also pay the wages of whiteness. The power of urban triage makes alienated social beings of those who hold to the fiction of triumphant individualism, and prevents the possibility of imagining wealth beyond private accumulation. It individualizes disorder, naturalizes pathology, and demands that one's relation to society, mediated by the state, is nothing but antagonistic. It calls others to join, but proclaims its house rules: good fences make good neighbors.

We might therefore consider *Bonfire* as the logical endpoint of a narrative that recognizes, yet is unable to transcend, its historical allegiance to racial power, the "stifling conformity imposed on whites" (Ignatiev and Garvey, 36): as the antiracist Race Traitor Collective, whose membership is composed of white members who call for the abolition of the white race, admit:

> Finally, we know how devilishly difficult it is for individuals to escape whiteness. The white race does not voluntarily surrender a single member, so that even those who step outside of it in one situation find it virtually impossible not to step back in later, if for no other reason than the assumptions of others. (Ignatiev and Garvey, 37)

Yet even if individual whites succeeded in singular acts of racial betrayal against the citadel of whiteness, such intention bears the burden not only of creating new "assumptions of others" in order to chart new modes of identity not allied to white privilege, but also of making such acts powerful enough to produce a general crisis in the structure that adheres whiteness to economic, legal, and political power. Treason to white privilege requires, then, a different kind of recognition, in which wealth is imagined and acted upon as a social right, to turn the work of state fascism into new coordinates of difficult, maybe even impossible, cooperation. Treasonous whiteness may, in fact, demand a new story about the United States, which turns multiculturalism not into a process of making whiteness more flexible to accommodate literate homeowners, model minorities, and talented tenths, but of inverting the parable of race into something far more treacherous to power's demand, a paradox or contradiction that whites must inhabit in order to refuse whiteness's imperative: "Indeed, it might be worth pondering the paradox that . . . black worldliness, the counter-tradition of America's most marked exclusion, is perhaps this country's only consistent universalism" (Singh, 514). This would be a different story of social recognition. Sherman's experience with the U.S. judicial and penal system may have radicalized him, turned his once inherited conservatism into "liberalism," but he is alone. Wolfe may indeed view his protagonist at some level as a racial hero of sorts because of his transformation, his refusal and inability to play by the rules of his former club of privilege. But Sherman's call to forget that he is white—the raised fist against the reconstituted community of white privilege—also contains its own parodic apparition returning as the ghost of aggressive masculinity. Sherman smiles slightly as he salutes, Wolfe's final ironic gesture telling us: never forget. Against the alienated and alienating smile of such allegiance, the possibilities of whiteness's betrayal lie in what white people choose not to forget, what determined faces they decide to encounter, and for what end they work to remember.

Conclusion

> We are the mothers and fathers
> who tell our children
> wipe your mouth of the M word
> wash your hands of it
> before you come to the table
> and give thanks
> for all the dead before you
> and all the living to come
> —Russell Leong, "Beware of the M Word"

The parable of multiculturalism is a story of many failures, but not one of defeat. It has expanded the orbit of the American literary constellation, sure enough, but still nervously wonders at what to make of its idealization. For those who reject other calls to revert to some form of mono-cultural return to Western culture as a basis for imagined community and common humanity, multiculturalism, in its broadest and most vague sense, offers not only egress from such cultural singularity, but also uncharted opportunities to see oneself and others anew. But tracing the age of multi-culturalism, as it emerged in the United States during the 1980s, helps us ask the question that has stood the test of time—what is to be done?—with another, for those who have remained attentive to that political urgency: what have we accomplished? This study has attempted to answer the latter question in hopes that the first remains vibrant in the minds of individuals who strive to imagine new ways of forging common humanity, who reach points of despair over what our best intentions have been used for, and who still believe, sometimes against the evidence, that stories of failures do not necessarily lead us down the road of historical defeat, the death march of history's end where some dance, while many others weep.

For that story, the one I call urban triage, makes legitimate the expan-sion of civil death for more and more people, which deepens the inevita-bility of social death for all. "Such is the work of fascism," Ruth Wilson

Gilmore observes, and, as Sherman discovers in Wolfe's novel, urban triage ultimately begins to gnaw away at those whom such social abandonment has benefited most. *The Bonfire of the Vanities* takes urban triage, and the particular brand of multiculturalism that has given such ethos credit, to its limit and gestures, unwittingly, at yet another triangulation of crisis, this one put forth by Thomas Rainboro, in 1637, at capitalism's birth: "Either poverty must use democracy to destroy the power of property, or property, in fear of poverty, will destroy democracy" (qtd. in Gilmore, "Terror," 35). The first to go in the destruction of democracy—and with this almost everyone can agree, though with different explanations—are those whose identities have made of them the persistent historical orphans of U.S. nationalism and its imperial presumption of economic and civilizational supremacy. But the gaze of the poor returns stares of indignation and shame, and gives us two messages: you made us this way, and you are not so far behind. That this mirror image provokes in our writers racial anxiety suggests that their newfound, partial entry into the cultural conversation might offer the salve of conscience, but only for a moment. Multicultural reveries awaken when we take the wrong turn and find ourselves in the spaces left behind, amidst people abandoned except to coerce and contain, imprison and incapacitate. And despite all our machinations to enjoy the small plots of property granted to us, to satiate our excess political desires in the bodies of others, to fantasize about our own small revolutions, we, like Wolfe, eventually get lost, stop, and peer at the built landscape we've destroyed, and can only utter "Astonishing."

Du Bois recognized that, in thinking through what was to be done by asking what had been accomplished throughout the long twentieth century, the color line, the famous phrase that is attributed to him, was only the beginning of the problem. He increasingly saw Rainboro's prophecy as a correct diagnosis for understanding not only America's "race problem" but also the world's dilemma, carved as it was in frantic colonial scrambles. Convinced that Black destitution found its counterpart in the world's dispossessed, Du Bois extended his analysis, which began with the Philadelphia Negro as a problem and ended with locating the problem in the dependence of civilization on the dehumanization of most of the world, especially the "dark workers of Asia, Africa, the islands of the sea, and South and Central America." "These are the ones," he pronounced at the end of *Black Folk: Then and Now*, "who are supporting a superstructure of wealth, luxury, and extravagance. It is the rise of these peoples that is the rise of the world" (338). The veil of *The Souls of Black Folk*, his painful metaphor for the condition of Blackness in the United States, cannot be lifted without a radical shift in sight; what Du Bois realized was that the partial or "second" sight given to Black people actually composed the most universal of visions. Call it a counterculture of modernity, Black Marxism, or revisionary (rather than revisionist) history, Du Bois discovered, toward the end of his life, that seeing the world through the looking glass darkly produced not partial knowledge, but different kinds of recognition, and that this worldly relation toward "these peoples" could provide the necessary cognitive map out of the grid of white supremacy, European colonialism, and capitalist misery. For this, J. Edgar Hoover of the FBI—who founded the Bureau to hunt down "Negroes, communists, and anarchists"—would deem him a threat to U.S. national security, even handcuff him just before he turned eighty-three, and the U.S. government would revoke his American passport. And Du Bois himself proclaimed that necessary social recognition could not be found in the United States: he announced his membership in the U.S. Communist Party from his new home in Accra, Ghana, in effect bridging worldwide socialism with transnational anticolonialism.

But differing sight does not necessitate physical exile, although geographical displacement is on occasion helpful. And such vision does not need utopia, though utopian urges abound because so little around us seems hopeful. If the era of urban triage marks one aspect of this age of human sacrifice, in which the Benjaminian state of emergency is the deepening of social death, then within multiculturalism lie the contradictions from which social recognition emerges out of specific crises. Racial anxiety produces numerous examples of failed vision, but also, sometimes, one moment that indexes responses that exceed their intentions, and work through crises differently from the answers offered by urban triage. Neither a valorization of the "local," nor a repudiation of global struggle, what is also provided is, I argue, a moment of political autonomy in a determined situation, multiculturalism's beneficiaries confronting figures of crisis of their making and providing a different, if not new, exertion of pressures against the seductive imperative to trigger triage at the moment of conflict. It is not abstractly resistant or subversive, and it is not a refusal of privilege; it is not a case study of bad subjects to ideology's hail: it is a realignment of racial power through imaginative, different recognition.

This study began with the modest proposal that in order to figure out what was to be done, we needed to understand what has been accomplished. Uncovering what urban triage has hidden of cities' palimpsests, the writers this study has investigated reveal deep anxiety over how a community of racial diversity mitigated social abandonment and sacrificed significant segments of U.S. humanity, multiculturalism's fix to urban triage's surpluses. It ends with a reading of Andrea Lee's short story, "The Days of the Thunderbirds," from her collection *Sarah Phillips* (1984), offering an example of what happens when those surplused come face-to-face with multiculturalism. Better known for her racial skepticism, class distance, and political hesitance, Andrea Lee's story bears the writerly markings of an "affirmative action baby," the children of the generation that took to streets, sat at lunch counters and the fronts of buses, gathered in churches, and set fire to stores, which enabled a trickle of young Black women and men to go to college. Lee herself attended Harvard. At first glance, Lee's stories seem to straddle the anxiety of Wideman with occasional flairs of unrepentant vitriol against the so-called Civil Rights Establishment that other affirmative action babies such as Shelby Steele, Stephen Carter, and Darryl Pinckney inveigh.

"The Days of the Thunderbirds" was written in the mid-1980s but takes place in the early 1960s, during which time the civil rights movement, at least its integrationist component, gained a substantial social legitimacy, which enabled middle-class Blacks to enter white or mixed spaces, for Black children to play with white children, and become a model for racial progress. In Lee's story, Sarah, the teenage narrator, attends Camp Greyfeather, an "integration" summer camp in the backwaters of Delaware designed to provide benign cross-cultural encounters: the motto for Camp Greyfeather is "Adventures in Understanding." Herself from Philadelphia's suburbs, Sarah befriends two other girls—Ellen, a Jewish girl from Baltimore, and Chen-cheu, the Chinese American "camp beauty," who hails from Oberlin, Ohio. The children's parents are on the frontlines of 1960s-style multiculturalism, mostly clergy and professors, whose progeny are selected deliberately to make the camp look like "illustrations for UNICEF posters." But to Sarah, such crossracial community is overloaded with the blandness of middle-class privilege. We learn, for example, that Chen-cheu's father is a professor in Oberlin, but not much more than that. And besides a "frightening exotic loveliness above her muscular swimmer's shoulders," Sarah reports, Chen-cheu displays a "calm, practical personality . . . and she talked with a flat Midwestern accent, as if she'd been brought up on a soddy" (68). The entire camp seems a picture-perfect image of moneyed racial harmony, and it is, until a gang of Black girls and boys from Wilmington, Delaware, known as the Thunderbirds, arrive to engage the camp in a kind of domestic cultural exchange. But as soon as the Thunderbirds arrive, mayhem and tension ensue. What begins as the Thunderbirds' disregard for camp protocol—they defiantly swing from a tree considered sacred and off-limits by camp counselors, they overload a canoe, they rap, they fool around when on a hayride, literally making hay—turns violent as the Thunderbirds scuffle with the boys and girls of the camp. This visit by the Thunderbirds is cut short, as a result, and the gang goes back to Wilmington and the encounter seems a failure.

Neither Sarah nor Ellen are personally involved in the fights, but Chen-cheu participates in a scuffle with three Thunderbird girls. After discovering that someone had stolen her t-shirts and new bathing suit, Chen-cheu protests. A fight ensues. It begins with hair-plucking and jostling, then Chen-cheu punches Belinda in the stomach. Sarah describes the rest of the scene: "Our counselor Molly came running down the path from the rec hall at precisely the moment when Chen-cheu, propelled by a nasty push, came flying out of the tent to sprawl in the dust and shriek out a string of curses that even Ellen and I had never heard her use. Her beautiful face was contorted and almost purple with rage, but she wasn't crying. None of us were. After that, we were separated from the Thunderbird girls" (78). For the moment, let us cite, but not overindulge, the possible allegorical reading of this scene, as a confrontation between accommodationist, integrationist ideals and its almost complete failure to address the material concerns and needs of the Black urban poor, between multicultural privilege and continued racial grievance. Certainly, Lee seems to suggest this line of reading as the story's denouement brings about what Sarah calls "adult justice," the mitigation of crisis by separating the campers and the Thunderbirds. The remedy for the potential for racial chaos is to lock out those who refuse to follow the terms of so-called rational integration, to send them back to the ghetto, to install a kind of benign neglect on the Thunderbirds. Both the campers and the Thunderbirds are rounded up, but the campers stay in their country reverie, while the gang is sent back to Wilmington with their chaperone, a sallow, unenthusiastic social worker. As the two groups are separated, Sarah, Ellen, and Chen-cheu attempt to forge a symbolic bridge, a desperate gesture to acknowledge the Thunderbirds' existence, as the adventure in understanding collapses precipitously: they feebly memorize and recite a song that the Thunderbirds performed earlier, as the gang's bus shambles away from the camp. Left behind is the hope that "some obscure misunderstanding was about to be cleared up," but the greater resignation that, as the logic of urban triage took hold once again, the failure and loss are insurmountable.

But what is curious in this story is Lee's choice to have Chen-cheu, the sole Asian American in the camp, fight the Thunderbirds. Chen-cheu is described as wholly Midwestern. She was raised in Ohio, but beyond that we know next to nothing about her upbringing: as the story points out, she might as well have been raised on a soddy. She is a placeless Asian, an Asian American girl hailing from the suburbs of America, just like the other placeless teenagers in the camp. It is Chen-cheu who lets out a string of curses that surprises even her best friends in the camp; it is she whose purple face expresses a rage that the other campers might feel but do not express; it is she who is the sole girl to fight. The cause of the fight is simple enough: someone takes her property, and she fights to get it back. It is the suburban fear and anger of racialized urban threat. But the fight is not the important matter, just as, to bring back Stuart Hall again, social crisis itself has little meaning. What's important in this story is the way in which people respond to the crisis. The narrative tells us that neither Chen-cheu nor the other girls cry: one response. The other is the very next sentence, the response of the crisis managers, the counselors and adults of the camp: the two groups are separated. For the adults, violence and theft are problems that can only be solved by separation, by sanctioning safe space, to reinstall the fiction of suburban bliss and urban violence. For the teenagers, however, the fight significantly becomes an object lesson, not in violation of property, but in the deep failure of the adults to understand that separation solves nothing, that the eruption of violence, the local sign of a much larger crisis, cannot be mitigated by remedies of containment. Chen-cheu and the others are not so much disappointed in the Thunderbirds as they are in the adults' attempt to maintain a multicultural fantasy by purging the very group that threatens that fiction.

As an Asian American person, whose scholarly work is anxiously lodged in institutions of knowledge and who participates in the political scales and structures that give rise to multiculturalism in the age of urban triage, I am struck by Chen-cheu's rage. It begins as a rage of the middle class and turns into something else, a different kind of anger, and along the way it exposes the utter failure of the counselors' structural remedies. It is an anger that demonstrates that deep gap in American life between spaces of privilege and spaces of poverty, the Maginot Line that the architects of contemporary U.S. social formation maintain at all costs. And it prophesies that the price of privilege is much costlier than cultural misunderstanding, the stakes so great that the struggle cannot but be engaged at every level. What this means, for criticism, is that we interrogate everything, every story, but we cede none of them either. For even here, in the space of multicultural artifice, those who find their anxiety, if they find their rage, *however it comes,* can violate that difficult line and begin to imagine how they might reconfigure what place they do occupy. Not without anxiety, we reconstruct stories of failure not to consolidate resigned defeat, but to alter our frames of recognition in a ceaseless dialectic. Multiculturalism, to this extent, need not serve as the fellow traveler of urban triage, nor the fantasy of exit from social confrontation, but as one level in which power wrought can be given back to those who have waited so long for the expansion of social wealth, the debt that has yet to be repaid. Like Chen-cheu, Ellen, and Sarah, those who have eyes to see and ears to hear, who locate themselves in the process of cultural production, can envision and imagine in their constrained spaces, and within these spaces labor to cooperate for the broadening of human life rather than collaborate in the deepening of social death. Abdicating neither racial identity nor common humanity, but transforming both in our analytic labor, we refuse to surplus anything, for "all stories are true," and they all help us map out a collective journey down that difficult, indefinite road.

Notes

1. Mapping Urban Triage and Racial Crisis

1. Catherine Saalfield and the late Ray Navarro make historical linkages between the insouciant apathy of the Reagan and Bush administrations' response to the AIDS epidemic and the discrimination experienced by Blacks, women, and the poor from the public health sector. To Saalfield and Navarro, "[E]very death related to HIV/AIDS complications is an act of racist, sexist, and homophobic violence" (351). And while this is certainly a rhetorical conflation, the utterance reveals an epistemology of the targeted, through which the eyes of those most damaged by state invasion of people's bodies or its abandoning of these bodies becomes the provisional space of objective sight, over and against the presumptuous universality of the state's vision. See Catherine Saalfield and Ray Navarro, "Shocking Pink Praxis," in Fuss, *Inside/out*, 341–69.

2. In 1985, Margaret Heckler, Reagan's director of the Department of Health and Human Services, outlined the administration's primary concern over the question of AIDS and public health. "We must *conquer* AIDS," asserted Heckler in a now infamous quote, "before it affects the *heterosexual* population . . . the *general* population. We have a very strong *public interest* in stopping AIDS before it spreads outside the *risk groups,* before it becomes an *overwhelming problem*" (emphases added). The imperial vantage that Heckler's statement assumes not only reinforces normative understandings of "public interest," in which damaged gay bodies are marked implicitly as a problem but not an "overwhelming" one, except insofar as these bodies might indeed run rampant over the "general," straight population. It also weaves in the discursive logic of urban triage as public health's main weapon and targets a group so that that group might be tagged unsalvageable. To the extent that a state agency sanctions the targeting of one group for the protection of another, in this case to quarantine gay men to "save" heterosexuals, it forms the ground upon which the state might justify the extension and expansion of such policy to other groups, if necessity demands it. It is not simply a case of the state's dependence on homophobic "common sense" that creates the conditions for this form of urban triage, but the extent to which that common sense is honed, made precise in its carving out of the saved and the damned, that we might consider the function of state power in its capacity to issue death to the dying. Heckler's comment is quoted in Jeff Nunokawa, "'All the Sad Young Men': AIDS and the Work of Mourning," in Fuss, *Inside/out,* 311.

3. The Master Plan for Higher Education, designed to project a fifteen-year vision for the state's educational policy, was unprecedented in scope, the first comprehensive attempt to coordinate the often competing and uncoordinated college and

189

university bodies across one state. It guaranteed state-financed higher education for all California students, on the heels of the steady growth of college enrollment through federally subsidized "G.I. Bills" following World War II. Anticipating both explosive growth and concomitant high economic development in the state, the creation of a coordinated higher education system in California was viewed as indispensable in the transformation and expansion of California's economic engine. For an excellent overview of the role of higher education in the production of a cold war labor force, see Barlow and Shapiro, "Educating the War Babies."

4. Moreover, the Master Plan of 1960 recommended the implementation of a policy of "diversion," that is, to divert lower division students—eligible for university or state college entrance—toward "readily accessible junior colleges" as a way to reduce the social wage of higher education and to stem the flow of much-needed capital on all campuses (including those newly created campuses).

5. The two most oft-cited renditions of the model minority myth emerged in the same year, 1966. In January, William Petersen penned an article entitled "Success Story, Japanese American Style" for the *New York Times* magazine, in which the author praised Japanese Americans for overcoming a long legacy of racist oppression that culminated in their World War II internment. Ten months later, *U.S. News & World Report* issued a similar report on Chinese Americans. The unnamed author of "Success Story of One Minority Group in the U.S.," mirrors Petersen's sentiment of this other Asian group, with explicit comparisons and denigrations of Black protests for increased state intervention: "At a time when it is being proposed that hundreds of billions of dollars be spent to uplift Negroes and other minorities, the nation's 300,000 Chinese Americans are moving ahead on their own, with no help from anyone else" (73). Between January and December, President Johnson's "War on Poverty" was in full swing, on the way to doubling funding for the poor between 1965 and 1968; this same year saw the emergence of the Black Panther Party.

6. The problem facing the Truman and later the Eisenhower administration was the American public's deep reluctance to funnel so much of its productive capacity into defense spending, particularly after World War II. The production of a "Red Menace" as the justification for continued expansionist and interventionist foreign policy was something of a public relations fiasco: the public simply did not see or did not want to see a crisis. And it was only the opening salvos of a civil war in Korea that gave seemingly material evidence to the supposed "threat" of communism. As Bruce Cumings has written, "If the Korean War became a total war for Koreans, it was for Americans a moment in the making and remaking of American hegemony; as [Secretary of State Dean] Acheson said, from this standpoint it was not a Korean War, it could have happened anywhere. Acheson also blurted out something else . . . in 1954: 'Korea came along and saved us'" (Cumings, 2: 761).

7. High wage levels and consumption patterns brought about by American Fordism afforded a predominantly white, skilled labor strata to enjoy these tenuous benefits of postwar capitalism, but did little to incorporate Blacks into the economic fold. The so-called underclass debate largely results from the structures of

intractable obstacle. See Blair and Fichtenbaum, "Changing Black Employment," and Sugrue, "Structures of Urban Poverty."

8. Alongside the vast purchasing power of a high-wage sector of U.S. labor arose the expansion of higher education through which members of the U.S. working class found themselves able to send their children to college. Between 1940 and 1970, the percentage of college-age people entering institutions of higher education rose from a mere 16 percent to 47 percent; those of the lower working class, whose presence in colleges was virtually nil in 1940, were able to put 15 percent of their children through college. In this period of economic expansion, suburban home ownership and higher education signified the emerging cultural standards of success for significant numbers of the white working class.

9. The job losses that resulted from the waning of Fordism continued well into the 1990s, but as M. V. Lee Badgett reports, workers of color suffered disproportionately: "Jobs were not uniformly lost, nor were they lost according to the race- and/or gender-blind forces of a recession, that is, affecting only certain regions, industries, and occupations" (113).

10. By no means a Marxist apologetic, Reich continues in his critique of 1980s financial speculation by warning of the larger consequences of such paper exchange cut loose from "real value": "An economy based on asset rearranging has a final disadvantage. It tends to invite zero-sum games, in which one group's gain is another's loss. As those engaged in rearranging the slices of the pie become more numerous and far more wealthy than those dedicated to enlarging the pie, social tranquility is threatened. Trust declines. As trust declines, the pie may actually shrink" (107–8).

11. See Edna Bonacich, "Asians in the Los Angeles Garment Industry," and Bonacich et al., eds., *Global Production: The Apparel Industry in the Pacific Rim.*

12. The waning of Fordism also led to the rise of what economists refer to as "Toyotism," a newer system of capitalist control that employs the specialized nature of flexible accumulation for its management. Briefly, a Toyotist concept of control diverges from Fordism along five arenas. First, rather than employing a mass of workers within a single company, Toyotist firms hold a limited number of "core" workers, selectively employing a smaller group for its parent company while "outsourcing" many of its operations. By subcontracting its processes, Toyotist companies secondly "vertically deintegrate" their system of supply, using a "just in time" logic that keeps their maintenance of inventory fairly low and puts pressure on the outsourced firms to feed necessary supply only during times of demand. Third, working against the idea of Fordism that high consumption must complement high productivity, Toyotism imagines its marketplace selectively and controls the production of goods by catering to "individual needs." Fourth, rather than restructuring its organization according to new trends in technology (a trend in U.S. companies in the early 1980s, which caused a severe backlash by displaced workers), a Toyotist company designs new technologies (such as robotics) to fit existing structures of production. And finally, while Fordist firms often own much of their capital and see banks as necessary evils, Toyotist companies hold little of their

own capital, and operate by debt finance, which in turn entails a more cooperative relationship with financial institutions. See Ruigrock and van Tulder, *The Logic of International Restructuring.*

13. The logic of capitalist accumulation put forth here ironically has been metaphorized by "radical" theorists who view the dismantling of rigid hierarchies and structures as a new logic of revolution (as opposed to the systematic, planned route of Marxism-Leninism). Deleuze and Guattari, for example, have likened this revolution to a "rhizome": "Let's sum up the principal characteristics of a rhizome: unlike trees or their roots, the rhizome connects any point with any other point, and none of its features necessarily refers to features of the same kind." See Deleuze and Guattari, *On the Line,* 47. While Deleuze and Guattari link this notion of rhizomorphic relations with issues of semiotic and textual concern, the idea of an autonomous "rhizome" extends to social relations. See Guattari and Negri, *Communists Like Us,* 17.

14. Wendy Brown argues in *States of Injury* that the result of the welfare state's legitimacy crisis and the concomitant economic panic during the 1970s—whose telltale signs were unemployment, fiscal misalignment, urban infrastructural decay, and capital flight—was to turn leftist and liberal critics of the state into its trenchant champions during the 1980s. "Indeed, Western leftists," Brown writes, "have largely forsaken analyses of the liberal state and capitalism as sites of *domination* and have focused instead on their implication in political and economic *inequalities*" (10). Neoconservative and neoliberal celebrations of the withering of Keynesian welfarism have effectively shifted the debate over state form and capacity that mask state *expansion* in a newer, meaner modality.

15. Manning Marable has referred to the domestic war against Black organizations as an example of U.S. "civil terrorism" involving concerted acts of repression that date back to the extralegal tactics of the FBI's COINTELPRO program of the 1960s and 1970s. See Marable, *How Capitalism Underdeveloped Black America,* 128–29, 246–48. Curiously, as Glenn Omatsu has reported, Asian American CBOs survived the repression of community organizations during the 1970s and early 1980s; he attributes this phenomenon to the perception that Asian American organizations posed less of a threat to the racial order. See Omatsu, "The 'Four Prisons' and the Movements of Liberation," 40–41.

16. As Gilmore notes, approximately 60 percent of California prisoners hail from the Los Angeles region, which includes Los Angeles, Ventura, San Bernadino, Riverside, and Orange counties ("From Military Keynesianism").

17. The racialization of urban space is all the more pronounced when we also take into consideration the extent to which residential segregation has *increased* in U.S. cities since the civil rights era. Systematic discrimination on the part of real estate agencies and federal "redlining" practices dovetail with the "neighborhood preference" of whites to live in racially homogeneous communities to make housing segregation the unspoken norm throughout the 1980s in almost every major U.S. city. For Douglas Massey and Nancy Denton, this "American apartheid" has contributed directly to the persistence of racialized "ghettoes." See Massey and Denton, *American Apartheid.*

18. The rhetorical danger of Wilson's thesis—and especially the title of his study—is articulated in a special forum entitled *The Declining Significance of Race?: A Dialogue among Black and White Social Scientists,* edited by Joseph R. Washington. Raymond S. Franklin has offered a complementary and corrective study that attempts to take into account Wilson's thesis while maintaining the significance of race in social analysis. See Franklin, *Shadows of Race and Class.*

19. As Michael Katz observes, the contemporary debate over the "underclass" (post-Moynihan thesis) emerged in 1977 with a *Time* magazine report on the "growing menace" of this group of people, "most of whose members were young and minorities." It was with the publication of Ken Auletta's book, *Underclass* (1982), that the term became firmly ensconced in popular discourse. Katz, however, finds questionable the imposition of moral categories to define urban poverty. See Katz, "The 'Urban Underclass,'" 4–5. See also "The American Underclass," *Time,* 14–15, and Auletta, *The Underclass.*

20. Murray began as a researcher for the Department of Justice and participated in crafting studies that attempted to unlock the connection between crime and social environment. See his *The Link between Crime and the Built Environment: The Current State of Knowledge.*

21. Murray's conclusion that race has no place in public policy—"Race is not a morally admissible reason for treating one person differently from another. Period."—ultimately leads to a naturalization of race as an instance of cultural mores (223). For to assume that race should not be considered in understanding the structures that determine social relations, even as one acknowledges that it exists, grants race almost noumenal status. It is therefore not at all surprising that Murray's notions of naturalized racial formations have led him to put forth, with Richard Herrnstein, the now infamous "Bell Curve" thesis.

22. Dove, *Selected Poems,* 14. This poem first appeared in her collection of poems entitled *The Yellow House on the Corner.*

23. I'm grateful to Richard Yarborough and Connie Razza for providing me with a corrective to Vendler's pedantic reading of "We Real Cool."

2. Fictionalizing Workers in the Barrio

1. I borrow this term from Elisa New in her study *The Regenerate Lyric: Theology and Innovation in American Poetry* (60).

2. For instance, in a different context, Ronald Takaki's study of plantation life and labor struggle in Hawaii, *Pau Hana* (1983), recounts the bitter interracial and interethnic tensions that occurred between various Asian immigrant groups and Portugese overseers or *lunas* during the latter half of the nineteenth century and into the first two decades of the twentieth. But *Pau Hana*'s story culminates in the momentuous labor strike in 1920, which brought Filipino, Japanese, and Chinese sugar cane workers together, a shining example, in Takaki's view, of class solidarity against plantation bosses and of an incipient "local" or even arguably Asian American identity formed in response to Hawaii's racial formation. The strike in 1920 sowed the seeds for even more interracial cooperation among various Asian workers in the

"all-race strike" of 1946, with which Takaki concludes *Pau Hana*. Takaki's cele-bration of Hawaii's multicultural labor history would eventually find its way into his Pulitzer Prize–winning *Strangers from a Different Shore* (1988), his chronicle of Asian American history and a still-assigned textbook in most Asian American studies courses in the United States. In both books, Takaki's narrative is, if not triumphalist, at least hopeful: the power of Asian American solidarity in Hawaii is enough to bring down the "Big Five" plantations, which would eventually lead to the dismantling of the plantation economy; the cultural interchange between vari-ous ethnic groups helped forge the concept of "local" culture and produce "pidgin English"; and the historical processes between the two strikes could be adequately described as nothing less than a "bloodless revolution."

But Takaki's bookends in *Pau Hana,* and indeed his selective reconstruction of Hawaiian history in *Strangers from a Different Shore,* occlude the islands' com-plexities, even contradictions, which on the one hand qualify his triumphalism and on the other signal the historical warrant under which Takaki wrote both books. Takaki's celebration of Hawaiian labor history must necessarily end in 1946, as the dissolution of the plantation economy that enabled the "all-race" cooperative spirit to emerge gave way to its contemporary formation, which is highly dependent on foreign (including U.S. mainland) tourism, an economy that splintered rather than solidified interracial cooperation. Moreover, Takaki's identification of these strikes as exemplary moments of *Asian American* labor history—as indices of Asian claims of their inherent Americanness—has been criticized by native Hawai-ian activists, who argue that the Asian American presence in Hawaii amounted to little more than a continuation of American colonial expansion, with little dif-ference among settlers of different racial groups. Takaki's own social warrant to write *Pau Hana* in 1983 and include selections in *Strangers from a Different Shore* (1988) coincided with the rise of a scholarly Asian American pan-ethnicity in the 1980s, one that consistently conflates Asian American struggles with Native Ha-waiian ones or, worse yet, ignores the uneven development and territorial contest that Native Hawaiians have engaged in against Asian American and even "local" interests. When viewed through the lens of complex history, Takaki's historiogra-phy lays bare that which it must submerge to form its coherent narrative, justify its interests, and make its fictive claim to truth, just as historical fiction, on the other end of the spectrum, depends so much on its relation to, and "original" rendering of, the past's events.

3. Two studies appropriate this term and use it as a metaphor to reflect on significant ideological and policy changes in Chicana/o struggles during a period of political retrenchment and reaction. See Burrola and Rivera, "Chicano Studies Programs at the Crossroads," and Maciel and Ortiz, *Chicanas/Chicanos at the Crossroads.* I will return to some of the findings in both of these projects later in the chapter.

4. See also Morales's comments in Gurpegui, "Interview with Alejandro Mo-rales," 10.

5. This project of reclamation is, as Ramon Saldívar argues, the underlying

ideological and cultural impetus for "Chicano narrative." Understanding that the means to narrate "history" amount to the capacity to determine a community's "reality," Saldívar claims this as the work of Chicana/o literature: "Rather than passively reproducing images of reality, the task of contemporary Chicano narrative is to deflect, deform, and thus transform reality by revealing the dialectical structures that form the base of human experience." See Saldívar, *Chicano Narrative: The Dialectics of Difference,* 5–7.

6. Márquez's interest in Morales's novels rests primarily in aesthetic judgment; for Márquez, fictional innovation of the postmodern sort offers instances in which Morales "risks the moment." Conversely, Márquez faults *The Brick People* when the narrative "lacks narrative focus" and instead degenerates into "flat," prosaic journalism. Ironic in this analysis is Márquez's notion that "postmodernist fiction" must be new, not "monotonous," since it is exactly the skepticism of innovation (the "grand narrative" of originality) that postmodernism is meant to propound. In this sense, boredom and tedious narrative would be central to, and not a "tack and distance from," postmodernist strategies; see Márquez, "The Use and Abuse of History," 81. Thus, while Lyotard would argue that the "post" in "postmodernism" does not imply this idea of "comeback, flashback, or feedback," he also argues that a postmodern "aesthetic" would amount to a refusal of nostalgia, or what Jameson calls "affect." For discussions on postmodernist "aesthetics," see also Lyotard, *The Postmodern Explained,* 80, 15; and Jameson, *Postmodernism,* 10.

7. Gutiérrez-Jones's reading of *The Brick People* is offered in the context of a larger critique of legal and social ideologies built on ahistorical visions of individualism; Morales's novel is, in this chapter, counterpointed to Richard Rodriguez's *Hunger of Memory.* Using insights from the work of critical race theory and critical legal studies, Gutiérrez-Jones attempts to situate particular Chicana/o works (Morales's, in this case) to put forth alternative visions that interrupt the predominance of protecting individual rights from political remedies for historical atrocities against groups (of color).

8. No doubt studies abound with regard to magical realism. Both Márquez and Gutiérrez-Jones place Morales's novel squarely in the tradition of Latin American writers who regularly deploy magical realist strategies. While the political usage and efficacy of magical realism deserve an extended debate, it should be said at the very least that on a stylistic or structural level, magical realist narratives entail a response to these moments of the fantastic and marvelous from both narrator and characters. Note the following delineation by Roland Walter between "fantastic" narratives and the narratives of magical realism: "As in the fantastic, in magical realism the reader is confronted with both a realistic and a magical level of reality. The main difference between the two modes, however, is the way the narrator and *the characters* react to and perceive the magical standards." See Walter, *Magical Realism in Contemporary Chicano Fiction,* 19.

9. While not definitively in the "magical realist" vein, Toni Morrison's celebrated 1987 novel *Beloved* reenacts the return of a magical or "ghostly" presence—Sethe's daughter—whose return compels only Sethe to work through and transform her

relationship to her slave past, and also the community to redeem and liberate itself from its alienating practices of their shared history. Simply put, no one in this segregated community on the outskirts of Cincinnati remains the same after Beloved's arrival.

10. This implicit gendering of capital processes and a "penetrated" feminine landscape is not insignificant, for this opposition continues throughout the narrative and helps to explain the patriarchal overtones for a nostalgia of community formation in Morales's vision. I am grateful to Tooktook Thongthiraj for this observation of the gendered implications of the Doña Eulalia story.

11. See Acuña, *Occupied America* (1981), 116–17; Romo, *East Los Angeles: History of a Barrio,* 4–6; Camarillo, *Chicanos in California,* 28–29. I am, of course, not suggesting at all that Chicano communities did not exist prior to the eradication of the Chinese, but rather that the exclusion of the Chinese was more or less coterminous with the massive arrival of Mexican labor through an unprecedented wave of immigration.

12. For a more complete history of the material conditions undergirding the process of racialization in California, see Almaguer, *Racial Fault Lines.*

13. To this extent, the novel's troublesome depiction of women, and particularly women of color, reveals that the "blindspot" is not Bulosan's alone, but one shared by U.S. labor during the 1930s and 1940s. That Bulosan narrates women of color and poor white women as figures of excess and violence invites a deeper historical critique of the betrayals that relegated women of color, and certain men of color, into terms of radical illegibility, in effect devaluing their labor and their capacity to organize within unionist and more broadly Popular Front formations. As Mike Davis and George Lipsitz have argued, labor's struggles in the context of the New Deal and World War II unevenly mitigated particular sections of the U.S. working class—namely, white men—which in turn consolidated the view that those who did not fall into prescribed versions of whiteness and masculinity would be little more than lumpen to a legible, legitimated "proletariat," sanctioned by the U.S. state and controlled from autonomous rebellion in corporate circuits (Davis, *Prisoners,* 80–82; Lipsitz, *American Studies,* 49). And, as Lisa Lowe reminds us, U.S. labor has historically remained trapped within this cultural logic of casting women of color outside the domains of organizing capacities: "The Asian 'American' woman and the racialized woman are materially in excess of the subject 'woman' posited by feminist discourse, or the 'proletariat' described by Marxism, or the 'racial or ethnic' subject projected by civil rights and ethno-nationalist movements" (*Immigrant Acts,* 163).

14. Benedict Anderson has written on the ideological service that "print-capitalism" helped facilitate, to allow seemingly disparate peoples to think of themselves as a coherent nation. See Anderson, *Imagined Communities,* especially chapter 3. For a concise discussion of Anderson's idea, see Brennan, "The National Longing for Form," 52.

15. As Elaine Scarry argues, because pain has for itself no referential content (it is not of or for anything), it can be invoked as a way to attribute meaning to a

certain idea, but this new idea is something different from "real" pain: "The very temptation to invoke analogies to remote cosmologies . . . is itself a sign of pain's triumph, for it achieves in its aversiveness in part by bringing about . . . this absolute split between one's sense of one's own reality and the reality of other persons" (4).

16. The passage of bringing the "barrio" into national meaning is a profound one, and could be opened up for further discussion using Scarry's section on "The Structure of War" (60–157). The passage from the novel itself warrants a brief citation: "Since the draft began, many Mexicans had volunteered. . . . And so they came and gathered from all the barrios: North Palatte, Cheyenne, Maravilla, La Loma, Austin. . . . From all Mexican neighborhoods the homeboys came ready to defend and die for *their home turf, the United States*" (250; emphasis mine). The conflation between the language of barrio ownership, "home turf," and a national community, "the United States," shows how violence, through its physicality and its lack of a singular discourse, brings about arbitrary relations and contingencies like that between the barrio and the national community.

17. The Los Angeles Police Department, according to Edward Escobar, emerged historically as the repressive arm of corporate and state interests to quell labor unrest, to break unionization attempts, and to keep the city "open shop." Not until the 1920s did the LAPD begin to reimagine itself as a professional organization of its own, independent from, but still structurally tied to, these same powerful interests. As Escobar notes, after 1923 the LAPD began compiling statistics correlating arrest records and racial background, and thus began a systematic march toward making criminality and race authoritative. By the 1940s, which is when Morales ends his story, the LAPD had produced fully developed racial theories of crime, which then spilled into official police policy and procedure toward its Chicana/o and other communities of color. Important to note is how the LAPD transformed itself into authoritative primary definers on the racialized backs of Chicana/os and other people of color, where earlier it had merely been seen as the protector of scabs, a repressive defender of white privilege. See Escobar, *Race, Police, and the Making of a Political Identity,* esp. 104–31.

18. Thus, Los Angeles and its barrios fall into the spatial history of border patrol predicated on a fear of disrupting by a "crowd," as Mike Davis has pointed out in his portrait of this insidious history of the LAPD. See "Fortress L.A.," in Davis, *City of Quartz,* 223–63, especially 228–29 and 250–51 for the discursive conflation of paranoia, crowd dispersal, technological surveillance, and militarized urban spacing. This regulation of crowds through the surveillance of various communities contributes to a regulation of the racial division of labor, which Mike Murashige refers to as the "warfare state." Thanks to Mike Murashige for allowing me to pilfer this contemporary usage of Antonio Negri's profound pun. See Murashige, "Race, Resistance, and Contestations of Urban Space."

19. I would argue that gender roles and constraints are even more delineated and buttressed in the course of this passage. The fear of Hickman the criminal, the murderer of a young girl, drives the residents of Simons to hold their children, especially their daughters, "by the hand" (172) and to celebrate Christmas, "the

birth of Christ in the safety of their homes" (175). This reassertion of a paternalistic domestic space in this moment of crisis meets up later in a spurious articulation of a familial domesticity that must be protected and nurtured through material accumulation. I will return to this marriage between money and family near the end of this chapter.

20. The exception to this assertion rests in the eyes of the women, the wives of the workers, who offer a critique of the photograph of the male workers (126–28). Here they exhibit a reading capacity that, as Gutiérrez-Jones points out, opens up a different space in which institutional power and its prevailing ideologies are put to the test: "The critical interpretations offered by these women are almost immediately silenced, yet in their brief surfacings it is clear that an apparently ontological battle is being waged and that the power clearly rests with the hacienda management, which can literally remake and destroy worlds by virtue of controlling the workers' desires" (89). But like the other examples given, this critical revision, which exposes the workers' reified positions, is quickly washed aside in Morales's narrative.

21. In a reading of Korean American artist Theresa Cha's seminal text, *Dictée,* Lisa Lowe expounds on this Althusserian axiom by demonstrating how dictation offers a means by which the imaginary relations structured by ideology can be challenged and exposed. A disjunction at the site of translation highlights and critiques the contradiction between ideological imperative and material conditions. See Lowe, "Unfaithful to the Original," 60–61.

22. The deployment and manipulation of semiotic codes in cultural expression and resistance has been discussed by Dick Hebdige, whose study on British youth suggests that the emergence of, for example, outlandish "punk" clothing styles displayed the youths' awareness of their subordinated position to societal norms and thus accentuated their rebellious stance toward such regulation: "When disaffected adolescents from the inner city . . . resort to symbolic and actual violence, they are playing with the only power at their disposal: the power to discomfit. The power, that is, to pose—to pose a threat. Far from abandoning good sense, they are acting in accordance with a logic that is manifest . . . they must first challenge the symbolic order which guarantees their subordination." See Hebdige, *Hiding in the Light,* 18. I am grateful to Mike Murashige for directing me to this important study.

23. A fascinating study of the discursive nature of the riots and their symbolic consequence both in the Anglo reaction and in their historical reverberances in Chicano historiography can be found in Mauricio Mazón's *The Zoot-Suit Riots.* Mazón suggests a correspondence between the white sailors' anxiety about the war, provoking a crisis in their ideas of masculinity, and their symbolic "castration" of the Other, personified in the zoot-suiter. Guillermo Hernández locates the figure of the *pachuco* in a satirical tradition embedded in Chicana/o literature; see Hernández, *Chicano Satire,* 20–30. George Lipsitz, among other labor historians, focuses on the riots' connection to the general unrest in labor (particularly by workers of color) during the war period; see Lipsitz, *Rainbow at Midnight,* 83–86. See also Acuña, *Occupied America* (1981), 326–29, and Romo, *East Los Angeles:*

History of a Barrio, 166–68. And of course, Louis Valdez's *Zoot Suit and Other Plays* provides even more ample coverage of the unrest.

24. This is what Gutiérrez-Jones finds laudable in Morales's novel. See Gutiérrez-Jones, *Rethinking the Borderlands,* 101–2.

25. Acuña has referred to this displacement of Chicana/o communities after World War II as a "siege" by "interests in the downtown [white] core." Romo specifies these interests in the "massive construction of freeways linking Anglo suburban communities. . . . Thousands of residents from Boyle Heights, Lincoln Heights, City Terrace, and surrounding neighborhoods were relocated." See Acuña, *A Community under Siege,* 19; Romo, *East Los Angeles: History of a Barrio,* 170.

26. In a study of working-class suburbs in Los Angeles between 1900 and 1940, Becky M. Nicolaides argues that blue-collar homeownership within small communities living alongside richer ones produced a different "version of the suburban ideal . . . [and] version of the American Dream." Because of the proliferation of these poorer suburbs, Los Angeles, in Nicolaides's view, counters the prevailing image of suburbia as a Parkian emblem of residential life free of urban poverty and corruption. Curiously, her analysis ends in 1940, a decade before powerful interests in places like Chavez Ravine convinced the city to use its power of eminent domain to disrupt the livelihoods that these homeowners had struggled so hard to build. Nicolaides does note that these working-class suburbs reached their numerical high point before World War II. Such residential expropriation in the 1950s onward in Los Angeles's Chicana/o communities is at least one reason for the strident militancy of Chicana/o youth in the 1960s who, inspired by the revolts in the grape fields of Delano, took over streets and schools to defend barrio-space from further contraction. See Nicolaides, "Where the Working Man Is Welcomed."

27. This is not to say that the home represents patriarchal idealization as such. Other works by Chicana/o writers open up the home in ways that displace Morales's vision of the home as sanctuary from labor's travails. Sandra Cisneros's trope of the house in *The House on Mango Street* (1986) highlights the extent to which the home is not a space of safety, but of violence, particularly for Chicanas. Likewise, Helena Maria Viramontes's short story, "Neighbors," in her collection *The Moths and Other Stories* (1985) offers a vision of a home that is neither safe from the violence of the street, nor a solution to the oppression experienced by those living in this East Los Angeles barrio. In fact, Viramontes seems to suggest, in the final image of Aura holding a shotgun toward the door, that the home signifies not safety and life, but the death of communal support. Earlier, Tomás Rivera's *y no se lo tragó la tierra* (1973) presents a house, under which the child dreams, that comes into being through the passage of several people, beyond that of familial bonds. And while Rivera's novel imagines collectivity where Cisneros's and Viramontes's stories highlight histories of domestic pain, tragedy, and survival, all three writers help bring to crisis Morales's notion of the home as panacea for the degradation and suffering of Chicana/o work outside the home.

28. Perhaps an index to the changing dynamics within Chicana/o historiography and cultural studies in responding to the conservatism of this era, Acuña's third

edition of *Occupied America* (1988) expurgates the Decker passage, and greatly submerges the work and contribution of communist organizers to Chicana/o workers' struggles.

29. For a discussion of the shift from "Chicano" to "Hispanic" in Chicano studies in the 1980s, see Muñoz, *Youth, Identity, Power,* 171–89.

30. Chicana/os and Latina/os have also served as the basis for testing and undermining other affirmative action measures, such the Supreme Court's decision in *Adarand Constructors, Inc. v. Peña* (1995), which deemed affirmative action in federal contractorships illegal and unconstitutional.

31. Compare this to the principles outlined in Juan Gómez-Quiñones's social history of the Chicana/o student movement in Southern California during the 1960s and 1970s: "The student movement is moving forward again . . . with a resurgence of militancy. . . . Students have made history. Today, the student movement, after ten years, must still continuously deepen the understanding of its role and make this understanding a force to face the major questions which confront the Mexican people. Students must assume the historical responsibilities incumbent upon them as a sector of the Mexican people with the seriousness this entails" (46–47).

32. Disparaging older forms of nationalism as intellectual and creative apartheid (clearly an attack on canon "well-wishers," but also a backhanded barb at cultural nationalists within groups of color), Kanellos links the new surge in multicultural creative production and interest to the new political economy geography that he sees as transnational: "As we move into a transnational world of European integration, [NAFTA], and many more such initiatives, our transnational peoples, our bilingual and multicultural literature, and the vision that literature bestows on the reader will become more crucial in identifying a place for the United States in the political, economic, and cultural geography of the twenty-first century" (4). Kanellos's comments coincide with those put forward by "transnational" critics such as Arjun Appadurai and Homi Bhabha, who makes the following claim about the United States in the new global condition: "But see even David Batstone's 'Virtually Democratic: Twenty Essentials for the Citizen in a Network Society,' an essay which heralds a new age of a 'network society' challenging the centralized power of nation-states and their borders: '[T]he network society will not usher in an era of utopia. It will initiate a radically new productive potential for global cultures, to be sure. But it will not resolve the perennial shame of rich and poor, standing side-by-side.'" From Batstone and Mendiola, *The Good Citizen,* 46–47.

33. It is important also to note that the task of building a home of one's own in one's community—in this case, the Simons barrio—cannot be regarded merely as a triumph of individual or even communal will. Instead, the *necessity* of making a living in one's community is part of the larger trend of segregation endemic to Los Angeles in the post–World War II era, not only as a result of enforced separation, but also because of the structural changes in the Los Angeles economy, which required Latina/o low-wage workers to locate their homes close to the industries

to which they were and are tied. See Massey and Denton, *American Apartheid*; Pulido, "Rethinking Environmental Racism"; and Rocco, "Latino Los Angeles: Reframing Boundaries/Borders."

3. Appropriations of Blackness

1. Gerald Horne recounts that "[a]s late as 1910 it was possible to say that African-Americans were less segregated than Asian-Americans," and that during the resurgence of the Ku Klux Klan in Southern California during the 1920s, Asian Americans, Latinos, and African Americans shared the brunt of the white supremacist group's violent attention (26). This racial attention toward Asian Americans resulted in part from the fact that throughout the latter half of the nineteenth century and into the early twentieth century, Asian Americans composed the largest nonwhite group in California. See Almaguer, *Racial Fault Lines*, 29.

2. "I grew up in the fifties and sixties in Los Angeles, in what used to be the very center of Los Angeles, around Jefferson and Normandy, near [the University of Southern California]. In those days, it was an African American place, and yet it had a Japanese American ghetto at the center of it. It was constituted of Japanese Americans returning from campus right after the war." From Murashige, interview with Karen Tei Yamashita, 340.

3. Hong's reading of Yamamoto's "A Fire in Fontana" traces the differential but "relational" connections between the two groups, and argues that despite their different histories, Japanese Americans and African Americans both suffer socially as a result of their denial of property rights. As Hong asserts, "Internment [of Japanese Americans] and segregation [against African Americans] are disparate but related manifestations of the privileging of private property rights that structures the liberal democratic state" (293). These property rights are sedimented in law so as to grant white racial identity privilege and access to property denied to people of color. In this way, Hong follows the argument made by Cheryl Harris. See Hong, "'Something Forgotten Which Should Have Been Remembered,'" and Harris, "Whiteness as Property."

4. See Marable, *Blackwater*, 146–54; Takagi, *The Retreat from Race*, 51–52; Omi and Winant, *Racial Formation in the United States*, 132–36; Takaki, *Strangers from a Different Shore*, 478–84; and *Who Killed Vincent Chin?*, directed by Christine Choy and Renee Tajima.

5. See Davis, *City of Quartz*, 267–322; Marable, "Black America," 244–64.

6. "[T]hough many universities have begun to reappraise their curricula in the humanities, adding texts by non-Western or female authors to Western civilization courses, there are fewer Black students attending college today than in 1975." See Lisa Lowe, "Canon," 52.

7. "Both directly and indirectly, African Americans and other minority groups provided Japanese Americans with a new social context from which to establish a different collective response to the Internment, to stimulate the working through of individual traumas, and to reveal the broader legal and social relevancy of the

Internment for current race relations." See Don Nakanishi, "Surviving Democracy's 'Mistake,'" 30. Nakanishi's article provides a contextualization of the "redress and reparations" movement, which culminated during the 1980s.

8. The reading list over the Black-Korean "conflict" would be enormous. A good synthesis of the scholarship written on this issue, along with interesting ethnographic research undertaken after the L.A. rebellion, is Nancy Abelmann and John Lie's *Blue Dreams: Korean Americans and the Los Angeles Riots.*

9. Such a split has been a central concern for Asian American activists in Southern California. Ed Park, professor of history at USC and an activist in the Korean American community, told me recently that Black and Chicano activists in Los Angeles have all but written off Korean Americans as potential political allies.

10. I am using the story as it is taken from Columbo, *Rereading America,* 366–73. Hereafter, all citations of "Fire" will be parenthetical in the main text.

11. I will refer to the narrator of the story as "Hisaye," following the typical practice of critics like Cheung and other Asian American critics to produce both narrative distance and affiliation between Yamamoto the writer and herself as the protagonist of the story. Cf. Cheung, *Articulate Silences,* 74–125, for a similar usage of Maxine Hong Kingston's first name in an analysis of *The Woman Warrior* and *China Men.*

12. Hong extends the terms, coined by Richard Bendix, of difference between "formal" citizenship and "substantive" citizenship. Whereas formal citizenship underscores the equality of rights every citizen enjoys within a particular state formation, substantive citizenship highlights the uneven and unequal access to resources that raced, gendered, and classed citizens suffer and/or enjoy in social practice. See Hong, "Something Forgotten Which Should Have Been Remembered," 309; see also Bendix, "The Extension of Citizenship."

13. See Omi and Winant, *Racial Formation in the United States,* 61–65, for a schematic of the conceptual march of race in U.S. "intellectual" history.

14. I am borrowing the phrase "common sense" from Omi and Winant, who use the term in the Gramscian sense; see *Racial Formation in the United States,* 67–69. Gramsci's more overt Marxist rendition can be found in Gramsci, *Selections from the Prison Notebooks,* 419–25.

15. Hong writes that the conflation between "aliens and non-aliens," the general systematic denial of citizenship rights to Japanese Americans, and the eventual internment is bound to the longer history in the United States of denying rights to people of color in order to found both social and legal definitions of whiteness. Hong considers the Alien Land Laws of 1913 and 1920, as well as the National Origins Act of 1924, the prequel to the enforced incarceration of Japanese Americans during World War II. Implicit in Hong's reading of "Fire," then, is the connection between race, citizenship, and property, an intersection with which I agree, even if my conclusions about the story may differ from Hong's.

16. In Okihiro, see especially chapter 2, "Is Yellow Black or White?" and chapter 5, "Perils of the Body and Mind."

17. Besides Okihiro, see also Takaki, "The 'Heathen Chinee' and American

Technology." For a brief overview of the "model minority" myth, see Osajima, "Asian Americans as the Model Minority." An example of "model minority" writing can be found in the article, "Success Story of One Minority Group in U.S."

18. See Cheung, *Articulate Silences*, 29–33, for a reading of Yamamoto's writing style in this cultural context.

19. This issue over the "reserve" and restraint of the Nisei (second-generation Japanese Americans) in response to political horrors such as the internment provoked dialogue between Nisei folks and their more vociferous children, Sansei (third generation), who solicited stories from their parents in the movement for redress and reparations from the U.S. government over this very issue of internment; see Takezawa, "Children of Inmates." The "cultural" aspect of Japanese, or for that matter, Asian reserve and seeming passivity, however, elides the numerous cases in U.S. history in which Asian Americans not only participated in political struggles, but actually instigated political agitation in the form of labor strikes and draft resistance. Japanese American farm workers, for example, struck with Mexican workers in 1903 in Oxnard, California. And the term "no-no boy" (which John Okada later used as the title of his novel) refers to the resistance of Japanese Americans interned who were compelled to sign loyalty oaths and pledge to serve in the U.S. military during World War II.

20. Readers of Asian American literature may be reminded of Frank Chin's assertion that Asian Americans are continually compelled to enact "racist love" toward their white oppressors, as they are confronted time and again with this binarism in racial formation between Black and white. Chin's response to this, in his polemic essay in the 1970s and in his subsequent creative work, was to attempt to mold a definitive space for Asian Americans. This attempt was replete with problems, as Chin not only employed masculinist assertions of Asian Americanness but himself appropriated certain forms and notions (read: stereotypes) of Blackness to fashion an extremely circumscribed Asian American identity. See Jeffrey Paul Chan et al., "Fifty Years of Our Whole Voice."

21. Robert Gooding-Williams reflects on a poll taken shortly after the Los Angeles uprisings in 1992 in which a significant number of whites agreed that African Americans "whined" too much about racial issues: "For many whites, then, black speech is not the speech of fellow citizens, but the always-complaining speech of spoiled children. . . . [T]he racial ideology of these white folk works against the possibility of recognizing blacks as partners in a broadly conceived social and political enterprise." See Gooding-Williams, "'Look, A Negro!'" 170–71.

22. Again, Gooding-Williams points out a similar way that the political purposes of the L.A. uprisings were evacuated, because African Americans are deemed without the presence of mind to fashion a viable political statement and thus must resort to senseless violence: "The motives bringing people to the streets were, no doubt, numerous. But it strains credulity to deny, as many conservative and liberal pundits immediately wanted to do, that the uprising in Los Angeles was not for many an act of political protest." See "'Look, A Negro!'" 170. See also Judith Butler, who writes cogently about the construction of the threatening Black body (of Rodney King) that

led to the eventual acquittal of the four police officers in "Endangered/Endangering: Schematic Racism and White Paranoia," 15–22, especially 19.

23. It is important to qualify here that Yamamoto's displacement of her narrative authority in the story submerges the political work that she herself undertook after leaving her job at the *Los Angeles Tribune*. During the 1950s, she participated with and contributed to the *Catholic Worker*, a pacifist organization and newspaper based in a Staten Island farm community. She has always considered herself a "Christian anarchist," as well as an avowed pacifist. See King-Kok Cheung's interview with Hisaye Yamamoto in Yamamoto, *Seventeen Syllables*, 81, 85.

24. Lawrence, "Beyond Redress."

25. "The possibility that . . . (some) Asian Americans may become an ethnic group that either assimilates into whiteness or transforms whiteness by becoming its ally is objectionable to mainstream Asian American intellectuals, whose discourse of the bad subject is predicated upon the insistence of a fundamental racial difference from whites. While this racial difference is (of course) articulated by Asian American intellectuals as a social and historical construction, it is also nevertheless quite often construed, implicitly, as an essential—and not a strategically essential—difference" (Nguyen, *Race and Resistance*, 169).

26. See Toji and Johnson, "Asian and Pacific Islander American Poverty."

27. See Edna Bonacich, "Asians in the Los Angeles Garment Industry," and Asian Immigrant Women's Advocates, "Immigrant Women Speak Out on Garment Industry Abuse."

28. An example of this can be seen in the work of Asian American activists against the New Otani Hotel in downtown Los Angeles, a luxury hotel owned by the Kajima Corporation, based in Japan. The New Otani management has refused to allow its workers the right to unionize; thus, a protracted campaign to boycott the hotel has ensued. What might have been seen as another example of interracial strife, between Asian and white management and African American/Latino workers, or even worse, as an instance of anti-Asian bashing, did not arise thanks to the intervention of the New Otani Support Committee, many of whom are longtime Asian American activists in Los Angeles. The Support Committee works to generate solidarity among community residents and provide general assistance to the workers and the local union (Local 11, SEIU) that represents the workers. But what is also important in the work of Support Committee members, as well as for the numerous Asian American students in the Los Angeles area who come out every week to the boycott pickets, is the making visible of an Asian American political identity on the picket line, not to erase their Asian body in favor of a class issue, but to highlight their status as Asians so as to articulate an adaptiveness to the new forms of racial politics in Los Angeles. Thus, when Asian Americans, alongside Black, Latino and White picketers, confront other Asians who patronize the hotel, the effect is jarring: for what is foreclosed is the possibility of the management to exploit what could have been a racial divide. For a brief, albeit dated, report on the New Otani workers' struggle, see Davis, "Kajima's Throne of Blood," 18–20. A portion of Davis's article is quoted in Dirlik, "Asians on the Rim," 18–19.

29. See Lawrence Chua's brilliant critique of Asian American cultural politics and racial/gender commodification in his essay, "The Postmodern Ethnic Brunch," 4–11. In it, he writes, "I think we are ready to dispose of the innocence of the Asian subject. It is time to turn to ash the supposedly innocent construct of an essential Asian subject, the corpse without a murderer." As an alternative, Chua proposes recuperating an idea of "Black" that is not unlike the "Black" category in 1970s oppositional British cultural politics. For the historical inflections of "Black" identity and politics in Britain, see Hall, "New Ethnicities," 441–49.

30. Edward Soja et al., "Urban Restructuring," 227.

4. Intellectual Cynics, Cynical Intellectualism, and Brokered Masculinities

1. Wideman's troubled questions rehearse a persistent concern in Black intellectual life, one shorthanded "racial uplift" in the late nineteenth and early twentieth centuries. As Kevin Gaines has argued, those who have composed the historical Black elite mobilized the term from its contested meanings and origins into a middle-class ideology whose emphasis on self-help, moral purity, patriarchal authority, racial solidarity, and the accumulation of wealth sought to distinguish these few—Du Bois's "talented tenth"—from the majority of Blacks in the United States (1–2). As a mode of survival during times of racial violence, systemic segregation and disenfranchisement, and visible articulations of white supremacy, racial uplift served at its best as both a model for a more general messianic liberation and a bulwark against white dehumanization; at its worst, uplift signaled a replication of class difference and the very racial fictions from which its proponents sought to be free. This tension within uplift ideologies, between liberatory leadership on the one hand and racial complicity on the other, has not diminished. Indeed, latter-day members of the talented tenth face even more difficulty in claiming this kind of representative status. Aside from dismissals of the Black elite as wholly self-serving and materialistic from scholars such as E. Franklin Frazier, Harold Cruse, and even Du Bois himself, the rise and fall of revolutionary and nationalist groups in the mid-1960s into the 1970s provided an alternative figure to which the community could look. The radical, often working-class man whose tactics of direct confrontation, systemic critique, and oppositional rhetoric replaced the entrepreneurial, status-conscious Black professional man or woman as the one who held the keys to liberation's promise.

2. In a 1991 interview with Rebekah Presson, Wideman defended what some reviewers of the novel considered a short-circuited exploration of the MOVE bombing, the ostensible "event" generating the narrative's orchestral maneuvers. Directed at two fellow Black writers who reviewed *Philadelphia Fire* (Ishmael Reed and Charles Johnson) but implicitly gestured at all of the novel's reviewers, Wideman's response—that they "missed the point in the same way"—is not atypical for a writer granting himself the privilege of fictional imagination, the capacity to move outside the domains of "fact-based" writing. Readers arrive at the purpose of the novel after concurring with a series of presupposed negations that Wideman lists to make his "point": "[I]t wasn't a piece of investigative journalism about MOVE.

There're lots of books that attempt to look at that organization—the history of that organization—and what happened to the people and biographies of the members. That isn't what I was after. The book is not even a fictionalized biography or history of the MOVE cult. It's a book about many things" (TuSmith, *Conversations*, 109). The battery of negative references to the novel—"wasn't," "isn't," "is not"—culminates in a final, rather amorphous affirmation of what the narrative "is," a "book about many things." If this mode of identifying and delineating genre is not surprising, it is also not insignificant in its attempt to dislodge the seeming centrality of MOVE to the novel's "purpose." Wideman's comment suggests that the reader who honors the disciplinary protocols of the genre in which he is writing, who understands that *Philadelphia Fire* is a novel, will assume the agency to discover these "many things" about the novel. Wideman's anxiety about critical judgment—and it would seem, political judgment, given the highly charged discourse around MOVE and the subsequent tragedy—becomes manifested in the double rhetorical strategy of displacement ("That isn't what I was after") and containment ("It's a book about many things"), even as he engages in a subtle adjudication of what the book ostensibly is not about: notice the shift from the bureaucratic naming of MOVE as an "organization" to the religious and politically inflected usage of "MOVE cult." Likewise, in an interview with Bonnie TuSmith, Wideman expresses his appreciation of recent French readers of his work for engaging in "serious discussions of the writing as writing." He contrasts these Continental close readers with unnamed American critics who are, in Wideman's mind, too quick to judge his work on political grounds: "A review, if it's longer than five hundred words, can sometimes be a platform for the critic to expound his or her own ideas about the subject you're writing about. Seldom does a critic hold back his or her own ideas or politics and say, 'Let's just see what *this* story or novel has to say. Let's give the benefit of the doubt and let's look at the world on *its* terms and closely scrutinize and figure out what those terms are before we hit it with the hammer of judgment.' I don't think that posture, that kind of treatment of books, is very prevalent. It seems rare." See TuSmith, *Conversations*, 195–97.

   3. Wideman's journalistic paragraph on page 97 is carefully crafted, so much so that Robert Morace holds the passage up as an exemplar of "clarity, specificity, discretion, objectivity, and authority"; the assumption that Morace holds undergirds the confluence between these five qualities, seeming pillars of journalistic integrity. But I locate three issues that Wideman's readers must accept as convincing, yet unarticulated, warrants in order for this passage to make as much sense as Morace seems to suggest it does. First, Wideman's journalism compels us to accept, however temporarily, the *decontextualized* status of the story, and by extension of the event itself. Perhaps it is easy to read this passage because of the familiarity of the structure of the event (the state unleashes its pent-up violence when its orders are not followed without the use of such force); perhaps its readability testifies to the use of a conventional cause/effect method to narrate the story (bullets fail, the bomb works; a bomb is dropped, a fire ensues; violence occurs, an investigation follows); decontextualized narrative in the form of journalism demands our assent

to its (at least) initial plausibility, its packaged digestibility must remain tasteful in our mouths in order for us to read on.

Second, this passage underscores journalism's use of *selective priority and specificity* in its narration of an event. The converse of decontextualization, selective priority enables the journalist to describe—within the constraints of authoritative "objectivity"—the main focus of the story, and the details that will help give meaning to that focus. Of course, though the story is told by one person, whose subjective eye cannot be simply dismissed, such priority is believable and acceptable because journalism, as a narrative mode, depersonalizes the author and validates its own discourse (style, rhetoric, structure) without the "intrusion" of the journalist: the journalist is instrumental, but ultimately expendable as the journalistic narrative lives on. This particular passage first highlights the surgical nature of the violence—bullets, water, and explosives failing to "dislodge" the MOVE members, as if these people were an unwanted growth—and locates that violence first and foremost in its infliction on property. If the police bombed the 6221 Osage Avenue rowhouse to "dislodge the occupants," such an action, the following sentence suggests, appears tragic primarily because the bomb does not accomplish its mission of dislodging, but rather decimates other people's homes (houses destroyed, people left homeless). The stitching together of the bomb dropped and property violated closes the circuit of causality and effectively leaves out the violence that the bomb (and the other weapons used in the siege) inflicted onto human bodies, the members of MOVE. Their deaths are a result not of any particular weapon, but specifically of their refusal to "obey a police order to leave their home."

The ambiguity produced by decontextualized narrative and selective priority of cause and effect leads to the third point of assent for credible journalism, the use of *indeterminate agency*. Here, journalistic "objectivity" yields a series of ambiguities between action and (human) agent, its careful deferral of responsibility diffusing and distancing the reader of the event from intent. The use and preponderance of passive voice most obviously exemplify the attempt to minimize the importance of the actors who put these events into motion—"a bomb was dropped," "houses were destroyed," "occupants . . . were said to be . . . ," "eleven [people] were killed," "no criminal charges should be brought"—and the infrequent qualifiers that finally do locate the agents of the action (that, for example, the bomb came from a state police helicopter) do not detract from the emphasis in this passage on selective moments of the events, not on those who enacted the tragedy. This is not to say that agency simply disappears. Instead, machinery substitutes for and filters human agency, the "bomb" and the "assault" rhetorically and metonymically assuming the role of activity even if they syntactically do not. The metonymic, even synecdochal, emblems of police violence that bear the brunt of accounting for this episode may serve to represent the state in its bare and horrifying rudiment, as a violent institution, but such substitution also enables those who pull the trigger, turn on the hose, and drop the satchel to place a mediating term, object, or duty between themselves and those who receive the force of their hidden action. Ironically then, the matériel of violence does the work of claiming determinate action, and enables the final sentence of the passage, the closure and vindication of those who "perpetrated the assault," to not begin with a transitional preface such as "surprisingly" or "inconceivably." The reader is asked (by the hidden authority of "objective" journalism) to read this suspension of responsibility as a logical extension of the way in which the story has been narrated, for the indeterminacy (or more specifically synecdochical substitution) of agency results directly in the dismissal and deferral of responsibility. Phyllis Frus makes the following analogy: "[J]ournalism shares the goal of objectivity which corresponds to the aesthetic ones elevated by the modernists. . . . By positing the world as objectively there and insisting on their ability to capture it accurately, practitioners of objective journalism contribute to the reification of modern consciousness." By reification, Frus alludes not only to the increasing erection of disciplinary boundaries, but also to the ways in which the establishment of such protocols produces worldviews equally compartmental. If journalism's objectivity has more to do with achieving a goal that only partially gets at the truth of a matter or event, such claims of objectivity become impossible, even misleading statements, as much an aesthetic ideology as that put forth by the high modernists in their heyday. See Frus, *The Politics and Poetics of Journalistic Narrative*, 5, 91. See also Norman Sims, ed., *Literary Journalism in the Twentieth Century*.

4. Biographer James Lord notes that Giacometti's surrealist work thematized through sculpture reflects "[i]ntimations of cruelty and violence, sexual anguish, and spiritual alienation." Lord cites Giacometti as stating the following: "In the finished work I have a tendency to rediscover—transformed and displaced—images, impressions, and events which had profoundly moved me . . . though I am often unable to identify them, which makes them for me always more disturbing" (*Giacometti: A Biography*, 126–27).

5. Madhu Dubey argues that the novel's tension is a "deliberate vacillation on the issue of literature's social value," and that it marks both the impossibility and the necessity of resolving the crisis between its form and its political desire. She specifically locates Wideman's deep discomfort with nationalist sensibilities as an ideal resolution for making sense of urban chaos. But by "advertising its literariness" and "strain[ing] to grasp the modernist solace of a distinctive stylistic signature," Wideman's novel fails to reach the very people to which it hopes to attend ("Literature and Urban Crisis," 593). My concern with Dubey's critique rests in part with her underlying warrant for such stylistic and therefore political legibility: while she brings to her reading of *Philadelphia Fire* the kind of political economic analysis necessary for understanding Wideman's urban landscape, Dubey seems to suggest that Wideman can and should forge a language that can adequately make sense of the terrain, if only he would dispense with his modernist anxieties. But this stylistic distress is the very crux of the novel: just as it refuses to admit easy transparency with its "urban audience," so, too, does *Philadelphia Fire* augment its own failed horizon of expectation and therefore highlights its implicit connections to the social context and contradictions that enable its narration.

6. Carolyn Adams et al. chronicle this "wrenching change" in Philadelphia's

political economy, highlighting the city's particular vulnerability to what were national postindustrial trends. They assert that, coinciding with the increasing racial segregation between suburb and city, the uneven access to work and home have all the more fractured an already racially divided metropolitan area (*Philadelphia,* 30–65). Of the 3.5 to 4 million jobs that Bennett Harrison and Barry Bluestone note were lost in the manufacturing sector of the U.S. economy between 1978 and 1982 (a total net loss of half a million jobs), Philadelphia alone—with a population of 1.6 million people—lost more than 35,000 net jobs, more than half of those lost in the larger metropolitan area, or a 3.03 percent annual loss (compared to the 1.46 percent of the aggregate of the twenty largest U.S. cities) (Harrison and Bluestone, *The Great U-Turn,* 37; Stull and Madden, *Post-Industrial Philadelphia,* 22–29). Four years later, 22,000 more jobs would be permanently lost within Philadelphia's city limits (Stull and Madden, 28).

7. "The manufacturing sector has traditionally provided the greatest prospects for black [economic] progress. . . . Blacks who would have traditionally been employed in manufacturing are unlikely to find comparable occupations in the service industries. They are more likely to hold lower-paying occupations with fewer skill requirements." See Blair and Fichtenbaum, "Changing Black Employment," 80, 82.

8. Accompanying the crisis in manufacturing, one of the bedrocks of Black employment, was a relative decline in wages, income, and especially wealth among African Americans in Philadelphia. Bennett Harrison and Lucy Gorham have offered the following figures to elucidate the evaporation of high-wage earnings by Blacks in the 1980s: although, between 1979 and 1987, the number of African Americans grew in the high-income bracket (defined here as an income greater than $50,000 in 1987 dollars) by 1.6 percent (from 7.9 to 9.5 percent), those in the low-income share rose even more sharply, up to 37.1 percent from 34.7 percent (Harrison and Gorham, "What Happened to African American Wages," 57). Certainly, this downward spiral of the Black economy has much to do with the movement of African American workers from "core" industries (manufacturing) to "periphery" sectors (paper, textile, service), the results of which are depressed wages, less security, and more instability in increasingly labor-intensive jobs. In addition, Melvin Oliver and Thomas Shapiro have noted that income disparities and depression constitute only part of the problem; if Blacks are earning less than whites, Blacks are able to save close to nothing, even those in supposedly stable jobs such as public sector work: "Blacks in public-sector jobs fare better both in comparison to other blacks and to government-sector whites in terms of net worth . . . [but] Black median net financial assets, again, remain stuck at zero, no matter what the sector of employment" (*Black Wealth, White Wealth,* 116). Thus, the coupling of the wage squeeze in the Black labor sector on the one hand, and the consistent financial insecurity of African Americans with regard to an inability to accumulate assets on the other, have cordoned Blacks into a racially stratified place in the larger labor market, an economic barrier from which there is little avenue to maneuver. Although it could be argued that the relative downward turn in wages for Blacks is a result of the increasing necessity for "human capital" development (i.e., higher education) as a

result of the evisceration of high-wage manufacturing jobs, Harrison and Gorham note the following to show that such economic depression fell upon African Americans across the board: "Suppose just blacks in 1987 are compared to blacks in 1979. Over this period, the absolute number of black men with a 4-year college education who received annualized earnings of at least $35,000 did increase, by 467,000. . . . But the number of well-educated African-American men receiving *low* wages grew even more, so that the fraction of all black male college graduates who had high wages actually *fell*—from 23.4 percent in 1979 to 19.5 percent in 1987. . . . For black women college graduates, the findings are even more discouraging. Between 1979 and 1987, despite a new addition to the American labor force of 407,000 black women with at least 4 years of college, the number earning $35,000 a year or more *declined* by 10,000, with the share of such women who received high earnings also dropping, from 12.4 percent of all black women college graduates to 7.6 percent" (66; their emphases).

9. One of the consequences of what Massey and Denton call "hypersegregation": a Philadelphia resident living within the city limits earned only sixty cents to every dollar made by a suburban dweller in neighboring (mostly white) Montgomery County throughout the first six years of the 1980s (Stull and Madden, 197–98).

10. And such debate, as Nancy Denton points out, reflects differing visions of Blackness within the context of hypersegregation, worldviews that may be contestatory and indeed contested, but remain no less Black: "[H]ypersegregated cities represent both the best and worst of worlds for blacks—while the majority of the black population is hypersegregated in places like Chicago or Philadelphia, these are also large cosmopolitan cities where highly skilled and highly educated blacks are best able to 'make it'" (66–67).

11. Michael Bernstein, tracking national unemployment figures, makes note of this political change in economic policy during the 1980s: "Unemployment, after rising to 9.7 percent in 1982, fell to about 7.5 percent in 1984–85, and to 5 percent by the end of 1988. But consistent with the Reagan administration's belief that an 'inflation threshold' existed, job idleness was not pressed below the 5 percent achieved at the end of 1988. In this, the Reagan White House sharply distinguished itself from the Keynesian-style full employment commitments of both Democratic and Republican predecessors" (Bernstein and Adler, 28).

12. Katz argues that while African Americans have never been able to look nostalgically to "better days" with regard to their social situation, their conditions within the new political economy portend even more dire conditions: prior to the postindustrial economy, "poverty existed within the context of hope." But by the late 1970s and well into the 1980s, Katz argues, "Deindustrialization and depopulation, not growth, shape the new context. . . . Poverty now increasingly exists within a context of hopelessness" ("Reframing the 'Underclass' Debate," 447).

13. That the Black destitute, a term I derive from John Dominic Crossan, are frequently referred to as the "Black underclass," when scholars want to make the distinction between the absolutely "unproductive" and the marginally productive

and struggling "working poor," warrants a much further discussion about the historical emergence of the term "underclass" and the political and social implications of the term's usage. It is a debate I cannot reproduce fully (besides what I have already mentioned), but suffice it to say the unspoken meaning of "underclass" as a group differentiated by their behavior from the "working poor" has drawn sharp criticism from scholars recent and past, even among those who continue to use the term in their analysis. It is not that those who employ the term think that structure has nothing to do with determining the behavior of the "underclass"; rather, what is also debated are the *ways* in which structure constrains and produces behavior, and *how* one views the structure in the first place. Charles Murray views the problem of the underclass as a structural problem, but his contention with the structure (the evil welfare state) is vastly different from my problem with the structure. I choose to employ the term "destitute" in my analysis and not "underclass" because my usage, to reiterate, must imply that the relationship between the destitute and the structure that produces that destitution is *always* exploitative, and that whatever behavior a destitute person might express is a result and reflection of that exploitation. I do not suggest that "underclass" cannot mean this as well—Manning Marable certainly uses the term "underclass" to report on the exploitation of the Black poor—but given the predominant usage of the term in both the academic and popular press, through the voices of nightly news commentators and politicians preaching clichéd, Nixonian "law and order" diatribes, the damaging weight of the term to place blame on those who occupy this group exceeds, for me at this moment of the debate, its potential analytical utility.

14. I revise the term "destitute" from John Dominic Crossan's distinction in ancient agrarian society in the era of Roman imperialism; see *The Birth of Christianity*, 320–22. Crossan in turn developed this categorical distinction from Gerhard Lenski's well-known study on social stratification, in which Lenski deploys and theorizes a group of people in agrarian society that he dubs the "expendables." What is striking in Lenski's analysis of this group is the extent to which his description of the perceptions of the expendables mirrors that of contemporary notions of the "underclass": "This class is often ignored in analyses of agrarian societies, and when dealt with is not usually recognized as possessing the distinctive characteristics of a class. . . . Rather, its members are treated as *deviant individuals*—individuals who lack either the *intelligence or moral character* necessary to function as *useful* members of society. As plausible as this view may appear, it contradicts the facts" (my emphases). Lenski makes clear that the misery of the expendables is a direct result of the privilege of the upper classes; see *Power and Privilege*, 281–82.

15. Elijah Anderson, using the conventional terminology that I avoid, articulates the attempt at symbolic legitimacy on the part of the Black poor against the destitute: "Though one may argue that the institutions of both the wider society and the local community have failed members of the black underclass, local working-class and middle-class residents often hold the people themselves to blame. Such a stance allows those who are better-off to maintain faith in the wider institutions,

particularly the work ethic, thus helping to legitimate their own position in the local system of stratification" (66). For the Black poor, the Black destitute embody all that must be abjected; the destitute are, in Anderson's words, the "social yardstick" by which the poor maintain their status, however exploited, within the contemporary social and economic circuit (66). Later, Anderson notes that "ghetto residents"—which I understand here to mean the Black poor, working and exploited—rarely use the term "underclass" but all the same employ the idea of Black destitution constructed by those up the economic echelon: "The category referred to by that term [underclass] is in effect socially constructed through public observations of relatively better-off residents concerned with their own status and identity" (68).

16. "The residual, by definition, has been effectively formed in the past, but it is still active in the cultural process, not only and often not at all as an element of the past, but as an effective element of the present. Thus certain experiences, meanings, and values which cannot be expressed or substantially verified in terms of the dominant culture, are nevertheless lived and practised on the basis of residue—cultural as well as social—of some previous social and cultural institution or formation." See Williams, *Marxism and Literature*, 122.

17. As Michael White explains, "urban triage" borrows its terminology from military medical discourse; triage is the assignment of urgency placed on those wounded soldiers brought into the field hospital, and the designation that determines who will receive immediate treatment, whose wounds can wait, and whose injuries are untreatable and must be abandoned. White cites this metaphorical usage of triage in the context of urban public policy: "It offers the prospect of choice among neighborhoods in a time of shrinking overall resources; some are designated for rescue while others are abandoned" (13–14). See also Peter Marcuse et al., "Triage as Urban Policy."

18. Elsewhere, Kelley takes to task liberal/left structuralist scholars such as Michael Katz for continuing to use "culture" as a determinant for defining the "underclass": structure "explains" behavior. But Kelley argues that this simple reversal from the conservative version of the "underclass" (behavior explains people's structural position) is still driven more by a "moral panic than by systematic analysis": "[H]ow do we fit criminals (many first-time offenders), welfare recipients, single mothers, absent fathers, alcohol and drug abusers, and gun-toting youth all into one 'class'?" (*Yo' Mama's*, 18).

19. See Michael Boyette with Randi Boyette, *"Let It Burn!"*; John Anderson and Hilary Hevenor, *Burning Down the House*; Hizkias Assefa and Paul Wahrhaftig, *Extremist Groups and Conflict Resolution*.

20. John Dominic Crossan offers this image of these racial itinerants: "The term *cynic*, from the Greek word for *dog*, reflects the deliberate disdain with which Cynics provocatively flouted the normal conventions of human life. Their philosophy was above all else populist and practical rather than elitist and theoretical. They not only practiced what they preached, their practice was their preaching and their preaching was their practice. They were to be found more in marketplace [the center of economic power] and temple courtyard [site of religio-political

power] than in study hall and classroom" (333–34). "The Cynics sought happiness through freedom," as Farrand Sayre summed them up. "The Cynic conception of freedom included freedom from desires, from fear, anger, grief and other emotions, from religious or moral control, from the authority of the city or state or public officials, from regard for public opinion and freedom also from the care of property, from confinement to any locality and from the care and support of wives and children. . . . The Cynics scoffed at the customs and conventionalities of others, but were rigid in observance of their own. The Cynic would not appear anywhere without his wallet [knapsack], staff and cloak, which must invariably be worn, dirty and ragged and worn so as to leave the right shoulder bare. He never wore shoes and his hair and beard were long and unkempt" (7, 18). See also Harold Attridge, *First-Century Cynicism in the Epistles of Heraclitus,* and R. Bracht Branham and Marie-Odile Goulet Cazé, eds., *The Cynics: The Cynic Movement in Antiquity and Its Legacy.* Substitute the Cynic with a MOVE member, and the practice of MOVE suddenly becomes more visible, more knowable. (It is also not coincidental, I think, that the meaning of cynic—dog—was applied not only to Diogenes, but also to John Africa: both were called, in their respective communities, "dog man.") Renunciation of civilization's accoutrements signifies rejection of, in the Greek Cynic case, Roman imperial idolatry and injustice, and for MOVE, the U.S. corruption into a "cancerous style of life" (John Africa, quoted in Boyette, "*Let It Burn!*" 39). In his latest novel, *Two Cities,* Wideman ruminates on John Africa's nickname, "Dogman."

21. It is, therefore, not surprising, as Wagner-Pacifici details, that prior to the violent repression of MOVE and the state-sanctioned murder of most of its members, the statement by Police Commissioner Sambor to evict the occupants of 6221 Osage changed from handling arrest warrants for suspected criminals to the now infamous statement against MOVE's cultural and political terrorism: "Attention MOVE, this is America. You have to abide by the laws of the United States." What Sambor was supposed to have read is as follows: "This is the Police Commissioner. We have warrants for the arrest of Frank James Africa, Ramona Johnson Africa, Theresa Brooks Africa, and Conrad Hampton Africa for various violations of the criminal statutes of Pennsylvania. We do not wish to harm anyone. All occupants have 15 minutes to peaceably evacuate the premises and surrender. This is your only notice. The 15 minutes start now" (qtd. in Wagner-Pacifici, *Discourse and Destruction,* 42). Margaret's willful destitution violates not simply criminal statutes, but she threatens the fundamental basis of law by refusing the life of disciplinary control made in America.

22. This is Wideman's most explicit moment of avowed criticism of the internal politics of the MOVE group, but attention toward this wrong immediately turns away from Margaret and her sense of betrayal to Cudjoe's fantasy of finding connection with King. What begins as a criticism of internal group dynamics through the lens of Black female subordination is subsumed by an overarching desire on the part of Cudjoe to look past Margaret and her travestied experience, and to focus instead on the other man, a classic triangulation of homosocial construction:

"He'd winced when she described King lifting the blanket off his bed. Then Cudjoe had leaned closer, tried to sneak a whiff of her. Scent of the sacred residue. Was a portion of her body unwashed since the holy coupling?" (15). Cudjoe's initial query after this moment of Margaret's testimony—"Was Margaret Jones still in love with her King[?]"—and his visceral fantasy of smelling King on her body reenact homosocial desire through the supposed safety of Margaret's "desire." His fixation on the "sacred residue" on Margaret's "body unwashed" reveals much more than what Kaja Silverman would view through a Freudian lens as a moment of simultaneous disavowal and fetishism of both sexual difference and destabilizing homosocial fantasy, the "external displacement of *male castration* onto the *female subject*"; such a moment in which Cudjoe "deposits his lack" onto Margaret through fetishistic smell simultaneously "recognizes" and submerges Margaret's sense of wrong, displacing her feminist internal critique into a reconstituted male libidinal economy that locates an imagined political community with another man's sexual conquest, and not with a woman's sexual injury (Silverman, 45–46). Where does this leave Margaret, in the midst of such male abandon? She remains subordinated, within masculinist constructions of "right," since "ain't nothing, nowhere any better" (15).

23. Kimberlé Crenshaw discusses how the law, even those laws meant to protect women and people of color from discrimination based on race and gender, continues to submerge the particular, intersectional experiences of women of color. But it is this very intersectionality, what other sociologists have called the "multiple oppressions" of women of color, that can be the basis from which a new jurisprudence can emerge. To paraphrase Crenshaw's conclusion, if the law attends to the experiences of women of color, it will also take care of men of color and white women. See "Mapping the Margins: Intersectionality, Identity Politics, and Violence against Women of Color."

24. Such elision of a "beloved" urban community has not gone unnoticed by readers of *Philadelphia Fire*. Jan Clausen, for example, laments the displacement of Margaret's potentially incisive observations of "intersectional" urban experience by Cudjoe's largely heterosexist rehearsals of masculinist anxiety, and Wideman's attention to Cudjoe's obsession with women's "dark creases" leaving open the "most problematic lapses . . . located precisely where issues of race, gender, and fatherhood emerge" (53, 54). Similarly, in a 1995 dissertation on the issue of "Afro-American manhood," Philip Auger makes special note of Wideman's construction of his main protagonist's "voyeuristic objectification" of women as indicative of the profound and "ironic" discursive failure to enact a narrative of male, presumably communal, wholeness. But no less critical is Darryl Pinckney's review of the novel, whose "unabashed androcentrism" (Michael Awkward's phrase) leads to the charge that *Philadelphia Fire* falls victim to the "feminist extremes" that, in its attempt to imagine a beloved community or as Pinckney puts it a "riches of belonging," has lost focus on the "enduring problem of blacks [read: Black men] in the general society." Pinckney faults Wideman for sliding toward self-referential, overly textual "academic abstractions," instead of focusing on what Wideman

does best, crafting the particular voice of the (male) Black poor: "One story about basketball says more about black life than all his previous novels combined." Interestingly, what connects these critics to one another, even if they are on opposite ends of the heterosexist-feminist spectrum, is their explicit problem (in the case of Clausen and Pinckney) or implicit confusion with Wideman's numerous narrative digressions; *Fire* gets "carried away" by multiple layers of language and reference that point out the failure of thematic coherence, the primacy of a postmodernist ethic, or at worst the "opportunism" of bumping competing dialogic discourses together. Such failure to achieve narrative "wholeness" seems to be, in all three critics' views, the central problem of resolving the questions of race and gender, Blackness and masculinity—a failure predicated on Wideman's "stylistic distress," to use Dubey's term again.

25. It is important to note here that Margaret does not take on an "originary" status, from which to understand the relations in the rest of the novel. Margaret herself, as we have seen, produces profoundly negotiated visions through her own experience, and her reconstruction of her time before, during, and after her participation in King's group. Instead, Margaret, like the idea of MOVE as a temporary eruption of Cynical critique, stands in as a "source," the basis upon which Wideman builds his narrative of understanding the contemporary situation in Philadelphia. To put it another way in a more political context, Wideman never attempts to get to an ideal, celebratory agency of resistance, but tries to look at how resistance is both enabled and determined by its reliance on already existing models, whether these models are available or not, and effective or not in the particular context in which that practice of resistance arises.

26. Margaret's resigned struggle through vertical community seems also to be the basis by which Cudjoe imagines his own reentry into community, his return to "Black responsibility." Casting an eye toward earlier generations—"He would liked to be named for something his father or grandfather had done well" (3)—and searching for the next through the figure of Simba—"He must find the child to be whole again" (8)—Cudjoe tries to establish a mythic line of paternity whose ideal continuity will bring about not the repetition of generational frustration and enervation, but the unfettered triumph of singular (male) accomplishment. By posing Simba as his fictive next-of-kin, Cudjoe locates the desire for horizontal community through the line of male descent; Simba acts as the idealized surrogate through which Cudjoe imagines both redemption from his abandonment of his own biological children and the liberation of the community he had forsaken and to which he now returns. But Simba's persistent absence and Cudjoe's consistent failure to find the child breaks this vision of unbroken agency and sends Cudjoe into other spaces in which he will see that masculinity is again and again negotiated, compromised, and settled before such wholeness can be achieved.

27. A bit more anxiously, Auger regards this section of the novel as an instance in which Wideman articulates the problem of these men playing basketball—that no one shares the ethic of teamwork, but instead attempts to play for his own sake, his own personal triumph: "[In] the one scene Wideman includes in which Black

men seem to be bonding, sharing the common language of the sport, the ideology is not one of teamwork for the sake of common gain. Instead, Cudjoe points out that the game promotes a less unifying ideology: 'The game's one on one on one. Every man for himself. You keep the pill as long as you can score'" (89).

28. Cudjoe's attention to O.T.'s body and bodily movements brings us back to the homosocial fantasy that Cudjoe imagined when Margaret described her brief sexual relations with King. There, Margaret became the site of triangulated desire that mediates between Cudjoe and King within the larger space of normative, heterosexual tyranny. Here, however, within the context of basketball, homosocial bonding is articulated through a palpable homoerotic transformation of O.T.'s body as Cudjoe admires O.T.'s virile masculinity ("big, black, graceful") through a coupling of both putatively masculine *and* feminine descriptions (broad shoulders *and* narrow waist, delicate steps *and* taller than his brother). The visual pleasure that O.T. gives Cudjoe moves into sound, the uncalculated, easy conversation in which both men are "enjoying" what the other is saying. For a moment, there is no mask, no making strange the model before Cudjoe. For just a moment, the fantasy not only of idealized masculinity through its visualization of O.T. and the unbrokered masculine community of eagerness in conversation contravenes the perceived threat of travestied heterosexist privilege, and offers so very briefly an alternative logic of homosocial commensality.

29. Even Wilson Goode in his apologetic autobiography staged his bureaucratic "triumphs" as Philadelphia's first Black mayor in the context of the political and economic disaster that devastated the city's Black, Brown, and poor white communities: "The Philadelphia I inherited as the city's first African American mayor was on the verge of collapse, slowly hemorrhaging to death from high inflation, a declining population [read: white flight to the suburbs], and anemic revenue base created by the exodus of thousands of jobs [read: capital flight, Federal defunding]" (189).

30. Frank Rizzo's personal bigotry, savagery, and megalomania are well-known. It was as police commissioner that Rizzo developed his Civil Defense Squad, a "countersubversive" division of the police department charged with infiltrating, monitoring, and ultimately destroying mostly, but not only, Black activist groups and organizations during the movement-filled 1960s. His reign of terror—which also included "planting" evidence of bomb and assassination "plots" against him and the city, driving out free-speech advocates, and encouraging the use of brutal force among the police rank-and-file against Black residents in the city—culminated in his mayoral tenure, during which Philadelphia's first encounter with MOVE would take place, in 1978, in the form of a massive year-long offensive and siege, and eventual shootout. Rizzo's electoral base consisted of poor white ethnics (many of whom were Italian American) who remained in the city as more affluent whites fled to the suburbs, a power bloc that attempted to reinforce white racial supremacy in the face of economic decline (to which Rizzo's economic policies ironically contributed). By the time Goode replaced this man, who was nicknamed "the Raider," as mayor (the intervening term of William Green notwithstanding),

Rizzo left a police force whose culture had learned from him an ethic of brutality, corruption, and vigilantism; had cultivated and sedimented racial segregation between Philadelphia's poor white and Black communities; and had created a political environment in which dissent would be met with surveillance and repression. So effective was Rizzo's CD squad in crushing Black activism and militancy that by 1967 the FBI would model its own counterintelligence program, COINTELPRO, after Philadelphia's CD squad. See Donner, *Protectors of Privilege*, 205.

31. Though the narrative does not name the area about which Timbo talks, we can infer from his references to these "eyesores"—former sites of industry—and to the rail line along which these abandoned buildings stand that the two men are driving in West Philadelphia, across the Schuylkill River from downtown Center City.

32. Carolyn Adams et al. examine the redevelopment of Center City Philadelphia and note that while economic growth has returned to this portion of the city, "the city's low-income and minority populations have borne the brunt of the hardships presented by the redevelopment process" (123).

33. The one figure who still struggles to remain committed is Wideman's friend, who loses tenure at the university because of his attempts to link the mission of the institution to community empowerment. But such an identity, which conflicts with the school's responsibilities and "priorities," warrants the "ax to fall" systematically on and against this man "who'd drawn an unlucky ticket in this lottery" (113). Yet there is nothing unlucky about such institutional rearrangement and fiscal austerity, but rather they represent a definitive retrenchment of what Ruth Wilson Gilmore calls the "production of private intellectuals" in institutions of "what should be the 'public production of use values.'" See Gilmore, "Public Enemies and Private Intellectuals."

34. A word must be said about that last sentence, more specifically the confluence of "instrumental and structural agency." Black prosperity does not derive from Black poverty, at least not directly. But as capital reorganizes itself to come out of its self-generated systemic crises in order to extract even more profit from surplus-saturated landscapes, middle-class Blacks become instruments, and instrumental, in the service of this reorganization, of the increasing privatization of public goods. The consequence of this siphoning of the public toward the private is indeed the anxiety that Cudjoe (and Wideman) feel(s) and from which he (they) try to escape, for what becomes increasingly visible is the movement of the formerly cherished idea of Du Bois's vanguardist "talented tenth" transmogrified into a cadre of crisis managers, whose racial contiguity with those dispossessed, policed, and imprisoned makes an explicit racial critique of this warfare state increasingly difficult. Not unlike the structural role that I have suggested Asian Americans undertake as instruments in the screen of multiculturalism, masking further economic disparity, residential displacement, and racialized corporatism in Los Angeles, Black prosperity may not derive from Black poverty and destitution, but Black prosperity is instrumental in contributing to the structured maintenance of that poverty, and a concomitant interiorized, subjective response of anxiety. What Wideman suggests in these encounters between Cudjoe and Timbo, and with

other men, is that when the anxiety of privilege meets the structures of domination, language—even the historical language of resistance—fails to imagine a narrative beyond one's brokered prosperity of negotiated settlement and another's dispossessed isolation of criminalized destitution. As Cudjoe and Timbo—and one might guess Wideman himself—reflect despondently of prior liberation struggles, "How could Cudjoe have thought it would fill novels?" (83). This apparent skepticism of the Black revolutionary hero is discussed in Jerry H. Bryant, *Victims and Heroes: Racial Violence in the African American Novel*, 274–79.

35. The litany is striking; let us count: there is (1) the unnamed white woman in Clark Park whom Cudjoe notices while he waits for Margaret (25), whose face reminds him of (2) Teresa, a coworker on Mykonos; there is the (3) unnamed woman, the "anonymous foxy friend" across the windowscape of his apartment (54); there is his (4) wife, Caroline, from whom Cudjoe has become alienated (56–58); and there are the guilty fantasies of (5) Sam's daughter, Cassandra (63–65), and (6) Rebecca (122–24). Two other characters pay close attention to white women: Wideman's autobiographical insertion of his musing on his (7) own wife (102), and Richard Corey, the white "traitor" of MOVE (modeled after Donald Glassey, a founding member of MOVE who turned government informant) who feels ashamed of his (8) white girlfriend Cynthia's shameless crying and exposed underwear after a mugging (173–74). This totals eight references of desire for white women.

36. Fanon's heterosexist warrants notwithstanding (the assumption of the heterosexual interraciality, the ease with which the white woman's body parts are signs of whiteness as such), others have taken up Fanon's psychosocial template, what Derrick Bell remarks as the "political implication in the black man's attraction for white women" (203). Citing Oliver Cox, Bell argues that such desire manifests more the Black man's desire for economic and cultural mobility represented by the woman's whiteness than her sexual attractiveness (203). It is the result of a white-capitalist patriarchy, bell hooks concurs, that Black men and white women compete (and sometimes copulate) for the favors of the "white daddy" (99) and thus Black male desire for white women reflects a sexualized response to the social emulation of white men. For Kobena Mercer, Fanon's importance rests not only in the politicization of the Black man/white woman relationship in terms of economic, social, political, and cultural power, but also in the very language of the Black male psyche itself: no longer individuated as a pathology, Black male sexuality must be viewed in terms of environmental concerns and consequently warrants a collective response (151–53). In other words, Mercer suggests, the therapeutic answer is not just psychoanalysis that focuses on the individual Black male subject, but a process that foregrounds the relation between that subject and his environment built by the forces of race and gender, and empowered by the state (153). Interracial sexual relations are, in this view, always relations of power, and thus this reading would view Cudjoe's fascination with white womanhood as a continual sign to broker power in the face of his diminished masculinity because of his Blackness.

37. Some men in the Black Power movement did have a "place" for Black women. For Carmichael, women's position was "prone"; for Cleaver, Black women

were "practice" for raping white women. It should not be understood, however, that Cleaver and Carmichael formed the crux of all thought concerning gender in racial liberation struggles.

38. And, as Coontz suggests, this rise in female-led households may contain a good sign, one that showcases how Black women's choices are a practical rejection of the normative patriarchy so encouraged by Murray. Coontz offers a feminist alternative reading to the depiction of a pathological "Black matriarchy" popularized by Daniel Patrick Moynihan in his infamous report to President Johnson in 1965. Challenging both Moynihan's conclusions of the necessity of governmental "benign neglect" and Murray's rather malicious call to cut all public assistance to poor mothers, Coontz foregrounds the benefits of programs like AFDC: "Women choose single motherhood partly because the general expansion of their options since the 1960s makes it more possible for them to forgo marriage or leave an unhappy relationship, partly because black women have a strong tradition of economic independence and collective childrearing that makes them less dependent on men than are many white women, and partly because the black community has always valued children, in or out of wedlock, more than has mainstream white culture. There is good reason to believe that these are healthy, not pathological, qualities" (252).

5. Whiteness, Virile Masculinity, and Viral Satire

1. Again, Wolfe's historical portrait is slightly off, as the first great wave of white settlers were of British and to a lesser extent Dutch stock, not to mention the enforced movement of African peoples.

2. David Reynolds's biography of Whitman locates the poet's struggle and eventual disappointment in existing American political protocols as a main conflict generating this new kind of verse. Like a corrupt system bent on compromising all ideals for its own maintenance, poetry needed, in Whitman's words, a new "living principle" through which to find restoration and salvation. See Reynolds, 111–53.

3. Written in the midst of a waxing Know-Nothing party whose populist appeal to a white Protestant working class seduced briefly even Whitman in his early nativist days, *Leaves of Grass* treats immigrants kindly and embraces newcomers as an exciting addition to U.S. urbanity. Immigrants punctuate Whitman's landscape and become the basis for his radical celebration of what was once considered the abject body, a testimony made most clear in the poem later entitled "I Sing the Body Electric":

> The man's body is sacred and the woman's body is sacred . . . it is no matter who,
> Is it a slave? Is it one of the dullfaced immigrants just landed on the wharf?
> Each belongs here or anywhere just as much as the welloff . . . just as much as you,
> Each has his or her place in the procession.

> Do you know so much that you call the slave or the dullface ignorant?
> Do you suppose you have a right to a good sight . . . and he or she has
> no right to a sight?
> Do you think matter has cohered together from its diffused float, and
> the soil is on the surface and water runs and vegetation sprouts for
> you . . . and not for him and her? (813)

Whitman engages and dismantles the seemingly primal opposition, that of gender and sexuality, and uses the celebration of both male and female bodies as his template to call into question more obvious social distinctions, between free person and slave, citizen and immigrant, rich and poor. Just as the body in *Leaves of Grass* no longer takes subordinate status to the tyrannical will of the soul, so does the tactile, visceral, bodily, and therefore *social* existence of the immigrant pose a direct commonality with that of the nativist. Whitman's challenge to his ostensibly white, male, nativist, materially privileged reader—the directly addressed anaphora "Do you"—is to consider these elemental commonalities (knowledge, sight, matter) through a discourse of rights: if bodily existence is common to all, and if bodily existence forms the foundation of social experience, then the rights of "you" (the white, nativist, rich citizen) must be the rights of "them" (the colored, foreign, poor outsider). Rights once again become inalienable, no longer the privilege of the center, but through Whitman's expanding field of his "I" persona encompassed for those whose social capacities are being curtailed and limited in state legislatures throughout the United States in 1855.

4. Smith's consideration of the "uneven development" of urban space derives from Marx's description of capital as the "annihilation of space by time." "Historically," Smith explains, "the earth is transformed into a universal means of production, and no corner is immune from the search for raw material; the land, the sea, the air and the geological substratum are reduced in the eyes of capital to a real or potential means of production, each with a price tag. . . . [But] as capitalism strives toward the annihilation of space by time, it also strives more and more to produce differentiated space as a means to its own survival" (*New Frontier*, 78, 89).

5. "The poem counters this nativist, antiforeign strain [of the Know-Nothings] in America by celebrating every *body* as a locus of divine and democratic energies and by insisting on the place of every *body* not only in the American procession but into the spiritual procession of the universe" (Erkkila, 125).

6. The term "token fantasy" is taken from Northrop Frye's classic definition of satire. Likening satire also to a "militant irony," Frye regards satire's token fantasy as "a content which the reader recognizes as grotesque, and at least an implicit moral standard, the latter being essential in a militant attitude to experience." See Frye, 223–24.

7. According to the New York City Landmarks Preservation Commission, the Bronx County Courthouse was built between 1931 and 1934. Designed by architects Max Hausle and Joseph H. Freedlander, the courthouse "is an exceptionally impressive example of publicly funded architecture of this period" ("Bronx County

Courthouse"). Costing eight million dollars in government subsidies during the depression, the construction of the building employed scores of artisans and sculptors "with welcome large-scale commissions" ("Bronx County Courthouse"; Moore). At the official dedication of the courthouse on June 16, 1934, Borough President James J. Lyons presented New York City mayor Fiorello La Guardia with a key to the building, but also apologized that the key was made of bronze rather than gold, an inadvertent sign of the courthouse's depression-era birth.

8. "The form of public buildings of the Depression years reflected the fact that they were in part required to be symbols of restored confidence in governmental authority. The Bronx County Building . . . combines in its form qualities we might wish to endure in our systems of law and government—clarity, dignity, harmony, efficiency, and concern for the needs of the public it serves" (Moore, 7).

9. According to Sylvia Moore, the hilltop site of the courthouse gave the building a position from which adjacent residents could look with a sense of "community pride." Emulating the Acropolis, the courthouse's location was meant to dominate the landscape in order to promote the communal feeling of security in what then Borough President Henry Bruckner referred to as the "Temple of Justice." The adjoining parks, rather than serving as a kind of dry moat, were meant to isolate the building from the rest of the community "so that there is nothing to obscure a full view of its form" (3).

10. "Entrances on all four sides make the structure highly accessible, a desirable feature for a public building" (Moore). "Near the southeast corner," states the Landmarks report, "a seated figure displays an elevation drawing of the courthouse itself—labeled the 'Bronx Unity Building.'"

11. Racial coding is best known in the discursive realm, in which phrases seemingly nonracial carry commonsensical racial meaning. Thus, in the 1980s, Reagan's use of the term "welfare queen" was well-understood by his intended white audience to mean poor Black women. As Omi and Winant observe, "The key device used by the new right in its effort to limit the gains of racial minority movements was 'code words.' These are phrases and symbols which refer indirectly to racial themes, but do not directly challenge popular democratic or egalitarian ideals" (123). The more recent campaign in New York City by then Republican mayor Rudy Giuliani to improve the "quality of life" can be seen as a racial code phrase to legitimize the city's push to privatize space for privileged elites and to further marginalize poor communities of color from city resources. For a discussion of the contemporary context of racial coding, see Omi and Winant, *Racial Formation in the United States*, 113–36.

12. Lisa Stokes, for example, attempts to ascribe a radical politics to Wolfe's writings by using a Bakhtinian model of the "dialogic" nature of the novel. "The very life of Wolfe's multi-voiced language and the energies exchanged between narrators and subjects undermine any conservative politics. . . . Wolfe's narratives empower readers by awakening their energies to the unresolved struggle between ideology and narrative." See "Tom Wolfe's Narratives," 22.

13. Income disparities help fill out the story that Sanjek tells: in the year that

Bonfire was published (1987), the Bronx had the lowest per capita income in the entire metropolitan area—$20,905, about 20 percent less than the national average—while a Manhattan resident earned almost twice the national average ($45,487) (Fitch, 277).

14. Yet just as the political economy of New York during the 1980s was not natural, so, too, was the assigning of racial tags to the transformed space of the city a calculated effort to vilify the very people bearing the brunt of New York's economic assassination. As Sanjek explains, the mayoral administrations since the late 1970s (Koch, Dinkins, Giuliani) have all attempted to transform New York into a "global city," one that centralizes its financial base in a FIRE economy. In 1995, Sanjek reports, Giuliani frankly acknowledged the profound shift of municipal public policy: no longer heedful of all New Yorkers, the mayor's administration concentrated its efforts on bringing money in while pushing (poor) people out. Asked if his unspoken strategy was to prompt poor people to move out of New York, Giuliani responded, "That's not an unspoken strategy. That is my strategy. We just cannot afford it. Those left out will have the option of moving elsewhere. That will help make New York City like the rest of the country" (Sanjek, 184). It should be noted, however, that Giuliani's comments are only the most blatant statements of what has been normative municipal policy in New York since Koch's administration.

15. And it is this construction of a new masculinity that finally troubles Kennedy about the novel. For Wolfe's satire, Kennedy inveighs, produces a masculine ethos that is in fact not new at all, but rather depends on an older mode of masculinity, one based on the idea of the fundamentally "bestial" nature of manhood: "This embrace of the bestial self . . . seems to be looking backward to a yet older, more celebrated myth of male self-empowerment—the frontier myth of imperial white manhood that depends on the mastery of threatening others" ("It's the Third World," 107). As evidence, Kennedy cites the final "mob" scene that takes place after Judge Kovitsky throws out the case against Sherman. Accosted by several of the spectators-turned-rioters, Sherman, behaving in a way quite unlike his earlier tentative inertia, shouts obscenities and violently fights each person who attempts to reach him. And in a Wolfian signal of his class demotion, Sherman yells in a frenzy to Kovitsky, "Judge . . . it don't matter! It don't matter!" (656), his incorrect grammar expressing his rebellion against the protocols of the proper. For Kennedy, this mob scene stages Wolfe's celebration of a "precapitalist model of masculinity," the racial logic of Wolfe's allegiance to whiteness: "Sherman comes to embody the national myth of imperial white manhood, his narrative descent into the urban depths re-allegorizing the frontier tale of the lone white male in the wilderness and his violent assertion of identity" (107).

Works Cited

Abelmann, Nancy, and John Lie. *Blue Dreams: Korean Americans and the Los Angeles Riots*. Cambridge: Harvard University Press, 1995.

Abu-Jamal, Mumia. "The Fictive Realism of John Edgar Wideman." *The Black Scholar* 28, no. 1 (1998): 75–79.

Acuña, Rudolfo. *A Community under Siege: A Chronicle of Chicanos East of the Los Angeles River, 1945–1975*. Los Angeles: Chicano Studies Research Center, University of California, Los Angeles, 1984.

———. *Occupied America: A History of Chicanos*. 2d ed. New York: Harper and Row, 1981.

———. *Occupied America: A History of Chicanos*. 3rd ed. New York: Harper-Collins, 1988.

Adams, Carolyn et al. *Philadelphia: Neighborhoods, Division, and Conflict in a Postindustrial City*. Philadelphia: Temple University Press, 1991.

Almaguer, Tomás. "Interpreting Chicano History: The 'World-System' Approach to Nineteenth-Century California." Institute for the Study of Social Change Working Papers Series #101. Department of Sociology, University of California at Berkeley, 1977.

———. *Racial Fault Lines: The Historical Origins of White Supremacy in California*. Berkeley and Los Angeles: University of California Press, 1994.

Althusser, Louis. "Ideology and Ideological State Apparatuses (Notes Toward an Investigation)." In *Lenin and Philosophy and Other Essays*, translated by Ben Brewster, 127–86. New York: Monthly Review, 1971.

"The American Underclass." *Time*, August 29, 1977, 14–15.

Anderson, Benedict. *Imagined Communities*. 2d ed. New York: Verso, 1991.

Anderson, Elijah. *Streetwise: Race, Class, and Change in an Urban Community*. Chicago: University of Chicago Press, 1990.

Anderson, John, and Hilary Hevenor. *Burning Down the House: MOVE and the Tragedy of Philadelphia*. New York: Norton, 1987.

Arrighi, Giovanni. *The Long Twentieth Century: Money, Power, and the Origins of Our Times*. New York: Verso, 1994.

Asian Immigrant Women's Advocates. *Immigrant Women Speak Out on Garment Industry Abuse*. A Community Hearing Initiated by AIWA, May 1, 1993. Oakland: AIWA, 1995.

Assefa, Hizkias, and Paul Wahrhaftig. *Extremist Groups and Conflict Resolution: The MOVE Crisis in Philadelphia*. Westport, Conn.: Praeger, 1988.

Attridge, Harold. *First-Century Cynicism in the Epistles of Heraclitus*. Harvard Theological Studies 29. Missoula, Mont.: Scholars, 1976.

Auger, Philip. "ReWrighting Afro-American Manhood: Negotiations of Discursive Space in the Fiction of James Baldwin, Alice Walker, John Edgar Wideman, and Ernest Gaines." Ph.D. diss., University of Rhode Island, 1995.

Auletta, Ken. *The Underclass.* New York: Random House, 1982.

Badgett, M. V. Lee. "Where the Jobs Went in the 1990–91 Downturn: Varying (Mis)Fortunes or Homogeneous Distress?" In *Civil Rights and Race Relations in the Post Reagan-Bush Era,* edited by Samuel L. Myers Jr., 99–147. Westport, Conn.: Praeger, 1997.

Baker, Houston. "Generational Shifts and the Recent Criticism of Afro-American Literature." *Black American Literature Forum* 15 (1981): 3–21.

———, ed. *Three American Literatures: Essays on Chicano, Native American, and Asian-American Literature for Teachers of American Literature.* New York: MLA, 1982.

Banks, James, A. *Teaching Strategies for Ethnic Studies.* 4th ed. Newton, Mass.: Allyn and Bacon, 1987.

Barlow, William, and Peter Shapiro. "Educating the War Babies: The Political Economy of Higher Education in California, 1947–1960." In *An End to Silence: The San Francisco State College Student Movement in the '60s.* New York: Pegasus, 1971.

Barrett, Lindon. "African American Slave Narratives: Literacy, the Body, Authority." *American Literary History* 7, no. 3 (fall 1995): 415–42.

———. "Black Men in the Mix: Badboys, Heroes, Sequins, and Dennis Rodman." *Callaloo* 20, no. 1 (1997): 106–26.

Barrow, Clyde W. *Critical Theories of the State: Marxist, Neo-Marxist, Post-Marxist.* Madison: University of Wisconsin Press, 1993.

Batstone, David, and Eduardo Mendiola, eds. *The Good Citizen.* New York: Routledge, 1999.

Beauregard, Robert A. "The Turbulence of Housing Markets: Investment, Disinvestment and Reinvestment in Philadelphia, 1963–1986." In *The Restless Urban Landscape,* edited by Paul Knox, 55–82. Englewood Cliffs, N.J.: Prentice Hall, 1993.

Bell, Derrick. "The Race-Charged Relationship of Black Men and Black Women." In *Constructing Masculinity,* edited by Maurice Berger et al., 193–210. New York: Routledge, 1995.

Bendix, Richard. "The Extension of Citizenship to the Lower Classes." In *Nation-Building and Citizenship.* Berkeley and Los Angeles: University of California Press, 1977.

Bennett, William J. *To Reclaim a Legacy: A Report on the Humanities in Higher Education.* Washington, D.C.: National Endowment for the Humanities, 1984.

Berger, Maurice et al., eds. *Constructing Masculinity.* New York: Routledge, 1995.

Bernstein, Michael A., and David E. Adler, eds. *Understanding American Economic Decline.* New York: Cambridge University Press, 1994.

Bérubé, Michael. *Public Access: Literary Theory and American Cultural Politics.* New York: Verso, 1994.

Blair, John P., and Rudy H. Fichtenbaum. "Changing Black Employment." In *The Metropolis in Black and White: Place, Power, and Polarization,* edited by George C. Galster and Edward W. Hill, 72–92. New Brunswick, N.J.: Rutgers University Center for Urban Policy Research, 1992.

Bloom, Allan. *The Closing of the American Mind: How Higher Education Has Failed Democracy and Impoverished the Souls of Today's Students.* New York: Simon and Schuster, 1987.

Bloom, Harold. *The Western Canon: The Books and Schools of the Ages.* New York: Harcourt Brace, 1994.

———, ed. *Tom Wolfe (Modern Critical Views).* Philadelphia: Chelsea House, 2001.

Bonacich, Edna. "Asians in the Los Angeles Garment Industry." In *The New Asian Immigration in Los Angeles and Global Restructuring,* edited by Paul Ong et al., 137–63. Philadelphia: Temple University Press.

Bonacich, Edna et al., eds. *Global Production: The Apparel Industry in the Pacific Rim.* Philadelphia: Temple University Press, 1994.

Boyer, M. Christine. "The City of Illusion: New York's Public Places." In *The Restless Urban Landscape,* edited by Paul Knox, 111–26. Englewood Cliffs, N.J.: Prentice Hall, 1993.

Boyette, Michael, with Randi Boyette. *"Let It Burn!": The Philadelphia Tragedy.* Chicago: Contemporary, 1989.

Branham, R. Bracht, and Marie-Odile Goulet-Cazé, eds. *The Cynics: The Cynic Movement in Antiquity and Its Legacy.* Berkeley and Los Angeles: University of California Press, 1996.

Brecher, Jeremy, and Tim Costello. *Global Village or Global Pillage: Economic Reconstruction from the Bottom Up.* Boston: South End, 1994.

Brennan, Timothy. "The National Longing for Form." In *Nation and Narration,* edited by Homi K. Bhabha, 44–70. New York: Routledge, 1990.

"Bronx County Courthouse." Ts. New York City Landmarks Preservation Commission, 1976.

Brooks, Gwendolyn. *Selected Poems.* New York: Harper and Row, 1963.

Brooks, Michael W. *Subway City: Riding the Trains, Reading New York.* New Brunswick, N.J.: Rutgers University Press, 1997.

Brown, Wendy. *States of Injury: Power and Freedom in Late Modernity.* Princeton: Princeton University Press, 1995.

Bryant, Jerry H. *Victims and Heroes: Racial Violence in the African American Novel.* Amherst: University of Massachusetts Press, 1997.

Bullard, Robert D. et al., eds. *Residential Apartheid: The American Legacy.* Los Angeles: Center for Afro-American Studies, University of California, Los Angeles, 1994.

Bulosan, Carlos. *America Is in the Heart.* 1946. Seattle: University of Washington Press, 1973.

Burnheimer, Charles, ed. *Comparative Literature in the Age of Multiculturalism.* Baltimore: The Johns Hopkins University Press, 1995.

Burrola, Luis Ramón, and José A. Rivera. "Chicano Studies Programs at the Crossroads: Alternative Futures for the 1980s." Working Paper 103, ts. Albuquerque: Southwest Hispanic Research Institute, University of New Mexico, 1983.

Butler, Judith. "Endangered/Endangering: Schematic Racism and White Paranoia." In *Reading Rodney King/Reading Urban Uprising,* edited by Robert Gooding-Williams, 15–22. New York: Routledge, 1993.

Calderón, Héctor, and José David Saldívar, eds. *Criticism in the Borderlands: Studies in Chicano Literature, Culture, and Ideology.* Durham, N.C.: Duke University Press, 1991.

California Liaison Committee of the Regents of the University of California and the State Board of Education. *A Master Plan for Higher Education in California, 1960–1975.* Sacramento: California State Department of Education, 1960.

Camarillo, Albert. *Chicanos in California: A History of Mexican Americans in California.* San Francisco: Boyd and Fraser, 1984.

Carby, Hazel. "Multi-Culture." *Screen Education* 34 (1980): 62–70.

Card, James. "Tom Wolfe and the 'Experimental Novel.'" In *Journal of American Culture* 14, no. 3 (1991), special issue on Tom Wolfe, edited by Marshall Fishwick, 31–34.

Carnoy, Martin. *Faded Dreams: The Politics and Economics of Race in America.* New York: Cambridge University Press, 1994.

Carter, Phillip. "Regents Vote Down Affirmative Action." *The Summer Bruin* (July 24, 1995).

Carton, Evan. "The Price of Privilege: 'Civil Disobedience' at 150." *The American Scholar* 67, no. 4 (1998): 105–12.

Cesairé, Aimé. *A Tempest.* Translated by Richard Miller. New York: Ubu Repertory Theater, 1993.

Chan, Jeffrey Paul et al., eds. *AIIIEEEEE! An Anthology of Asian American Literature.* 1974. Reprint, New York: Mentor, 1991.

———. "Fifty Years of Our Whole Voice: An Introduction to Chinese and Japanese American Literature." In *AIIIEEEEE! An Anthology of Asian American Literature,* 3–38. Revised edition. New York: Mentor, 1991.

Chan, Sucheng. *Asian Americans: An Interpretive History.* Boston: Twayne, 1990.

Chang, Edward T. *Amerasia* 19, no. 2 (1993).

Chatterjee, Gargi, and Augie Tam. "Is There an Asian American Aesthetics?" In *Contemporary Asian America: A Multidisciplinary Reader,* edited by Min Zhou and James V. Gatewood, 627–35. New York: New York University Press, 2000.

Cheung, King-Kok. *Articulate Silences: Hisaye Yamamoto, Maxine Hong Kingston, Joy Kogawa.* Ithaca, N.Y.: Cornell University Press, 1993.

———. "Double-Telling: Intertextual Silence in Hisaye Yamamoto's Fiction." *American Literary History* 3, no. 2 (1991): 277–93.

———. "The Dream in Flames: Hisaye Yamamoto, Multiculturalism and the Los Angeles Uprising." *Bucknell Review* 39, no. 1 (1995): 118–30.

———. "Hisaye Yamamoto and Wakako Yamauchi." In *Words Matter: Interviews with Twenty Writers of Asian Descent,* edited by King-Kok Cheung, 343–82. Honolulu: University of Hawai'i Press, 2000.

———, ed. *An Interethnic Companion to Asian American Literature.* New York: Cambridge University Press, 1997.

———, ed. *Words Matter: Interviews with Twenty Writers of Asian Descent.* Honolulu: University of Hawai'i Press, 2000.

Christian, Barbara. *Black Feminist Criticism: Perspectives on Black Women Writers.* New York: Pergamon, 1985.

———. "The Race for Theory," *Cultural Critique* 6 (1987): 51–63. Reprinted in *Making Face, Making Soul/Hacienda Caras: Creative and Critical Perspectives by Feminists of Color,* edited by Gloria Anzaldúa, 335–45. San Francisco: Aunt Lute, 1990.

Chu, Patricia P. *Assimilating Asians: Gendered Strategies of Authorship in Asian America.* Durham: Duke University Press, 2000.

Chua, Lawrence. "The Postmodern Ethnic Brunch: Devouring Difference," *Muæ* 1 (1995): 4–11.

Cisneros, Sandra. *The House on Mango Street.* 1984. New York: Vintage, 1991.

Clausen, Jan. "Native Fathers," *Kenyon Review* 14, no. 2 (1992): 44–55.

Cohen, Ed. "Tom Wolfe and the Truth Memoirs: A Historical Fable," *Clio* 16, no. 1 (1986): 1–11.

Coleman, James W. *Blackness and Modernism: The Literary Career of John Edgar Wideman.* Jackson: University Press of Mississippi, 1989.

Columbo, Gary, Robert Cullen, and Bonnie Lisle, eds. *Rereading America: Cultural Contexts for Critical Thinking and Writing.* 2d ed. Boston: Bedford, 1992.

Connell, R. W. *Masculinities.* Berkeley and Los Angeles: University of California Press, 1995.

Coontz, Stephanie. *The Way We Never Were: American Families and the Nostalgia Trap.* New York: Basic, 1992.

Crawford, Sheri F. "Rebel-Doodle Dandy." In *Journal of American Culture* 14, no. 3 (1991), special issue on Tom Wolfe, edited by Marshall Fishwick, 13–18.

Crenshaw, Kimberlé. "Mapping the Margins: Intersectionality, Identity Politics, and Violence against Women of Color," *Stanford Law Review* 43, no. 6 (1991): 1241–99.

Crenshaw, Kimberlé, and Gary Peller. "Reel Time/Real Justice." In *Reading Rodney King/Reading Urban Uprising,* edited by Robert Gooding-Williams, 56–72. New York: Routledge, 1993.

Crossan, John Dominic. *The Birth of Christianity: Discovering What Happened in the Years Immediately after the Execution of Jesus.* New York: HarperSanFrancisco, 1998.

———. *A Long Way from Tipperary: A Memoir.* New York: HarperSanFrancisco, 2000.

Cumings, Bruce. *The Origins of the Korean War.* 2 vols. Princeton: Princeton University Press, 1981–1990.

Davis, Mike. "*Chinatown,* Part Two? The 'Internationalization' of Downtown Los Angeles," *New Left Review* 164 (1987): 65–84.

———. *City of Quartz: Excavating the Future of Los Angeles.* New York: Vintage, 1989.

———. *Ecology of Fear: Los Angeles and the Imagination of Disaster.* New York: Metropolitan, 1998.

———. "Kajima's Throne of Blood." *The Nation,* February 12, 1996, 18–20.

———. "Los Angeles Was Just the Beginning." In *Open Fire,* edited by Greg Ruggiero and Stuart Sahulka, 220–43. New York: Verso, 1993.

———. *Prisoners of the American Dream: Politics and Economy in the History of the U.S. Working Class.* New York: Verso, 1986.

DeGowin, Elmer L., and Richard L. DeGowin. *Bedside Diagnostic Examination.* 4th ed. New York: Macmillan, 1981.

Deleuze, Gilles, and Félix Guattari. *On the Line,* translated by John Johnston. New York: Semiotext(e), 1983.

Denton, Nancy A. "Are African Americans Still Hypersegregated?" In *Residential Apartheid: The American Legacy,* edited by Robert D. Bullard et al., 49–81. Los Angeles: Center for Afro-American Studies, University of California, Los Angeles, 1994.

Dirlik, Arif. "Asians on the Rim: Transnational Capital and Local Community in the Making of Contemporary Asian America." *Amerasia* 22, no. 3 (1996): 1–23.

Donner, Frank. *Protectors of Privilege: Red Squads and Police Repression in Urban America.* Berkeley and Los Angeles: University of California Press, 1990.

Dove, Rita. *Selected Poems.* New York: Vintage, 1993.

———. *The Yellow House on the Corner.* Pittsburgh: Carnegie-Mellon University Press, 1980.

D'Souza, Dinesh. *The End of Racism: Principles for a Multicultural Society.* New York: Free Press, 1995.

———. *Illiberal Education: The Politics of Race and Sex on Campus.* New York: Free Press, 1991.

Dubey, Madhu. *Black Women Novelists and the Nationalist Aesthetic.* Bloomington: Indiana University Press, 1994.

———. "Literature and Urban Crisis: John Edgar Wideman's *Philadelphia Fire.*" *African American Review* 32, no. 4 (1998): 579–95.

Du Bois, W. E. B. *Black Folk: Then and Now.* New York: Kraus-Thomson, 1975.

———. *The Souls of Black Folk.* 1903. New York: Dover, 1994.

Dumm, Thomas L. "The New Enclosures: Racism in the Normalized Community." In *Reading Rodney King/Reading Urban Uprising,* edited by Robert Gooding-Williams, 178–95. New York: Routledge, 1993.

Duran, Livie Isauro, and H. Russell Bernard, eds. *Introduction to Chicano Studies: A Reader.* New York: Macmillan, 1973.

Edsall, Thomas Byrne. *The New Politics of Inequality.* New York: Norton, 1984.
———. *Power and Money: Writing about Politics, 1971–1987.* New York: Norton, 1988.

Edsall, Thomas Byrne, with Mary D. Edsall. *Chain Reaction: The Impact of Race, Rights, and Taxes on American Politics.* New York: Norton, 1992.

Ellison, Ralph. *Invisible Man.* New York: Random House, 1952; Vintage, 1990.

Epstein, Edward, and Henry K. Lee. "UC Students Rally for Affirmative Action." *San Francisco Chronicle,* October 13, 1995.

Erkkila, Betsy. *Whitman: The Political Poet.* New York: Oxford University Press, 1988.

Escobar, Edward. *Race, Police, and the Making of a Political Identity: Mexican Americans and the Los Angeles Police Department, 1900–1945.* Berkeley and Los Angeles: University of California Press, 1999.

Espiritu, Yen Le. *Asian American Panethnicity: Bridging Institutions and Identities.* Philadelphia: Temple University Press, 1991.

Evans, Peter B., Dietrich Rueschemeyer, and Theda Skocpol, eds. *Bringing the State Back In.* New York: Cambridge University Press, 1985.

Fanon, Frantz. *Black Skin, White Masks.* Translated by Charles Lam Markmann. New York: Grove, 1952, 1967.

Feldman, Allen. *Formations of Violence: The Narrative of the Body and Political Terror in Northern Ireland.* Chicago: University of Chicago Press, 1991.

Ferguson, Russell et al., eds. *Out There: Marginalization and Contemporary Cultures.* New York and Cambridge: New Museum of Contemporary Art and MIT Press, 1990.

Ferman, Barbara. *Challenging the Growth Machine: Neighborhood Politics in Chicago and Pittsburgh.* Lawrence: University of Kansas, 1996.

Fisher, Dexter, and Robert B. Stepto, eds. *Afro-American Literature: The Reconstruction of Instruction.* New York: MLA, 1979.

Fishwick, Marshall, ed. *Journal of American Culture* 14, no. 3 (1991).
———. Introduction to special issue on Tom Wolfe. *Journal of American Culture* 14, no. 3 (1991): 1–10.

Fitch, Robert. *The Assassination of New York.* New York: Verso, 1996.

Foucault, Michel. *Madness and Civilization: A History of Insanity in the Age of Reason.* Translated by Richard Howard. New York: Vintage, 1988.

Franklin, Raymond S. *Shadows of Race and Class.* Minneapolis: University of Minnesota Press, 1991.

Frye, Northop. *Anatomy of Criticism: Four Essays.* New York: Atheneum, 1967.

Frus, Phyllis. *The Politics and Poetics of Journalistic Narrative: The Timely and the Timeless.* New York: Cambridge University Press, 1994.

Fusfeld, Daniel R., and Timothy Bates. *The Political Economy of the Urban Ghetto.* Carbondale: Southern Illinois University Press, 1984.

Fuss, Diana, ed. *Inside/out: Lesbian Theories, Gay Theories.* New York: Routledge, 1991.

Gaines, Kevin K. *Uplifting the Race: Black Leadership, Politics, and Culture in the Twentieth Century.* Chapel Hill: University of North Carolina Press, 1996.

Galster, George C., and Edward W. Hill, eds. *The Metropolis in Black and White: Place, Power, and Polarization.* New Brunswick, N.J.: Rutgers University Center for Urban Policy Research, 1992.

García, Mario T. "History, Literature, and the Chicano Working-Class Novel: A Critical Review of Alejandro Morales's *The Brick People*." *Crítica* 2 (1990): 189–201.

Gates, Henry Louis, Jr., ed. *Black Literature and Literary Theory.* New York: Methuen, 1984.

———, ed. *Reading Black, Reading Feminist: A Critical Anthology.* New York: Meridian, 1990.

Gates, Robert A. *The New York Vision: Interpretations of New York City in the American Novel.* Latham, Md.: University Press of America, 1987.

Gayle, Addison, ed. *The Black Aesthetic.* Garden City, N.Y.: Anchor, 1971.

Gilmore, Ruth Wilson. "From Military Keynesianism to Post-Keynesian Militarism: Finance Capital, Land, Labor, and Opposition in the Rising California Prison State." Ph.D. diss., Rutgers University, 1997.

———. "Globalisation and U.S. Prison Growth: From Military Keynesianism to Post-Keynesian Militarism." *Race and Class* 40, no. 2–3 (1998): 171–88.

———. "Public Enemies and Private Intellectuals: Apartheid USA." *Race and Class* 35, no. 1 (1993): 69–78.

———. "Terror Austerity Race Gender Excess Theater." In *Reading Rodney King/ Reading Urban Uprising,* edited by Robert Gooding-Williams, 23–37. New York: Routledge, 1993.

Gilroy, Paul. *"There Ain't No Black in the Union Jack": The Cultural Politics of Race and Nation.* Chicago: University of Chicago Press, 1991.

Goldberg, David Theo. *The Racial State.* Malden, Mass.: Blackwell, 2002.

Gómez-Quiñones, Juan. *Mexican Students Por La Raza: The Chicano Student Movement in Southern California 1967–1977.* Santa Bárbara, Calif.: Editorial La Causa, 1978.

Goode, W. Wilson, with Joann Stevens. *In Goode Faith.* Valley Forge, Penn.: Judson, 1992.

Gooding-Williams, Robert. "'Look, a Negro!'" In *Reading Rodney King/Reading Urban Uprising,* edited by Robert Gooding-Williams, 157–77. New York: Routledge, 1993.

———, ed. *Reading Rodney King/Reading Urban Uprising.* New York: Routledge, 1993.

Gordon, Avery F., and Christopher Newfield, eds. *Mapping Multiculturalism.* Minneapolis: University of Minnesota Press, 1996.

Gramsci, Antonio. *Selections from the Prison Notebooks.* Edited by Quintin Hoare and Geoffrey Nowell Smith. New York: International, 1971.

Grandjeat, Yves Charles, and Alfonso Rodríguez. "Interview with Chicano Writer Alejandro Morales." *Confluencia* 7, no. 1 (1991): 109–14.

Grünzweig, Walter, Roberta Maierhofer, and Adi Wimmer, eds. *Constructing the Eighties: Versions of an American Decade.* Tübingen, Germany: Gunter Narr Verlag, 1992.

Guattari, Félix, and Toni Negri. *Communists Like Us: New Spaces of Liberty, New Lines of Alliance.* Translated by Michael Ryan. New York: Semiotext(e), 1990.

Guillory, John. *Cultural Capital: The Problem of Literary Canon Formation.* Chicago: University of Chicago Press, 1993.

Gurpegui, José Antonio, ed. *Alejandro Morales: Fiction Past, Present, Future Perfect.* Tempe, Ariz.: Bilingual, 1996.

———. "Interview with Alejandro Morales." In *Alejandro Morales: Fiction Past, Present, Future Perfect,* edited by José Antonio Gurpegui, 5–13. Tempe, Ariz.: Bilingual, 1996.

Gutiérrez, Ramón A. "Community, Patriarchy and Individualism: The Politics of Chicano History and the Dream of Equality." *American Quarterly* 45, no. 1 (1993): 44–72.

Gutiérrez-Jones, Carl. *Rethinking the Borderlands: Between Chicano Culture and Legal Discourse.* Berkeley and Los Angeles: University of California Press, 1995.

Hall, Stuart. "New Ethnicities." In *Stuart Hall: Critical Dialogues in Cultural Studies,* edited by David Morley and Kuan-Hsing Chen, 441–49. New York: Routledge, 1996.

Hall, Stuart et al. *Policing the Crisis: Mugging, the State, and Law and Order.* London: Macmillan, 1978.

Hall, Stuart, and Martin Jacques, eds. *New Times: The Changing Face of Politics in the 1990s.* New York: Verso, 1990.

Harlow, Barbara. *Resistance Literature.* New York: Methuen, 1987.

Harris, Cheryl I. "Whiteness as Property." *Harvard Law Review* 106, no. 8 (1993): 1707–91.

Harrison, Bennett. *Lean and Mean: The Changing Landscape of Corporate Power in the Age of Flexibility.* New York: Basic, 1994.

Harrison, Bennett, and Barry Bluestone. *The Great U-Turn: Corporate Restructuring and the Polarizing of America.* New York: Basic, 1988.

Harrison, Bennett, and Lucy Gorham, "What Happened to African American Wages in the 1980s?" In *The Metropolis in Black and White: Place, Power, and Polarization,* edited by George C. Galster and Edward W. Hill, 56–71. New Brunswick, N.J.: Rutgers University Center for Urban Policy Research, 1992.

Harry, Margot. *"Attention, MOVE! This is America!"* Chicago: Banner, 1987.

Harvey, David. *The Condition of Postmodernity: An Enquiry into the Origins of Cultural Change.* Cambridge, Mass.: Blackwell, 1990.

———. *The Limits to Capital.* New York: Verso, 1999.

———. *The Urban Experience.* Baltimore: The Johns Hopkins University Press, 1989.

Hatamiya, Leslie T. *Righting a Wrong: Japanese Americans and the Passage of the Civil Liberties Act of 1988.* Stanford: Stanford University Press, 1993.

Hebdige, Dick. *Hiding in the Light: On Images and Things.* New York: Routledge, 1988.

Hernández, Guillermo E. *Chicano Satire: A Study in Literary Culture.* Austin: University of Texas Press, 1991.

Himes, Chester. *If He Hollers Let Him Go.* 1945. London: Pluto, 1986.

Hirsch, E. D. *Cultural Literacy: What Every American Needs to Know.* Boston: Houghton Mifflin, 1987.

Hogue, W. Lawrence. *Race, Modernity, Postmodernity: A Look at the History and Literatures of People of Color Since the 1960s.* Albany: State University of New York Press, 1996.

Hong, Grace Kyung Won. "Interethnic and Interracial Relations in the Short Stories of Hisaye Yamamoto." M.A. thesis, University of California, Los Angeles, 1995.

———. "'Something Forgotten Which Should Have Been Remembered': Private Property and Cross-Racial Solidarity in the Work of Hisaye Yamamoto." *American Literature* 71, no. 2 (1999): 291–310.

hooks, bell. "Doing It For Daddy." In *Constructing Masculinity,* edited by Maurice Berger et al., 98–106. New York: Routledge, 1995.

Horne, Gerald. *Fire This Time: The Watts Uprisings and the 1960s.* Charlottesville: University Press of Virginia, 1995.

Hutcheon, Linda. *Irony's Edge: The Theory and Politics of Irony.* New York: Routledge, 1995.

Ignatiev, Noel, and John Garvey, eds. *Race Traitor.* New York: Routledge, 1996.

Jackson, Sandra, and José Solís, eds. *Beyond Comfort Zones in Multiculturalism: Confronting the Politics of Privilege.* Westport, Conn.: Bergin and Garvey, 1995.

Jackson, Thomas F. "The State, the Movement, and the Urban Poor: The War on Poverty and Political Mobilization in the 1960s." In *The "Underclass" Debate: Views from History,* edited by Michael B. Katz, 403–39. Princeton: Princeton University Press, 1993.

James, Joy. *Resisting State Violence: Radicalism, Gender, and Race in U.S. Culture.* Minneapolis: University of Minnesota Press, 1996.

Jameson, Fredric. *Postmodernism, or The Cultural Logic of Late Capitalism.* Durham: Duke University Press, 1994.

Jaye, Michael C., and Ann Chalmer Watts, eds. *Literature and the Urban Experience: Essays on the City and Literature.* New Brunswick, N.J.: Rutgers University Press, 1981.

Jordan, June. *Technical Difficulties: African-American Notes on the State of the Union.* New York: Pantheon, 1992.

Kamp, David. "The White Stuff." *Vanity Fair,* September 1998.

Kanellos, Nicolás. *Hispanic American Literature: A Brief Introduction and Anthology.* New York: Harper Collins, 1995.

Katz, Michael B. "Reframing the 'Underclass' Debate." In *The "Underclass" Debate: Views from History,* edited by Michael B. Katz, 440–78. Princeton: Princeton University Press, 1993.

———. "The Urban 'Underclass' as a Metaphor of Social Transformation." In *The "Underclass" Debate: Views from History,* edited by Michael B. Katz, 3–26. Princeton: Princeton University Press, 1993.

———, ed. *The "Underclass" Debate: Views from History.* Princeton: Princeton University Press, 1993.

Katz, Michael B., and Thomas J. Sugrue, eds. *W. E. B. Du Bois, Race, and the City: "The Philadelphia Negro" and Its Legacy.* Philadelphia: University of Pennsylvania Press, 1998.

Kelley, Robin D. G. "Confessions of a Nice Nego, or Why I Shaved My Head." *Speak My Name: Black Men on Masculinity and the American Dream.* Edited by Don Belton, 12–22. Boston: Beacon, 1995.

———. *Yo' Mama's Disfunktional! Fighting the Culture Wars in Urban America.* Boston: Beacon, 1997.

Kennedy, Liam. "'It's the Third World Down There!': Urban Decline and (Post) National Mythologies in *Bonfire of the Vanities.*" *Modern Fiction Studies* 43, no. 1 (1997): 93–111.

———. *Race and Urban Space in Contemporary American Culture.* Edinburgh: Edinburgh University Press, 2000.

Kim, Claire Jean. *Bitter Fruit: The Politics of Black-Korean Conflict in New York City.* New Haven: Yale University Press, 2000.

Kim, Elaine H. *Asian American Literature: An Introduction to the Writings and Their Social Contexts.* Philadephia: Temple University Press, 1982.

Kingston, Maxine Hong. *The Woman Warrior: Memoirs of a Girlhood among Ghosts.* 1976. New York: Vintage, 1989.

Knox, Paul, ed. *The Restless Urban Landscape.* Englewood Cliffs, N.J.: Prentice Hall, 1993.

Lawrence, Charles. "Beyond Redress: Reclaiming the Meaning of Affirmative Action." *Amerasia* 19, no. 1 (1993): 1–6.

Lee, Andrea. *Sarah Phillips.* 1984. Boston: Northeastern University Press, 1993.

Lee, Rachel. *The Americas of Asian American Literature: Gendered Fictions of Nation and Transnation.* Princeton: Princeton University Press, 1999.

Lenski, Gerhard E. *Power and Privilege: A Theory of Social Stratification.* New York: McGraw-Hill, 1966.

Leong, Russell. "Beware of the M Word." In *Places and Politics in an Age of Globalization,* edited by Roxann Prazniak and Arif Dirlik, ix–xii. Lanham, Md.: Rowman & Littlefield, 2001.

Lin, Jan. *Reconstructing Chinatown: Ethnic Enclave, Global Change.* Minneapolis: University of Minnesota Press, 1998.

Lipsitz, George. *American Studies in a Moment of Danger.* Minneapolis: University of Minnesota Press, 2001.

———. *Rainbow at Midnight: Labor and Culture in the 1940s.* Urbana: University of Illinois Press, 1994.

———. *Time Passages: Collective Memory and American Popular Culture.* Minneapolis: University of Minnesota Press, 1990.

Lord, James. *Giacometti: A Biography.* New York: Farrar, Straus & Giroux, 1983.

Lowe, Lisa. "Canon, Institutionalization, Identity: Contradictions for Asian American Studies." In *The Ethnic Canon: Histories, Institutions, and Interventions,* edited by David Palumbo-Liu, 48–68. Minneapolis: University of Minnesota Press, 1995.

———. *Immigrant Acts: On Asian American Cultural Politics.* Durham, N.C.: Duke University Press, 1996.

———. "Unfaithful to the Original: The Subject of *Dictée.*" In *Writing Self, Writing Nation: Essays on Theresa Hak Kyung Cha's "Dictée,"* edited by Norma Alarcón and Elaine H. Kim, 35–69. Berkeley: Third Woman, 1994.

Lubiano, Wahneema. "Like Being Mugged by a Metaphor: Multiculturalism and State Narratives." In *Mapping Multiculturalism,* edited by Avery F. Gordon and Christopher Newfield, 64–75. Minneapolis: University of Minnesota Press, 1996.

———. "Toni Morrison." In *African American Writers,* edited by Valerie Smith, 321–33. New York: Scribner's, 1991.

Lubove, Roy. *Twentieth-Century Pittsburgh.* Vol. 2, *The Post-Steel Era.* Pittsburgh: University of Pittsburgh Press, 1996.

Lyotard, François. *The Postmodern Explained.* Translated by Don Barry et al. Minneapolis: University of Minnesota Press, 1992.

Maciel, David R., and Isidoro D. Ortiz, eds. *Chicanas/Chicanos at the Crossroads: Social, Economic, and Political Change.* Tucson: University of Arizona Press, 1996.

MacKinnon, Catherine A. *Toward a Feminist Theory of the State.* Cambridge: Harvard University Press, 1989.

Maitino, John R., and David R. Peck. *Teaching American Ethnic Literatures: Nineteen Essays.* Albuquerque: University of New Mexico Press, 1996.

Maki, Mitchell T. et al. *Achieving the Impossible Dream: How Japanese Americans Obtained Redress.* Urbana: University of Illinois Press, 1999.

Marable, Manning. *Beyond Black and White: Transforming African-American Politics.* New York: Verso, 1995.

———. "Black America: Multicultural Democracy in the Age of Clarence Thomas, David Duke, and the Los Angeles Uprisings." In *Open Fire,* edited by Greg Ruggiero and Stuart Sahulka, 244–64. New York: Verso, 1993.

———. *Blackwater: Historical Studies in Race, Class Consciousnesss, and Revolution.* Niwot: University Press of Colorado, 1993.

———. *How Capitalism Underdeveloped Black America: Problems in Race, Political Economy, and Society.* Boston: South End, 1983.

Marcuse, Peter, P. Medoff, and A. Pereira. "Triage as Urban Policy." *Social Policy* (winter 1982): 33–37.

Márquez, Antonio. "The Use and Abuse of History in Alejandro Morales' *The Brick People* and *The Rag Doll Plagues*." In *Alejandro Morales: Fiction Past, Present, Future Perfect*, edited by José Antonio Gurpegui, 76–85. Tempe, Ariz.: Bilingual, 1996.

Marx, Karl. *Capital*. Vol. 1. Translated by Ben Fowkes. New York: Vintage 1977.

Massey, Douglas S., and Nancy A. Denton. *American Apartheid: Segregation and the Making of the Underclass*. Cambridge, Mass.: Harvard University Press, 1993.

Mazón, Mauricio. *The Zoot-Suit Riots: The Psychology of Symbolic Annihilation*. Austin: University of Texas Press, 1984.

Mbalia, Doreatha D. *John Edgar Wideman: Reclaiming the African Personality*. Selingsgrove, Penn.: Susquehanna University Press, 1995.

Medcalf, Linda J., and Kenneth M. Dolbeare. *Neopolitics: American Political Ideas in the 1980s*. Philadelphia: Temple University Press, 1985.

Mercer, Kobena. *Welcome to the Jungle: New Positions in Black Cultural Studies*. New York: Routledge, 1994.

Mills, Nicholaus, ed. *Culture in an Age of Money: The Legacy of the 1980s in America*. Chicago: Ivan R. Dee, 1990.

———. "The Culture of Triumph and the Spirit of the Times." In *Culture in an Age of Money: The Legacy of the 1980s in America*, edited by Nicholaus Mills, 12–13. Chicago: Ivan R. Dee, 1990.

Mirandé, Alfredo, and Evangelina Enríquez. *La Chicana: The Mexican American Woman*. Chicago: University of Chicago Press, 1979.

Mohanty, Satya P. *Literary Theory and the Claims of History: Postmodernism, Objectivity, Multicultural Politics*. Ithaca, N.Y.: Cornell University Press, 1997.

Mollenkopf, John H., and Manuel Castells, eds. *Dual City: Restructuring New York*. New York: Russell Sage, 1991.

Moore, Sylvia. "Bronx County Building." Ts. New York: Bronx County Historical Society, 1972.

Morace, Robert. "The Facts in Black and White: Cheever's *Falconer*, Wideman's *Philadelphia Fire*." In *Powerless Fictions? Ethics, Cultural Critique, and American Fiction in the Age of Postmodernism*, edited by Ricardo Miguel Alfonso, 85–112. Atlanta: Rodopi, 1996.

Moraga, Cherríe, and Gloria Anzaldúa, eds. *This Bridge Called My Back: Writings by Radical Women of Color*. 2d ed. Latham, N.Y.: Kitchen Table, 1983.

Morales, Alejandro. *The Brick People*. 1988. Houston: Arte Público, 1992.

Morita, Jennifer K. "Diversity Rally Draws 3000." *Daily Bruin*, October 13, 1995.

Morley, David, and Kuan-Hsing Chen, eds. *Stuart Hall: Critical Dialogues in Cultural Studies*. New York: Routledge, 1996.

Morrison, Toni. *Beloved*. New York: Signet, 1991.

Moya, Paula M. L. *Learning from Experience: Minority Identities, Multicultural Struggles*. Berkeley and Los Angeles: University of California Press, 2002.

Muñoz, Carlos, Jr. *Youth, Identity, Power: The Chicano Movement*. New York: Verso, 1989.

Murase, Ichiro Mike. *Little Tokyo: One Hundred Years in Pictures.* Los Angeles: Visual Communications/Asian American Studies Central, 1983.

Murashige, Michael S. "Karen Tei Yamashita." In *Words Matter: Interviews with Twenty Writers of Asian Descent,* edited by King-Kok Cheung, 320–42. Honolulu: University of Hawai'i Press, 2000.

———. "Race, Resistance, and Contestations of Urban Space." Ph.D. diss., University of California, Los Angeles, 1995.

Murray, Charles. *The Link between Crime and the Built Environment: The Current State of Knowledge,* vol. 1. U.S. Department of Justice: National Institute of Justice, 1980.

———. *Losing Ground: American Social Policy, 1950–1980.* New York: Basic, 1984.

Myers, Samuel L., Jr., ed. *Civil Rights and Race Relations in the Post Reagan-Bush Era.* Westport, Conn.: Praeger, 1997.

Nakanishi, Don. "Surviving Democracy's 'Mistake': Japanese Americans and the Enduring Legacy of Executive Order 9066." *Amerasia* 19, no. 1 (1993): 30.

Nakanishi, Don T., and Tina Yamano Nishida, eds. *The Asian American Educational Experience: A Source Book for Teachers and Students.* New York: Routledge, 1995.

Nakayama, Thomas, and Judith Martin, eds. *Whiteness: The Communication of Social Identity.* Thousand Oaks, Calif.: Sage, 1999.

Negri, Antonio. *Marx beyond Marx: Lessons on the Grundrisse.* Edited by Jim Fleming. Translated by Harry Cleaver, Michael Ryan, and Maurizio Viano. New York: Autonomedia, 1991.

———. *Revolution Retrieved: Selected Writings on Marx, Keynes, Capitalist Crisis and New Social Subjects, 1967–1983.* London: Red Notes, 1988.

New, Elisa. *The Regenerate Lyric: Theology and Innovation in American Poetry.* New York: Cambridge University Press, 1993.

Nguyen, Viet Thanh. *Race and Resistance: Literature and Politics in Asian America.* New York: Oxford University Press, 2002.

Nicolaides, Becky M. *My Blue Heaven: Life and Politics in the Working-Class Suburbs of Los Angeles, 1920–1965.* Chicago: University of Chicago Press, 2002.

———. "'Where the Working Man Is Welcomed': Working-Class Suburbs in Los Angeles, 1900–1940." *Pacific Historical Review* 68, no. 4 (1999).

Noble, David. *Progress without People: New Technology, Unemployment, and the Message of Resistance.* Toronto: Between the Lines, 1995.

Nolan, James L., ed. *The American Culture Wars: Current Contests and Future Prospects.* Charlottesville: University of Virginia, 1996.

O'Connell, Shaun. *Remarkable, Unspeakable New York: A Literary History.* Boston: Beacon, 1995.

O'Connor, James. *The Fiscal Crisis of the State.* New York: St. Martin's, 1973.

———. *The Meaning of Crisis.* New York: Blackwell, 1987.

Okihiro, Gary. *Margins and Mainstreams: Asians in American History and Culture.* Seattle: University of Washington Press, 1994.

Oliver, Eileen Iscoff. *Crossing the Mainstream: Multicultural Perspectives in Teaching Literature*. Urbana, Ill.: National Council of Teachers of English, 1994.

Oliver, Melvin, James Johnson, and Walter Farrell. "Anatomy of a Rebellion: A Political-Economic Analysis." In *Reading Rodney King/Reading Urban Uprising*, edited by Robert Gooding-Williams, 117–41. New York: Routledge, 1993.

Oliver, Melvin, and Thomas M. Shapiro. *Black Wealth, White Wealth: A New Perspective on Racial Inequality*. New York: Routledge, 1995.

Omatsu, Glenn. "The 'Four Prisons' and the Movements of Liberation: Asian American Activism from the 1960s to the 1990s." In *The State of Asian America: Activism and Resistance in the 1990s*, edited by Karin Aguilar-San Juan, 19–69. Boston: South End, 1993.

Omi, Michael, and Howard Winant. *Racial Formation in the United States: From the 1960s to the 1990s*. 2d ed. New York: Routledge, 1994.

Onishi, Norimitsu. "Affirmative Action: Choosing Sides." *New York Times*, March 31, 1996.

Ong, Paul, Edna Bonacich, and Lucie Cheng, eds. *The New Asian Immigration in Los Angeles and Global Restructuring*. Philadelphia: Temple University Press, 1994.

Osajima, Keith. "Asian Americans as the Model Minority: An Analysis of Popular Press Image in the 1960s and 1980s." In *Reflections on Shattered Windows: Promises and Prospects for Asian American Studies*, edited by Keith Osajima, 165–74. Pullman: Washington State University, 1988.

Palumbo-Liu, David. *Asian/American: Historical Crossings of a Racial Frontier*. Stanford: Stanford University Press, 1999.

———. Introduction to *The Ethnic Canon: Histories, Institutions, and Interventions*, edited by David Palumbo-Liu, 1–27. Minneapolis: University of Minnesota Press, 1995.

———, ed. *The Ethnic Canon: Histories, Institutions, and Interventions*. Minneapolis: University of Minnesota Press, 1995.

Peck, Dennis L., and J. Selwyn Hollingsworth, eds. *Demographic and Structural Change: The Effects of the 1980s on American Society*. Westport, Conn.: Greenwood Press, 1996.

Petersen, William. "Success Story, Japanese-American Style." *New York Times Magazine*, January 9, 1966.

Philadelphia County Trial Division. Court of Common Pleas. Report of the Grand Jury. May 15, 1986.

Philadelphia Special Investigation Commission. Dissenting Statement of Commissioner Bruce W. Kauffman. March 6, 1986.

Pick, Christopher, ed. *What's What in the 1980s: A Dictionary of Contemporary History, Literature, Arts, Technology, Medicine, Music, Cinema, Theatre, Controversies, Fads, Movements and Events*. Vol. 1. Detroit: Gale Research, 1982.

Pinckney, Darryl. "'Cos I'm a so-o-oul man': The Back-Country Blues of John Edgar Wideman." Review of John Edgar Wideman's *Philadelphia Fire* and *Fever. Times Literary Supplement* 4612, August 23, 1991, 19–20.

Pollack, Sheldon D. *The Failure of U.S. Tax Policy.* University Park: Pennsylvania State University Press, 1996.

Porter, Carolyn. *Seeing and Being: The Plight of the Participant Observer in Emerson, James, Adams, and Faulkner.* Middletown, Conn.: Wesleyan University Press, 1981.

Prazniak, Roxann, and Arif Dirlik, eds. *Places and Politics in an Age of Globalization.* Lanham, Md.: Rowman and Littlefield, 2001.

Pulido, Laura. *Environmentalism and Economic Justice: Two Chicano Struggles in the Southwest.* Tucson: University of Arizona Press, 1996.

———. "Rethinking Environmental Racism: White Privilege and Urban Development in Southern California." *Annals of the Association of American Geographers* 90, no. 1 (2000): 12–40.

Reed, Ishmael. *Flight to Canada.* 1976. New York: Atheneum, 1989.

———. *New and Collected Poems.* New York: Atheneum, 1988.

———, ed. *MultiAmerica: Essays on Cultural Wars and Cultural Peace.* New York: Penguin, 1998.

Reich, Robert. "A Culture of Paper Tigers." In *Culture in an Age of Money: The Legacy of the 1980s in America,* edited by Nicholaus Mill, 95–108. Chicago: Ivan R. Dee, 1990.

Reynolds, David S. *Walt Whitman's America: A Cultural Biography.* New York: Knopf, 1995.

Richard, Jean-Pierre. "*Philadelphia Fire,* or the Shape of a City." *Callaloo* 22, no. 3 (1999): 603–13.

Rocco, Raymond A. "Latino Los Angeles: Reframing Boundaries/Borders." In *The City: Los Angeles and Urban Theory at the End of the Twentieth Century,* edited by Allen J. Scott and Edward W. Soja, 365–89. Berkeley and Los Angeles: University of California Press, 1996.

Rodriguez, Richard. *Hunger of Memory: The Education of Richard Rodriguez.* New York: Bantam, 1988.

Roediger, David R. *Towards the Abolition of Whiteness: Essays on Race, Politics, and Working Class History.* New York: Verso, 1994.

———. *The Wages of Whiteness: Race and the Making of the American Working Class.* New York: Verso, 1991.

Romo, Ricardo. *East Los Angeles: History of a Barrio.* Austin: University of Texas Press, 1983.

Rotella, Carlo. *October Cities: The Redevelopment of Urban Literature.* Berkeley and Los Angeles: University of California Press, 1998.

Rubenstein, Richard L. *The Age of Triage: Fear and Hope in an Overcrowded World.* Boston: Beacon, 1983.

Ruggiero, Greg, and Stuart Sahulka, eds. *Open Fire.* New York: Verso, 1993.

Ruigrock, Winifried, and Rob van Tulder. *The Logic of International Restructuring.* New York: Routledge, 1995.

Ruoff, A. La Vonne Brown, and Jerry W. Ward, Jr., eds. *Redefining American Literary History.* New York: MLA, 1990.

Saldívar, Ramón. *Chicano Narrative: The Dialectics of Difference.* Madison: University of Wisconsin Press, 1990.

Sánchez, George J. *Becoming Mexican American: Ethnicity, Culture and Identity in Chicano Los Angeles, 1900–1945.* New York: Oxford University Press, 1993.

Sánchez, Rosaura. *Telling Identities: The Californio "Testimonios."* Minneapolis: University of Minnesota Press, 1995.

Sanjek, Roger. *The Future of Us All: Race and Neighborhood in New York City.* Ithaca: Cornell University Press, 1998.

Sassen, Saskia. *The Global City: New York, London, Tokyo.* Princeton: Princeton University Press, 1991.

San Juan, Jr., E. *Hegemony and Strategies of Transgression: Essays in Cultural Studies and Comparative Literature.* Albany: State University of New York Pess, 1995.

Sayre, Farrand. *The Greek Cynics.* Baltimore: J. H. Furst, 1948.

Scarry, Elaine. *The Body in Pain: The Making and Unmaking of the World.* New York: Oxford University Press, 1985.

Schwartz, Bonnie Fox. *The Civil Works Administration, 1933–1934: The Business of Emergency Employment in the New Deal.* Princeton: Princeton University Press, 1984.

Scott, Allen J., and Edward W. Soja, eds. *The City: Los Angeles and Urban Theory at the End of the Twentieth Century.* Berkeley and Los Angeles: University of California Press, 1996.

Scruggs, Charles. *Sweet Home: Invisible Cities in the Afro-American Novel.* Baltimore: The Johns Hopkins University Press, 1993.

Scura, Dorothy, ed. *Conversations with Tom Wolfe.* Jackson: University Press of Mississippi, 1990.

Shomette, Doug, ed. *The Critical Response to Tom Wolfe.* Westport, Conn.: Greenwood Press, 1992.

Silko, Leslie Marmon. *Almanac of the Dead.* New York: Penguin, 1991.

Silverman, Kaja. *Male Subjectivity at the Margins.* New York: Routledge, 1992.

Simon, William E. *A Time for Truth.* New York: Reader's Digest, 1978.

Sims, Norman, ed. *Literary Journalism in the Twentieth Century.* New York: Oxford University Press, 1990.

Singh, Nikhil Pal. "Culture/Wars: Recoding Empire in an Age of Democracy." *American Quarterly* 50, no. 3 (1998): 471–522.

Small, Stephen. *Racialised Barriers: The Black Experience in the United States and England in the 1980s.* New York: Routledge, 1994.

Smith, James. "Tom Wolfe's *Bonfire of the Vanities*: A Dreiser Novel for the 1980s."

In *Journal of American Culture* 14, no. 3 (1991), special issue on Tom Wolfe, edited by Marshall Fishwick, 43–50.

Smith, Neil. *The New Urban Frontier: Gentrification and the Revanchist City.* New York: Routledge, 1996.

———. *Uneven Development: Nature, Capital and the Production of Space.* 2d ed. New York: Blackwell, 1990.

Smith, Valerie. *Not Just Race, Not Just Gender: Black Feminist Readings.* New York: Routledge, 1998.

———. *Self-Discovery and Authority in Afro-American Narrative.* Cambridge: Harvard University Press, 1987.

Soja, Edward, R. Morales, and G. Wolff. "Urban Restructuring: An Analysis of Social and Spatial Change in Los Angeles." *Economic Geography* 59 (1983): 227.

Sonenshein, Raphael J. *Politics in Black and White: Race and Power in Los Angeles.* Princeton: Princeton University Press, 1993.

Squires, Gregory D. *Capital and Communities in Black and White: The Intersections of Race, Class, and Uneven Development.* Albany: State University of New York Press, 1994.

Stefancic, Jean, and Richard Delgado. *No Mercy: How Conservative Think Tanks and Foundations Changed America's Social Agenda.* Philadelphia: Temple University Press, 1996.

Stepto, Robert B. *From behind the Veil: A Study of Afro-American Narrative.* Urbana: University of Illinois Press, 1979.

Stokes, Lisa. "Tom Wolfe's Narratives as Stories of Growth." In *Journal of American Culture* 14, no. 3 (1991), special issue on Tom Wolfe, edited by Marshall Fishwick, 19–24.

Stull, James N. "The Cultural Gamesmanship of Tom Wolfe." In *Journal of American Culture* 14, no. 3 (1991), special issue on Tom Wolfe, edited by Marshall Fishwick, 25–30.

Stull, William, and Janice Fanning Madden. *Post-Industrial Philadelphia: Structural Changes in the Metropolitan Economy.* Philadelphia: University of Pennsylvania Press, 1990.

"Success Story of One Minority Group in the U.S." *U.S. News & World Report,* December 26, 1966, 73–78. Reprinted in *Roots: An Asian American Studies Reader,* edited by Amy Tachiki et al., 6–9. Los Angeles: UCLA Asian American Studies Center, 1971.

Sugrue, Thomas J. *The Origins of the Urban Crisis: Race and Inequality in Postwar Detroit.* Princeton: Princeton University Press, 1996.

———. "The Structures of Urban Poverty: The Reorganization of Space and Work in Three Periods of American History." In *The "Underclass" Debate: Views from History,* edited by Michael B. Katz, 85–117. Princeton: Princeton University Press, 1993.

Takagi, Dana. "Post-Civil Rights Politics and Asian-American Identity: Admissions and Higher Education." In *Race,* edited by S. Gregory and R. Sanjek. New Brunswick, N.J.: Rutgers University Press, 1994.

———. *The Retreat from Race: Asian-American Admissions and Racial Politics.* New Brunswick, N.J.: Rutgers University Press, 1993.

Takaki, Ronald. "The 'Heathen Chinee' and American Technology." In *Iron Cages: Race and Culture in the Nineteenth Century,* edited by Ronald Takaki, 215–49. New York: Knopf, 1979.

———. *Iron Cages: Race and Culture in the Nineteenth Century.* New York: Knopf, 1979.

———. *Pau Hana.* Honolulu: University of Hawaii Press, 1983.

———. *Strangers from a Different Shore: A History of Asian Americans.* Boston: Little, Brown, 1989.

Takezawa, Yasuko I. "Children of Inmates: The Effects of the Redress Movement among Third Generation Japanese Americans." *Qualitative Sociology* 14, no. 1 (1991): 39–56.

Tatum, Charles M. *Chicano Literature.* Boston: Twayne, 1982.

Thomas, Gail E., ed. *U.S. Race Relations in the 1980s and 1990s: Challenges and Alternatives.* New York: Hemisphere, 1990.

Tilly, Charles. *Durable Inequality.* Berkeley and Los Angeles: University of California Press, 1998.

Toji, Dean S., and James H. Johnson. "Asian and Pacific Islander American Poverty: The Working Poor and the Jobless Poor." *Amerasia* 18, no. 1 (1992): 83–91.

Trimmer, Joseph, and Tilly Warnock, eds. *Understanding Others: Cultural and Cross-Cultural Studies and the Teaching of Literature.* Urbana, Ill.: National Council of Teachers of English, 1992.

Trotter, Joe William, Jr. "Blacks in the Urban North: The 'Underclass Question' in Historical Perspective." In *The "Underclass" Debate: Views from History,* edited by Michael B. Katz, 55–81. Princeton: Princeton University Press, 1993.

TuSmith, Bonnie. *All My Relatives: Community in Contemporary Ethnic American Literatures.* Ann Arbor: University of Michigan Press, 1993.

———, ed. *Conversations with John Edgar Wideman.* Jackson: University Press of Mississippi, 1998.

United States. General Accounting Office. *The Urban Underclass: Disturbing Problems Demanding Attention.* Washington, D.C.: GAO, 1991.

Valdez, Luis. *Zoot Suit and Other Plays.* Houston: Arte Público, 1992.

Varsava, Jerry A. "Tom Wolfe's Defense of the New (Old) Social Novel; Or, The Perils of the Great White-Suited Hunter." In *Journal of American Culture* 14, no. 3 (1991), special issue on Tom Wolfe, edited by Marshall Fishwick, 35–42.

Vendler, Helen. "Rita Dove: Identity Markers." *Callaloo* 17, no. 2 (1994): 381–98.

Villa, Raul. *Barrio-Logos: Space and Place in Urban Chicano Literature and Culture.* Austin: University of Texas Press, 2000.

Wagner-Pacifici, Robin. *Discourse and Destruction: The City of Philadelphia versus MOVE.* Chicago: University of Chicago Press, 1994.

Wald, Priscilla. *Constituting Americans: Cultural Anxiety and Narrative Form.* Durham: Duke University Press, 1995.

Waldron, John V. "Uncovering History in the 'Postmodern Condition': (Re)Writing the Past, (Re)Righting Ourselves in Alejandro Morales' *The Brick People.*" *Confluencia* 7, no. 2 (1992): 99–106.

Wall, Cheryl A., ed. *Changing Our Own Words: Essays on Criticism, Theory, and Writing by Black Women.* New Brunswick, N.J.: Rutgers University Press, 1989.

Wallace, Michele. *Black Macho and the Myth of the Superwoman.* New York: Dial, 1978.

Walter, Roland. *Magical Realism in Contemporary Chicano Fiction.* Frankfurt: Verveurt Verlag, 1993.

Washington, Joseph R., ed. *The Declining Significance of Race?: A Dialogue among Black and White Social Scientists.* Philadelphia: University of Pennsylvania Afro-American Studies Program, 1979.

Weiler, Conrad. *Philadelphia: Neighborhood, Authority, and the Urban Crisis.* New York: Praeger, 1974.

Weisenburger, Steven. *Fables of Subversion: Satire and the American Novel, 1930–1980.* Athens: University of Georgia Press, 1995.

West, Cornel. *Beyond Eurocentrism and Multiculturalism.* 2 vols. Monroe, Maine: Common Courage, 1993.

———. *Race Matters.* New York: Vintage, 1994.

White, Michael. *American Neighborhoods and Residential Differentiation.* New York: Russell Sage, 1987.

Whitman, Walt. *Leaves of Grass.* In *American Poetry: The Nineteenth Century,* vol. 1. Edited by John Hollander. New York: Library of America, 1993.

Who Killed Vincent Chin? Directed by Christine Choy and Renee Tajima. Filmmaker's Library, 1989.

Wideman, John Edgar. *Brothers and Keepers.* New York: Penguin, 1984.

———. *Fatheralong: A Meditation on Fathers and Sons, Race and Society.* New York: Vintage, 1994.

———. *Fever: Twelve Stories.* New York: Penguin, 1989.

———. "The Night I Was Nobody." In *Speak My Name: Black Men on Masculinity and the American Dream,* edited by Don Belton, 23–27. Boston: Beacon, 1995.

———. *Philadelphia Fire.* New York: Henry Holt, 1990.

———. *Two Cities.* Boston: Houghton Mifflin, 1998.

Williams, Raymond. *Marxism and Literature.* New York: Oxford University Press, 1977.

Williams, Rhonda. "Accumulation as Evisceration: Urban Rebellion and the New Growth Dynamics." In *Reading Rodney King/Reading Urban Uprising,* edited by Robert Gooding-Williams, 82–96. New York: Routledge, 1993.

Wilson, William Julius. *The Declining Significance of Race: Blacks and Changing American Institutions.* 2d. ed. Chicago: University of Chicago Press, 1980.

Winant, Howard. *Racial Conditions: Politics, Theory, Comparisons.* Minneapolis: University of Minnesota Press, 1994.

Winslow, Gerald R. *Triage and Justice: The Ethics of Rationing Life-Saving Medical Resources.* Berkeley and Los Angeles: University of California Press, 1982.

Wolfe, Tom. *The Bonfire of the Vanities.* New York: Farrar, Straus & Giroux, 1987.

———. *Radical Chic & Mau-Mauing the Flak Catchers.* New York: Farrar, Straus & Giroux, 1970.

———. "Stalking the Billion-Footed Beast: A Literary Manifesto for the New Social Novel." *Harper's,* November 1989, 45–56.

———. "The Years of Living Prosperously." *U.S. News & World Report,* December 1989–January 1990, 117.

Wong, Sau-ling Cynthia. *Reading Asian American Literature: From Necessity to Extravagance.* Princeton: Princeton University Press, 1993.

Yamamoto, Hisaye. "A Fire in Fontana." *Rafu Shimpo,* 21 December 1985. Reprinted in *Seventeen Syllables and Other Stories,* edited by King-Kok Cheung, 150–57. New Brunswick, N.J.: Rutgers University Press, 1994.

———. "A Fire in Fontana." In *Rereading America: Cultural Contexts for Critical Thinking and Writing,* ed. Gary Columbo et al., 366–73. 2d ed. Boston: Bedford, 1992.

———. *Seventeen Syllables.* Edited by King-Kok Cheung. New Brunswick, N.J.: Rutgers University Press, 1994.

———. *Seventeen Syllables and Other Stories.* Revised ed. New Brunswick, N.J: Rutgers University Press, 2001.

Žižek, Slavoj. *The Sublime Object of Ideology.* New York: Verso, 1989.

Index

James Kyung-Jin Lee is assistant professor of English and Asian American studies at the University of Texas at Austin.

81-3 "AAs derive ~~a const~~ racial id.s through a constrt
mediat" - (82)
(83) triangular mediat ; blk - white - Asian

Not unlike // or exactly the same as Maeda's
comment re: triangulat → in Babylon Chains of

87 visual overdeterminat of Black bodies
presented as "signs" thru which they can'spk
                 the only   AAs